Tradition and Change in American Party Politics

Tradition and Change in American Party Politics

JOYCE GELB
CITY COLLEGE OF THE CITY UNIVERSITY OF NEW YORK
and
MARIAN LIEF PALLEY
UNIVERSITY OF DELAWARE

THOMAS Y. CROWELL COMPANY
NEW YORK   ESTABLISHED 1834

Library of Congress Cataloging in Publication Data

GELB, JOYCE, 1940–
    Tradition and change in American party politics.

    Includes bibliographical references and index.
    1. Political parties—United States. I. Palley,
Marian, 1939– joint author. II. Title.
JK2265.P26 1975   329'.02   74-30134
ISBN 0-690-00196-7

U-QU-RK
Copyright © 1975 by
Thomas Y. Crowell Company, Inc.

*To the Memory of Samuel Lief and Rose Klein
and for Frances Lief and Irving Klein*

Preface

For several years both authors of this book have been teaching courses on political parties in the United States and have been finding increasingly that the materials which are available for use by undergraduates are inadequate, given the questions being raised by today's students. Students have been asking about the constraints of the environment upon parties. They want to know about the effects of technology on parties. They have become more interested in the impact of class and ethnicity upon political participation and parties. Increasingly questions about the structure of the party system have related to public policy concerns. We embarked upon the writing of this book in response to these expressions of concern by the students we encountered in our classes.

We have tried to relate the standard materials on political parties to the more contemporary concerns of our students. In so doing we have tried to present neither a radical critique of society—assuming the complete futility of saving our institutions—nor an unquestioning acceptance of parties in the political system. Rather we have probed and reexamined the role of parties in the United States inasmuch as we perceive that throughout the history of the United States political parties have been deliberately given a very limited role to perform. The circumscribed role of parties is due to the fact that the majority of Americans have a very strong fear of centralized power and an antipathy toward powerful parties. We have suggested that this particular phenomenon be called *antiparty politics*. Throughout this volume reference is

vii

made to this pervasive concern in American society as we show its effects upon the role of parties in the political system.

As all authors feel a sense of gratitude to the people who helped them in their work, we too have people we wish to thank for their assistance to us as we worked to complete this project. Several students at the University of Delaware and The City College of New York worked dutifully as research assistants for us during different stages of our work. George Hale, Daniel Harkins, Douglas Hiland, Paul Lee, Martin Milner, and Bruce Luger all performed many tedious tasks while trying to retain their good humor. We would like to thank our colleagues for their observations and insights on the problems we were considering. Henry Reynolds, Jerrold Schneider, and James Oliver all at the University of Delaware, and Howard Palley, of the University of Maryland read or discussed sections of the manuscript with us and made many useful suggestions. Henry Reynolds also performed all the data analysis which appears in Chapters 5 and 6. The students in our classes on political parties at the University of Delaware and at The City College of New York provided us with the opportunity to "test" the materials in this book, which then enabled us to react to their criticisms and comments. The editorial staff at Thomas Y. Crowell was always helpful to us and we particularly want to thank Herb Addison and Joan Greene for their aid and assistance. The manuscript was typed in its many drafts by Donna Carter, Melanie Wallace, Sandra Atlas, and Gladys Hartman to whom we wish to express our most sincere thanks. The University of Delaware provided one of us with a Summer Research Grant (1972) which facilitated research and writing on this project. Also, the University of Delaware's Computer Center was available to us for the necessary analysis of data. Finally we wish to thank our husbands and children for their extreme tolerance without which this work would never have been completed.

JOYCE GELB, *New York, New York*
MARIAN LIEF PALLEY, *Newark, Delaware*

Contents

Introduction
to Chapters 1
and 2

In the first two chapters of this book, we will provide a foundation for our analysis of political parties in the American political system. Chapter 1 examines the theoretical and historical roots of American parties as well as the antipathy to them. Chapter 2 discusses the impact on parties of environmental changes largely produced by technology. Contemporary changes in economic and social patterns, in particular, are related to the American tradition of antipartyism.

1

1

Parties in Perspective

For students of American politics, the two-party system in the United States has long enjoyed a dominant place in political life. Although nowhere mentioned (at least specifically) in the Constitution, parties have been viewed traditionally as major institutions in American politics; groupings distinguished from other, largely social and economic organizations by their monopoly of the electoral function. There have been, of course, throughout the history of the nation, a variety of groups that have attempted to influence policymaking.[1] In the 1830s Alexis de Tocqueville remarked that: "in no other country in the world has the principle of association been more successfully used or applied to a greater multitude of objects than in America." [2] It is, however, the purpose of this book to stimulate a new dialogue on the roles and functions of political parties—the two-party system—in America's postindustrial society.

Essentially, we are eager to explore two major questions regarding political parties and politics in the United States:

1. How effectively do our parties serve as the major linkage between the government and the people?

[1] These groups, as distinguished from political parties, have been called interest groups and have been defined as ". . . any group that, on the basis of one or more shared attitudes, makes claims upon other groups in society for the establishment, maintenance, or enhancement of forms of behavior that are implied by the shared attitude." David Truman, *The Governmental Process* (New York: Knopf, 1951), p. 33.

[2] *Democracy in America* (New York: Vintage Books, 1954), p. 193.

2. Given our ever changing political culture, how crucial are parties to the maintenance of the legitimacy of governmental institutions and to national unity?

Throughout this book reference is made to the prevalence of *antiparty politics* in the United States. Insofar as the term is used with considerable frequency, it is necessary at the outset of this volume to provide the reader with a clear understanding of how the authors are using it. *Antiparty politics* is the short-hand phrase used to describe the negative response—almost a fear—Americans have toward political parties. It refers to a general unwillingness to participate in party activities or to provide parties with any greater authority or responsibility than is absolutely necessary to nominate and elect candidates to public elective office or to perform as agents of policymaking.

CONTRASTING VIEWS ON THE FUNCTIONS OF POLITICAL PARTIES

PARTIES AS CENTRAL TO AMERICAN POLITICS

Political parties have been seen by some political scientists as "by far the most important part of the representative structure in complex democratic societies."[3] For those who hold this view political parties are seen to perform many functions. Among these functions are expressing and aggregating interests, formulating public policy alternatives, containing conflict, fostering popular participation in government, linking the individual to his government, politically socializing the citizen, recruiting and training political leaders, organizing government, and institutionalizing the idea of a "loyal opposition." There is general agreement among most analysts, however, that the primary function of the party in the United States is its electoral function—nominating and electing officials to public office.[4]

Leon Epstein has identified two conflicting theories of representation: an "older more traditional one, where elected public office-holders, individually or collectively, decide policy"; and a second theory where "the office-holder is considered the agent, although he may also be a leader, of an organized following that determines policy." The essence of the second theory Epstein

[3] Seymour Martin Lipset, "Party Systems and the Representation of Social Groups," in Roy C. Macridis, ed., *Political Parties* (New York: Harper and Row, 1967), p. 43; see also William Chambers, "Party Development and the American Mainstream," in William Chambers and William Dean Burnham, eds., *The American Party Systems* (New York: Oxford University Press, 1967), pp. 3–32.

[4] See William Chambers, "Parties and Nation Building in America," in Joseph La Palombara and Myron Weiner, eds., *Political Parties and Political Development* (Princeton, N.J.: Princeton University Press, 1966), p. 89; Avery Leiserson, "The Place of Parties in the Study of Politics," in Macridis, ed., *Political Parties,* p. 31; and Macridis, "The History, Functions and Typology of Parties," ibid., p. 17.

concludes "is not that it makes for policy agreement among a party's office-holders, but that it makes for this agreement as the result of decisions of an organized party leadership." [5] For those political scientists accepting this second conception of party, party is seen as a most valuable instrument in maintaining an operative representative government. There are, however, very few cases which can be used to garner evidence to support the reality of this view in contemporary American experience. Congress and state representative bodies organize on the basis of party identification and some states have systems in which parties retain strong controls via the caucus on individual legislator's voting behavior. Nonetheless, even those who accept the desirability of cohesive parties recognize that American parties fall far short of the ideal type. Strong party government, as it has existed in Great Britain and some other continental countries, cannot be transferred to a system that has a separation of powers and an historic tradition of federalism.

THE DIMINISHED ROLE OF PARTIES

Thus there is a growing body of political analysts who find the role of the party to be an increasingly limited one in a complex postindustrial society. In fact some critics suggest that we may have been overestimating the role and function of parties for years. [6] Daniel Bell has suggested that there has been an expansion in the power of the intellectuals in our postindustrial society. He has noted that, "the technical intelligentsia becomes a claimant, like other groups, for public support (though its influence is felt in the bureaucratic and administrative labyrinth rather than in the electoral system and through mass pressure.)" [7] The implication of Bell's remarks is clear. In the world he describes, the role for political parties diminishes as experts and technocrats gain public importance as purveyors of essential knowledge and skills, either as government advisers or as brokers for various interest groups.

Perhaps it is becoming the case increasingly that for the average citizen "nonpolitical" voluntary organizations and public bureaucracies are providing both greater frequency and intensity of political experience than the political parties. It may be that citizen encounters with party organizations are less and less frequent and more limited in scope—for most people limited to the act

---

[5] Leon D. Epstein, *Political Parties in Western Democracies* (New York: Praeger, 1967), p. 292.

[6] See Anthony King, "Political Parties in Western Democracies: Some Skeptical Reflections," *Polity* 4 (Winter 1969): 114–41; Morton Grodzins, "Parties and the Crisis of Succession in the U.S.: The Case of 1800," in La Palombara and Weiner, *Political Parties*, p. 317, for the view that parties have functioned ineffectively as agents of political moderation, but rather, have exacerbated conflicts and made their resolution more difficult.

[7] Daniel Bell, "Notes on the Post Industrial Society (I)," *The Public Interest*, 6 (Winter 1967): 35.

of voting only, if that. One additional point should be made here. That is, along with this perspective on the contemporary role of parties as perhaps being less than central in American politics there is a perceived relationship between interest groups and citizenry. Voluntary associations, it has been suggested, are the prime means by which "the function of mediating between the individual and the state is performed. Through them the individual is able to relate himself effectively and meaningfully to the political system." [8]

There are no mass membership parties in the United States. As a result political party activists are now and always have been few in number.[9]

It has been argued by some political analysts that party organizations, once "part channel of protest, part source of protection, part surveyors of visions of the future" are institutions which are becoming "more remote, alien and quasi-institutional in character." [10] Or as Chambers has put it, the two major parties are awkwardly large and unspecialized in areas of differentiated political roles—"if party was king in a democratic polity, it no longer reigns." [11] From this point it is not far to the view, lamented by some, unlamented by others, that parties as we have known them may even disappear.[12]

THE SYMBOLIC ROLE OF PARTIES

A third view accepted by some political scientists sees parties as still active on the electoral scene, but in largely a symbolic fashion, as reference

[8] Gabriel A. Almond and Sidney Verba, *The Civic Culture: Political Attitudes and Democracy in Five Nations* (Boston: Little, Brown, 1965), p. 245.

[9] Maurice Duverger has classified political parties as *mass parties* if the following criteria are met:

Recruitment of members is a fundamental activity, both from political and financial standpoints. . . . The mass-party technique in effect replaces the capitalist financing. Instead of appealing to a few big private donors, industrialists, bankers, or important merchants, for funds to meet campaign expenses—which makes the candidate (and the person elected) dependent on them—the mass party spreads the burden over the largest possible number of members, each of whom contributes a modest sum.

. . . It is characteristic of the mass party that it appeals to the public.

The cadre party corresponds to a different conception: the grouping of notabilities for the preparation of elections, conducting campaigns and maintaining contact with the candidates. Influential persons, in the first place, whose name, prestige, or connections can provide a backing for the candidate and secure him votes; experts, in the second place, who know how to handle the electors and how to organize a campaign; last of all financiers, who can bring the sinews of war. Quality is the most important factor: extent of prestige, skill in technique, size of fortune. What the mass party secures by numbers, the cadre party achieves by selection.

For Duverger the American party system falls clearly into the latter category. Maurice Duverger, *Political Parties* (New York: John Wiley, 1954), pp. 63–64.

[10] Otto Kircheimer, "The Transformation of the Western European Party Systems," in La Palombara and Weiner, *Political Parties*, p. 199.

[11] Chambers, in Chambers and Burnham, *The American Party Systems*, p. 15.

[12] Kircheimer, in La Palombara and Weiner, *Political Parties*, p. 200.

points at the ballot box.[13] This notion takes off in large part from a broader conception of politics as essentially symbolic action. One of the best statements on symbolic politics was presented by Murray Edelman when he wrote:

> The basic thesis is that mass publics respond to currently conspicuous political symbols: not to 'facts', and not to moral codes embedded in the character or soul, but to the gestures and speeches that make up the drama of the state . . . The mass public does not study and analyze detailed data about secondary boycotts, provisions for stock ownership and control in a proposed space communications corporation, or missile installations in Cuba . . . It ignores these things until political actions and speeches make them symbolically threatening or reassuring and it then responds to the cues furnished by the actions and speeches, not to direct knowledge of the facts . . . It is therefore political actions that chiefly shape men's political wants and knowledge, not the other way around.[14]

Thus a more modest view of parties emerges: "a relatively durable social formation which seeks offices and power in government . . . which links leaders at the centers of government to a significant popular following in the political arena and its local enclaves, and generates in-group perspectives or at least symbols of identity and loyalty." [15]

An even more cynical view regarding the symbolic role of political parties sees an analogy between the decreasing significance for the partisan electoral process in twentieth-century politics and of the English monarchy at the beginning of the nineteenth century, with both institutions continuing to exist despite a lack of relevance to a new society.[16] Eric Nordlinger finds a decline in the manifest functions of the electoral system, that is, in the mobilization of votes, the filling of governmental offices, and the like, while he sees the electoral system and by extension, political parties as continuing to provide: (a) a common reference point for society; (b) a set of rituals, ceremonies, and symbols that tend to integrate society and produce a unified political system; and (c) the legitimization of governmental authority.[17] In a convergence of these points it can be suggested that the nineteenth-century system of political parties, distinguished as suggested earlier by its central role in electoral politics, is, in anything more than a symbolic sense, inadequate to meet the demands of a complex postindustrial society.

[13] Everett Carll Ladd, *American Political Parties* (New York: W. W. Norton, 1970), p. 24.

[14] Murray Edelman, *The Symbolic Uses of Politics* (Chicago: University of Illinois Press, Illinois Books Edition, 1960), p. 172.

[15] Chambers, in Chambers and Burnham, *The American Party Systems,* p. 5.

[16] Eric Nordlinger, "Representation, Governmental Stability and Decisional Effectiveness," in J. Ronald Pennock and John W. Chapman, eds., *Representation* (New York: Atherton Press, 1968), p. 124.

[17] Ibid.

SUMMARY

Thus parties are seen by some scholars as being central to American politics, while others view parties as having a diminishing role in contemporary American society, and still a third group of analysts suggest that parties perform what they have called a symbolic function in American politics. It seems that each of these views of American parties has some truth. Insofar as parties nominate candidates for public office they do in fact remain central to the political process. But, as technology demands an increasing political role for experts, the role for the party in the political process seems to be declining. Furthermore, as long as we attribute to parties a centrality in the political process, assuming that they perform a significant function regarding the participatory ideals of American democracy, the third view of parties—parties as symbols—holds part of the answer. In fact, it is our belief that the American two-party system has served historically to perform some specific and important functions—notably in the nominating and electing of officials to public office—in our society, but because of the *antiparty tradition* in the United States, the role of the two major parties has always been limited and is perhaps becoming more limited given the demands of our modern technological society. The parties that have always provided a symbolic referent for the American people may become even more symbolic in their functions.

ANTIPARTYISM IN THE AMERICAN POLITICAL CULTURE

ANTIPARTYISM, PLURALIST PARTIES, AND PROPARTYISM

Antiparty trends have always been significantly entrenched in American political culture. Parties in America have changed little in either form or structure since the days prior to the civil war. American parties arose first as congressional factions and then participation was extended to the masses, unlike some European parties, which arose from the masses to gain political power through electoral parliamentary activity. Even more important, parties in America have been rooted in an ambivalent theoretical ground, best symbolized by the Constitution. The Constitution sought to contain and limit, rather than maximize, the majority political power, that power which is a major aim, at least in theory, of the two-party system. In fact, George Washington in his "Farewell Address" warned against "the baneful effects of the spirit of party."

A significant portion of political thought in the eighteenth century viewed parties as evil in the truest "antiparty" sense; as destructive of consensus and productive of tyranny and as a counterpoise to civic virtue and objective citizen judgment, after the tradition of Rousseau. For example, in his *Social Contract* Rousseau condemned political parties, for they disturbed the general will through the introduction of private designs. Thus he stated, "it is therefore of the utmost importance for obtaining the general will, that no partial society be formed in the States, and that every citizen speak his opinion entirely from himself."

Alexander Hamilton was a renowned proponent of the "nonpartisan" view that is today still prevalent among proponents of nonpartisanship, and among some adherents of "reform" politics and advocates of "participatory democracy." Throughout his entire public career Hamilton conveyed the impression that he would have liked to witness the abolition of political parties. He concluded *Federalist 85* by warning against "an obstinate adherence to political parties." [18]

To Madisonians, modified antiparty, or "pluralist" parties (factions) remained evil but their existence was viewed as a necessary part of a free state. James Madison recognized that "the latent causes of faction" are in human nature and thus he foresaw the development of political parties regardless of whether or not people desired them to exist. In the tenth paper of *The Federalist* he wrote:

> A landed interest, a manufacturing interest, a mercantile interest, a moneyed interest, with many lesser interests, grow up of necessity in civilized nations, and divide them into different classes, actuated by different sentiments and views. The regulation of these various and interfering interests forms the principal task of modern legislation, and involves the spirit of party and faction in the necessary and ordinary operations of government.

Factions (parties) then, are to be constrained, not eliminated, Madison continued. "The inference to which we are brought is, that the causes of faction cannot be removed; and that relief is only to be sought in the means of controlling the effects." In this view, parties should not be suppressed but rather constrained, through such devices as federalism, separation of powers, and the creation of a large and diverse territorial republic. Such checks and balances act to prevent the formation of a permanent majority—or mass party—which could dominate the political system and upset the desired balance of power. Parties then become just another set of actors competing for influence in the political arena. This, probably the dominant view of American parties, has sought a constitutional government that would check and control

---

[18] For a detailed analysis of Hamilton's evaluation of political parties see Gerald Stourgh, *Alexander Hamilton and the Idea of Republican Government* (Stanford, Calif.: Stanford University Press, 1970), pp. 110–20.

parties, rather than a system of party government under the Constitution.[19]

There is no room in this view for the idea that parties can reinforce rather than undermine liberty. In fact, none of the founding fathers saw parties as the functional providers of a wide variety of services necessary to the political system and unlikely to be performed as well by alternative institutions. Certainly the traditional urban political machine that provided services to the needy, that "served certain latent social functions, functions no one intended but which presumably would have had to be served by another means if not that one," [20] fell outside the intended role of parties as perceived by the Madisonians.

This ambivalent, even hostile, view toward parties has been widely prevalent and successful in the United States. This is not to say, however, that there have not been two viable parties during most of American history, though there is a tendency toward one-party dominance. A short review of party history will show that, only from 1814 to 1832 was there only one party in the United States. In the early years of the Republic (1796 to 1814) there were two parties—the Federalists and the Republican-Democrats—though there was very little interparty competition. From 1832 to 1852 there was interparty competition between the Whigs and the Democrats, although the Democrats controlled Congress for most of the period, and won the presidency in four out of six tries. The Whig party was held together largely by its opposition to the Democrats. They did not have a positive party program, and won the presidency in two cases by nominating military heros. In the period after 1852 regional politics based largely on slavery, led to the demise of the Whigs, the rise of the Republicans, and the temporary split in the ranks of the Democrats in 1860. These regional splits culminated in the Civil War. After the war the Democrats and the Republicans remained as the two major parties—though third parties developed and often nominated candidates for national office. From 1868 to 1912 the Republicans controlled the White House continuously with the exception of the two terms won by Democrat Grover Cleveland. During this time there was two-party competition at the national level, though there was once again one-party supremacy. This era, as just noted, saw the development of several third parties—most prominent of these were the Populists. In the 1890s however, the Populists were largely absorbed into the Democratic party—which continued to lose presidential elections until Woodrow Wilson's victory in 1912. This Democratic success was due to the split in the ranks of the Republican party when Theodore Roosevelt ran for the

---

[19] Richard Hofstadter, *The Idea of a Party System* (Berkeley: University of California Press, 1969), p. 53. This entire section is heavily reliant on Hofstadter's threefold typology of party concepts in the United States.

[20] Edward C. Banfield and James Q. Wilson, *City Politics* (New York: Random House, 1963), p. 126.

presidency as the candidate of the Progressive party rather than support Republican President Taft in his bid for reelection. Wilson remained in the White House for eight years, and then Republicans were returned to the presidency for three terms. During the time frame, 1892–1932, though the Republicans were the majority party nationally, the Democrats contested congressional seats and dominated the politics of some states and localities. It was not until Franklin D. Roosevelt was elected president in 1932 that the Democratic party became the majority party in the national political arena. It has retained this position to the present day, with the Republican party contesting elections at all governmental levels—having been victorious nationally in four presidential contests (1952, 1956, 1968, and 1972). We have had a tendency toward one-party dominance in American national politics— though a second party has been always able to sustain itself, and often provide strong national competition (see Table 1).

Table 1. Political Party Affiliations in Congress and the Presidency: 1789–1976

Year	Congress	House		Senate		President
		Majority party	Principal minority party	Majority party	Principal minority party	
1974–1976	94th	D-290	R-144	D-60	R-38	R (Ford)
1972–1974	93rd	D-244	R-191	D-57	R-43	R (Nixon)
1970–1972	92nd	D-245	R-180	D-54	R-44	R (Nixon)
1968–1970	91st	D-243	R-192	D-58	R-42	R (Nixon)
1966–1968	90th	D-248	R-187	D-64	R-36	D (Johnson)
1964–1966	89th	D-295	R-140	D-67	R-33	D (Johnson)
1962–1964	88th	D-258	R-176	D-68	R-32	D (Kennedy)
1960–1962	87th	D-263	R-174	D-64	R-36	D (Kennedy)
1958–1960	86th	D-283	R-154	D-66	R-34	R (Eisenhower)
1957–1958	85th	D-233	R-200	D-49	R-47	R (Eisenhower)
1955–1956	84th	D-232	R-203	D-48	R-47	R (Eisenhower)
1953–1954	83rd	R-221	D-211	R-48	D-47	R (Eisenhower)
1951–1952	82nd	D-234	R-199	D-49	R-47	D (Truman)
1949–1950	81st	D-263	R-171	D-54	R-42	D (Truman)
1947–1948	80th	R-245	D-188	R-51	D-45	D (Truman)
1945–1946	79th	D-242	R-190	D-56	R-38	D (Truman)
1943–1944	78th	D-218	R-208	D-58	R-37	D (F. Roosevelt)
1941–1942	77th	D-268	R-162	D-66	R-28	D (F. Roosevelt)
1939–1941	76th	D-261	R-164	D-69	R-23	D (F. Roosevelt)
1937–1938	75th	D-331	R-89	D-76	R-16	D (F. Roosevelt)
1935–1936	74th	D-319	R-103	D-69	R-25	D (F. Roosevelt)
1933–1934	73rd	D-310	R-117	D-60	R-35	D (F. Roosevelt)
1931–1933	72nd	D-220	R-214	R-48	D-47	R (Hoover)
1929–1931	71st	R-267	D-167	R-56	D-39	R (Hoover)

Table 1. Political Party Affiliations in Congress and the Presidency: 1789–1976

Year	Congress	House Majority party	House Principal minority party	Senate Majority party	Senate Principal minority party	President
1927–1929	70th	R-237	D-195	R-49	D-46	R (Coolidge)
1925–1927	69th	R-247	D-183	R-56	D-39	R (Coolidge)
1923–1925	68th	R-225	D-205	R-51	D-43	R (Coolidge)
1921–1923	67th	R-301	D-131	R-59	D-37	R (Harding)
1919–1921	66th	R-240	D-190	R-49	D-47	D (Wilson)
1917–1919	65th	D-216	R-210	D-53	R-42	D (Wilson)
1915–1917	64th	D-230	R-196	D-56	R-40	D (Wilson)
1913–1915	63rd	D-291	R-127	D-51	R-44	D (Wilson)
1911–1913	62nd	D-228	R-161	R-51	D-41	R (Taft)
1909–1911	61st	R-219	D-172	R-61	D-32	R (Taft)
1907–1909	60th	R-222	D-164	R-61	D-31	R (T. Roosevelt)
1905–1907	59th	R-250	D-136	R-57	D-33	R (T. Roosevelt)
1903–1905	58th	R-208	D-178	R-57	D-33	R (T. Roosevelt)
1901–1903	57th	R-197	D-151	R-55	D-31	R (T. Roosevelt) R (McKinley)
1899–1901	56th	R-185	D-163	R-53	D-26	R (McKinley)
1897–1899	55th	R-204	D-113	R-47	D-34	R (McKinley)
1895–1897	54th	R-244	D-105	R-43	D-39	D (Cleveland)
1893–1895	53rd	D-218	R-127	D-44	R-38	D (Cleveland)
1891–1893	52nd	D-235	R-88	R-47	D-39	R (B. Harrison)
1889–1891	51st	R-166	D-159	R-39	D-37	R (B. Harrison)
1887–1889	50th	D-169	R-152	R-39	D-37	D (Cleveland)
1885–1887	49th	D-183	R-140	R-43	D-34	D (Cleveland)
1883–1885	48th	D-197	R-118	R-38	D-36	R (Arthur)
1881–1883	47th	R-147	D-135	R-37	D-37	R (Arthur)
1879–1881	46th	D-149	R-130	D-42	R-33	R (Hayes)
1877–1879	45th	D-153	R-140	R-39	D-36	R (Hayes)
1875–1877	44th	D-169	R-109	R-45	D-29	R (Grant)
1873–1875	43rd	R-194	D-92	R-49	D-19	R (Grant)
1871–1873	42nd	R-134	D-104	R-52	D-17	R (Grant)
1869–1871	41st	R-149	D-63	R-56	D-11	R (Grant)
1867–1869	40th	R-143	D-49	R-42	D-11	R (Johnson)
1865–1867	39th	U-149	D-42	U-42	D-10	R (Johnson) R (Lincoln)
1863–1865	38th	R-102	D-75	R-36	D-9	R (Lincoln)
1861–1863	37th	R-105	D-43	R-31	D-10	R (Lincoln)
1859–1861	36th	R-114	D-92	D-36	R-26	D (Buchanan)
1857–1859	35th	D-118	R-92	D-36	R-20	D (Buchanan)
1855–1857	34th	R-108	D-83	D-40	R-15	D (Pierce)
1853–1855	33rd	D-159	W-71	D-38	W-22	D (Pierce)
1851–1853	32nd	D-140	W-88	D-35	W-24	W (Fillmore)
1849–1851	31st	D-112	W-109	D-35	W-25	W (Fillmore) W (Taylor)

Table 1. Political Party Affiliations in Congress and the Presidency: 1789–1976

Year	Congress	House Majority party	House Principal minority party	Senate Majority party	Senate Principal minority party	President
1847–1849	30th	W-115	D-108	D-36	W-21	D (Polk)
1845–1847	29th	D-143	W-77	D-31	W-25	D (Polk)
1843–1845	28th	D-142	W-79	W-28	D-25	W (Tyler)
1841–1843	27th	W-133	D-102	W-28	D-22	W (Tyler)
						W (W. Harrison)
1839–1841	26th	D-124	W-118	D-28	W-22	D (Van Buren)
1837–1839	25th	D-108	W-107	D-30	W-18	D (Van Buren)
1835–1837	24th	D-145	W-98	D-27	W-25	D (Jackson)
1833–1835	23rd	D-147	AM-53	D-20	NR-20	D (Jackson)
1831–1833	22nd	D-141	NR-58	D-25	NR-21	D (Jackson)
1829–1831	21st	D-139	NR-74	D-26	NR-22	D (Jackson)
1827–1829	20th	J-119	AD-94	J-28	AD-20	C (John Q. Adams)
1825–1827	19th	AD-105	J-97	AD-26	J-20	C (John Q. Adams)
1823–1825	18th	DR-187	F-26	DR-44	F-4	DR (Monroe)
1821–1823	17th	DR-158	F-25	DR-44	F-4	DR (Monroe)
1819–1821	16th	DR-156	F-27	DR-35	F-7	DR (Monroe)
1817–1819	15th	DR-141	F-42	DR-34	F-10	DR (Monroe)
1815–1817	14th	DR-117	F-65	DR-25	F-11	DR (Madison)
1813–1815	13th	DR-112	F-68	DR-27	F-9	DR (Madison)
1811–1813	12th	DR-108	F-36	DR-30	F-6	DR (Madison)
1809–1811	11th	DR-94	F-48	DR-28	F-6	DR (Madison)
1807–1809	10th	DR-118	F-24	DR-28	F-6	DR (Jefferson)
1805–1807	9th	DR-116	F-25	DR-27	F-7	DR (Jefferson)
1803–1805	8th	DR-102	F-39	DR-25	F-9	DR (Jefferson)
1801–1803	7th	DR-69	F-36	DR-18	F-13	DR (Jefferson)
1799–1801	6th	F-64	DR-42	F-19	DR-12	F (J. Adams)
1797–1799	5th	F-58	DR-48	F-20	DR-13	F (J. Adams)
1795–1797	4th	F-54	DR-52	F-19	DR-13	F (Washington)
1793–1795	3rd	DR-57	F-48	F-17	DR-13	F (Washington)
1791–1793	2nd	F-37	DR-33	F-16	DR-13	F (Washington)
1789–1791	1st	AD-38	OP-26	AD-17	OP-9	F (Washington)

KEY: AD-Administration; AM-Anti-Masonic; C-Coalition; D-Democrat; DR-Democrat-Republican; F-Federalist; J-Jacksonian; NR-National Republican; OP-Opposition; R-Republican; U-Unionist; W-Whig. Figures are for the beginning of the first session of each Congress.

SOURCES:

Congressional Quarterly Service, *Historical Review of Presidential Elections from 1788 to 1968* (Wash., D.C.: Congressional Quarterly Service, 1969), p. 24.

U.S. Bureau of the Census, *Historical Statistics of the United States, Colonial Times to 1957* (Wash., D.C., 1960), pp. 9139–45.

Congressional Digest (May 1974), p. 161.

The 1974–1976 data is not complete because there were undecided cases reported.

Pluralism has extended from among the parties to within the parties. In American politics individual liberty has been a most highly prized tradition valued more than equality and certainly more prized than the order that might arise from centralized authority. Our political system historically has dispersed power. Thus our political parties, which parallel our government institutions, reflect our primary value, freedom. Our national perspective toward parties has developed with skepticism, often taking the form of negativism toward politics and its extension, parties.[21]

Though these antiparty views prevail in the American political tradition, there is also a positive stream of thought regarding parties that has run through American history. There is a third, less prevalent view of parties, that is, the "majoritarian" or proparty view. This conception sees parties as inevitable and good, and supports the notion that opposition should be welcomed and institutionalized within a partisan framework. Thus, the American Political Science Association's Committee on Political Parties issued a report in 1950 that called for more responsible parties. "The fundamental requirement of accountability," the report stated, "is a two-party system in which the opposition party acts as the critic of the party in power, developing, defining and presenting the policy alternatives which are necessary for a true choice in reaching public decisions. The opposition most conducive to responsible government is an organized party government." [22] This perspective is found largely among political scientists, and was more recently articulated by Lawrence O'Brien, the national chairman of the Democratic party in 1969 and from 1970 to 1972. The 1972 Democratic convention approved the appointment of a Democratic Charter Commission to report to a national convention meeting in 1974. Among other issues they considered were the possibility of regularly scheduled biennial conventions to bring divergent interests in the party together and to develop national policy for the party. They also considered national party membership as distinct from state party membership, dues to be paid by national Democrats, and the establishment of the post of national chairman, as a full-time, elected position.[23] Despite the appointment of the Democratic Charter Commission and the support of some Democrats for strong proparty rhetoric, it is unlikely that strong party politics will emerge in this country, since the majoritarian view rarely has permeated the American psyche.

[21] Morton Grodzins, "Party and Government in the United States," in Robert A. Goldwin, ed., *Political Parties USA* (New York: Rand McNally, 1964), p. 133.

[22] "Toward a More Responsible Two Party System: A Report of the Committee on Political Parties, American Political Science Association," *American Political Science Review* 44 (Supplement, September 1950): 1–2.

[23] *Congressional Quarterly Weekly Report* 30 (December 21, 1972): 3095. For additional discussion of the Democratic party committees and commissions of 1974, see Chapter 11.

THE EVOLUTION OF CONTEMPORARY ANTIPARTYISM

The dominant attitudes that affected the American view toward parties seem to have remained reasonably constant throughout American history, despite changes in our overall political culture. Most Americans appear to be highly suspicious of parties. This can be witnessed today in split ticket voting; "independent" (as opposed to partisan) identification, particularly among young people; and the upsurge of nonparty (and nonpartisan) groups and channels of expression. Jack Dennis has found that "anti-party norms and images are present as a living part of the political culture." [24] Elections themselves fare only a little better, with the popular belief in elections as an agency of participatory democracy apparently rating considerably lower than the belief that one *should* vote.[25] The American public sees politics as creating conflict where none exists and confusing issues in the truest antiparty sense. Dennis concludes that while parties may carry on as before—as sources of electioneering and builders of short-term consensus—ultimately they will lack the strong pillars of support that can be decisive in time of crisis.

Dennis's analysis is buttressed by other studies completed recently by political analysts. As cited by David Broder, The Center for Political Studies at the University of Michigan reported a considerable increase in public distrust in, and alienation from, governmental representatives: [26]

| | White (percent) | | | Black (percent) | | |
Believe Government Run By:	1958	1966	1970	1958	1966	1970
People's Representative for Benefit of All	74	51	41	78	63	34
By Big Interests for Themselves	18	34	48	12	23	63

A 1970 Yankelovich poll found that only 16 percent of the students questioned believed that parties offer any political alternative.[27] And, a Gallup poll in 1968 found that 84 percent of those polled said that they chose the *person,* not the party, when making their voting choice.[28] Even if this is an exaggeration of the reality of voter selection techniques, it is interesting that a vast majority of those questioned answered the way they did—perhaps indicating their belief that

[24] Jack Dennis, "Support for the Party System by the Mass Public," *American Political Science Review* 60 (September 1966): 615.

[25] Jack Dennis, "Support for the Institution of Elections by the Mass Public," *American Political Science Review* 64 (September 1970): 830.

[26] David Broder, *The Party's Over* (New York: Harper and Row, 1972), p. xxii.

[27] *Newsweek,* October 28, 1971, p. 47.

[28] Broder, *The Party's Over,* p. 199.

party is not the appropriate "major cue" for voting in the United States. The view presented by the 1968 Gallup Poll received some support from the 1972 election results which showed six out of every ten voters splitting their tickets.[29]

The preceding discussion has suggested a limited, even negative role for American parties. A number of key factors must be understood when considering the evolution of the American two-party system into its present form.

1. In the United States there are single-member districts and plurality elections operative for both legislative and executive positions, especially at the national level, but to a considerable extent also at state and local levels.[30] In the single-member district, be it for a legislative or executive position, the "winner takes all." The victorious candidate, who in most cases receives at least a plurality of the votes cast, wins the election. There is complete victory or complete defeat. That is to say, there is no partial victory, or sharing of victory by two or more candidates in proportion to the number of votes received on election day. In 1968, for example, Richard Nixon received 43.4 percent of the popular vote, which gave him 56.9 percent of the electoral vote, and made him president of the United States. The American two-party system gives one party a majority or a plurality and then exaggerates it; this is sometimes called the "snowball effect." [31] This electoral mechanism contrasts with a multimember district system or a system that utilizes proportional representation [32] where the division of seats in each district tends to reflect more accurately the actual party preferences of the voters.

2. At the same time, as Robert Dahl reminds us, in any party system, aggregation must take place somewhere; either within the party, as is the case in the United States, or within the legislative body, which is the operative mode in many multiparty systems and in nations that utilize proportional representation.[33] In the United States and Great Britain, both nations with two-party systems, candidates must appeal to a wide spectrum of voters. Thus, prior to the election they usually feel compelled to present moderate positions on issues based on compromise. In France, which has had a multiparty system, such compromise has usually occurred after the election. The resultant process in France requires bargaining among political leaders after the fact of the election, whereas the American and the British systems require appeals to the voters—as well as bargaining among political leaders. Unlike a multiparty

---

[29] *The Gallup Opinion Index* (December 1972): 12.

[30] It should be noted that Maurice Klain has observed that the phenomenon of single-member districts is very much overstated regarding the states. Maurice Klain, "A New Look At Constituencies: The Need for a Recount and a Reappraisal," *American Political Science Review* 49, no. 4 (December 1955): 1105.

[31] Gerald Pomper, *Elections in America* (New York: Dodd, Mead, 1968), p. 45.

[32] For a good discussion of the types of proportional representation see John G. Grum, "Theories of Electoral Systems," *Midwest Journal of Political Science* 2 (November 1958): 357–76. See also Klain, "A New Look at Constituencies."

[33] Robert Dahl, *Polyarchy* (New Haven: Yale University Press, 1971), pp. 223–24.

parliamentary system where coalitions are often formed after the election with bargaining going on for cabinet positions, little or no opportunity for postelectoral bargaining exists in the presidential system, and thus, at least on a superficial level, there appears to be national two-party hegemony.

3. A corollary of points one and two taken together must be that it is unlikely that third parties will gain more than a transient national political role. Thus, for example, the United States has never developed a mass working-class party. This is due in large measure to the fact that since most American workers—after 1828—were included in the political party system, the parties developed as nonelite organizations virtually from their inception.[34] Furthermore, class cohesion was weakened by ethnic and religious differences, and belief in the United States as "the land of opportunity" in which anybody could succeed meant that most workers believed that their condition was temporary.

Marc Karson has noted that "the following characteristics of twentieth century America will help explain the weakness of socialism within organized labor and the absence of an American labor party: (1) The vitality of American capitalism, (2) The middle class psychology of American workers, (3) The American's faith in individual rights, (4) The conservative features of the American political system, (5) The anti-Socialist position of the Roman Catholic Church, (6) The anti-Socialist leadership of Samuel Gompers, a dominant figure in American trade unionism from approximately 1880 to 1924." [35] Horatio Alger concluded his book, *Struggling Upward or Luke Larkin's Luck,* "so closes an eventful passage in the life of Luke Larkin. He has struggled upward from a boyhood of privation and self-denial into a youth and manhood of prosperity and honor. There has been some luck about it, I admit, but after all he is indebted for most of his good fortune to his own qualities."

4. A "centrist" stance by both major parties, reflecting in part the absence of a feudal society in the United States, has led to reasonably nonclass oriented party politics. This may be contrasted with many European party systems that tend to be more programmatic and class oriented in their appeal. Thus Louis Hartz has suggested that: "Actually socialism is largely an ideological phenomenon, arising out of the principles of class and the revolutionary liberal revolt against them which the old European order inspired. It is not accidental that America which has lacked a feudal tradition has uniquely lacked also a socialist tradition." [36] The phenomenon of "centrist" politics has been further reinforced by the broad diversity—ethnically, religiously, and regionally—of

---

[34] See Robert Dahl, "Some Explanations," in Robert Dahl, ed., *Political Oppositions in Western Democracies* (New Haven: Yale University Press, 1966), p. 363.

[35] Marc Karson, *American Labor Unions and Politics* (Boston: Beacon Press, 1965; originally published Southern Illinois University Press, 1958), p. 286.

[36] Louis Hartz, *The Liberal Tradition in America* (New York: Harcourt, Brace, 1955), p. 6.

the American public that has led the parties to draw upon multiple groups in an effort to broaden national appeal. This has led some political scientists to speak of a "consensus" system, in which substantive differences are blurred and obscured rather than made the foci of party politics. This is not to say that some groups do not have better access to decision makers than other groups—and thus can effect policy decisions that are beneficial to their special interests.

5. The "separation of powers" system has made it difficult for a chief executive, even if his party controls the majority in Congress, to dominate the legislative branch of government. President John F. Kennedy noted the difficulties a president has in dominating Congress. "The Congress looks more powerful sitting here," the president said at the end of 1962, "than it did when I was there in Congress. But that is because when you are in Congress you are one of 100 in the Senate or one of 435 in the House . . . that . . . power is divided . . . but the collective power of the Congress, particularly the bloc action, . . . is substantial power." [37] According to Arthur Schlesinger, "Kennedy was fully sensitive—perhaps oversensitive—to the limitations imposed by Congress on the presidential freedom of maneuver." [38] "Before my term has ended," Kennedy said in his first State of the Union address, "we shall have to test anew whether a nation organized and governed such as ours can endure. The outcome is by no means certain." [39]

6. The federal system and its extensions have militated against the development of a national political party. This is due to the decentralized system created by federalism,[40] in which party organizations traditionally built their strongest organizations at the state and local levels. It has been suggested by political scientist Theodore Lowi that parties are both the creations and agents of decentralization; [41] in the latter sense, once parties become established, they have a stake in the maintenance of those state and local boundaries that they dominate electorally.

7. Unlike many of their European counterparts, American parties have never developed a mass, dues paying base, with ancillary agencies to buttress the party structure. There are no dues paying national Republicans or Democrats, and generally there are very few states that have party organizations with systematic dues paying systems.[42] Perhaps Americans are not prepared to "join" parties in the traditional sense in which they join other organizations.

[37] Arthur M. Schlesinger, Jr., *A Thousand Days* (Boston: Houghton Mifflin, 1965), p. 593.
[38] Ibid., p. 567.
[39] Ibid.
[40] Grodzins, in Goldwin, *Political Parties USA,* p. 130.
[41] Theodore Lowi, "Party Policy and Constitution in America," in Chambers and Burnham, *The American Party Systems,* p. 243.
[42] "Amateur" party organizations in California, Wisconsin, Chicago, and New York City are exceptions to this rule. See Epstein, *Political Parties in Western Democracies,* p. 123.

In contrast Carter and Herz state, "British political parties are among the largest in the world. Nearly one-quarter of all those eligible for the franchise belong to one or another of the political parties. . . ." [43]

Antiparty attitudes have been reinforced by the push of postindustrial society. Several very important influences on the party system caused by the changing social and economic relationships of contemporary postindustrial society should therefore be examined.

The increased importance of technology, especially electronic data processing, survey research, public relations, and mass electronic media, most notably television, have all had the effect of weakening the monopoly that parties formerly had on the electoral process. There has also been fragmentation and personalization of politics, caused in part by the decentralized nature of fund raising to meet the increased campaign costs resulting from the use of technology. These trends have, at the same time, created the possibility of more efficient contacts between candidates and citizens than have been maintained in the past.

Increased affluence for many Americans has led to more leisure time, which has sometimes resulted in greater political participation affecting all shades of the political spectrum. Also, mass education has led to more critical and often more intense antiparty questioning of the political system. These two contemporary trends have resulted in movements that have tried, often unsuccessfully, to effect internal party reforms as well as to force an issue orientation for candidates pursuing public office. One notable success for this genre of politics was the 1972 Democratic National Convention. The reforms presented by the McGovern Commission [44] led to changes in the delegate selection process and limited the power of party leaders in the presidential nomination process. But given the failure of presidential candidate McGovern, it is possible that party leaders will return to the convention in 1976 with greater force than they had in 1972. After all, nobody likes to lose when the purpose of the game is victory!

One effect of technology on government has been the rise of the "technocrat" in politics. This relatively recent phenomenon has added a new dimension to the historical inability of parties to represent the members of the polity who are not party members. The nonelected decision maker, who often has technical expertise (hence the term "technocrat"), has either through public

---

[43] Gwendolen M. Carter and John H. Herz, *Major Foreign Powers* (New York: Harcourt, Brace, 1972), p. 81.

[44] For a discussion of the McGovern Commission Report see Chapter 11.

or private government influence and hierarchial authority become more dominant in policymaking. As technical expertise increases in importance it is likely that the role of the voter, who has long been viewed by political scientists as someone whose sole political function is that of political consumer choosing political entrepreneurs from among competing elites, will have to be reevaluated. Similarly the role of party activists will have to be reconsidered. The new and broader context within which parties are viewed will have to include public and private technocratic decision makers.[45]

REPRESENTATION AND PARTICIPATION

Hannah Arendt has indicted modern political parties, contending that although parties are supposed to serve the needs of mass democracy, by making representative government possible where participatory democracy cannot become operative due to vast population, they have failed. She contends that "huge party machines have succeeded everywhere to overrule the voice of citizens." [46] This is not an accurate picture of parties in America today. Parties today may be unloved by many citizens, under attack from numerous competing directions, and left behind in key policymaking decisions, but they can be one of the avenues of access to the political decision-making process if they are understood and properly used by the citizenry.

Parts of the public remain vitally interested in political participation—as numerous demonstrations, protests, reform movements, and calls for "participatory democracy" will affirm. Parties can provide a degree of political stability and a means by which organization and numbers can overcome influence based on wealth and status; it is the latter role that our parties initiated when millions of voters were enfranchised in the first half of the nineteenth century. Today, however, Americans remain confused about just how they want their party system to operate and what they hope it will accomplish. There has never been agreement as to whether elected officials

[45] With this view in mind it might be useful to heed Sanford Lakoff's observations on public and private governments . . . "the separation of public and private implies and generates a dual system of government public and private. Both sectors of government regulate the affairs of members, both exercise influence over nonmembers, and both serve as contexts for the expression and resolution of conflict. To estimate the ordinary prospects for autonomy in any society it is therefore essential to analyze the structure and operation of both types of government and the pattern of their interaction."

Sanford A. Lakoff, "Private Government in the Managed Society," in J. Roland Pennock and John W. Champman, ed., *Voluntary Associations* (New York: Atherton, 1969), pp. 170–71. Given Lakoff's observation, and given the apparent breakdown in the separation between the sectors, it becomes important increasingly to keep in mind the power and influence of members of nongovernmental institutions in affecting public decisions.

[46] Hannah Arendt, "Reflections on Violence," *New York Review of Books* (February 27, 1969), p. 31.

should serve their constituencies, their parties, or their consciences most effectively. Thus the question arises, Can the American political system continue
to provide representative government to its citizenry? Can representation in
its instrumental, symbolic, and authority conferring roles be sustained? [47]

In 1774 in a speech to the electors of Bristol, Edmund Burke observed that:
"Parliament is not a congress of ambassadors from different and hostile interests, which interests each must maintain, as an agent and advocate, against
other agents and advocates; but Parliament is a deliberative assembly of one
nation, with one interest, that of the whole—where not local purposes, not
local prejudices, ought to guide, but the general good, resulting from the
general reason of the whole. You choose a member, indeed; but when you have
chosen him, he is not a member of Bristol, but he is a member of Parliament
. . ." If Edmund Burke's perspective on representation is still operative today,
then the question of the relationship between representation and the participatory needs of the citizenry remains quite real—especially given the nature of
some of the contemporary demands for quotas and functional representation
by minority groups. Additional questions should be raised here as well. Assuming that Burke's perspective on decisions for the polity is not accepted as
reasonable and viable for the last third of the twentieth century, then how in
fact can group and individual participation be increased in decision making,
especially national decision making, when the average size of a congressional
district has grown from 30,000 in 1790 to almost 500,000 today? How can
one resolve the dilemma posed by Robert Dahl: "At one extreme . . . the
people vote but they do not rule; at the other, they rule—but have nothing
to rule over." [48] By increasing the range and stability of party support can
participation in politics and parties be made more of an ongoing process than
simply voting at regular intervals? Does the inequality of distribution of economic resources in America ensure a political system in which participation
is effectively limited by class and status? If parties can no longer serve as
effective "linkages" between the citizen and his government, what is likely to
be the consequence for the future of representative democracy? And, finally,
can the parties make any contribution toward resolving these dilemmas when
our antiparty heritage appears to be running rampant?

[47] Malcolm Jewell and Samuel Patterson, *The Legislative Process in the United States* (New
York: Random House, 1966), pp. 29–34.
[48] Robert Dahl, "The City in the Future of Democracy," in Terrence Cook and Patrick Morgan,
eds., *Participatory Democracy* (New York: Harper and Row, 1971), p. 97.

2
Politics and Participation in Contemporary Society

In Chapter 1 we suggested that political parties have historically provided the forum whereby coalitions of groups and individuals support candidates for public office—at all levels of political organization. We have been socialized to believe that this system of choosing our elected officials provides us both with a forum for public participation in the electoral process and with an adequate system of representing the disparate interests of the members of the voting American public. These assumptions rest to a considerable extent on the belief that our elected officials at least set the parameters for public policy decision making. However, if the choices that must be made within the political system are so intricate that nonelected technocrats must make the decisions, can the parties remain viable instruments of power in the American political system? Will they matter? Certainly local politics—which deals with issues such as education, the provision of law enforcement, and maintenance of local services—will not be as prone to technocratic "takeover" as national decisions on research and development in science policy (especially weaponry). But, even on the local level, questions relating to garbage disposal, for example, can go beyond the limits of knowledge and understanding of the local polity and its elected representatives.

As the United States approaches the twenty-first century it is rapidly being transformed into a *postindustrial society*. A postindustrial society is based on services—as opposed to the extraction of raw materials as in preindustrial society, and the production of goods as in industrial society.[1] This change is

---

[1] This definition of postindustrial society was provided by Daniel Bell, "Labor in a Post-Industrial Society," *Dissent* (Winter 1972): 166.

21

taking place in part as a result of the state of our industrial and agricultural technology. Because of the advanced state of our technology, often incomprehensible to the general population as well as our elected decision makers, technical decisions increasingly have to be made by a "scientific estate." Such decisions affect not only national security, but also the most diverse aspects of domestic social policy in the United States.

The role of the government in our collective lives has been increasing steadily as the delivery of services by the public sector has grown. At the same time, traditional distinctions between the "public" and "private" sectors of economic life have been more or less obliterated in a society in which these sectors are inextricably linked.

Government has become involved in all aspects of technology—from the assumption of most costs for research and development to regulation and coordination. " 'Big government' becomes the necessary adjunct of the technological society, for the state is the custodian of the advanced technology." [2]

The rise of big government based on technology and the provision of a wide range of social services has not been an unmitigated blessing for the American people. This is because the technological society is inevitably a society requiring both massive scale, and its concomitant, complex organization or bureaucracy. The creation of new large-scale institutions that impinge on many aspects of daily life appear to the individual citizen to limit his ability to control his destiny. Feelings of powerlessness and alienation among all sectors of society are the consequences.

When trying to determine the relationships between technology and politics in contemporary society it becomes apparent that often there are more theories than hard data. In this chapter we have on occasion presented theories unsubstantiated by survey data. It is important to keep in mind that there can be many views on a particular subject, and many arguments can be presented to substantiate positions. When views without data support are presented herein they are intended simply as *our* views and are to be recognized as such.

The assumption underlying this discussion of technology and styles of participation in contemporary politics is that technology has produced significant social and economic changes in American life. Technology and affluence have been closely linked for a large number of Americans and both together have apparently given rise to an emerging participatory political style for the middle class. At the same time the relative economic position of other groups has remained below or just about at subsistence level. The new technology has made the extent of deprivation common knowledge and produced predispositions to different political styles among the poor and near poor. In general, what is striking about the political styles emerging in our technological society

[2] Everett Carll Ladd, Jr., *American Political Parties* (New York: Norton, 1970), p. 259.

is that they provide an especially "good fit" with our antiparty tradition.

Political parties represent incremental politics, insofar as they epitomize, often by necessity, compromise, conciliation, and gradual change. Political parties in the U.S., representing wide coalitions of interests, present positions to the voting public that are perceived to be widely acceptable. To be acceptable, they must have broad enough support so that the candidates will not lose elections. "Usually—though not always—what is feasible politically is policy only incrementally, or marginally, different from existing policies. Drastically different policies fall beyond that pale." [3]

Technology is altering many aspects of American society as we approach the twenty-first century. The general pace of life has affected expectations among all Americans. Life is faster; we can fly almost any place in the world in hours, we can make connections to talk to anybody in the country in seconds, and as a partial result of this speedup in communications, the nation seems to be losing regional differences and to be becoming more homogeneous. The South, for example, once a clearly distinct area, has become much like the rest of the nation. The speed with which information can be disseminated is reflected by computer connections between police departments whereby a person's identity can be traced any place in the nation in minutes! At the present time, System for Electronic Analysis and Retrieval of Criminal Histories (SEARCH) is being used in five Middle Atlantic States, and plans are being made to expand the program nationally. In less than five minutes SEARCH can ascertain whether an individual has a criminal record in any of the cooperating states.[4] Can we expect people who live in this kind of society to wait twenty years (or maybe more) for increments of change of the type represented by political parties?

Superimposed on the nature of technological decision making, the changing educational level of the polity, the improved communications network, and the expansion of leisure time among Americans all seem to be reinforcing demands for participation among diverse groups of Americans. In order to maintain a stable and legitimate political order, the participatory needs of the citizenry will have to be met, whether via parties or some alternative route.

CHANGING ECONOMIC RELATIONSHIPS

Let us now consider more specifically some of the changes occurring in postindustrial America.

It should be apparent to anyone who has been living in the United States

---

[3] Charles E. Lindblom, *The Policy Making Process* (Englewood Cliffs, N.J.: Prentice-Hall, 1968), p. 26.

[4] Interview with Donald Payne, Assistant Director, Delaware Agency to Reduce Crime, June 21, 1972.

during the period since World War II that many people are the beneficiaries of the great affluence resulting from the scientific achievements that have reached fruition in the past thirty years. At first blush, the statistics are startling. For example, in 1968 the Gross National Product (GNP) was $900 billion, and in 1974 it was over $1 trillion. This compares to the GNP for 1950 which was approximately $285 billion, and for 1900 which was approximately $17 billion.[5] As an indicator of tangible consumer purchasing power, it should be noted that in 1965 94.1 percent of all homes in the United States had black and white television sets and 5.1 percent of all homes in the United States had color televisions. By 1969, 98.5 percent of all American homes had black and white televisions and 35.7 percent of all American homes had color televisions. Also, in 1958, 1,084,652,000 aircraft miles were clocked by United States commercial airlines. By 1968, the comparable figure had increased to 2,580,500,000 miles—an increase of approximately 1.5 billion miles in ten years. In addition to moving by air, Americans also move around by automobile. In 1968, 83,698,100 cars were registered in the United States. This averages out to over one car per consumer unit for all Americans.[6]

All of these figures tend to indicate that as a nation we are becoming increasingly affluent. At the same time that this obvious wealth is being shared by great numbers of people in the United States, there are people subject to the most abject poverty. Though we like to believe that the problems of poverty are *not* as severe as they were ten or twenty years ago, in reality the situation has not improved too much. There were, for example, according to findings of the National Nutrition Survey—a survey mandated by the U.S. Congress in December 1967—"statistics in some areas [which] showed that infant mortality was as high as 40, 60, even 80 per 1,000 live births compared to 17 per 1,000 on the national average." [7]

Also, as one looks at income distribution data, unemployment statistics, public assistance rolls, and the like for the United States, it is clear that not everybody is as well off as we might like to believe. While many people believe that American income distribution has become considerably more equal as the nation has grown more prosperous, that is not entirely true as Table 2 shows. The relative shapes of the lowest and highest fifth have remained more or less constant over time and the concentration of great wealth in the hands of a

---

[5] In 1957 prices. *Historical Statistics of the United States: Colonial Times to 1957* (Washington, D.C.: Bureau of the Census, 1960), p. 139.

[6] Seymour Kuntz, ed., *New York Times Encyclopedic Almanac, 1970* (New York: 1969), pp. 425, 672.

This figure does not assume that all American consumer units possessed one plus cars in 1968. In fact, some families did own more than one car, while other consumer units owned no automobiles.

[7] U.S. Congress, *Congressional Record,* 92nd. Cong., 1st. sess., 1971, 117, pt. 5:7363.

Table 2. Income Distribution in U.S.

	1962ᵃ (percent)	1970ᵇ (percent)
Top Fifth	57.2	41.6
Fourth Fifth	15.6	17.4
Middle Fifth	11.4	23.5
Second Fifth	8.6	12.0
Lowest Fifth	7.2	5.5

SOURCES: [a] This data was drawn from chart 5–15 "Distribution of Wealth, 1962," in Office of Management and Budget, *Social Indicators* (Washington, D.C.: Government Printing Office, 1973), p. 164.

[b] This data was drawn from U.S. Department of Commerce, Bureau of the Census, *Current Population Reports,* Series P-60, no. 80, *Income in 1970 of Families and Persons in the United States* (Washington, D.C.: Government Printing Office, 1971), p. 28.

few continues unchanged. At the same time Table 3 does indicate a decline in the absolute number of poor in America.

In 1974, the Bureau of the Census reported $4,540 as the poverty level for an urban family of four. There were in March 1974, 23,000,000 (11 percent of the total population) people living in purchasing units with incomes of less than

Table 3. Persons Below the Low Income Level ($6,960): 1959–1971

Year	All Persons (in millions)
1959	39.5
1960	39.9
1961	39.6
1962	38.6
1963	36.4
1964	36.1
1965	33.2
1966	30.4
1967	27.8
1968	25.4
1969	24.3
1970	25.5
1971	25.6

SOURCE: Table derived from Table 5–17 "Persons Below the Low Income Level: 1959–1971," *Social Indicators,* p. 183.

this designated poverty level. The Bureau of Labor Statistics (BLS) has also been in the business of setting up "low income" levels. In 1971 their "lower" budget guideline figure for a family of four living in an urbanized area (most of the nation) was $6,960 (1971) a year. If $7,000 a year, a close approximation of $6,960 is used—then 30.1 percent of all Americans were members of consumer units with incomes that fell below the BLS "lower" budget guideline. One-fifth of all family units had incomes which fell between the lower figure of the BLS and the "intermediate" budget for an urban family of four, which the BLS set at $10,644 (1971).[8] By 1974 the BLS budget figures had been changed as a result of inflation with the "lower budget" figure changing to $8,181 and the "intermediate budget" figure changing to $12,626. However, the size of the population in each group changed only by a small margin. Members of those consumer units which fell between the "lower" and "intermediate" budget levels are in this chapter referred to as the "working class." [9] There are some individuals who identify with the working class whose incomes are higher than those referred to herein. However, for the purposes of analysis it is convenient to define an easily identifiable population group.

Further, the uneven distribution of essential social services underscores the fact that affluence is not spread among all Americans. Health is an interesting service to examine. In 1972 nearly $60 billion was spent on health care by Americans; this figure represented approximately 7.9 percent of consumer expenditures in that year.[10] However, because most health care is private and very expensive, not all people have the same access to health facilities.

> . . . health delivery services are non-existent for many in our population. If they do exist, they are too few and too far between. It is easy to say that we need to get nutrition into our health delivery system, if there is no delivery system, then what? [11]

EFFECTS OF INCREASED AFFLUENCE ON AMERICANS

Thus it is evident that some people are benefiting more from our nation's affluence than others. It should also be evident that the increased wealth is

[8] Calculated from figures from U.S. Bureau of the Census, *Current Population Reports*, Series P-60, no. 80, *Income in 1970 of Families and Persons in the United States* (Washington, D.C.: Government Printing Office, 1971), pp. 40, 59.

[9] U.S. Department of Labor, Bureau of Labor Statistics, *3 Budgets for an Urban Family of Four Persons 1969–1970* (Washington, D.C.: U.S. Department of Labor, Bureau of Labor Statistics, 1972), pp. 1, 7; U.S. Department of Labor, Bureau of Labor Statistics, *Autumn 1973 Urban Family Budgets* (Washington, D.C.: U.S. Department of Labor, Bureau of Labor Statistics, 1974), p. 1; U.S. Department of Commerce, Bureau of the Census, *Consumer Income* (Washington, D.C.: U.S. Department of Labor, Bureau of the Census, 1974), Series P-60, no. 96, p. 1.

[10] *Information Please Almanac* (New York: Dan Golen Paul Assoc., 1973), p. 84.

[11] U.S. Congress, *Congressional Record*, 92nd. Cong., 1st. sess., 1971, 117, pt. 5:7635.

having continuing effects on the entire system. The question which must be asked at this point is: What are the effects of increased wealth on the American population in our postindustrial society?

The first factor that should be examined, especially as it relates to the political process, is the nature of changing educational and occupational opportunity, more readily available now than even as recently as twenty years ago. Access to *information* about all aspects of life is more readily available than ever before in recorded human history. Information retrieval systems have led to a speeding up of information gathering, as computer systems in general have led to new and faster ways to collect and store massive quantities of information. In the human sphere, for example, we know that the government authorities can readily collect data about all citizens—to be used at later dates for any number of undisclosed reasons. We have developed an educational system in the U.S. that reaches great numbers of people. In 1940, the median educational achievement level in this nation was 8.6 years; [12] in 1970 it was 11 plus years. The percentage of the college age population attending college in 1945 was 15 percent; in 1970 the comparable figure was 50 percent (for all post-high school education).[13]

There are a variety of explanations for the increased educational levels of the American public. It has been hypothesized that many people have encouraged schooling because access to social status—a sign of financial success—has seemed to come to individuals as a result of educational achievements. Higher level of education has appeared to mean higher status jobs with paying better salaries, than jobs that require less education. It has also been observed that whereas an industrial society in its "youth" creates low-skilled jobs, a more mature industrial society, especially one generating *cybernetic* achievements, eliminates low-skilled jobs. Thus in order to find and retain employment, a certain degree of advanced skill development is now required. This leads many people to seek advanced educational degrees. In some mass production industries, many routine assembly line jobs have been replaced by machines. Thus low skilled individuals are *not* needed to produce the products; skilled technicians are required. An additional result of this situation has been the demand for increased personnel in the service component of society, leading to an expansion of the professional and managerial component of society.

These factors superimposed on the post-World War II era—in which returning GIs who might never have had the opportunity to gain a college education were given financial support through the GI Bill of Rights—led to an expansion of the college educated population in the late 1940s and early 1950s. There were 2.2 million people who took advantage of that provision of the GI Bill.[14]

---

[12] *Historical Statistics,* p. 214.
[13] *New York Times,* January 10, 1972, p. 28.
[14] *Congress and the Nation,* vol. 2, 1965–68 (Washington, D.C.: Congressional Quarterly Service, 1969): 456.

Today these men and women are among the managers and the professional service core of our technological society, and are among those individuals responsible for creating jobs for the skilled (but not the unskilled), and for encouraging education for the nation's youth.

Education, changing economic relationships, and cybernetics have therefore been interacting to change relationships in society. As the demand for trained personnel increases, and the demand for untrained personnel declines, the disparities in economic fulfillment between these two groups do *not* decline. In fact, such gaps become more apparent to many people—especially to those people who feel marginal to the affluent society—particularly unemployed workers, but also some professionals who are dissatisfied with society as it exists.

The changes in educational and job opportunities that have been caused by alterations in the technological base of society have had another effect on the general population—i.e., other than the effect of producing an expanded, educated, skilled professional group. There have been, due to the changing nature of economic relationships, increases in the extent of leisure time to which we as a nation have access.

Quite evidently there are different kinds of leisure. Our only concern here, however, is the relationship of leisure to politics. Though the family that is barely eking out a subsistence income may appear to have "spare" time, it is *not* apparent that they have truly acquired leisure. The worker who now works a thirty-hour week, however, has acquired a certain amount of leisure time. Also, individuals who spend more years in school often have more flexible schedules and consequently greater access to leisure. Many other examples can be found of individuals in our postindustrial society who have acquired considerably more leisure than either their parents or their grandparents ever knew.

What do people do with their leisure? Will the individual whose work week is reduced from five days to four days become involved to any extent in learning about politics or participating in the political process? Will the ever increasing school age population (both in terms of absolute numbers and proportionate to the size of the nation's entire population) impact the political system—through gaining more knowledge of its workings and outputs, or through participatory efforts?

There are unfortunately no definitive empirical studies that provide an answer to these questions. It is clear, however, that some people will find leisure time a burden, whereas others will take advantage of their "free time" for self-improvement and the like, or to participate in some way in the political process. In the past decade, we have seen students, for example, participate in the political process, first in antiwar movements and later in movements to reform their universities. Many of these students appear to believe that in the affluent society, the "good" life is possible for all.

The school-age population that was fully employed was among the harshest critics of these politically participating students. Thus student participation in the political process was *not* solely an "age-cohort" movement. Student participation in the political process was an "age-education-leisure cohort" movement. Surveys have shown that 15 percent of college students did some campaign work in 1970—three times the number of older adults.[15] Many young activists—an elite of sorts in themselves—have sought to "destructural-ize" both political and technological society—with possibly significant results for the political system. Similarly, the increased number of political "ama-teurs" mobilized in the 1960s and 1970s (often affiliated with the New Demo-cratic Coalition [NDC]), and usually comprised of educated middle-class women and professional and managerial men, is another instance of leisure time being used for participation in the political process. The unsuccessful campaign by Senator Eugene McCarthy in 1968 to gain the Democratic party nomination for president, and the 1972 campaigns by Senator McGovern, are examples of political participation by people with increased amounts of leisure time. Also interest in such independent nonpartisan groups as Ralph Nader's "Public Citizen," the Center for the Study of Responsive Law, and Common Cause together with continued grass roots support for suburban politics, are indications that some leisured members of society are using their time to try to influence the political system. Whether or not large numbers of the working class—who are recently being exposed to shorter work weeks with fewer hours on the job, will become politically involved beyond voting, is a question which has yet to be answered.

Some politically oriented groups that have developed as a result of having more leisure time are *not* keyed into the job-oriented two-party system that has existed for so many years in the United States. Increasingly professional and other well off citizens are more concerned with the *issues* of politics than with party. In fact, in September 1973, it was estimated that fully 33 percent of all registered voters were "independents" [16] who claimed to be unaffiliated with any political party. The "independents" tend to be younger, more middle class, and more educated. This is the highest percentage of "independents" in U.S. history.

Why has there been this increase in "independent" voters in the U.S.? What has caused this changing political identification pattern among Americans? Part of this changing identification pattern can be related to the generalized antiparty attitudes held by many members of the polity. Perhaps these views are surfacing now in light of the increased educational levels and changes in the variety of leisure activities available to many Americans. It has been estimated that adults in the United States watch on an average of two and

---

[15] Frederick G. Dutton, *Changing Sources of Power: American Politics in the 1970's* (New York: McGraw-Hill, 1971), p. 35; see Chapter 6 for a discussion of the youth vote; see also Kenneth Keniston, "You Have to Grow Up in Scarsdale to Know How Bad Things Really Are," *New York Times Magazine* (April 27, 1969), p. 21 for an analysis of young radicals.
[16] *The Gallup Opinion Index* (October 1973): 20.

a half hours of television each day.[17] Some of the entertainment sector provides social/political commentary as well. In addition, 62,107,527 newspapers are purchased each day.[18] In 1969, Huntley and Brinkley (NBC) and Cronkite (CBS) spoke nightly to about 30 million people.[19] Thus the information inputs to us are vast.

Not all people receive equal access to this information. Generally, the college educated public reads more news, and watches more television news than people with less education.[20] In addition, political participation increases with education. Therefore, it is likely that those people most likely to have up-to-date political information are those people who are most likely to be active participants in the political process. As all indications are that the available job opportunities will continue to be in areas that demand college education, more and more people will be socialized by their educational experience to pay attention to current political happenings, to question the decisions of policymakers, and to try to influence the political process. For example, decisions on environmental issues are not satisfactory to increasing numbers of people who feel that industrial interests get more hearings from decision makers than the rank and file voters who want pollution controls. Increasingly more and more citizens are questioning the uses of technology and the influence of dominant economic groupings in creating societal problems.

Since the two political parties as they have existed to date in the United States have not always provided an adequate forum to cope with changing conditions, and have not sufficiently met the demands for more complete participation in decision making by rank and file voters, new ways may develop to fill the void being created by these changing relationships. Such new ways— perhaps taking the form of community organization or more traditional interest groups—may develop because in a complex social setting citizens are perhaps no longer satisfied by channeling their views into only two partisan alternatives.

CHANGING STYLES OF POLITICAL PARTICIPATION

THE NEW MIDDLE-CLASS STYLE

Given the assumptions on the effects of technological society discussed above it is understandable that some groups are increasingly conscious of the

[17] Robert McNeil, "Electronic Schizophrenia: Does Television Alienate Voters?" *Politeia* I (Summer 1972): 5.
[18] *Information Please Almanac* (New York: Simon and Schuster, 1972), p. 374.
[19] Ladd, *American Political Parties*, p. 260.
[20] See William A. Glazer, "Television and Voting Turnout," *Public Opinion Quarterly* (Spring 1965): 86.

need for participation in the political system. Since different economic groups in the United States are affected differently by technology and affluence, the major socioeconomic groups have begun to develop—and in some cases resurrect from earlier groups—distinct styles of political participation. In this section three major socioeconomic group styles will be considered: the middle-class "reform" style, the nonwhite "community" style, and the white poor and white working class "entrenchment" style. Not all members of the groups to be discussed favor the styles associated with their socioeconomic group. The styles being considered are merely that group's *predispositions* to political style. This typology does not include the upper class, because their wealth and social status apparently provide them with easy access to policymakers.[21]

> Our concern here is with the nature of the individual's attachment to the body politic and, more particularly, with the value premises underlying the choices made by certain classes of voters. Our hypothesis is that some classes of voters (provisionally defined as "subcultures" constituted on ethnic and economic lines) are more disposed than others to rest their choices on some conception of "the public interest" or the "welfare of the community." To say the same thing in another way, the voting behavior of some classes tends to be more public-regarding and less private—(self—or family—) regarding than that of others.[22]

Although the orthodox application of this typology can be disputed, it is useful as a "take-off" point for this discussion. Studies completed by James Q. Wilson and Edward C. Banfield point to the fact that voters in "some income and ethnic groups are more likely than voters in others to take a public regarding rather than narrowly self-interested view of things, i.e., to take the welfare of others, especially of the community as a whole into account as an aspect of their own welfare." [23] Public regarding or "reform" voters are also likely to be committed to political principles, making the compromise traditionally associated with our two-party system often difficult to obtain. According to Banfield and Wilson, the middle-class, white, Anglo-Saxon Protestant ethos stresses the procedure, the desirability of rule by the "best qualified" (or "experts"), and the ideal of "good government" (honesty, efficiency, and impartiality). This translates politically into at large representation, nonpartisanship, a strong executive, and master planning. The contrasting "private regarding" or working-class ethic emphasizes family and personal needs and loyalties

---

[21] For example see C. William Domhoff, *Who Rules America?* (Englewood Cliffs, N.J.: Prentice-Hall, 1967). Some upper-class members behave, it should be noted, much as do the middle-class "reformers" described below.

[22] James Q. Wilson and Edward C. Banfield, "Public-Regardingness as a Value Premise in Voting Behavior," *American Political Science Review* 58:876.

[23] Ibid., p. 885. See pp. 35–36 for a discussion of the significance of their typology.

and is best expressed through ward politics, the boss, and the machine.[24] Banfield and Wilson have also suggested that some Anglo Saxons and to a lesser extent Jews—groups found predominantly in the middle- and upper-income brackets in this country—have a tendency to be "public regarding." What effect has this tendency toward "public regardingness" and increased issue orientation had upon political participation by individuals of this background? [25] Have these new attitudes by politically active groups in the U.S. affected political decision making and the party system? What kinds of changes are likely as a result?

The issues that divide the public- and private-regarding groups often center around social programs. Some members of the middle and upper-middle classes may be more willing than the working classes to see tax increases to expand and provide more equitable social programs. The working classes, who may benefit ultimately from the programs being supported by the more public-regarding groups, in the short run see infringements upon their own lives in the form of higher taxes to pay for services from which others will reap the benefits.[26]

The policies the "public-regarding" middle classes support include programs that they perceive as benefiting the wider community. Very often in the history of reformism in American politics, this has led to demands for procedural changes in the nominating process, structural changes in the governing process, and policy changes on specific issues. Such demands have occurred within and outside of the party structure. The successes of party reform, historically most often initiated by people from the middle classes, can be seen at the local and state levels of government in some areas. For example, nonpartisan elections in Wisconsin cities and towns for all judges, municipal councils, town officials, and county board members are required by state law and are a testament to the diligence of the Progressives in Wisconsin who also, early in the twentieth century, brought a comprehensive primary law to the state of Wisconsin.[27] By 1917 all but four states had provisions for primary elections for at least some nominations. These reforms were in response to "bossism": the attitude expressed by William Marcy Tweed, Tammany Hall boss (New York City) at the turn of the twentieth century when he said, "I don't care who does the electing, just so I can do the nominating." [28] More recently, cities such as New York, Chicago, and Philadelphia have had middle-class groups

[24] James Q. Wilson and Edward Banfield, "Political Ethos Revisited," *American Political Science Review* 65 (December 1971): 1048.

[25] See Chapter 5 for a discussion of who participates in politics and how.

[26] See for example Patricia Cayo Sexton and Brendan Sexton, *Blue Collars and Hard Hats* (New York: Vintage Books, 1971), pp. 69–70.

[27] Leon D. Epstein, *Politics in Wisconsin* (Madison: University of Wisconsin Press, 1958), p. 37.

[28] Quoted by John W. Gardner in *Common Cause Report* (November 1971): 1.

who try, with varying success, to roust the "bosses" and open up party politics to "the people." The party in question, in big cities with party organizations and partisan elections is almost always the Democratic party, since cities have in the past been the power preserves of the party that welcomed immigrant groups. If Mike Royko is correct, middle-class reformers have a long way to go, particularly in Chicago. In 1971 Mayor Daley won 70 percent of the vote and handily defeated a reform candidate, a liberal Democrat running as a Republican under the reform banner. The size of Daley's victory prompted Royko to cite an unidentified observer, who said: "This proves that if you put together a coalition of independents, blacks, liberals, and Republicans, there is no way Daley can keep you from getting twenty-nine percent of the vote." [29]

In New York City, for many years there has been an organization that has tried to coordinate internal party reform groups. In the 1950s and early 1960s the coordinating group was known as the Committee for Democratic Voters (CDV). In the late 1960s and 1970s the group has been called the New Democratic Coalition (NDC). This group has been successful in electing numerous representatives to Congress, the state legislature, and the city council. They were able to wrest domination, though not complete control, of the Manhattan Democratic Party Organization ("Tammany") from the incumbents, who were led by Carmine DeSapio, machine "boss" of the 1950s.

Middle-class reformers have also operated in the Republican party, though notably with less frequency and with less noise, and usually on the statewide or national convention level. Thus there are similar types of movements in the Republican party. In 1952, for example, Republican party irregulars—"reformers"—were able to gain the nomination for president for Dwight Eisenhower away from Senator Robert Taft (Ohio) who had the support of the party organization. In 1972 Representative Paul McCloskey (Republican representative from California) entered primary elections in an attempt to take the Republican party nomination away from President Nixon. McCloskey's support was not too different in character from the support gained by Democratic Senator Eugene McCarthy in 1968 when he entered primaries in order to force President Johnson to surrender the presidency. In other words, McCloskey's supporters were usually white, middle class, issue oriented, and often young voters.[30] In New Hampshire, for example, McCloskey workers were active in trying to get students to register—since they expected that their candidate would benefit most from youthful participation in the voting process.

As noted above, reformers in the Republican party emerge without the noise and fanfare often associated with reform in the Democratic party; thus, nation-

[29] Mike Royko, *Boss* (New York: E. P. Dutton, 1971), p. 215.
[30] Interview with John Doble, a McCloskey worker in New Hampshire (December 31, 1971).

ally a "liberal" Republican organization, the Ripon Society, has been working quietly behind the scenes for years in an effort to make the GOP more "progressive."

For others, an antiparty form—"reform" or "good government" outside the party system—has been the desired goal. Certainly the "nonparty politics" that often pervades suburbia is "an out-right reaction against partisan activity, a refusal to recognize that there may be persistent cleavages in the electorate and an ethical disapproval of permanent group collaboration as an appropriate means of settling disputes." [31] Robert Wood suggested when he wrote these words back in 1959 that suburban communities were reasonably homogeneous, and therefore the nonpartisanship of their electoral system was representative of "a highly integrated community life with a powerful capacity to induce conformity." [32] This form evolved when suburban populations were rather similar—most being middle to upper class. By the 1970s, however, when 35 percent of the total U.S. population is suburban, it is no longer the case that the "public-regarding" subgroups in our society alone control suburbia.[33] Quite to the contrary, all classes are represented in suburbia, and increasingly the problems of the inner city are coming to American suburbs, though many suburbs continue to utilize the nonpartisan form of electoral politics.

Since a majority of suburbs have nonpartisan elections, reform of local party politics is not an issue for many members of America's middle class in the 1970s. It should be noted here that many of our large cities also have adopted nonpartisanship as a legacy of the successes of earlier reformers. Thus cities such as Boston, Los Angeles, Milwaukee, Minneapolis, and Newark, N.J., have nonpartisan elections, and party politics does not revolve as easily around local issues and personalities. Also many of our middle-sized cities have retained as their legacies from earlier reformers nonpartisan elections and council-manager or commission forms of government. Often a city will have a council-manager or commission form of government in which elected officials are chosen on a nonpartisan ballot.[34] A majority of American cities have, in fact, adopted nonpartisan electoral systems.

Other middle-class reformers have moved into traditional pressure group activity in order to seek changes in both the party system and the governmental process. It is interesting to note, for example, the middle-class orientation of

[31] Robert Wood, *Suburbia: Its People and Their Politics* (Boston: Houghton Mifflin, 1959), p. 155.

[32] Ibid., p. 154.

[33] This figure is based on census estimates that appeared in the *New York Times,* June 21, 1970, p. 54.

[34] See Charles R. Adrian, *State and Local Governments* (New York: McGraw-Hill, 1967), pp. 222–27, for a discussion of commission and council-manager forms of government. Adrian notes that these forms of government are most common in middle-sized rather than small or large cities.

the public lobby Common Cause (public regardingness is its theme) formed by John W. Gardner in 1970. Jack T. Conway, president of Common Cause, characterizes the membership as "highly intelligent, highly educated, highly professional, highly white, highly suburban or small town."

What is most important about the "new middle-class politics" or reform, however, is not necessarily the distinction Banfield and Wilson make between class determined political ethos. It should be noted that despite the appealing simplicity of the "public regarding" and "private regarding" categories, middle-class and working-class groups may not actually conform to these ideal types.[35]

The "public regardingness" concept is probably not a completely accurate way to analyze middle-class politics, for even the most well intentioned proposals will not distribute benefits equally to all. It may well be asked what is "public regarding" about many classic reform concepts; metropolitan reorganization that dilutes black voting strength, city manager and nonpartisan forms of government and politics that limit the power of the masses in decision making, and high levels of public expenditures for programs that will benefit the middle and upper classes in some way?[36] A notable failure of "reform" politics has been its inability to include effectively working-class people and nonwhite minority groups and actually speak in the name of the "whole community," if, indeed, it is ever possible to do so. Thus, the most important influence of the "new middle-class" politics has been less in terms of specific political proposals and more in terms of a new political "style": one which emphasizes *issues, voluntarism,* and *participation.*

These values were reflected in American politics in the McGovern Commission Report issued by the Democratic party in 1970. The McGovern Commission called for democratization of the process used to select the delegates to the Democratic National Convention, which nominates the presidential and vice-presidential candidates of the party. In most states, largely middle-class groups participated eagerly at the grass roots level in precinct party caucuses as an expression of acceptance of the report's intent.[37]

It is well to remember, however, that until recently the greatest victory of the amatuer spirit—or the new "middle-class" style—occurred not in the Democratic but in the Republican party and not on the "left" of the Republi-

---

[35] See Raymond Wolfinger and John Osgood Field, "Political Ethos and the Structure of City Government," *American Political Science Review* 60 (June 1966): 324–26 for the view that the theory needs modification and James Q. Wilson and Edward Banfield, "Political Ethos Revisited": 1062, for the finding that a significant number of voters' attitudes do not display the consistency along "ethos" lines that they had anticipated.

[36] See Chapter 7 for a more detailed discussion of the impact of reform style politics on local government.

[37] For a more complete discussion of the McGovern Commission Report and its implications see Chapter 11.

can party (as in the case of the Democrats and Republicans discussed above) but on the "right," with Barry Goldwater winning the presidential nomination in 1964. Grass roots volunteers took over the Republican nominating machinery at the local level, supporting a candidate for whom rigid adherence to principle and a refusal to compromise were all important. Both the Goldwater and McGovern victories indicate that possibly the most important contribution of the middle-class "style" of politics has been its participatory aspect: its emphasis on personal contact and insistence on adherence to ideologies or issues.

Today the "new politics" is no longer the province of the liberal wing of the Democratic party and no longer leads invariably to the support of liberal candidates. Conservative "law and order" mayoralty candidates Stenvig (Minneapolis) and Yorty (Los Angeles) mobilized hundreds of middle-class Americans to do door-to-door canvassing for them in 1969. George McGovern's Democratic presidential candidacy in 1972 was brought about by many of the same techniques that made Barry Goldwater his party's nominee in 1964. In 1972 in California, for example, prior to the June 7 primary, McGovern's middle-class campaigners mounted a massive personal contact campaign that involved thousands of volunteers in a get-out-the vote drive in which 75 percent of the states 23,000 precincts were canvassed by primary day.[38] Democratic party organizations in key states such as Illinois and Ohio turned out to be hollow shells—as the only and productive field organizations belonged to McGovern's volunteer troops.

Hence, the "reform" ethic is not only the province of the left or left of center and the middle-class "style": participation, issue orientation, voluntarism, may well have signaled important changes in American parties and politics.

COMMUNITY PARTICIPATORY STYLES AMONG NONWHITES

We have noted already that despite the apparent affluence of large numbers of Americans, many millions of people in this nation are living at or below the subsistence level and many millions more can be classified as "subaffluent." It is clear that nonwhites, blacks, American Indians, and Spanish-speaking Americans,[39] far out of proportion to their percentage in the total population, are the individuals least likely to be enjoying the benefits of postindustrial society. Of the nearly 5 million black families in the U.S. in 1970, 55.5 percent (2,735,040) had incomes below $7,000 a year.[40] This compared to 30.1 percent

---

[38] *New York Times,* June 4, 1972, pp. 1, 15.

[39] Orientals are not included in this classification because they are often not poor.

[40] U.S. Department of Commerce, Bureau of the Census, *Current Population Reports,* Series P-60, no. 80, "Income in 1970 of Families and Persons in the United States" (Washington, D.C.: Government Printing Office, 1971), p. 60.

for the whole U.S. population and 28.3 percent for the white population. Also, though nonwhites in 1970 comprised 13 percent of the total population of the United States, the Nixon administration estimated they comprised 38.6 percent of those eligible for the Aid to Families with Dependent Children (AFDC) program.[41] Certainly the majority of consumer units receiving AFDC and other forms of public assistance are whites—but again, not in proportion to their numbers in the total population.

Anthropologist Oscar Lewis noted the pessimism and powerlessness of the poor: "On the level of the individual the major characteristics are a strong feeling of marginality, of helplessness, of dependence and of inferiority." [42] Technology, which has created the anomaly of large islands of poverty in a society of affluence has, however, also contributed to the creation of mass discontent among the poor. If poor people—a disproportionate number of whom are nonwhite—have the same visual access to the media images as the affluent, and are as aware of the speed of change as the affluent, how has this affected their political participation? This question has become increasingly important as the accoutrements of the jet age and instant communication have become entrenched in society.

Television confronts the viewer with the images of affluence. Toothpaste, soap, detergents, paint, and beer advertisements present pictures of affluent Americans—usually white, but also nonwhite—using their products. Television entertainment also underscores the affluent society, with the "typical" television family shown as white, suburban, and middle class, using all the products advertised on the screen throughout the day. The same images of the middle class—usually upper-middle class—reach the suburban livingroom with its viewers as reach the ghetto livingroom with its viewers. The obvious difference lies in the "fit" to reality. The "fit" is more appropriate to the suburban middle class than to the poor. The poor do *not* live in the life-style portrayed on the television screen. But they are being reminded over and over again that the screen image is apparently the norm. One can be reminded just so many times of how well others live—and how one ought to live to be living up to social expectations—before there may be an "explosion." The "explosion" has taken two general forms. Though crime rates have always been higher in the poor neighborhoods than in the affluent areas there seems to be a growing awareness of this phenomenon! Some black and white radicals discuss these crimes as political acts of violence against a repressive society.[43]

[41] U.S. Congress, Senate, Committee on Finance, The Family Assistance Act of 1970, H.R. 16311, revised and resubmitted to the Committee on Finance by the administration (Washington, D.C.: Government Printing Office, 1970), p. 25. AFDC public assistance category is the family assistance category.

[42] *La Vida* (New York: Random House, 1965), p. xlvii.

[43] See, for example, Eldridge Cleaver, *Soul on Ice* (New York: McGraw-Hill, 1968), p. 14.

Also, in the second half of the 1960s, racial disorders broke out in many American cities. Group violence in America, however, is not a new condition. We have a tradition of intergroup conflict—blacks and whites, Protestants and Catholics, et al. The causes of the disorders in the 1960s cannot be narrowed down to one particular situation or event; they were not group pitted against group as much as they were one group against society. There were, however, multiple and interrelated—oftentimes unmeasurable—causes of these outbreaks.[44] One of these causes was related to the media insofar as the conditions of affluence have been, and continue to be, bombarding the television viewing audience. Throughout the history of the United States material rewards of affluence have not been available to the poor black population of the U.S. because of discrimination—and because of the history of powerlessness that riddles poor communities.

In addition to these conditions, the media have a tendency to present crisis news in the same manner in which they present football games, complete with play by play action and instant replays. Thus the disorders in Detroit, for example, were broadcast throughout the Detroit viewing area. The disorders were therefore seen in livingrooms throughout the state of Michigan, and they spread throughout the state within hours. In July of 1967 the same type of situation occurred in the Newark, N.J., viewing area—where within hours, violence spread throughout northern New Jersey. The Kerner Commission reported:

> Reports of looting, sniping, fire and death in Newark wove a web of tension over other Negro enclaves in northern New Jersey. Wherever Negro ghettos existed—Elizabeth, Englewood, Jersey City, Plainfield, New Brunswick—people had friends and relatives living in Newark. Everywhere the telephone provided a direct link to the scenes of violence. The telephoned messages were frequently at variance with reports transmitted by the mass media.
>
> As reports of excessive use of firearms in Newark grew, so did fear and anger in the Negro ghetto. Conversely, rumors amplified by radio, television and the newspaper, especially with regard to guerrilla bands roaming the streets—created a sense of danger and terror within the white communities.[45]

It should be added that the existing lag between technology and public policy and the contrast between the slowness of political accommodation and the instant nature of telecommunications have produced, especially among the nonwhite poor, a reluctance to participate in the two-party system. The media have provided for protest groups the promise of instant television coverage

---

[44] See H. Palley and M. Palley, "Social Policy Analysis: The Use of Social Indicators" *Welfare in Review* 9 (March–April 1971): 8–13, for a discussion of this phenomenon.

[45] *Report of the National Advisory Commission on Civil Disorders* (Washington, D.C.: Government Printing Office, 1968), p. 69.

for demonstrations. Publicity for "the cause" has seemed to be a way for the powerless to circumvent the time consuming process of building political organization.

However, some nonwhites have continued to use the two-party system in order to influence public policy.[46] To the extent that nonwhites do participate in party politics, like working-class whites, they are most concerned with politics as a means of obtaining jobs and financial resources. They are far less interested in reforming political institutions than in using them as access routes to the middle-class status some whites have now acquired.

Alternative channels for participation have been sought by nonwhites in political institutions other than parties. Nonwhites have been among those seeking to counter bureaucratic bigness and impersonality through new forms of political participation. Community participation received its impetus from the Community Action Programs (CAP), which were developed as a result of the Economic Opportunity Act of 1964. Title II, Section 202 of the Economic Opportunity Act (EOA), which called for the development of CAPs, also mandated the "maximum feasible participation of the poor." Though in March 1972, there were 977 operational CAPs in the United States, in 1974 the Office of Economic Opportunity was dismantled. However, despite its formal demise, the concept of community participation seems reasonably well entrenched in poor communities. Since 1964 welfare rights groups, tenant organizations, block associations, Model Cities councils, and most recently groups seeking "community control" over educational, health, housing, and law enforcement agencies have come to supplement the original call for increased participation by the urban (predominantly) black and Spanish speaking poor. These organizations are akin to middle-class civic associations in many of their goal orientations. What is new about these organizations, however, is that people previously uninvolved politically are being mobilized to participate in politics. These activities have increasingly led to a more "politicized" society as more specific issue demands have been made by the nonwhite poor citizenry. Moderate party organizations have often lost ground before more militant and outspoken community groups. Although some blacks have continued to be involved in the two-party system (and several cities have elected black mayors), if parties decline in influence, the question of how in conditions of relative economic scarcity allocation of resources can be accomplished more equitably looms large.[47]

[46] See Chapter 6 for a discussion of black voting.
[47] See Chapters 6 and 7 for a discussion of blacks in political parties.

THE ENTRENCHMENT STYLE AMONG THE WHITE POOR AND THE WHITE WORKING CLASS

We have considered the nonwhite poor in the U.S. and have asked how they react to the "new society" that is being built upon the affluence and technology of postindustrial America. Now let us look at a group that numerically is larger than the nonwhite poor. This group is the white poor. In 1971 28.3 percent of white families fit into the category of consumer units with a total family income below the BLS "lower budget" figure of $7,000 per year.[48] (By 1974, this figure had changed to approximately $8,200 per year.) Included in this group are those people who live on incomes below the poverty level (as defined at the beginning of this chapter). Some of these people live in consumer units where the head of the household is employed. Others live in consumer units where the head of the household is unemployed. In some instances, the latter units are receiving public assistance payments of some type; in other units, unemployment insurance may be collected for short periods of time; and, in still other units, aged individuals and couples may be living on fixed retirement incomes in the form of social security insurance payments or other pension plans.

How do these people react to the affluence of America? The white poor are receiving the same media messages as the nonwhite poor. They also have the same inadequate social services as the nonwhite poor, and thus one can make the same generalizations about disparities in services and goods provisions for both groups. Intergenerational poverty is a factor among poor whites as it is among poor nonwhites. They suffer the same frustrations. We know, for example, that during the black ghetto disorders, whites looted stores along with blacks.[49] The white poor identify with the "silent majority" and with notions of the "Forgotten Man" and "Middle American." Many of these people resent the rebellious children of the upper-middle class who have the benefits of wealth and education, yet cause social disruption in society. Many believe, too, that if the nonwhite population would start cooperating with the political system, instead of disrupting society, and if the upper-middle class and rich would reach to *their* needs instead of reacting exclusively to the needs of nonwhites, a more equitable society for all would result.[50]

Geographically this poor white population is distributed across the nation,

[48] Calculated from data in U.S. Bureau of the Census, *Current Population Reports,* "Income in 1970 of Families and Persons in the United States," p. 59.
[49] For example, 15 percent of arrests in 1967 riots in twenty-two cities were of whites. *Report of the National Advisory Commission on Civil Disorders,* pp. 129, 172.
[50] See Teresa E. Levitin and Warren E. Miller, "The New Politics and Partisan Realignment," Center for Political Studies, University of Michigan (unpublished paper presented at 1972 Annual Meeting of American Political Science Association), for the finding that the "Silent Majority" is "composed largely of working-class people, people with low incomes and limited educations" (p. 34).

but is most heavily concentrated in the South where it was reported that in 1971 34.3 percent of the white population have incomes below $7,000 a year.[51] These people came out in large numbers to support George Wallace's presidential candidacy in 1968, and have helped in recent years to elect conservative southern congressional delegations and conservative southern governors.[52] Traditionally, the poor white population in this country has been very patriotic and has volunteered large numbers of young men for the armed services. The eleven states of the old Confederacy had 24.6 percent of the nation's population, but provided 28.5 percent of the total army enlistments for fiscal year 1971.[53]

Another group that perceives itself as marginal to the political decision-making process but in which there is a high level of political participation—in all forms—is the working class. This is the population which it was reported in 1971 had incomes between $7,000 a year and $10,000 a year representing 20.4 percent of the white population.[54] (By 1974, this BLS range had changed to approximately $8,200 to $12,600.) Their attitudes are often like those of the poor whites, for although economically more secure than the white poor, workers often do not feel economically secure. They believe that they are not receiving all that they deserve from the political system—especially given their contributions to industrial society in the form of "labor." These people perceive policymakers as giving to the poor—especially the nonwhite poor who are not contributing to society—at their expense. They know that they are working hard, but that they have trouble making ends meet because inflation eats up their raises. They know that government services are far from adequate, and they insist that whereas large sums of money are going to the marginally employed and unemployed poor, little is going to them. They feel that they deserve some greater benefits from the postindustrial society that they keep moving.[55]

[51] Bureau of the Census, *Current Population Reports*, p. 59. It is interesting to note that in a poll conducted by Gallup in August 1972, of those people with incomes in the $3,000 to $4,900 a year category, 45 percent categorized themselves as "conservative" and 30 percent as "middle of the road." Of these same people 44 percent categorized Nixon as "conservative" and 29 percent as "middle of the road." Thus there was clearly some similarity in their self-identification and their identification of Nixon on a liberal conservative continuum. The *Gallup Opinion Index* (August 1972): 8–9.

[52] The poor whites have a tendency not to vote and not to be active participants in the political system just as poor blacks have this tendency. The former may vote when they feel especially threatened. For example, in November 1971, poor whites came out in record numbers to vote *against* Charles Evers, a black, for governor of Mississippi.

[53] This data was provided by the Selective Service Commission to Senator William Roth (Delaware), who made it available to the authors.

[54] This is of course an approximation of the $10,644 figure used by the BLS as an intermediate budget for an urban family of four.

[55] See for example, Pete Hamill, "The Revolt of the White Lower-Middle Class," in Louise Kapp Howe, ed., *The White Majority* (New York: Vintage Books, 1970), pp. 10–22.

Thus the very poor white and unemployed are concerned with issues such as public welfare and jobs. The working classes are most interested in issues such as inflation and job security. The latter group supports candidates who discuss specific issues and policy alternatives that they perceive will help them. They are not likely to be enamored of candidates who are glamorous and upper-middle class in background and who do not appear to understand their problems. Thus by 1969, John Lindsay of New York had lost most of the working class support he had in 1965 when he first ran for mayor of New York. As a candidate and as mayor for four years, he had proven to the satisfaction of large numbers of the city's working class that he was concerned not with their immediate needs, but with a broader conception of "community."

"Among other things, Lindsay's problems show that for Americans weary of a government overly attentive to selfish interest groups a switch to a government that ignores those interest groups can be a bold new shift to disaster—the hazards therein would not seem to be mitigated by scientifically correct solutions purveyed by sophisticated, throbbing public relations machinery." [56]

The type of political organization that has in the past best exemplified the political style of the working class and the lower class has been old-style machine politics. The well functioning machine often has been able to provide economic security to some members of the working class, as well as providing social and economic mobility for other people of working-class origin. People have supported machine candidates in order to provide job security for themselves or a friend or relative, in order to acquire a job, and in recognition of the fact that these politicians will get the necessary programs for the neighborhood from the decision makers. In addition, the candidates of the machines are from the community and known to the people, and know what the people want and need. Such ward based local politicians relate exclusively to the narrow needs and demands of the people in their district. They take care of getting streets paved and street lights fixed—not in another part of the city, but in their own section.

This "material" style of politics existed in American cities when the waves of immigrants arrived during the second half of the nineteenth century and early twentieth century and persists on the ward level in working-class areas in many cities today where reformers have thus far failed to penetrate.[57]

Where the old-style political machine has begun to atrophy, new political behavior patterns have begun to emerge amongst the white poor and the white working class. The attachment to party does not seem as strong as it was in the past. In part this behavior is due to fears of racial unrest and rapid progress

---

[56] Steven R. Weissman, "Why Lindsay Failed as Mayor," *Washington Monthly* 4 (April 1972): 53.

[57] The political machine will be discussed more fully in Chapter 7.

for blacks at the expense of the white working class. In part it may be related to a perception held by many white workers that middle-class "reformers" have taken over the Democratic party, and have moved it to the left of center—away from what they believe to be an accurate representation of their economic and social interests. Thus in 1968, George Wallace received considerable working-class support for his third-party candidacy for president.[58] The same pattern held in Wallace's 1972 campaign for the Democratic nomination for president. When it came to pulling down a lever for a presidential candidate in 1972 it has been estimated that 54 percent of the "blue-collar" voters chose the Nixon lever. Though the white working class still tends to identify with the Democratic party, their political behavior in the past decade may portend a willingness to move away from supporting the Democratic party, if the Democratic party does not respond to its demand for representation and participation.

THE NEW POLITICS

It is apparent that although large numbers of Americans are reasonably secure economically, many other citizens are not enjoying the benefits of the affluent society; if one uses the figure of 25 million people in poverty (as defined by HEW), 12 percent of the total population, and if one adds those people whose incomes provide just marginal economic security, the working class, the figure represents 50 percent of American families. Thus 50 percent of all American families in our postindustrial affluent society are either poor or just marginally "making ends meet." [59]

On the basis of this information, it would be naïve to suggest that the economics of scarcity has been left behind. It is possibly the case that for those people who are the prime beneficiaries of the affluent society "scarcity" is no longer an issue. For the middle-class, nonmaterial issues, such as ecology, may be meaningful. For the half of the population that is not as economically secure as the middle classes, the more material rewards of politics are still more relevant than the community oriented, ostensibly nonmaterial politics of the middle class. For example, controls on industrial pollution may be a meaningful issue for people who live in areas where they are benefiting from industrial development. On the other hand, there are areas of the United States, most

[58] See S. M. Lipset and Earl Raab, *The Politics of Unreason* (New York: Harper and Row, 1970), p. 361 (Table 46); and Philip E. Converse, Warren E. Miller, Jerrold Rusk, and Arthur Wolfe, "Continuity and Change in American Politics: Parties and Issues in the 1968 Election," *American Political Science Review* 63 (December 1969): 1102 for the finding that Wallace's center of occupational gravity was among white skilled workers.

[59] One-half of American families have incomes below $10,000, Bureau of the Census, *Current Population Reports,* p. 59.

notably Appalachia, where residents might be far more economically secure if there were industrial pollution, as a necessary side product of industrial development. Similarly, controlling the number of air-conditioning units that can be installed in a city so as to prevent the overutilization of power sources is a fine issue if you have an air conditioner installed in your home. If you do not already have an air-conditioning unit, it is reasonable to expect a preference to see more units built, so that you may be just as comfortable as your economically more secure neighbors.

The marginally secure working classes and the poor classes in the United States do not perceive their interests as similar and therefore do not recognize the political reality that requires them to work together to influence the political system if they ever expect to experience the economic security of the upper middle class. The poor and the working classes would benefit (as would the middle class), for example, from more extensive government funding of health programs. The high costs of health care, especially in the case of long-range illness or accidents, can economically wipe out the working-class (or middle-class) family. Preventive medical care is often prohibitive due to the high costs of doctors' visits. The very poor who now use public health services receive care in overcrowded, understaffed facilities. In order to receive this care, they must go through the degrading experience of applying for assistance. If both groups were able to recognize—in this example—that they would both benefit from a more extensive government supported health program, then they could start pressuring decision makers collectively for this change. Similarly, both groups would benefit from better public schools and public recreational facilities.

The average working class person does not, however, perceive a commonality of interests with the poor—whom he may identify as nonwhite. Rather he believes rightly or wrongly that the very poor want his job and are therefore threatening his own economic security. In addition to the economic component of group conflict, *status anxiety* remains a major political motivation for whites of marginal socioeconomic status who feel their hard fought position in society is threatened. "Groups within the nonestablished and the disestablished are engaged in bitter and continuing conflict." [60]

At the present time, a de facto alliance often exists between the reformist middle classes (and upper-class businessmen) and the poor (who are often nonparticipants or minimal participants at least in the traditional political arena). To a considerable extent it was such a coalition of upper-middle class reformers and the "underclass" who supported the unsuccessful presidential campaign of George McGovern. Reformers tend to exclude the working class from consideration because they charge workers with narrow-mindedness and

---

[60] Ladd, *American Political Parties,* p. 275; see his pp. 267–71 for a good discussion of status anxiety.

bigotry. The reformer can recognize the problems of the very poor, perhaps in a paternalistic way, but does not perceive the problems of the working class as clearly. Members of the working class are often shunted aside as reactionary bigots both by the poor and the reform-minded middle class.[61]

Of course, it may be argued that if indeed technocrats make most crucial decisions, especially at the national level, even providing the information necessary for the development of parameters within which policy alternatives can be explored, political coalitions may not really matter. It is our belief that they do matter. The technocrats also provide the information to state and local governmental units, but we all have some understanding of schools, hospitals, and the other issues that affect our everyday lives. Also, though most people know very little about national defense—which amounted to over 30 percent of the recommended outlays in President Nixon's federal budget for fiscal 1975 ($95.047 billion out of a total budget of $304.4 billion)—we do have thoughts on spending priorities, and on federal education programs, public welfare programs, where highways should be built, and the like. It is therefore likely that even at the national level, for the foreseeable future, decision makers, if they want to be reelected, will have to consider the judgments of their constituents in setting the outer limits of social policy. It should be underlined that as constituents, citizens must be counted as voters, community and group leaders, and interest group members. As long as appropriations must be approved by congressional decision makers, the elected Congress will have to react to the political pressures from their districts. Thus, they will have to be sensitive to the demands of political coalitions, and they will have to continue to set the limits for policy and program development which will be implemented by the unelected and therefore politically less responsive policy program developers.

It has been the contention of this chapter that as technology pervades politics and as government gets larger—in order to provide some services and "monitor" others—the desire for representation and participation (though not necessarily party politics) remains a potent force.

We have seen that the very poor, traditionally marginal participants in the political process, have often been leaders in seeking to develop institutions outside of partisan politics through which to gain power. The affluent middle class, while retaining some allegiance to partisan modes, has moved toward

---

[61] Some writers see a potential for coalition between the "professional and managerial class," which may also be viewed as a "new working class," a product of our postindustrial society, and the "old working class." While the former have high incomes and are well educated they are employed in subordinate positions by large public and private bureaucratic organizations and are directly or indirectly dependent on federal political decisions for their economic well being. It is possible, although hardly imminent, that this "new working class" may join the "old working class" and provide the basis for a new progressive coalition. See Michael Harrington, "Old Working Class, New Working Class," *Dissent* (Winter 1972): 60–61.

a more issue oriented, voluntaristic style of political participation. The working class remains an uncertain ally of the ward-based machine style of politics as we move toward the twenty-first century.

The increasing concern by some Americans with participation in politics, formed partly as a result of the technological, postindustrial society in which we live, will continue to place the resolution of controversial issues on the political agenda and may make conflict resolution in the traditional, centrist two-party mold more difficult in the future.

Introduction to Chapters 3 and 4

The next two chapters attempt to develop the idea that the candidates—not the party—are the major focus of contemporary campaigning.

Party professionals have been replaced by a "new class" of campaign professionals who utilize techniques such as computer technology, survey data, and sophisticated media appeal in order to put their employers—the candidates —across to the public. We will suggest that, though all of these new techniques

47

associated with the "new political technology" affect the voting public, thus far at least, the most significant impact of the "new technology" has not been directly on the voters. Rather, it has been on the politicians, due in large measure to their reliance on these "new" techniques. As a result, a changed role for parties in the electoral process seems likely.*

A major factor in the newly circumscribed role played by parties in election campaigns has been the direct primary, which initially loosened party control over the nominating process.** While campaigners continue to rely on personal contact on a door-to-door basis, there can be no doubt that *skills and money* have replaced party organization as key political resources.† The new style of politics stems in part from previous changes in the role and function of party organization and, in turn, the new politics has created further changes in parties.

* See Harold Mendelsohn and Irving Crespi, *Polls, Television, and the New Politics* (Scranton, Pa.: Chandler, 1970), p. 7.

** See Chapter 8 for a further discussion of the direct primary.

† See Robert Agranoff, "Introduction to the New Style of Campaigning: The Decline of Party and the Rise of Candidate-Centered Technology" in Agranoff, ed., *The New Style in Election Campaigns* (Boston: Holbrook, 1972), p. 11.

3

The New Political Technology: The Use and Effects of Polling and Public Relations

It was suggested in Chapter 1 that the major function of American political parties in the past was to nominate, campaign for, and elect candidates to public office at all levels of government. In recent years, however, new private organizations have come to dominate at least a significant segment of the ground once occupied by political parties in the electoral process. Insofar as this has occurred, there is another force operating in American politics reinforcing our antiparty tradition. The private organizations are the pollsters, public relations or political management consultants, and the media. Let us examine each in turn in order to evaluate its impact on the American party system.

It is our view that the "new political technology" has already had a major impact on the electoral process: on the manner in which candidates are selected, our expectations of candidates, the functioning of national nominating conventions, and the party structure and nature of campaigning for public office.

POLLS IN THE MODERN CAMPAIGN

GENERAL PERSPECTIVE

Rather than assume that any comprehensive coverage of the complex field of polling will be included here, let us begin by underlining the fact that only enough material to provide the basis for conversance in the field of politics, and especially political parties, will be included.

Some polling is commissioned in order to determine the popularity of candidates and officials while other polls are carried out in an attempt to gain some insight into the distribution of popular attitudes or extent of information on public issues.

If an individual is considering the possibility of campaigning for public office—given the costs and the time commitment involved—he will, if he has the funds, commission a poll to determine his chances for victory.

A candidate or potential candidate may also try to gain information from a poll regarding his name recognition by voters, his popularity, his "image," and the "correct" positions to take on issues. Polls may even reveal which issues a candidate ought to concentrate his campaign upon and may also help the candidate to determine the effectiveness of his campaign appeals over time. Of course, polling is a very expensive enterprise. (For example, it was estimated by the Finance Committee to Reelect the President that Richard Nixon's 1972 campaign costs included $1.6 million for polling.) [1] Potential candidates and declared candidates often cannot afford this type of campaign method. However, big city mayoralty hopefuls and state and national political contenders do often hire pollsters to gain better insight into their chances of winning an election, and to learn how to best go about campaigning for the desired office. For example, in September 1960 Joseph Alsop noted in the *Washington Post* that:

> The truth is that Senator Kennedy has made lavish use of a professional polling firm, Louis Harris and Associates, ever since he began promoting his presidential candidacy. The Senator's strategy has always been much influenced by Mr. Harris' findings about the state of public opinion, about the issues capable of generating votes and about Kennedy's standing with the electorate.

It has been estimated that an average poll, with a sample size of 1,000 people, costs approximately $10,000 [2]—which can be an awesome figure if one does not have funding. Of course, in order to raise the money necessary to run a respectable campaign, one must first prove to one's potential contributors that there is a reasonably good chance of electoral victory. A favorable poll will be invaluable in proving this vote-getting ability. Most people do not want to underwrite a sure loser. [3] Incumbents can raise money more easily than insur-

---

[1] Report of the Finance Committee to Reelect the President, as reported by Thomas W. Madron and Carl P. Chelf, *Political Parties in the United States* (Boston: Holbrook, 1974), p. 233.

[2] Dan Nimmo, *The Political Persuaders* (Englewood Cliffs, N.J.: Prentice-Hall, 1970), p. 96.

[3] The possible exception to this rule might be the person who is willing to underwrite financially a candidate, who though he has little or no chance at victory, may be articulating views that the financial supporter wishes to have expressed to the polity.

gents, and people with private funding sources often can raise the necessary additional money to embark on early campaigning. It is very difficult for the financially unsupported person, without private wealth, who is not already a politically "known factor" to raise the necessary money to enable him to enter into politics—especially if he aspires to high political office.

PRIVATE VERSUS PUBLIC POLLING

The type of polling we have been discussing is private polling. Political candidates or hopefuls, as well as elected officials, commission polls in order to gain some scientific data to support their claims of personal popularity as well as to determine the most popular issues to support. Once in office, as noted above, officials will sometimes commission private polls to gauge the extent of their popularity—especially if they are interested in running for reelection. Thus President Johnson, who was known for paying close attention to the polls, became the first president of the United States to hire a private polling firm, Oliver Quayle & Co., to report to him on a continuing basis.[4] In 1968, he paid close attention to the private polls, and it is believed that his lack of popularity among the American voters was one of the more salient reasons for his stepping down after just one term as the elected president of the United States. All the polls indicated that his popularity among Democratic voters had fallen substantially. In February 1968, Gallup (a public poll) had estimated his support for nomination among Democrats at 52 percent, with Robert Kennedy receiving 40 percent. By March, these figures had changed to 45 percent for Johnson and 44 percent for Kennedy. In the presidential "trial heats" Johnson's popularity was on the wane, too. In December 1967, Gallup estimated 44 percent of the voters favored Johnson, 36 percent favored Richard Nixon, and 12 percent favored George Wallace. By February 1968, the figures had changed to 39 percent for Johnson, 39 percent for Nixon, and 11 percent for Wallace. Harris Poll figures (another public poll) showed Johnson in even a worse light. In March 1968, Harris estimated 39 percent for Johnson, 39 percent for Nixon, and 12 percent for Wallace. The trial heats between Johnson and New York's Governor Nelson Rockefeller looked especially bad for Johnson. By March 1968, Harris had Rockefeller outpolling Johnson 41 percent to 34 percent. Thus, "trial heats" can provide prospective candidates with a dynamic view of their electoral chances. Perhaps one note of caution should be expressed. Candidates sometimes do very badly in early polls, and then go on to mobilize support and win elections. Thus New York Governor Nelson Rockefeller did very poorly in the early 1966 and 1970 polls

---

[4] William H. Honan, "Good Case of the Poll Sniffles," *New York Times Magazine,* August 21, 1966, p. 34.

against Democratic opponents Frank O'Connor and Arthur Goldberg. Yet, he went on to win reelection as governor of New York. Money was *not* however, a factor for Rockefeller! [5] Also, George McGovern, who polled only 3 percent in a poll in January 1972, won the Democratic nomination in July of the same year, much as another "dark horse," Eugene McCarthy, had defied pollsters by achieving significant primary successes in 1968.

In addition to the privately commissioned polls, there are also public polls (the Harris and Gallup polls noted above are public polls), which candidates and potential candidates do not commission. The public polls are paid for by newspapers, magazines, and radio and television networks. These polls will give information on candidate popularity, as well as information on the array of voter attitudes and information on specified public issues. Candidates, potential candidates, and financial backers pay attention to these polling results as well as to the results of the private polls.

All polls measure public attitudes and information levels with regard to issues and candidates. But whereas private polls measure attitudes and information in regard to issues specified by the contracting individuals, public polls do not. It is because public polls may not provide the types of information a candidate may need at a given time, that private polls are commissioned. Unlike private polls, whose results may remain hidden from the public if unfavorable to a candidate (or "leaked" to the press if they may damage an opponent), nonprivate polls are usually well publicized. The polling of attitudes toward potential candidates—both private and public—can and does take place months or even years before the actual campaign and election.

SOME SPECIFIC USES OF POLLS

The public position a candidate takes if he is influenced by the polls (apparently candidates and potential candidates are likely to be at least partially influenced by survey results), is likely to be drawn from what the pollsters find the public wants from a candidate.

For example, polls influenced the decision of Representative Henry Helstoski, running for U.S. Congress from New Jersey in 1966 to moderate his views on ending bombing in North Vietnam. Polls demonstrating voter concern about "Black Power" led senatorial candidate Edward Brooke in Massachusetts in 1966 to appear on television decrying "violence." Robert Griffin, successful Republican senatorial candidate from Michigan, was influenced by polls in the same year to emphasize centrist rather than conservative issue posi-

---

[5] Rockefeller sought to take advantage of his "underdog" status and benefit from gradually building momentum for his candidacy.

tions.[6] Polls can harm a candidate's chance for electoral victory if potential voters feel that he has absolutely no chance of winning—with a possible reaction of "why vote?" They can also hurt if victory appears to be too imminent, for the candidate may be tempted to just "take it easy," because he expects to win anyway. Thus, in 1948 "all the polls were catastrophically off in predicting Truman's defeat, and Dewey, taking counsel from them, was defeated."

It is also helpful to any campaign hopeful to do well in early polling so as to garner the necessary financial and manpower support. One apparent exception to this "rule" was George McGovern, who in 1972 began the "primary trail" with a 4 to 5 percent showing in national polls, which as noted above, dropped to 3 percent in January 1972, but went on to receive his party's nomination largely through organizational efforts.[7] By doing well in the early polls, it is sometimes possible to garner the impetus to gain a wanted nomination to the detriment of any potential political foes. An example of this process could be seen just prior to the 1968 Republican Convention when Richard Nixon emerged as the overwhelming choice of Republicans, according to the Gallup Poll.[8] Polls may also be used by a losing party to determine the reason for failure. In 1968 Republicans studied "marginal" congressional districts—when their loss had been by a margin of less than 5 percent—to determine why their candidates had failed.[9]

SAMPLING AND THE ACCURACY OF PREDICTIONS

Questions may be raised about the accuracy of surveys used so extensively today by candidates running for public office. Distortion of results is clearly possible especially when private polls are utilized. But it is also important to examine the results of the public polls because of the wide disparities that can emerge among the pollsters depending upon how their samples were chosen and how successful they were in contacting the individuals in their selected sample. Thus, Jules Abels reported rather disparate results in public polling just prior to the 1966 New York State gubernatorial election. (See Table 4.)

A general rule in polling has been set by George Gallup and Saul F. Rae. They suggested that ". . . the size of the population has little bearing on sample size whenever the sample size is less than 5 percent of the population." [10] It has been estimated that in order to have a systematic poll of any

---

[6] Dan Nimmo, *The Political Persuaders,* pp. 91–93, 110.

[7] See *New York Times,* June 11, 1972, pp. 1, 54.

[8] Richard M. Scammon and Ben J. Wattenberg, *The Real Majority* (New York: Coward, McCann, and Geohegan, 1970), p. 149.

[9] Dan Nimmo, *The Political Persuaders,* p. 94.

[10] *The Pulse of Democracy* (New York: Simon and Schuster, 1940), p. 48, quoted in Nimmo, *Political Persuaders,* p. 96.

Table 4. New York Gubernatorial Poll, 1966 (Percent)

	Rockefeller	O'Connor	FDR, Jr.	Adams
Daily News	39.0	41.6	11.7	7.7
ABC	33.0	35.0	14.0	5.0 (Rest Undecided)
NBC	40.0	27.0	14.0	6.0 (Rest Undecided)
Actual	45.0	38.0	08.6	8.4

SOURCE: Jules Abels, *The Degeneration of Our Presidential Elections* (New York: Macmillan, 1968), p. 43.

population—be it a congressional district or the nation—a properly chosen sample of 1,000 adults will be within 5 percent of accuracy. The 1,000 member sample should be chosen so that there is a representation of the constellation of major differentiating characteristics in the polity being sampled. For example, if results of this type of sampling tell the pollster that in a nationwide survey of 1,000 adults, 40 percent of respondents say they approve of the way the president is handling his job, the chances are ninety-nine out of a hundred that somewhere between 36 and 44 percent of American adults hold this opinion. If our sample size had been 4,000, our range of error would have been 2 percent, permitting us to estimate that 38–42 percent so evaluate the president's performance. With interviews costing approximately $10 each, a 1 percent error range will cost $170,000. The pollsters and clients are usually willing to accept a 4 percent range in surveys.[11]

There are two principal sampling techniques used by pollsters; probability and nonprobability sampling.[12] Briefly, a probability sample does not choose people to be interviewed on the basis of their individual characteristics. Rather by giving every person an equal opportunity to be chosen, there is the probability that every segment of the population will be represented proportionally. In a nonprobability sample, people are selected on the basis of specific characteristics or even convenience. For example, if 12 percent of the population is black, then 12 percent (or 120 of sample 1,000) of the sample should be black. In general, nonprobability samples are no longer used by pollsters because of the factors of chance and because the ordinary tests of statistical accuracy are not applicable. For example, a pollster utilizing nonprobability sampling techniques must recognize that the sample selection depends not only on chance but on the sample selector. Shopping centers can be selected as places to interview people—the centers being chosen because they represent a particular

[11] Nimmo, *Political Persuaders,* p. 96.
[12] Nimmo, ibid., has a good discussion of how samples are chosen for polls. See pp. 95–108.

neighborhood's income, ethnic composition, and other relevant characteristics. Also mailing questionnaires is a method used to collect information for nonprobability samples. Clearly motivation to respond varies, and the most highly motivated and educated people will respond and thus be overrepresented in the sample. This factor leads one to question the validity of nonprobability samples. It should be noted, however, that there is still some modified nonprobability polling in use today; both mailed questionnaires and telephone polls are used in some surveys. Since there is an error range of plus or minus four percentage points in a poll with a sample of 1,000, it is clear that all the pollster is telling the voter or the candidate is that within a range of eight percentage points, he can predict what will happen at the polls. Of course, when elections are won by margins of one or two percentage points—as has been the case of two successful presidential candidates since 1960 (JFK's 1960 margin was 118,550 popular votes and Nixon's 1968 margin was 510,314 popular votes)—polling may not tell us too much about what the future has in store for us vis-à-vis political office holders.

It should be noted that the kinds of questions asked by survey respondents may significantly determine their replies and sometimes impugn the validity of the survey. Thus, for example, pollster Louis Harris during the New Hampshire presidential primary in 1964 tested three different types of polls. These techniques were: (1) first choice volunteered by respondents; (2) the voters choosing from a list of candidates and possible write-ins; (3) a "secret" written ballot by the voter. Harris actually received different results with each type. It might be expected that the secret ballot would most reflect the actual outcome. In reality, however, the "first choice" most clearly reflected the views of the electorate.[13]

THE THREE-WAY RACE AND THE LARGE UNDECIDED VOTE

When there are three-way competitions for public office, the problems of polling and prediction—both private and public—become more complicated, by more than simply a factor of one. Some of the traditional assumptions about two-party alignment do not hold, and personality and issues can begin to play a more significant role in voting behavior. For example, in 1968 when George Wallace ran as the American Independent party candidate for president of the United States, he received votes from people who had previously not defected from voting for one of two major political parties. Thus the estimates of regularly voting Democrats and Republicans had to be adjusted. Also, in this case, it appears that some people who were leaning toward voting for

[13] Harold Mendelsohn and Irving Crespi, *Polls, Television, and the New Politics* (Scranton, Pa.: Chandler, 1970), pp. 113–14.

George Wallace prior to the actual election shifted their preference at the end of the campaign. The possible reasons for these shifts include the traditional American adage: "Why Waste a Vote!" Some pollsters were unaware of the extent of voter switching until just prior to the tallying of the votes on Election Day.

Of course, when one is trying to predict elections on the basis of three candidates rather than two, a 4 percent error factor can become more significant. The proportion of the vote any one candidate is likely to receive is reduced because the range of alternatives has been raised from two to three. One additional point may be raised here. If there are more than two candidates contesting a position there may be increased levels of voter volatility.

Another factor that complicates predictions is the "undecided" vote. There has always been an "undecided" vote with which pollsters have had to contend. If it is small, then the problems of prediction are not as complicated as when the "undecided" vote is bigger. With the rise in the number of independent voters, the problems the pollsters will have to face regarding early predictions are reasonably obvious. If 33 percent of the eligible voters are not registered in a political party, then, at least in theory, it is possible that 33 percent of the electorate is, at the outset, "undecided." [14] Added to this must be the consideration that there are those voters registered in political parties who are also "undecided"—since not all registered voters are necessarily automatons voting for the party in which they have registered. It is important to remember that traditionally, the less committed a voter has been to a party—even if he is registered in a party—the less likely he has been to vote. If this still is the case—and it is becoming questionable as the "independent" category is increasing in size—what portion of these "undecideds" can the pollster expect to vote, and for whom? A wide range of error in polling can result if the pollster predicts that nonvoters will vote! [15]

In 1968, the number of potential voters was overestimated by preelection surveys. In 1972 the size of Nixon's victory was so great that any miscalculations in the size of the turnout did not affect significantly the pollster's prediction. Problems of turnout overestimation may have occurred in New York City in 1969 when a three-way race and a large number of undecided voters chose among Republican conservative John Marchi, Democrat Mario Procaccino, and Liberal John Lindsay. The respected *Daily News* poll predicted a Lindsay victory margin of 21 percent and Quayle (for NBC) predicted a 15 percent Lindsay victory margin. Lindsay's actual winning margin was only 7 percent.[16]

In Great Britain, most major polls erroneously predicted Laborite Harold Wilson the victor in 1970 national elections (while Conservative Edward

---

[14] It should be noted that in practice not all registered Independents are uncommitted to a party.
[15] Mendelsohn and Crespi, *Polls, Television,* p. 110.
[16] *New York Times,* November 5, 1969, p. 32.

Becker (in percent)		March 7 Primary (in percent)	
Muskie	42	Muskie	47.8
McGovern	26	McGovern	37.6
Yorty	4	Yorty	6.0
Hartke	2	Hartke	2.7
Mills	2	Mills	4.1
Other	4	Kennedy	.9
Undecided	20	Humphrey	.3
		Edward T. Coll	.3
		H. M. Jackson	.1
		McCarthy	.1

SOURCE: "New Hampshire Results," *Congressional Quarterly Report* (March 11, 1972), p. 539.

Heath actually won). The error occurred because of incorrect calculations on the turnout of Laborite voters. In the 1972 New Hampshire primary, a high proportion of the "undecideds" voted for McGovern. While McGovern was favored by only 26 percent of surveyed votes in a preprimary poll, he actually received 37.6 percent of the final vote.[17]

The examples cited should indicate an important aspect of polling; polls are not predictions of election results, a fact clearly borne out by Hubert Humphrey's poor survey showings in the early days of the 1968 presidential campaign and George McGovern's disastrous percentages in the early days of the contest for the Democratic presidential nomination in 1972. Polls are simply measurements of opinion at a given point in time, reflections of trends, and it must be remembered that politics is a dynamic process.[18] In addition, since polls often are not made on a nationwide basis, in a presidential election they often do not consider the impact of the electoral vote.

IMPACT OF POLLS ON VOTER EXPECTATIONS AND BEHAVIOR

The obvious question that must be asked at this point is: What impact does all of this polling, during prenomination and electoral campaign periods— sampling personality, "image," and issues—have on voters' expectations and

[17] In theory, Muskie could have lost 5 percent of his 42 percent of the estimated poll vote, and could have gained half of the undecided vote.

[18] See Mendelsohn and Crespi, *Polls, Television,* p. 108. Polls are often released to the public four weeks after the survey is completed.

behavior? There is thus far little evidence to support the view that polls do induce voting behavior change. But let us consider the "underdog" effect, and then analyze the "bandwagon" effect.

The "underdog" effect implies the development of "sympathy" for the presumed loser whose support is consequently increased. [19] This may result in a larger voter turnout than previously anticipated. The presumed "underdog" vote can thus turn the tide of an election away from the assessments of the pollsters made prior to the actual casting of votes on election day. However, there does not appear to be much systematic evidence available to prove or disprove this effect. [20]

The "bandwagon" effect is associated with the notion that as a candidate's chances for nomination or election improve—in this instance according to the polls—he will gain increased support, often at the expense of the other contenders for the same office. In the case of a nomination, for example, if one candidate is doing especially well in the polls, rank and file members of his own party, as well as other potential candidates, may begin to rally to his support prior to the granting of the actual nomination. The latter group may do this for a variety of reasons; the most obvious being the high costs of running a campaign. If the chances of winning are seen as unlikely, why not "go with a winner!" However, rank-and-file voters may support a "sure loser" if there are other motives driving them besides electoral victory for their candidate. (Thus in 1972, though Richard Nixon was far ahead in the polls prior to the New Hampshire primary, Representative Paul McCloskey remained in the New Hampshire primary race to the end. [21] His supporters knew he would not win, but they remained loyal to him in order to provide a broadening of the discussion of foreign policy alternatives for the Republican party.) Hubert Humphrey came up in the Gallup Poll from fifteen points behind his rival Nixon (and just seven points ahead of third-party contender Wallace) in September 1968 to a close forty-two–forty position, only two points behind Nixon by November 2, defying the bandwagon effect.

It is possible, however, for modified "bandwagon" effects to occur when, for example, a third-party candidate looks reasonably strong at the outset of the campaign. As the campaign proceeds, the polls indicate that one of the major party candidates—in this case more than the two major parties are running candidates—is ahead. This may lead to the falling away of support

---

[19] Ibid., pp. 17–18.

[20] Ibid., p. 25.

[21] A poll for the *Boston Globe* by the Becker Research Corporation, January 17–24. Among 1,035 New Hampshire Republicans preferences were: Nixon 71 percent, McCloskey 14 percent, Ashbrook 4 percent, Paulsen 1 percent, Others 1 percent, Undecided 9 percent. *Congressional Quarterly Weekly Report* (February 26, 1972): 427. Another poll for the *Boston Globe* by Becker, March 4–5, showed: Nixon 69 percent, McCloskey 14 percent, Ashbrook 5 percent, Undecided 10 percent. *Congressional Quarterly Weekly Report* (March 11, 1972): 539.

from the third-party candidate to the person the polls point to as being ahead. The specter of a wasted vote may lead people who *had* intended to support the perceived "sure loser" to switch.

Generally, there is little empirical evidence to support the relationship between polls and the "bandwagon" effect, just as there is little empirical evidence to support the relationship between the polls and the "underdog" effect.

Most voters are not easily led astray by poll results because their political attitudes and commitments have been formed long in advance of the campaign itself. If the impact of the campaign process is regarded as (1) reinforcement of the vote of the faithful, (2) activation of the views of the latent or wavering voter, and (3) conversion of the opposition (the most difficult to achieve),[22] it may be observed that there may not be a large number of voters in any given election (perhaps less than one-quarter—though these voters may be critical for victory) who may even be potentially influenced by poll results or other campaign attempts.

IMPACT OF POLLS ON ACTIVISTS, LEADERS, AND ELECTED OFFICIALS

ABILITY OF CANDIDATES TO RAISE MONEY

It is clear that while polls could potentially have an effect on voting behavior, generally the effect apparently is not causal in nature. What relationship exists between the outcome of the polls and the behavior of the party activists, party leaders, and elected officials? The first question we will examine will be the relationship of the polls to fund raising. Alexander Heard has observed that "the giving, receiving, and handling of political money is a unique and especially important form of political action . . . it ranks next to voting itself in deserving study." [23] A political corollary of this economic rule might well be that as the possibility of political success increases, the smell of success will beget money. Thus it appears to many observers of the political scene that if one looks like a winner—and the polls tell the potential campaign contributors who looks like a winner just as it tells the candidates, party leaders, and voters who looks like a winner—one will be better able to gain the access to the funds that are necessary to run a competitive political campaign in our era of campaigning with mass media, polling, and public relations.

In the months prior to the 1972 presidential primaries, the number of

[22] Lewis Froman, "A Realistic Approach to Campaign Strategies and Tactics," in David W. Abbott and Edward T. Rogowsky, eds., *Political Parties: Leadership, Organization, Linkage* (Chicago: Rand McNally, 1971), pp. 286–90.

[23] Alexander Heard, *The Costs of Democracy* (Chapel Hill: University of North Carolina Press, 1960), p. 3.

presidential hopefuls multiplied within the Democratic party. During the eighteen months prior to the nominating convention, at least twelve Democrats campaigned for this party's endorsement.[24] They were not all successful in raising the money needed to run a primary campaign. Senator Harris, for example, after only one month of active campaigning and a $50,000 debt, had to drop out of the contest because he was unable to raise the funds necessary for campaigning. He had not looked like a winner to people who might have funded his campaign.[25] On the other hand, Senator Muskie, Senator Humphrey, and Senator McGovern all were able to raise funds for all-out campaigns during the months prior to the campaign. The polls prior to the primary elections indicated that Senator Muskie was the favored candidate of 35 percent of the Democratic voters, Senator Humphrey of 32 percent of the Democratic voters, and Senator McGovern of 6 percent of the Democratic voters. The other candidates split in the preferences of the 27 percent of the remaining Democratic voters:

Table 5. GALLUP POLL: Preference for a Democratic nominee among 605 Democrats out of a sample of 1,450 adults (in percent)

	Feb. 4–7, 1972	Jan. 7–10, 1972	Feb. 4–7, 1972 *	Jan. 7–10, 1972 *
Muskie	29	32	35	39
Kennedy	24	27	—	—
Humphrey	23	17	32	29
McGovern	5	3	6	3
Jackson	3	2	4	3
McCarthy	3	5	4	8
Chisholm	2	2	3	2
Lindsay	2	5	5	7
Yorty	1	2	1	2
Hartke	1	†	1	†
No preference	7	5	9	7

* These were the results when Kennedy's name was eliminated and the second choices of Kennedy supporters were divided among the other candidates.
† No significant support registered.
SOURCE: *Congressional Quarterly Weekly Report* (February 26, 1972), p. 434.

[24] During this eighteen-month period, in addition to the frontrunners, Senators Muskie and Humphrey, at different times, Senators McGovern, Hughes, Harris, Jackson, and Hartke, and Representative Chisholm, Mayor Lindsay, Mayor Yorty, Governor George Wallace, and ex-Senator McCarthy, campaigned for the Democratic party nomination for president.
[25] For a timely and personal account of a candidate's interrelated problems of political fund raising and media exposure, see Fred R. Harris, "The Frog Hair Problem," *Harper's* (May 1972): 12–20.

In this instance, it seems that much of Senator McGovern's financial backing came from individuals who were trying to broaden the spectrum for policy discussions and decisions within the Democratic party. It is unlikely that the majority of McGovern's early financial supporters perceived a likely victory by the senator.

ABILITY OF CANDIDATES TO SUSTAIN ORGANIZATIONAL MOMENTUM

Polling takes on an additional significance as candidates campaign for the nomination of their party or for the election to public office. If a candidate or a potential candidate appears to be losing electoral support, or if a new candidate is not gaining to the point of being a meaningful contender as revealed by the polls, his funding and his organizational momentum may dissipate (if it ever existed) or may not develop at all if it is a newly developing campaign. The phenomenon described as the "bandwagon effect" for voters and potential voters may affect campaign organization even more. In fact, it appears that the major impact of poll results may well be not on voters but on politicians and party activists. If the likelihood of victory is not great, why participate in the organization of a campaign. In the winter months of 1972 just prior to the New Hampshire primary election, the organizational momentum that Paul McCloskey's campaign had derived in the last months of 1971 waned considerably as the polls indicated that he had no real chance of electoral victory. As the polls indicated this, his funding came to a grinding halt. Much of the organized manpower that had formed around McCloskey fell apart. By the end of the campaign, he had no new funds to speak of, and very little organization with which to wage a contest in the New Hampshire primary election in March 1972—though as noted previously, his campaign did provide a forum for discussions of foreign policy issues. Again, the apparent exception was George McGovern's 1972 capture of the Democratic presidential nomination against all odds. This was due, at least in part, to the fact that his battle was an uphill one in which primary successes, themselves virtual surveys of voter opinion, created the momentum leading to the necessary monetary contributions and good staff morale.[26]

ABILITY OF CANDIDATES TO GAUGE PUBLIC OPINION

One very important use of private polling data is the gauging of constituent interests. By gaining some understanding of what the voters "want" from the political system, the potential candidate and/or candidate can address himself

---

[26] See Chapter 11 for a discussion of primaries and presidential nominations.

to the issues that have the potential of gaining the most support. Simultaneously, he can play down those issues that have the potential of losing the most support. Also, the issues that are potentially the most divisive for a particular electorate can be sidestepped in order to avoid antagonizing potentially large numbers of voters. There are certainly some people who are suspicious of "synthetic candidates" who derive their positions from the polls. But, the results of polls can, to a considerable extent, provide candidates with the kind of information to use in order to present themselves in the best possible light. In the 1972 presidential primaries, most of the candidates for convention delegates votes did not take positions on the exact extent of a guaranteed national minimum income. To do so might have won votes among the potential beneficiaries, but similarly might have lost votes among the tax-paying nonbeneficiaries. George McGovern did present a proposal for income redistribution. However, he was forced to backtrack as he came closer to the nomination.[27] In this instance, the basic value concerns of many Americans, which run counter to the notion of government responsibility for nonworking individuals viewed as neither caring for themselves nor contributing to society, prevailed.[28]

THE ROLE OF OPINION LEADERS

Just as organizational staffing and other vital elements for campaign success can be influenced by polling results, so too can opinion leaders be drawn to support particular candidates if there is reasonable evidence for success among the voters on election day. While empirical evidence is lacking on this point, politicians often believe that the support of rank-and-file voters, to a considerable extent, follows the support of the opinion leaders. Therefore, the bandwagoning of endorsements—especially among respected party and public officials, interest group leaders, entertainment celebrities, and media commentators— can be significant in collecting votes and raising money. Prominent citizens may provide useful cues for voters who are not too clear on the merits of candidates seeking a particular political office.

This phenomenon helps to explain the push by potential and actual candidates to gain as many endorsements by visible personalities as possible. If, however, a candidate or potential candidate is assumed to have little or no chance of victory, as determined by the polls, he will find it difficult to gain the necessary opinion leader endorsements to give what often is the necessary impetus to a campaign for public office. The importance of support from

---

[27] *New York Times,* June 9, 1972, p. 18.
[28] *Congressional Quarterly Weekly Report* (September 2, 1972): 2274.

"opinion leaders" ought not, however, to be overstated. By the spring of 1972, Senator Edmund Muskie had received the support of sixteen senators, nine governors, and thirty-two congressmen.[29] Obviously, Muskie recognized the importance of these "testimonials" or he would not have endeavored to get such support so early in the presidential campaign. It is interesting to note that Muskie's presidential nomination chances faltered despite these endorsements, perhaps an indication of the lack of viability of traditional party organization. When Muskie's chances for the nomination declined, many of those who had endorsed him joined the McGovern and Humphrey bandwagons.

It should be stressed that despite the "pulse-taking" character of public opinion surveys, there is often little relationship between the findings of the polls and the positions taken by the elected officials on specific matters of public policy. Thus, despite the poll results which indicate that a majority of citizens favor electoral college reform (81 percent) and gun control (71 percent), Congress has voted for neither.[30] Hence, unlike elections, desires expressed in polls can be and have been ignored by political leaders.

Still, polling does represent a means of fast communication between the public and incumbent and potential public officials. The views strongly held by the public can influence the campaign positions and strategies of candidates for public office. Such candidate response to survey data may be viewed with cynicism regarding the apparent lack of relationship between political principles and desire for electoral success. Yet, the democratic potential in terms of enhancing participation in decision making by the masses inherent in this aspect of political technology appears to be great, although its utilization thus far has been uneven.

To date, then, the apparent significant results of polling have been on candidates for elective office and political activists, including campaign workers and contributors.

It may be argued that polls simply are a more sophisticated refinement of the proverbial precinct captain who once stood on the street corner assessing the views of his constituents.[31] Nonetheless, it appears that surveys and the specialized agencies that conduct them have modified the nature of campaigns by reducing the role of party organization and impelling the individual candidate to conduct his own campaign—relying heavily on the data and strategy provided by pollsters.

[29] Verbal report of the press secretary of the "Muskie for President Committee" to author on June 7, 1972.

[30] Reprinted by permission of George Gallup Field Enterprises, 1972 and American Institute of Public Opinion, 1969.

[31] See Frank J. Sorauf, *Party Politics in America,* 2d. ed. (Boston: Little Brown, 1972), p. 248 for a statement of this view.

POLITICAL CONSULTANTS AND ELECTRONIC COMPUTERS

The use of computers in election campaigns is not limited to the analysis of survey results. Today's computers can aid in determining where advertisements should be placed and how to schedule the events of an entire campaign by determining where to spend the most time. Research can be done on "key" precincts, which reflect voting patterns in the state or other area, and on voting patterns in previous elections to determine the margin of victory necessary in the present one. The extent of ticket splitting and potential "switching" and the degree of turnout and political productivity of an area can be analyzed (a clearly "opposition" area would be ignored by campaign planners).

Insofar as constituent files are essential for any well organized campaign, "information technology" techniques (automatic or electronic data processing) have been developed for use by campaigners. To a considerable extent technology can do what campaign workers can do! One firm—Merrill Research Associates—offers demographic studies, redistricting and reapportionment plans, and opinion surveys. Other companies involved with campaign technology offer additional services. Thus Scientific Political Services, Inc., will do public opinion surveys on current issues, and will screen elected officials casework requests, in order to make a client more responsive to constituent needs. All of this is done in an effort to develop a more complete file on every registered voter and a better voter profile of the district.[32] The goal is to mount an efficient campaign that will maximize the candidate's potential strengths and best use his limited time.[33]

Elections can even be "simulated." In 1960, a simulation (never actually used) done for John F. Kennedy revealed a special interest in the Catholic issue and correctly predicted the candidate would both win and lose votes as a result. Computers can also direct voter mail and recorded telephone appeals, as well as voter registration. Mail and telephone messages are increasingly significant areas of campaigning for they appear to provide a more personal type of contact between the candidate and voters. In 1970, for example, Governor Rockefeller, running for reelection in New York State, used electronic data to gear his campaign to specific pivotal groups: personal letters were sent to voters whose families had mental health problems to stress the governor's efforts in this area; to staunch Republicans who might fail to vote due to overconfidence in the governor's victory; and to Jews, stressing the governor's commitment to their interests.[34] The governor also arranged to be photographed with local politicians who had high popularity ratings in his polls.

---

[32] Robert L. Chartrand, "Information Technology and the Potential Campaigner," in Robert Agranoff, ed., *The New Style in Election Campaigns* (Boston: Holbrook, 1972), p. 130.

[33] See Nimmo, *Political Persuaders,* pp. 76–77, and James Perry, *The New Politics* (New York: Clarkson N. Potter, 1968), p. 161.

[34] See *New York Times,* October 12, 1970, p. 43.

A very interesting example of the interplay of computer technology with traditional campaigning techniques occurred in Wyoming in 1970. Almost one year before the scheduled election, information was compiled for every person in the state's strongest Democratic precincts. For each person, name, address, phone number, party affiliation, and registration status was collected. This information, which was derived from precinct voter lists, telephone books, and city directories was then punched onto computer tape. Then the computer printed out, alphabetically according to surname, as well as by street and house number, this information onto multiple sets of 3 x 5 cards. Four months before the election one set of cards was distributed to precinct leaders so that the cards could be used in a voter registration drive. On Election Day, sets of cards were again distributed to precinct leaders in order to facilitate the traditional "get out the vote" campaigns in the strong Democratic precincts. All registered Democrats and Independents were contacted and encouraged to vote. The effect of this interplay of modern tactics with traditional strategy was that very few registered Democrats or Independents failed to vote.[35] This example seems to indicate that a marriage of the "new technology" and traditional party organization is not impossible, although to date instances of party cooptation of the new techniques have been limited.[36]

In addition to polling and the use of computers, a group of people who can handle the new political technology have emerged: the *New York Times* estimated that in 1970 more than half the candidates for senatorial and gubernatorial slots utilized the services of out-of-state paid political consultants.[37]

The use of private political public relations advisers was pioneered in California by Whittaker and Baxter, which filled the vacuum left in that state by weak party organization identification.[38] In recent decades, numerous political consultants have created campaign organizations for candidates, providing what one writer calls "a bridge between the past and future." [39]

Spencer Roberts, one of the best known of professional political consulting firms, has virtually usurped the former role of party by opening candidate campaign headquarters, distributing brochures, purchasing time on media,

[35] Andrew E. Manatos, "What Do You Get When You Get-Out-the-Vote?" *Politeia* 1 (Summer 1974): 41.

[36] It should be noted that the Democratic and Republican National Committees do utilize electronic data processing—the Republicans provide state organizations with technical assistance while the Democrats provide support for some congressmen and other party candidates. The aid of the two committees—while reaching only a limited number of total candidates—has included data banks of voting patterns, computerized mailings, and processed voter lists. Chartrand, in Agranoff, ed., *New Style*, pp. 134–37. See also Robert Agranoff, "The Role of Political Parties in the New Campaigning," in Agranoff, ed., *New Style*, pp. 96–114, for the view that some party organizations at the state and national level have already begun to play a vital role in managing the new technology of campaigns.

[37] *New York Times*, November 5, 1970, p. 28.

[38] Nimmo, *Political Persuaders*, pp. 35–36.

[39] Perry, *The New Politics*, p. 17.

conducting voter history surveys and demographic studies through its own processing subsidy, and coordinating volunteer and organizational efforts—in short, managing the entire campaign. In its home state of California, Spencer Roberts has even developed mailing lists of Republican partisans and maintained important contacts with that party's reliable activists.

An article in the *New York Times,* five and one-half months prior to the 1972 election, made an observation regarding political consultants worth noting: "To sophisticated political observers, Joe Napolitan is probably more famous than Joe Staszak. But, believe it or not, they're both in the same business: the election of political candidates."

"Their styles are a trifle different. Joe Napolitan takes polls, hires camera crews and packages images. Joe Staszak holds rallies, hires precinct workers and hands out sample ballots. Joe Napolitan is called a political consultant. He operates in the United States, Europe and South America. Joe Staszak is called a political boss. He operates in the first district of Baltimore city. Joe Napolitan is former president of the American Association of Political Consultants. Joe Staszak is Polish. What Joe Napolitan gets paid for his services is called a fee. What Joe Staszak is paid is called 'Walkaround' money. . . ." [40]

In 1966, Joseph Napolitan ran the Pennsylvania Democratic gubernatorial campaign for Milton Shapp, a wealthy industrialist. In January 1966, only 5.2 percent of the state's voters had heard of Shapp. But 7,000 radio spots, 34 prime time television shows, 30 pamphlets, 60 headquarters, and a single mailing to 1.5 million voters later—all organized by Napolitan—Shapp won the Democratic primary and went on in 1970 (though not in 1966) to become the state's governor. [41]

The advent of public relations in electoral politics has reinforced trends toward personalization of politics and the disintegration of party organizational machinery. Shapp's primary victory in 1966 was achieved in opposition to the wishes of Pennsylvania's strong party organization. Perhaps only a Napolitan-like campaign could have made his victory possible. As V. O. Key noted in 1956, "Party hierarchical structures cannot survive if they are not successful in selecting candidates slates. The results will be competing centers of power—competing informal hierarchies based on localities, regions, groups, personal followings. . . ." [42] "Republican" Governor Rockefeller's victorious campaign in New York State in 1966 was organized and directed by public relations consultant Jack Tinker. Rockefeller won running a candidate-focused campaign based on perhaps the most sophisticated "new politics" campaign

---

[40] *New York Times,* May 22, 1972, p. 35.
[41] Perry, *New Politics,* p. 51.
[42] V. O. Key, Jr., *American State Politics: An Introduction* (New York: Alfred A. Knopf, 1956), p. 167.

yet mounted in the United States. The governor's success was not tied to his party; seven of his fellow Republicans seeking congressional seats lost the same year.[43]

Increasingly private, nonpartisan groups representing individual candidates are occupying a major position in what has been a major arena of party activity in America. To summarize, there have been several important changes in modes of campaign communication reflected by this trend toward the use of professional public relations.[44] To begin with, it is the candidate and not the party that tends to be the focal point of the campaign. Also, the acquisition of campaign resources, development of campaign organization and campaign strategy, and media utilization have become candidate decisions and not party organization decisions. In addition, the new campaign techniques and resultant styles have led to the emergence of a "new class" of political professionals who have the skills of public relations, the media, polling, and management. It is the skills of large-scale industry that are being demanded by campaigners and not the skills of party precinct workers. The new campaign professionals have brought with them the habit of doing systematic research about the products they are trying to market. Thus, as discussed earlier in this chapter, there has been an increased reliance on polling in campaigns. Finally, the new kinds of campaigning include wide use of both electronic and printed media presentations.

The words of Joe Napolitan, a leading political consultant, are instructive for those who may doubt the antiparty thrust of the new politics: "My preference is for candidates to talk directly to the people who are going to vote for them, without any filter between them and the voter. It's no coincidence that party organization and machine politics have entered their death stage with the advent of electronic campaigning and I for one think this is good. . . ." [45] It is the candidate mailings, news events, and computer-generated organizations aided by paid political professionals that are emerging with a near-monopoly on most aspects of campaigning. For all of the above reasons, there has been a substitution of candidate-centered campaigns for party-centered campaigns—an operational mode much in keeping with our antiparty tradition.

---

[43] Perry, *New Politics*, p. 134.

[44] This discussion relies heavily on Agranoff, ed., *New Style*, pp. 4–5.

[45] Joseph Napolitan, *The Election Game and How to Win It* (Garden City, N.Y.: Doubleday, 1972), p. 112.

4

The Use and Effects
of the Mass Media

THE IMPACT OF TELEVISION ON VOTING BEHAVIOR

According to Marshall McLuhan, "T.V. is revolutionizing every political system in the Western world; . . . the political candidate who understands T.V.—whatever his party goals or beliefs—can gain power unknown in history." [1]

In this chapter we will examine the impact of television, radio, and newspapers on voting, nominations, and campaigns. We will focus on the role of the media—especially television—in the emergence of candidate-centered politics, at the increasing expense of party-focused politics. Just as the technology of polling, computers, and the like have proven congruent with our antiparty environment, so too have the electronic media.

As personality via television packaging is becoming a more significant influence on elections, the future potential for antiparty politics—especially given the decentralized and fragmented nature of American parties—is reinforced. A candidate for political office now can go straight to the people. He can bypass even the remaining amenities of party discipline. Media candidates can be followed by media decision makers. Parties even today control many campaigns less than individual candidates and their designated assistants, espe-

[1] "Interview with Marshall McLuhan," *Playboy* (March 1969): 61–62.

cially media experts. It is possible to run a campaign for high political office without the strong support of one of the two major parties if television is available to you. Nominations for local, state, and national office even by the major parties are increasingly being brought to the people via television reporting and television campaigning. Furthermore, given the increased number of "independents" in the U.S. who have little or no partisan loyalty, and who receive their information on candidates and issues largely from television, the future for strong party politics seems dim. Many television advertisements already deliberately omit mention of the candidate's party, for fear of alienating potential voters. A major theme that will dominate this discussion of the "new political technology" is the inability of party organization to recoup its losses in the arena of nominations and election campaigns. Party organizations lack the centralization, coordination, resources, and skills—at least thus far—to compete with the merchants of a new, antiparty style of campaigning.

As media campaigns continue to reach a broader and more diverse audience, partisanship as a specific appeal is further reduced in importance.

POLITICAL INFORMATION RECEIVED FROM TELEVISION

It is difficult to say with certainty exactly what the impact of the electronic media—especially television—has been on voters. Survey findings do indicate that television is the most popular of all the media for news and information. In 1971, it was the preferred medium of 60 percent of the population.[2] Furthermore, television is perceived as the least biased, most believable, and most complete of the mass media. Thus when Roper asked, "If you got conflicting or different reports of the same news story from radio, television, the magazines, or the newspapers, which of the four versions would you be most inclined to believe—the one on radio or television or magazines or newspapers?" The largest number of those surveyed responded television. In 1971, television was seen as most credible by 49 percent of those questioned, whereas a similar figure for 1959 was 29 percent.[3] In contrast, computers were regarded by half the voters as "untrustworthy" as recently as 1964.[4]

If all of this information is superimposed on the amount of time the average American adult views television, some interesting questions can be asked. It has been estimated that Americans watch an average of two and one-half hours of television each day. Voting turnout tends to be higher among television

---

[2] This data is from a Burns Roper survey reported by McNeil, "Electronic Schizophrenia: Does Television Alienate Voters?" *Politeia* 1 (Summer 1972): 6.

[3] Ibid.

[4] Harold Mendelsohn and Irving Crespi, *Polls, Television and the New Politics* (Scranton, Pa.: Chandler, 1970), p. 202.

viewers than among nonviewers.[5] And further, television watchers who read newspapers as well have the highest voter turnout rates—with reading probably more significant in affecting turnout than television viewing. It has been postulated that the increment of time spent watching television (and reading newspapers) was not as significant as the actual watching (or reading) of the medium itself.[6]

Given the amount of time the average adult American spends watching television—even assuming most of this time is given to viewing shows with no obvious political or social "message," some political and social content may emerge—especially during campaigns, when spot announcements become more numerous. For example, Richard Nixon, in his 1968 presidential campaign, used sixty-second "spot" advertisements on such audience favorites as "Laugh-In," "Monday Night at the Movies," and "Edge of Night," as well as major football games. Even shows that focus primarily on entertainment often have nonovert messages for subgroups in society. Thus "My Three Sons" depicts the average happy American family living in near perfect security and harmony in a near perfect and harmonious suburb. For people who are less fortunate, who are poverty stricken, or left to live in decaying cities, bitterness may arise. For the aspiring subaffluent classes, goal orientation may develop. For those people living in similar suburban affluence, cynical reactions about the emptiness of this type of life may arise. Thus, even entertainment may cause social and ultimately political reactions.

In addition, politics itself has come to be viewed as part of the entertainment process, as aspirants for high level political office appear with increasing frequency on late night "talk" shows (such as Johnny Carson, Merv Griffin) and the like.

IMPACT OF MEDIA ON POLITICAL BEHAVIOR

It seems clear that exposure to media has affected all segments of the electorate. With the increased utilization of media campaigning by the candidates, especially at the national level, "the flow of short-term political stimuli—both during campaigns and in the lengthy lulls between them—has effectively penetrated all segments of the electorate. The more or less immediate circumstances that surround any given election have eroded and probably will continue to erode the stabilizing influences associated with the electorate's partisan loyalties."[7] This analysis of the impact of the media on party loyalty

[5] A. C. Nielsen, *National Audience Composition Report,* January 1967.

[6] From Gallup Survey 576K, December 1956, quoted by William A. Glaser, "Television and Voting Turnout," *Public Opinion Quarterly* 29 (Spring 1965): 79.

[7] Edward C. Dreyer, "Media Use and Electoral Choices," *Public Opinion Quarterly* 35 (Winter 1971–72): 553.

appears to be congruent with the changing balance of party registration in the U.S. in the 1970s. As already noted, the proportion of independents in the electorate has increased markedly in the past several years.[8] It is reasonable to suggest that given the increased and continuous flow of information to the voter—even assuming the lack of a depth of knowledge by much of the voting public—the willingness to stay steadfast and firm in one's partisan loyalties has diminished. Events are relayed rapidly to the public in a manner that makes all viewers participants in the events, and many viewers livingroom decisionmakers. Our dependence on party for "political cues" has diminished as we make our own voting decisions in part based upon media inputs. Certainly voter independence has always existed to some extent in the United States. It is however an increasing tendency, building upon our antiparty tradition. These trends are likely to continue, since there has been a greater tendency for younger voters rather than for older voters to register as "independents." It is the younger voters who have been brought up in an age of electronic media and who have had the greatest opportunities for education. Many young voters may have more detailed information than we associate with information levels of the average American, thus reinforcing issue and/or candidate orientation, and reducing party identification as the primary influence in making voting choices.

If it were true, however, that increased access to information was a sufficient cause to increase political participation in the aggregate, a direct positive relationship between increased media utilization and voting should be apparent. This situation does not, however, exist. In fact, if one looks at presidential elections from 1960 to 1972, it is clear that as the proportion of households with televisions increased, the proportion of the voting age public who actually voted declined.[9] Thus, the percentage of the population eligible to vote, actually casting votes for presidential electors in successive elections was:

1960	1964	1968	1972
64%	62.9%	61.6%	55%

SOURCE: U.S. Bureau of the Census, *Statistical Abstract of the U.S.,* 1971 (Washington, D.C.: Government Printing Office, 1971), p. 366.

As Angus Campbell has pointed out, television has neither increased the general level of interest in nor broadened the total range of information about

[8] See Chapter 2 for a discussion of changing party identifications and the increased and changing role of the "independents" in American politics.

[9] Exceptions were the southern states of Alabama, Arkansas, Florida, Georgia, Louisiana, Mississippi, North Carolina, South Carolina, Tennessee, Texas, and Virginia (plus the new states of Alaska and Hawaii). In these states the percentage increased due to the ability of blacks to vote after the passage of the Civil Rights Act of 1965. U.S. Bureau of the Census, *Statistical Abstract of the United States: 1971,* 92d ed. (Washington, D.C., 1971), p. 366.

elections.[10] The reasons for this condition in an era of increased media use and declining party identification are difficult to isolate. Campbell suggests that at the time television entered the political arena, radio and the press had already saturated the population with political information. In the late 1940s, for example, 90 percent of the population listened to the radio and 80 percent read a daily newspaper.[11] Hence, there was little room for further expansion. It is possible that television is a more passive medium than radio; as it has replaced radio as the major vehicle for news, interest in politics has ended with viewing for many. Perhaps television itself satisfies the participatory needs of segments of the electorate, especially for those who are the least politically involved.

It is sometimes thought that television has been able to reach the "uninvolved" and interest them in politics. However, as suggested above, those who follow politics the most on television are also the most likely to follow politics in the press and magazines. Television appears weaker than newspapers in reminding people of all classes to vote. As Glaser reminds us, the impact of television watching is connected with life-style, family behavior, and behavioral predispositions.[12] Thus, television has a different impact on disparate groups of voters. For the low involvement voter, the "style" or entertainment value of a television campaign (as opposed to the substantive "content") may prove to be exciting and involve the viewer in a campaign that previously was of little interest to him. For the highly motivated and interested party identifier, television provides information and reinforcement of his previous political identification.[13]

TELEVISION AND THE VOTING DECISION

Influence on actual voting preferences with regard to media campaigning by candidates during the intense campaigning period prior to an election does more to reinforce already existing positions and candidate preferences than to switch decided voters from one candidate to another candidate.[14] The firmly decided voter with strong partisan loyalties, group commitments, and issue orientations will vote for the candidate of his party. However, the "indepen-

---

[10] Angus Campbell, "Has Television Reshaped Politics?" *Columbia Journalism Review* (Fall 1962): 10–13.

[11] Ibid., p. 13.

[12] Glaser, "Television and Voting Turnout," p. 86.

[13] See Dan Nimmo, *The Political Persuaders* (Englewood Cliffs, N.J.: Prentice-Hall, 1970), p. 185, and Kurt Lang and Gladys Lang, *Politics and Television* (Chicago: Quadrangle Books, 1968), p. 218.

[14] Kurt Lang and Gladys Lang, "The Mass Media and Voting," in E. Burdick and A. Brodbeck, eds., *American Voting Behavior* (Glencoe, Ill.: Free Press, 1959), pp. 218–19.

dents," who are becoming an increasingly significant segment of the voting public, can be influenced and may augur a more significant role for television in campaigns in the future![15] Although many "independents" have partisan leanings and often hold strong issue positions which lead them to a particular candidate thus preordaining their electoral choice, there remain many undecided independent voters who especially in a close election can help determine which candidate will be successful. It is to these voters too that media campaigns are directed, as well as to the voters with decided votes who need to be reinforced so that they will actually cast their ballot. It is the recognition of the fact that a plurality of voters *preferring* a candidate will not elect him to office, but that rather, the candidate with the *plurality of votes* will be successful, that has led to expensive media campaigning.

A good illustration of the effects of television on voting behavior may be seen in the famed Kennedy-Nixon debates of 1960. They provided a good example of the use of the media in reinforcing candidate-oriented politics as well as party-focused politics. Insofar as Kennedy was successful in the debates, he was able to influence voters to vote for Kennedy the man and the Democrat.

It has been suggested by numerous election analysts that the "Great Debates" won the election for John Kennedy.[16] Kennedy recognized the significance of staging as he had during the primary campaign in West Virginia. He made use of decisiveness in answering questions and of appropriate television gestures. He had the appearance of many voters' perception of a president. Richard Nixon did not understand television. He permitted himself to be put on the defensive under Kennedy's attacks. According to Theodore White, in 1960 Nixon's "clean masculine quality" did not come through on black and white television; his worst features—deep eyewells, heavy brows, thick beard, and meaningless smile (like that of a commercial announcer) were emphasized by the television cameras.[17] Joe McGinniss blames Nixon's poor performance on the fact that television showed the "real" Nixon, who, grumpy and aloof, refused to follow the advice of his technicians to sleep more before the debates. As a result, Nixon came across looking haggard, hungry, too eager. Norman Mailer saw Nixon as a church usher; Marshall McLuhan saw a railroad lawyer selling out a small town.[18] According to these views, Nixon failed to realize the vast audience for all four of the debates—over 50 percent of the electorate. (In 1960, it was estimated that the electorate favored campaigns wholly con-

---

[15] See Chapter 5 for a discussion of the rational versus the irrational voter controversy.

[16] See, for example, Theodore H. White, *The Making of the President, 1960* (New York: Atheneum, 1961), p. 353, for the results of Gallup and Roper polls which indicate that Kennedy's success in the debates turned the election tide in his favor.

[17] Ibid., p. 275.

[18] Joe McGinniss, *The Selling of the President* (New York: Pocket Books, 1969), p. 25.

ducted by radio and television by a margin of five to four.) [19] With all of those people watching television campaigns, and with first impressions being very important on television, Nixon lost votes, some of which became Kennedy's margin for victory.

The above views present an overly simplistic portrait of the impact of television on voting decisions. It appears that Kennedy's debate performance increased his support among weak Democrats, Independents, and undecideds who were unsure of him because of his age and religion.[20] This might have provided his winning margin. For the most part, a distinction became evident between *personally* favorable reactions to Kennedy (affected by television) and *political* ones (affected by party, family, etc.). A group of researchers found among individuals they studied that while most viewers found Kennedy personally appealing, Democrats tended to view his performance as that of an ideal president; while Republicans saw Nixon as the more statesmanlike and stable, and therefore more politically acceptable.[21] Thus, voters tend to bring their personal choices in line with their perceptions.[22] The debates did reactivate the Democratic leanings of some of the less politically involved and reinforced the partisan dispositions of the more involved.

Whatever the impact of the debates on actual individual voting behavior in 1960, they may have had other more significant inputs into the political process. For example, Kennedy's generally favorable "video" impact may have helped to build worker morale during the campaign, and the "image" he established during the debates may have served him well once he was elected president. The same may have held true for Milton Shapp whose "new politics" gubernatorial campaign, though defeated in 1966, apparently made him a familiar "name" and aided his victory in Pennsylvania in 1970.

Of course, the influence of television on perceptions of political events and personalities may in the long run significantly influence voting behavior. The growing independent group may be one evidence of McLuhan's view that television is causing us to leave the "age of political parties." [23] And while media oriented campaigns may not convert the party "faithful," they may in some circumstances produce heightened interest in issues, leading to a higher voter turnout among independent and weak partisans than has been the case traditionally. It then becomes possible for "swing" voters with marginal or no party ties, subject to techniques of mass persuasion to profoundly alter

[19] Edward W. Chester, *Radio, Television, and Politics* (New York: Sheed and Ward, 1969), p. 115.

[20] Lang and Lang, *Politics and Television,* pp. 222–36; Chester, *Radio, Television, and Politics,* p. 122.

[21] See Nimmo, *Political Persuaders,* p. 189.

[22] Lang and Lang, *Politics and Television,* p. 238.

[23] McLuhan, "Interview," p. 72.

election outcomes, as apparently occurred in a Maryland senatorial race as far back as 1950.[24]

At this juncture, it is certainly clear that a disastrous television performance can be detrimental to the political aspirations of candidates. In 1968, for example, George Romney's statement that he had been "brainwashed" with regard to Vietnam policy became a *cause célèbre:* "Not only did millions of Americans know that George Romney stated he had been brainwashed; millions of them saw him say it on their home T.V. screens." [25] Romney's quest for the presidency all but ended with this televised *faux pas.*

The media have exercised significant influence in recent years at party nominating conventions. In numerous instances, the media seem to have usurped the role of party organization in structuring convention events. Extensive media coverage may also have increased public cynicism about the usefulness of parties as presented by the conventions. Television in particular has become an integral part of the convention machinery and process. For example, in 1968, the CBS and NBC networks played a key role in advancing the candidacy of Senator Edward Kennedy in order to achieve dramatic momentum with which to entertain their prime-time audience, despite the lack of factual basis to the "Kennedy boomlet." In 1968, $40 million worth of equipment, manned by thirty crews, was present at the Democratic convention.[26] Television has also been significant in structuring convention viewing in new ways. Network reporters interrupt roll-call votes for interviews with delegates and candidates; analysis by "experts" often takes the place of key speeches on the convention floor. In 1968, the disorders on the Chicago streets during the Democratic convention were deemed more "newsworthy" than a Humphrey seconding speech. Theodore White has written: "to permit American conventions to become . . . a quarry for dramatic fragments by competitive television networks is to let camera values control the atmosphere of politics." [27]

In 1972 the Democrats apparently sought to cope with some of the exigencies of media coverage by streamlining their convention. They limited nominating and seconding speeches to a few minutes each and barred "spontaneous" demonstrations in order to hasten the proceedings. As in 1968, ABC, one of the three major networks, indicated its view of continuous gavel-to-gavel coverage by covering the day's convention activities in one and one-half

---

[24] See Walt Anderson, *Campaigns: Cases in Political Conflict* (Pacific Palisades, Calif.: Goodyear Publishing Company, 1970), pp. 145–60. See Chapter 5 for a discussion of voting and voter turnout.

[25] Theodore H. White, *The Making of the President, 1968* (New York: Atheneum, 1968), p. 58. Romney's actual statement was not viewed widely; it was the national evening television news that publicized the "misstatement."

[26] Ibid., p. 327.

[27] Ibid., p. 388.

hour summaries. In doing so it captured a significant share of the audience, apparently a reflection of low viewer tolerance for the lengthy parliamentary party gathering. The extensive coverage of conventions presented to the American public by the television networks may have added a veneer of cynicism to the already existing American antipathy to political parties. The Nielsen ratings in New York City during the 1972 Democratic convention indicated that before 11 P.M. of each televised convention day, half of the television sets in the area were turned to programs other than the convention.[28]

In 1972 the role of television at the conventions remained significant. Intra-party squabbles prevented newly nominated Democratic candidate George McGovern from making his acceptance speech until 3 A.M. (Eastern time) and he missed his greatest opportunity to receive free time before a vast awake nationwide audience.

Warren Weaver, writing in the *New York Times* wrote of the 1972 Republican convention as "the first genuine multimedia political convention, deploying a wide range of slides, films and live television events to keep the delegates entertained enough so they would look alert to the great television audience outside. The greenest political amateur could recognize that the Republican convention, with its entertainment celebrities, split second scenario and prime time schedule, was being aimed at the national television audience rather than the 1,348 delegates in the hall." [29]

As suggested earlier, it is our belief that television has significantly affected the kind of campaign a candidate for elective office will run. The campaign style must be geared to the media—especially television. This requires the use of public relations and media professionals—an added expense to campaigning. Candidates must raise the money to run this kind of campaign. They do so in large part via independent candidate-focused committees. Insofar as party as a political cue-giver has diminished in significance, voters must be convinced to vote for a candidate, not necessarily for a party. The result is more candidate-oriented campaigns and fewer party-focused campaigns.

METHODS OF MEDIA UTILIZATION: THE CASE OF TELEVISION

THE TECHNIQUES

There are a variety of advertising methods used by the merchandisers of political candidates to have their "products" viewed by the American public.

[28] *New York Times,* July 12, 1972, p. 83.
[29] *New York Times,* August 24, 1972, p. 46. The creator of "The Dating Game" was assigned the task of making a suspenseless convention visually interesting. It should be noted that for color television viewers, the decor was red, white, and blue.

Since 1952, the role of radio and television in campaigning has been particularly significant. Television, and to a lesser extent radio, increases the costs of campaigning, but for the candidate with sufficient funding, it simplifies the problems of exposure to mass publics. Let us look first at the role of television in campaigning, since it is, in terms of cost and utilization, the most important form of media advertising for political campaigns. The role of radio and other media in campaigning will be discussed later in this chapter.

Paid television exposure takes on several basic forms, depending largely on the advice of media consultants to specific candidates. There are spot announcements, staged conversations or panel shows, five-minute tailers, telethons, and filmed documentaries,[30] as well as "created news events."

Spot announcements are often the most popular broadcasts used by politicians. They enable the candidate to reach a large number of viewers at relatively low cost per viewer and allow the candidate to address people he could not easily reach by any other means.[31] A spot in "Monday Night at the Movies" in 1968 would reach more people of voting age than another type of broadcast lasting a half hour at a similar time.[32] The spot would undoubtedly attract people who would not watch a longer political program. In the 1968 election campaign, the candidates chose to spend three-fourths of their television budget for spot announcements. This narrowed the viewers' opportunity to hear a serious discussion of the issues and did not permit the viewers to observe the candidate long enough to judge his personal qualities.[33] In 1966, for example, Governor Rockefeller, running for reelection in New York State, reached 91 percent of New York City's homes ten times in seven days—and it was estimated that his 1970 media campaign was even more extensive.[34] In 1968, there were over a million airings of spots during the presidential election period.[35]

Filmed documentaries are used also to present candidates to the television viewing public. For example, on the day Edmund Muskie announced his 1972 candidacy for president a press conference and a message to the voters were filmed and were shown that night on television as a documentary. President Nixon's brief television campaign in Wisconsin in 1972 consisted largely of news cuts with cabinet officers explaining their support for the president.[36] Skillfully executed half-hour documentaries have been credited with aiding the

[30] See Nimmo, *Political Persuaders,* pp. 149–55, for a discussion of these various techniques of advertising candidates.

[31] Ibid., p. 118.

[32] Ibid.

[33] For a discussion of the use of radio in campaigning, see pp. 86–87.

[34] James Perry, *The New Politics* (New York: Clarkson N. Potter, 1968), p. 136.

[35] Frederick G. Dutton, *Changing Sources of Power: American Politics in the 1970's* (New York: McGraw-Hill, 1971), p. 212.

[36] "The News Look: Latest Thing in Political Ads," *Congressional Quarterly Weekly Report* (April 15, 1972): 858.

gubernatorial campaign of Shapp (Pennsylvania 1966), Mike Gravel's senatorial race in Alaska in 1968, and Humphrey's presidential candidacy in 1968.[37] Such documentaries often seek to emphasize the "human" side of the candidate as well as his past accomplishments.

Television debates, which seek to present issues in a more rational and relatively clear manner, are used primarily in close, local elections. For a "safe" incumbent holding national or statewide office (President Nixon in 1968, for example) the debate is seen as a source of unwarranted publicity for a less well known opponent and is therefore assiduously avoided. It is for this reason that incumbent presidents since 1960 have successfully exercised pressure on Congress not to suspend Section 315 of the Federal Communications Act, which provides for "equal time" for all presidential candidates, regardless of party affiliation. Such a suspension could clear the way for several million dollars of free network time to be awarded to the two major candidates for debate, and perhaps result in new prominence (as in the case of John F. Kennedy in 1960) for the challenger.

Telethons can be very successful for last-minute saturation of large audiences, but they can be total disasters if not produced with the precision of other media presentations. Thus Theodore White, in his discussion of the 1960 Democratic primary in West Virginia, points out that when Hubert Humphrey ran a telethon on a local television station, which was truly spontaneous—i.e., not professionally produced—it was an unmitigated disaster. An elderly lady caller caused Humphrey to lose his television presence when she said: "You git out! You git out of West Virginia, Mr. Humphrey." [38] Humphrey learned his lesson by 1968, and the night before the November election held an effective, celebrity studded two-hour telethon that reached a large viewing audience.

Television panel shows have also been used by candidates to receive public exposure. In 1968, Spiro Agnew, the Republican candidate for vice-president, was often seen on morning and late-evening panel shows. Also, more contrived panel shows, produced for the candidate by his own staff, have been used with varying success. "The imaginative character of the Edward Kennedy campaign for the Senate in 1962 . . . was apparent in the way Kennedy utilized his brain trust. To counteract his absence of a public record and to create the impression that he was a statesman rather than a politician, members of the brain trust appeared several times in a taped 'panel discussion' type of television program during which they invented a new concept in American politics, i.e., that of 'relevant experience.' . . ." [39] Among the members of the brain trust to appear on this show were Professors Robert Wood of MIT and James

[37] See Joseph Napolitan, *The Election Game and How to Win It* (Garden City, N.Y.: Doubleday, 1972), Chapters 2, 6, and 7.

[38] White, *Making of the President, 1960,* p. 132.

[39] Murray B. Levin, *Kennedy Campaigning: The System and Style as Practiced by Senator Edward Kennedy* (Boston: Beacon Press, 1966), pp. 154–55.

MacGregor Burns of Williams College. In 1968, President Nixon utilized the so-called "Hillsboro" format—a handpicked preselected panel and carefully edited questions, which were, nevertheless, supposed to demonstrate the candidate's "spontaneity" to the viewer. Five-minute tailers, another media form, are so-called because they appear at the end of regularly scheduled programs (and use commercial time rather than program time). In the 1971 mayoralty campaign in Baltimore, for example, there was a program tailer that examined the role a black man could play in Baltimore politics. It flashed pictures of candidate George Russell as an active leader in the community. Tailers and spots in particular, can be tailored to open and conclude news programs, in order to present the advertisement as a virtual part of the news format.

All of the aforementioned techniques for television coverage are costly. At all times, therefore, free publicity on network news programs is the method most preferred by campaigning politicians. In fact, the cost of media campaigning is so expensive that during the 1970 gubernatorial campaign in California, Jesse Unruh, the Democratic candidate for governor, made a special effort to do newsworthy things—attending sky diving competitions, carnivals, and the like—so that he could get the television exposure that he could not otherwise afford.[40]

In 1970, Lawton Chiles, U.S. Senate candidate, walked across his native state of Florida in order to gain free publicity. Consider for a moment the candidacy of George Wallace in 1968. Though he did not reach the people as much via paid television as did his opponents—all third-party candidates spent a combined total $2,450,651 on media campaigning in 1968 compared to $22,504,858 for Republicans and $15,447,989 for Democrats—he reached the people via news programs.[41] As a prominent and controversial third-party candidate, he received 13 percent of the total popular vote cast in that election.

Candidates may also appear on national news programs such as "Face the Nation" and "Meet the Press," and submit to often difficult questions from skilled political analysts. As suggested above, the most widely used method of television advertising by political candidates is spot announcing. Actually, the philosophy of this advertising style has not changed much since 1952. In the 1952 campaign, Rosser Reeves of the Ted Bates Agency, who was responsible for planning Eisenhower's pioneering television effort, was quoted as saying: "I think of a man in a voting booth who hesitates between two levers as if he were pausing between competing tubes of toothpaste in a drugstore. The brand that has made the highest penetration in his brain will win his choice." [42] Campaign spots would run something like this: An unseen voice would ask

[40] Jeremy Larner, "Jesse Unruh and His Moment of Truth," *Harpers* 242 (April 1971): 62–68.
[41] *Congressional Quarterly Weekly Report* (December 5, 1969): 2442.
[42] Robert Bendiner, *White House Fever*, as cited by Jules Abels, *The Degeneration of Our Presidential Elections* (New York: Macmillan, 1968), p. 57.

Mr. Eisenhower, "What about the high cost of living?" Reply: "My wife Mamie worries about the same thing. I tell her it's our job to change that on November 4." [43]

In 1964, Doyle Dane Bernbach Agencies developed spots for Democratic candidate Lyndon B. Johnson which, like the 1952 spot just noted, attempted to discredit the position of the opposition candidate on some specific issue or set of issues. However, appeals were now more often made on the basis of highly emotional and sometimes divisive themes in order to "sell a candidate." Thus, on the issue of nuclear weapons the following spot was developed:

> A small girl picks petals from a daisy as she sits in a meadow; a background voice begins a countdown; the countdown ends, a nuclear explosion is heard and a mushroom cloud appears; the voice says, "These are the stakes: To make a world in which all of God's children can live or go into the dark." [44]

The intent of this spot, withdrawn because of protest from the Republicans, was to imply that GOP candidate Barry Goldwater would, if elected, lead the country into nuclear war.

Other volatile public issues, including communism and racism, have been emphasized by some campaign spots. In 1970, Senator Vance Hartke complained to the Federal Communications Commission about television spots sponsored by Richard Roudebush, his Republican senatorial opponent. The Roudebush people later removed the spot, but not before Indiana viewers saw an actor dressed as a Vietcong guerrilla load and point a rifle at them. "The weapons the Vietcong uses to kill American service men are given to them by Communist countries," said a voice. "Senator Vance Hartke voted for a bill to permit American trade with those Communist countries. Isn't that like putting a loaded gun in the hands of our enemies? Vote for Dick Roudebush. Roudebush thinks the way we do." [45]

Race was the key issue in the 1970 campaign for the governorship of South Carolina. Albert Watson campaigned against John C. West, the lieutenant governor and a political moderate. One of Watson's first television commercials of the campaign was withdrawn after it had been widely denounced as racist and unrelated to the problems of the state. It showed film clips of blacks rioting in Los Angeles and opened with the message, "Are we going to be ruled by the bloc. . . ?" [46]

Several obvious problems relating to information accuracy arise, especially with regard to the television spot type of campaigning discussed above. With the exception of the truly spontaneous telethon or the truly spontaneous panel

---

[43] Quoted by Nimmo, *Political Persuaders,* p. 149.
[44] Ibid., pp. 150–51.
[45] "The Selling of the Candidates 1970," *Newsweek* 76 (October 19, 1970): 38. The allegation regarding Hartke's vote was untrue.
[46] *New York Times,* October 24, 1970, p. 13.

METHODS OF MEDIA UTILIZATION 81

show—both unpreferred forms of media advertising by candidates—the candidates are being presented to mass publics as images who may state positions in only outline form, since time is a factor, and being too specific may lose more votes than it may gain. Thus positions are not clarified for the benefit of the viewer. Often, the position of a candidate on an issue may be presented too briefly to be meaningful, or may be taken out of a broader issue context. This type of situation presents the voters with a subtle form of political distortion and does not provide totally accurate information. The situation can become exacerbated if a candidate presenting the view of the opposition cannot respond immediately—as is the case with "canned" television presentations during campaigns. In 1970, Illinois Republican Senator Ralph Tyler Smith asked leading questions in his spots during his campaign against Adlai Stevenson, III. "Why doesn't Adlai Stevenson speak out against busing? . . . Why doesn't he denounce those students who try to force our universities to close? . . . What has Adlai got against the FBI and the Chicago police? . . . Why doesn't he admit he is a liberal and end the pretense?" the advertisement asked. The camera focused on a picture of Stevenson and a voice repeated: "Why doesn't he?" Before the picture disappeared a small message revealed the questions were paid for by supporters of Senator Smith.[47]

Often, candidates do not even appear in their own spots. In 1966, for example, Rockefeller in New York State had one commercial replete with ukuleles and Hawaiian dancing girls as well as scenic locale. The message: during his terms as governor, Rockefeller had built roads in New York State that would stretch all the way to Hawaii.[48]

"Without question the new technology introduces not only the possibility but indeed the likelihood of systematic deception in electoral politics." [49] Senator Clair Engle (D., Calif.) nearly made this prophecy come true in 1964. The senator announced for reelection in a televised spot that "the medical people have given me the green light and I am running." Only after a medical inquiry did the news break that the senator had brain surgery, was paralyzed, and could hardly move or speak. Even though he withdrew late in the race, and died shortly thereafter, he still received 100,000 votes in the primary election.

The spot commercial reflects a refinement of the sloganeering and image building that have always been present in American politics (for example, "Tippecanoe and Tyler Too" in Harrison's 1840 presidential campaign). What differentiates the new approach from the old is the greatly enlarged size of the popular audience, increased information about the nature of the electorate being reached, and the decline of party organization as both the sponsor and the source of identification for television viewers.

[47] "The Selling of the Candidates," *Newsweek:* 34.
[48] Nimmo, *Political Persuaders,* p. 151.
[49] Ibid., p. 195.

If Marshall McLuhan is correct candidates need not be blatantly dishonest in order to gain a good television image. According to McLuhan, "cool" candidates who are bland and "low intensity" are best suited to the television medium because they permit the viewer to fill in his own details. John F. Kennedy personified this kind of candidate for McLuhan. Whether valid or not (the appeal of George Wallace, who has appeared frequently on television from 1964–72 in quests for national influence, although he admittedly prefers mass rallies, would appear to challenge McLuhan's contention) the concept of the "cool" candidate has influenced numerous would-be office holders. Richard Nixon, who in the 1960 presidential campaign ignored his television advisers, spoke in ad-lib fashion and feared accusations of "Madison Avenue" campaigning, reassessed this position in 1968.[50] Nixon's first move in 1968 was to appoint a seasoned advertising and television professional as a key campaign aide.

Nixon apparently learned from his mistakes in 1960. He was repackaged as "The New Nixon." Thus when he emerged as a television campaigner in 1968, he looked honest, sincere, and vigorous. He no longer looked tired and overanxious.[51]

"The biggest mistake in my political life was not to learn how to use television," noted Hubert Humphrey. For McLuhanites his image was too emotional, too hot, too unfiltered. Humphrey seeking the Democratic nomination in 1972 learned from his experiences in 1968 and was a somewhat "cooler" media candidate than he had been four years earlier. His statements on television were shorter and more to the point. Eugene McCarthy in 1968 was the perfect McLuhanite television candidate—with gentle wit, warmth, and sincerity, yet given to understatement and irony.

THE ROLE OF MEDIA-ORIENTED CAMPAIGNS IN WINNING ELECTIONS

THE COSTS

Senator Charles Mathias (R., Md.) has suggested that: "If you have to be rich or have rich friends and backers to reach high office, then democracy is a fraud. This is the most undemocratic flaw in our system, and nothing is done about it." [52]

[50] Chester, *Radio, Television, and Politics,* pp. 118, 269.
[51] McGinniss, *Selling of the President.* The impact of McLuhanism on Nixon's campaign strategy is amply documented by McGinniss's appendix.
[52] Quoted by Richard Harris, "A Fundamental Hoax," *The New Yorker* 47 (August 7, 1971): 38.

There are certainly instances where expensive media campaigning is unnecessary. If a very well known and popular incumbent is campaigning for reelection in a state or local contest, he will probably not require the media exposure his opponent will need to reach the public. For example, in June 1972 Senator Margaret Chase Smith (R., M.) spent less than $10,000 to win the Republican senatorial primary. Her opponent, Robert Monks, spent nearly $250,000.[53] There is, however, somewhat of a paradox evident here. If the incumbent is well-known and popular, he can probably raise the necessary funds to run an effective media campaign! It should be noted that geographically limited local districts, particularly those in remaining strong party areas, can make little effective use of media messages. The media would be wasteful in reaching a much larger area than necessary to influence voters in the specific congressional or state legislative district and would probably reach only a few more voters than party canvassers.

But for many candidates the high costs associated with media campaigning are a reality. Let us look at the estimated costs for media campaigns for the past several years. First, it is obvious that the larger a constituency the greater the expense of running for office. It is more expensive to run for president than to run for the Senate. It usually costs more to run for the Senate than to run for the House of Representatives. In 1972, 106 candidates for Senate seats spent a total of $26,446,393, while 1,010 candidates for the House of Representatives spent $39,959,376.[54]

According to estimates released by the General Accounting Office of the U.S. Government, the total cost of the 1972 presidential campaigns, including congressional primaries and elections was at an all time high. Additional data on election costs, gathered by *U.S. News and World Report,* estimates the price of acquiring the presidency at from $35 million to $60 million; a state governorship at $50,000 to $5 million; a Senate seat from $250,000 to $5 million; and a seat in the House of Representatives from $30,000 to $300,000. These expenditures have steadily increased and the likelihood is that this trend will continue. Estimates of costs also vary depending on the type of constituency and the contest at stake, and with the urban versus rural nature of the area.

The actual costs are staggering and their implications place Senator Mathias's statement in a more meaningful context. It was estimated by the Federal Communications Commission that the costs for radio and television time in the 1968 primary and general election campaigns were $58 million, and that in 1972 these costs exceeded $60 million.[55]

---

[53] *New York Times,* June 21, 1972, p. 28. Senator Smith was, however, defeated in the general election.

[54] *Congressional Quarterly Weekly Report* (September 22, 1973): 2515.

[55] U.S. Bureau of the Census, *Statistical Abstract of the United States: 1973,* 94th ed. (Washington, D.C., 1973), p. 384.

TELEVISION

Television is charged with having contributed greatly to the growth in campaign expenditures. The presidential candidates account for a high percentage of total spending on television in general elections. Approximately half of the television costs in 1968 and in 1972 were attributed to the candidates for president and vice-president. It was originally thought that television would siphon money from radio campaigning rather than significantly increase overall costs. However, the costs per vote went from 19 cents in 1952 to 29 cents in 1960 and 35 cents in 1964. The price per vote in 1968 moved to 60 cents.[56] Even discounting the inflation and costly campaign technology, television is labeled as the culprit that has added enormously to the cost of mobilizing each vote. Television costs include buying time on networks (at rates which vary from city to city and within cities), travel, production, and fees to media consultants.

The cost of T.V. has brought forth the need for big money which has contributed further to the idea that one must be rich to run for political office. Thus, the question which one must ask is; from where does this money come? The Citizen's Research Foundation estimated that there were 89 people who contributed $30,000 or more to presidential campaigns in 1968, for a total of $6.8 million. Also, 424 contributors made political donations of over $10,000 to presidential candidates for a total of $12 million. In 1972, the year of Watergate, Nixon received $37.6 million in donations of over $100 and McGovern received $13 million in contributions of over $100.[57] Relatively few people donate a rather large portion of the funds necessary to run a modern and very costly political campaign. It would be naïve to assume that large campaign contributions do not bring with them greater access to the political decision makers.[58]

As mentioned in the discussion of polling techniques, it is often impossible for a political unknown who may be perceived as a sure loser to raise the money necessary to get the party's endorsement. Similar difficulties occur with regard to the even more costly media. In the 1972 Wisconsin presidential primary— just one step in winning the nomination—the costs incurred by the six leading contenders were estimated to be more than $1 million with the Jackson forces spending $400,000; the Humphrey campaign spending $160,000; McGovern forces, $250,000; and the Muskie staff, $163,000.[59]

It is clear that wealthy contenders who utilize their own resources to mount

[56] Report of the Twentieth Century Fund Commission on Campaign Costs in the Electronic Era, *Voters' Time* (New York: The Twentieth Century Fund, 1968).
[57] *Congressional Quarterly Weekly Report* (September 1, 1973): 2382.
[58] Ibid. See Chapter 10 for a further look at campaign costs and attempts at reform.
[59] *Wilmington Morning News* (Delaware), April 5, 1972, p. 2.

extensive media campaigns are among the "winners" in the "new politics"; among them are Shapp, Rockefeller, the Kennedys, and countless others.

How does all of this expensive campaigning, based heavily on television campaigning, influence electoral victory or defeat? *Advertising Age,* a trade paper in the advertising business, suggested the following in 1968:

> How did Richard Nixon win the Presidency? Partly, at least, because he out-spent the competition in advertising. The extent to which that was true was again pointed up today with the Television Bureau of Advertising's release of 1968's biggest clients in network TV. Nestled among the top 100, in 79th place, between Schlitz Brewing Co. and Monsanto is United Citizens for Nixon and Agnew with an estimated net time talent budget of $3,922,600. In addition, $175,000 was reported by the Nixon for President Committee.
>
> Hubert Humphrey, the Democratic runnerup, was in 109th place, bracketed between Sperry Rand Corp. and Standard Oil of New Jersey. His budget: $2,826,000.

It should be noted, however, that although Humphrey spent less and was less successful, he too relied heavily on "new politics" techniques in his 1968 race. Some students of contemporary politics profess to see a voter "backlash" in response to what appears to be oversaturation of the air waves by media oriented campaigns. Consider the case of John V. Lindsay, who ran as the Liberal party candidate for mayor of New York in 1969. He made heavy use of media campaigning, surveys, and political consultants and his victory was attributed to the use of these techniques. But by 1972, many people were saying that Americans were tired of "image" politics. The defeat of John V. Lindsay, the handsome, "cool," charismatic mayor of New York City, in Wisconsin and other primaries where he staged expensive television campaigns during his 1972 quest for the Democratic presidential nomination has been cited as a case in point. Lindsay received only about 7 percent of the Wisconsin and Florida primary vote. It is well to remember that even in 1969, when Lindsay won his "new politics" victory in New York, Peter Flaherty became mayor of Pittsburgh, Pennsylvania with limited funds and virtually no media projection. And, even the wealthy must ultimately rely on their ability to engender additional financial resources in order to wage a campaign successfully.

Television appeals by the candidates have made it easy for them to go straight to the voters—for both financial support and ultimately votes—often bypassing the party. Thus it is possible to see an eclipse in the role of parties in the electoral process taking place during this era of television campaigning. Antiorganizational candidates such as Shapp in Pennsylvania (1966) and Ottinger in New York (1970) have been able to prevail in the nominating process, at least in primary elections (where party cues are of very little importance) by virtue of personal wealth and impressive media presentations. The reach of television has now extended even to judicial candidacies, as the 1973 New York Democratic primary victor in New York's race for prestigious chief judge of the Court of Appeals won nomination (though not the general election) by a similar combination of money and media.

RADIO—STILL A KEY INFLUENCE

> On March 4, 1933, people huddled around radios with desperate intensity. Unable though they were to see the wire-taut muscles in Roosevelt's face while he delivered his inaugural speech, their response to his confident voice and message turned despair into hope edged with excitement. . .
>
> Never before in all human history had a speech been heard by so many people; never before had an address produced such an immediate, widespread, or profound impact upon a nation's psychology. A new mood of hopeful expectation had been achieved through the alchemy of a man, his message, his rhetoric, and far-flung radio audience.[60]

It has been estimated that 80 million people heard some of President Franklin Roosevelt's "fireside chats." The huge audience appeal of radio not only helped to generate confidence and excitement about politics, it also provided the forum for the image of the president as a strong national leader. During Roosevelt's twelve years in the White House radio emerged as a very important campaign tool. Candidates began to spend increasing portions of their campaign funds on radio because of the large number of people who could be contacted via this medium. (For example, in 1950, 95 percent of all American homes had at least one radio.)[61]

The vastness of the radio audience is still a phenomenon of the 1970s, and the potential power of radio as a campaign device has not been lost to contemporary political managers. Thus, expenditures for radio time during the primary and general election increased from $10.8 million in 1964 to nearly $21 million in 1968.[62] This rise in radio time expenditures was marked particularly by increased use of radio advertisements during the primary campaigns.

If the question of radio utilization in campaigns is probed further, then the trend of increased use of radio time for campaigning becomes clearer. In 1952, $3.1 million was spent on radio time during the general election campaign. This figure increased to $7.1 million in 1964 and to approximately $13 million in 1968–72. In 1968, for example, Senator McCarthy in the New Hampshire primary used 7,200 radio spots in three weeks.[63]

[60] E. J. Wrange and B. Baskerville, *Contemporary Forum* (New York: Harper and Row, 1962), p. 136, quoted by Mendelsohn and Crespi, *Polls, Television,* p. 262.

[61] In 1932 the Democrats allocated 17 percent of their $1,170,000 campaign funds for radio time, and the Republicans allocated 20 percent of their $2,670,000 campaign expenditures for radio time. See ibid., p. 260.

[62] Herbert Alexander, *Financing the 1968 Election* (Lexington, Mass.: Heath, Lexington, 1971), p. 93.

[63] Chester, *Radio, Television, and Politics,* p. 60.

Certain questions must be considered regarding such heavy utilization of radio in an era of television campaigning. While more money is spent on television than radio during the general campaign, the radio audience is not ignored by the major candidates during either the primaries or the general election. Who makes up the radio audience? The suburban commuter driving in the car to work, the housewife doing her daily chores, the elderly, who were brought up on radio, black and other ethnic voters loyal to a particular "station," and perhaps young voters who are still "hooked" on radio as a result of their rock-and-roll teens.[64] The Nixon campaign in both 1968 and again in 1972 relied heavily on radio for the presentation of detailed policy statements, which were not appropriate for television, and for statements of interest to special clienteles. Also utilized were interview programs, talk shows, and call-in shows.

THE PRESS—IMPACT ON OPINION LEADERS

It has been indicated elsewhere in this chapter that there is a reasonably strong relationship between education and newspaper and magazine reading, with the printed word increasing as a more salient influence on members of the polity as educational achievement level increases. The latter also correlates highly with propensity to vote. It is true, however, that a majority of American people place more trust in the information they receive from the electronic media than from the print media. Of course, prior to the advent of radio and television, the printed word was the only effective means for the mass dissemination of political information, and the effect of the press historically as affecting campaign outcomes is interesting to examine. From 1796 to 1940 there were thirty-six presidential campaigns. In only eighteen of these contests did the successful candidate have the support of a majority of newspapers.[65] Thus, even when newspapers were the major source of mass disseminated information, it apparently was not necessary to have their support to win elections!

The printed word in campaigning has not been ignored in the age of electronic media. It was estimated in 1968 that a total of $20 million was spent on newspaper advertising during the primary and general election campaigns by candidates at all levels.[66] In addition to paid advertisements placed in foreign-language as well as the English press, news stories provide information

[64] Nimmo, *Political Persuaders,* p. 134.
[65] In two of these years, 1804 when Jefferson was elected for a second term, and 1820, when Monroe was elected, there were no campaigns. Frank Luther Mott, "Newspapers in Presidential Campaigns," *Public Opinion Quarterly* 8 (1944): 362.
[66] Alexander, *Financing the 1968 Election,* p. 112.

to the general public—and especially to opinion leaders or the "attentive public," who are most likely to read through the details of printed stories—to help fill in the issue outlines which are presented on television. It has been estimated that 49 percent of a national sample followed the 1968 campaign regularly in the press whereas 89 percent of the public followed it on television.[67] To borrow from Marshall McLuhan—the press, which is a hot medium, fills in the gaps left by television, a cool medium. Only by following the press can a more complete knowledge of contemporary issues be had. Furthermore, often it is not the editorial policy in magazines and newspapers which influences readers, it is the choice and presentation of news stories. Speaking about the 1968 presidential campaign, Doris Graeber has suggested that the information provided by the press was not complete. "The reader did not gain much insight into the substance of the issues or the merits which the candidates attached to various policy options. However, he could tell which issues seemed most important to a particular candidate and how the candidate rated himself and others in the ability to cope successfuly with the manifold problems of the presidency." [68] It is particularly instructive to view Graeber's comments on press treatment of candidates and issues in relation to our discussion of the "new politics." According to her analysis, the image of candidates everywhere was based on personal qualities with little information about the candidate's political philosophy or executive ability. The public's diet of campaign information was "bland, uniform and filling." [69] The print media appear to reinforce candidate and personality centered campaigning almost as much as do their electronic colleagues.

OTHER CAMPAIGN TECHNIQUES

In addition to the costs for electronic and print media, as well as political consultants and sophisticated survey research, already discussed, most campaigns also utilize direct phone messages, direct mail (and phone) appeals, and the traditional billboards, handouts, bumper stickers, and buttons. The point to be made about the latter is the decreasing proportion of a candidate's budget they appear to comprise. Agranoff has estimated costs of a million-dollar statewide campaign as follows: [70]

[67] Doris Graeber, "The Press as Opinion Resource during the 1968 Presidential Campaign," *Public Opinion Quarterly* 35, no. 2 (1971): 169.

[68] Ibid., p. 182.

[69] Ibid., pp. 168, 182.

[70] Robert Agranoff, "Introduction to the New Style of Campaigning: The Decline of Party and the Rise of Candidate-Centered Campaign Technology," in Agranoff, *The New Style in Election Campaigns* (Boston: Holbrook, 1972), pp. 33–34.

headquarters	$95,000
personnel	127,000
candidate and staff travel	46,500
special events	8,500
research (polls etc.)	75,000
direct mail	90,000
television	375,000
radio	40,500
newspapers	15,500
outdoor advertising	42,000
agency fees	25,000
literature and stickers	25,000
telephone banks	35,000

While it may be suggested that other forms of campaigning including bill-boards, personalized letters, and recorded phone messages may reach a large number of voters at lower cost per voter, at least until now, contemporary candidates for major political office have chosen to rely very heavily on television.

IMPLICATIONS OF THE NEW POLITICAL TECHNOLOGY

Undoubtedly, the wizardry of electronic media has captivated the intellectual's attention. Its techniques are fascinating. A person mastering something as simple as the hand camera can turn an absolute idiot into a stylist, charismatic leader of men, a super personality who gazes thoughtfully into futures, trudges compassionately through slums and understands instinctively the desperate yearnings of hard hats and housewives.[71]

If it is true, as suggested earlier, that "the criteria used in the world of toothpaste and women's bras (can be applied) to the world of politics," then perhaps any candidate can be successfully marketed to the American public. If this is a correct assessment of American politics then there are grave implications for democracy in the United States. However before this assessment can be accepted totally, the notion of marketability of any candidate should be examined.

In addition to "image making," candidates must rely on reportage by television, radio, and the press, for support for political views by the public, ability to recruit volunteers to build strong organizations, and ultimately, even party support. Outside support is more difficult to manipulate for a candidate than his own paid presentations. In this context, it is well to remember too that

[71] *New York Times,* May 22, 1972, p. 32.

manipulative techniques utilizing the "new political technology" do not necessarily insure a successful candidacy. While it is true, for example, that New York's former Governor Rockefeller spent $600,000 more on media presentations alone than his opponent Arthur Goldberg spent on his entire campaign in 1970,[72] it is also true that Rockefeller is an indefatigable street campaigner whose issue orientation (somewhat right of center) perhaps accorded more with the views of the electorate than did Goldberg's. Still, though it may be erroneous to attribute Rockefeller's success only to the "image" purchased by a millionaire's funds, the polls, consultants, and media undoubtedly helped to develop the "image" the voters selected on Election Day in New York State.

While we have sought to view the "new political technology" and television in particular as a force for social change, unlike McLuhan, we do not see it as a revolutionary development, *yet.* It is, however, clear that the thrust of the "new politics" is personality, and not party or even issues.

Our "new politics" may be contrasted with the centralized British system. There each candidate for a parliamentary seat is limited to a total of $3,400 in campaign expenditures and each campaign is managed by a centrally appointed party manager. But even in staid Britain, advertising managers are being hired by candidates for prime minister (exempt from the above rules), and in the election of 1970, the Conservative party used a television spot showing scissors snipping away at a pound note if the rival Laborites were elected. The march of technology and the "new politics" is apparently inexorable.

[72] *New York Times,* October 25, 1970, p. 14.

Introduction
to Chapters 5
and 6

The next two chapters will analyze one of the most important—and increasingly enigmatic—roles of party in American politics: that of party identification and voting. An electorate that has traditionally been loyal to the two-party system—with remarkable stability—may be undergoing significant and unprecedented changes. Many of the changes which have been evident in the past decade, at least in part, have been produced by the antiparty trends docu-

91

mented in the previous chapters. Our focus here is on the relevance of party identification to the voting decision, those forces which seem to be limiting the role of partisanship in voting, and the expected impact of new patterns on the future of American parties.

5
Voting in America

According to Robert Dahl, writing in *Polyarchy,* a pluralistic state is distinguished from other forms of government by the right to participate in politics and public contestation of issues. It is these functions that elections most clearly provide for the citizen within the political system.

In this chapter we are interested in examining several key aspects of voting in American politics: Why do people vote? Who votes? How important is party identification today as a source of voting behavior? Is voting rational?

THE CITIZEN WHO IDENTIFIES AND VOTES

First, a word about voting in general. Although the act of voting is the major vehicle by which Americans participate in the political system, it should be noted that voting is only one source of political influence. Other sources, including pressure group activity for political purposes, litigation, protest, expert leadership, party activism, public office holding, and status related to wealth, may often prove to have greater impact on the political system for individuals and groups than voting per se. Interest groups with money, status, and organizational skill, may, for example, obtain great power despite their inability to mobilize large blocs of voters.

WHY DO PEOPLE VOTE?

Some people vote because they perceive it to be their civic responsibility to do so. This attitude tends to be reinforced by peer group pressure. Union members, for example, are more likely to vote than nonunion members, in part because the "organization" seeks to educate its members to the need to vote, thus effectively mobilizing them for political participation. The AFL-CIO may spend between half to $1 million a year on drives to register union members. In 1972 the AFL-CIO national Committee on Political Education (COPE) reported expenditures of over $1.27 million on election campaigns for the presidency and congress. The Voluntary Community Action Program of the United Auto Workers (UAW-V-CAP) reported 1972 campaign expenditures of over $580,000.[1] Members of labor unions comprise approximately one-seventh of the adult population of the United States, and together with their spouses and other immediate family members of voting age make up about one-quarter of the potential American electorate.

People do not necessarily vote because they think their vote will "count," or make a difference in the electoral outcome, particularly in national elections where the constituency is vast. However, even in such elections, votes can make a difference; in 1960, Nixon lost Michigan by 1.1 percent, Minnesota by 1.4 percent, Illinois by 0.2 percent, and New Jersey by 0.8 percent. In 1940, .002 percent of the vote (2 votes out of every 1000) gave Michigan's electoral votes to the Republicans, not the Democrats.[2] In fact, the 1960 and the 1968 presidential elections were decided by less than one-half of 1 percent of the vote. A 1964 study of "late voting" in California revealed that although voters knew (through media presentations) of Goldwater's apparent loss to Johnson in the presidential election because the eastern polls had already closed due to time differences, large numbers of the people who voted (and most of those who planned to did, despite the broadcast returns) voted for the candidate they had favored previously.[3] Thus, although their votes did not really "count," they had been motivated sufficiently to vote, and their vote had a symbolic, if seemingly irrational, quality.

Reinforcement to vote is significant; contact with party workers, peer groups, and family members who are strong politicos, may be important influences in motivating individuals to vote. A Gallup study has suggested that greater party activity in stimulating voting might have altered the outcome of the 1968 presidential election. The Gallup organization estimates that 19 million people made plans to vote during the course of the 1968 campaign for a candidate other than the one they finally chose on November 5.

Persons contacted by party workers are more likely to vote. "In Massachusetts, Senator George S. McGovern (Dem., S.D.), won all the 102 conven-

---

[1] *Congressional Quarterly Weekly Report* (March 17, 1973): 577–78.

[2] Archibald and Helen Crosley, "Polling in 1968," *Public Opinion Quarterly* 33 (March 1969): 11.

[3] Kurt Lang and Gladys Engel Lang, "The Late Vote: A Summary of Findings and Implications," *Voting and Non-Voting* (Waltham, Mass.: Ginn and Company, 1970), p. 165.

tion seats after displaying his ability to field a political army of committed volunteers. It was much the same technique that McGovern had employed successfully to win the April 4 Democratic primary in Wisconsin." [4] In Wisconsin, McGovern fielded 3,000 canvassers to identify voters as supporting, leaning toward, or opposing him. On Election Day, voters supporting or leaning toward McGovern were reminded by telephone to vote and in some cases provided with transportation to the polls. Gene Pokorny, the senator's Midwest regional coordinator summarized the role of canvassing: "Organization is a very simple thing. You build, you create, you reinforce. . . . All politics is names. Get their names and telephone numbers and put them on three-by-five cards. The guts of politics is three-by-five cards." [5] On the basis of a drive in which canvassing played a reinforcing role, McGovern finished first in Wisconsin (with 29.5 percent of the vote) in a field of six candidates. Gerald H. Kramer concludes his study of canvassing by suggesting that door-to-door canvassing in a presidential campaign acts to increase voting but "there is little effect on voter preferences for national or local offices." [6]

Some people vote because they come from politically active and interested families and their parents' view of political participation has been inculcated in them. Hess and Torney report that "following the identification model, children may become politically active if their parents are active. Children may learn to value modes of political involvement which they observe in their parents." [7]

Other citizens are committed strongly to one of the two major parties—probably also inherited from their parents—and therefore feel committed to register and vote for the candidate of their preferred party. (See Table 6.) According to Hess and Torney, "The family also presents examples that children may emulate. Probably the most significant socialization of this kind involves parental affiliation with a political party. Despite some variability in reported data, there is evidence that the family exerts an important influence upon the child's preference. . . ." [8]

People who belong to relatively high status occupational groups and perceive their stake as citizens in maintaining the kind of society in which they believe they best can continue to thrive, will vote to maintain the system. Low turnouts by workers and low-income people may be due in part to their

[4] Andrew Glass, "Political Organization Adds Needed Muscle for Humphrey and McGovern Victories," *National Journal* 4 (April 29, 1972): 714.

[5] Ibid., p. 715.

[6] "The Effects of Precinct-Level Canvassing on Voter Behavior," *Public Opinion Quarterly* 34 (Winter, 1970–71): 572.

[7] Robert D. Hess and Judith V. Torney, *The Development of Political Attitudes in Children* (Chicago: Aldine, 1967), p. 96.

[8] Ibid.

Table 6. Party Identification and Participation, 1972 (in percent)

	Strong Democrat	Weak Democrat	Independent Leaning Democrat	Independent	Independent Leaning Republican	Weak Republican	Strong Republican
Voted	79.6	70.5	71.5	53.4	75.9	79.4	87.3
Did Not Vote	20.4	29.5	28.5	46.6	24.1	20.6	12.7
	100	100	100	100	100	100	100
	(329)*	(587)	(242)	(281)	(245)	(320)	(245)

* Figures in parentheses refer to the number of cases.
SOURCE: The Center for Political Studies (C.P.S.) of the University of Michigan data made available through the Inter-University Consortium for Political Research (I.C.P.R.).

inability to perceive their economic self-interest in terms of complex political and economic issues. High status individuals, however, are in a better position to perceive and defend their position in society. For example, Seymour Martin Lipset contends that "Where economic relationships are not easily visible to those affected, general insight into complex social problems can result from education and no doubt contributes to the higher voting among the more educated groups." [9]

Sometimes voters deliberately vote as a bloc, seeking to influence electoral results. A good example is the record turnout of black voters (who often have not been active electoral participants) who almost unanimously cast their votes for one man in order to influence the election of black mayors in Cleveland, Ohio; Gary, Indiana; and Newark, New Jersey. In 1960, according to one account, Chicano voters (who had been organized into Viva Kennedy! clubs) made the difference between John F. Kennedy's victory and defeat in two states. In New Mexico, Kennedy received a 20,000 vote plurality among Chicanos and carried the state by 2,000 votes. In Texas, Kennedy received a 200,000 vote plurality among Chicanos and carried the state by less than 50,000 votes.[10] Bloc voting may be accentuated in presidential elections by the operation of the electoral college's "winner take all" principle, which awards all electoral votes within each state to the candidate with a plurality of popular votes. This system has enhanced the political influence of large states with many electoral votes; these states often have large urban (metropolitan) concentrations of "ethnic" voters who are able through bloc voting to influence their state's popular—and hopefully, for them—electoral vote total. An example of such influence is the so-called "Jewish" vote. Jews, as a group, tend to vote in large numbers, and because of their geographically strategic locations in states with large electoral college voting blocs, such as New York, Pennsylvania, and Illinois, often have been able to induce presidential candidates to affirm their warm and continued support for the state of Israel and for social reform measures. It should be noted that the deliberate withholding of votes has been a tactic employed by groups seeking to gain a foothold in organized politics, particularly on the state and local level. In 1970, in Alabama, for example, Dr. John Cashin, running for governor on the National Democratic party of Alabama ticket (an all-black party) was able to get 90 percent of the black vote. Although Cashin lost the election to George Wallace, it is certain that the lesson of his impressive vote-getting appeal among blacks will not be lost among future (white) candidates for public office in Alabama.

[9] Seymour Martin Lipset, *Political Man* (Garden City, N.Y.: Anchor Books, 1963), p. 197.
[10] Mark Levy and Michael Kramer, *The Ethnic Factor* (New York: Simon and Schuster, 1972), pp. 77–78.

WHO IS THE VOTER?

It seems clear that a number of components go into the citizen's decision to vote in elections. Voting behavior itself has been, for better or worse, one of the most studied aspects of political behavior in America.

One way of answering the question "Who is the voter?" is to examine the role of party identification in voting. Following the voluminous work of the scholars at the Survey Research Center (SRC), now known as the Center for Political Studies (CPS), of the University of Michigan, we may discuss two kinds of forces that influence voting behavior: the long term—party identification—and the short term—political personalities, social forces and issues, etc. The SRC, which has sampled voters continuously in presidential elections since 1948, believes that the psychological attachment of the voter to his party, accompanied by high political interest and a sense of political efficacy, is the most important aspect of his voting behavior.[11] Dividing the electorate into strong partisans, weak partisans, and independents, the SRC has attempted empirically to validate the idea that there is a "core" voting group strongly committed to each of the major parties. This "core" is comprised of those voters who are best informed politically, most active, and most likely to vote in all elections. Congressional elections tend to attract "core" voters because issues and personality are less salient than in presidential elections; hence, such elections are good tests of relative party strength.

Party identification in the United States has, at least until recently, been remarkably stable.[12] Party loyalty has often survived change of residence (i.e., city to suburb), income, and status. Party loyalty may be sufficiently strong in many instances to overcome cross-pressures—or conflicting pulls upon the voter. In 1960, when John F. Kennedy, a Democrat and a Catholic, ran against Richard M. Nixon, a Republican and a Protestant, and religious feelings ran high, Protestant Democrats were more likely to behave as Democrats while Catholic Republicans were more likely to behave as Republicans.[13] The SRC estimated that in past elections (not including 1972) party supplied 60 percent of the vote; issues, and personality, 40 percent.[14] Through its threefold classification (see Table 7) the SRC has sought to deal with a paradox of American politics; the high percentage of Americans who identify with parties (most often the party of their parents); considerable stability of party loyalty (the

---

[11] See especially Angus Campbell, Phillip E. Converse, Warren E. Miller, and Donald E. Stokes, *The American Voter* (New York: Wiley, 1964), and Angus Campbell, et al., *Elections and the Political Order* (New York: Wiley, 1966).

[12] It is interesting to speculate on the actual change in voter identification. That is, as voters move in opposite directions to different parties, these movements may cancel out in the net figures.

[13] Phillip E. Converse, "Religion and Politics: The 1960 Election," in Campbell, et al., *Elections and the Political Order,* p. 123.

[14] Phillip E. Converse, Warren E. Miller, Jerrold Rusk, and Arthur Wolfe, "Continuity and Change in American Politics: Parties and Issues in the 1968 Election," *American Political Science Review* 63 (December 1969): 1096.

SRC estimated in *The American Voter* that 56 percent of presidential voters had never crossed party lines in presidential elections); *and* low voting turnouts in many elections. A study in 1958 found that while only 25 percent of French voters could identify their father's party preference, 76 percent of the American electorate could, indicating a far higher level of continuity of party identification in American politics.[15]

In the studies of the 1950s and 1960s which were done by those associated with the SRC, the strength of a voter's identification with a party was the major key to "who votes." Gerald Pomper, a political scientist studying this era, estimated that between 1952 and 1964 close to four out of five persons in each of the elections retained the same underlying party loyalty. Also, during the same time frame over 20 percent of the electorate admitted changing their party loyalties.[16]

The SRC itself has recognized, however, that despite the relative stability of party loyalty in the aggregate, individual voting behavior is fluctuating. Thus in a 1972 voting study completed by several scholars associated with the SRC, it was noted that: "At the same time that the general population was becoming increasingly detached from the parties, as evidenced by the growing number of Independents, a parallel increase in the tendency to vote for the other party was occurring among the partisans."[17] For example, 11 percent of all Democrats who voted for Nixon, and who voted also for a congressional candidate voted for a Republican congressional candidate. A 1972 Gallup Poll reported that one-third of all Democrats voted for Republican Nixon, far exceeding the rate of defection of the previous five presidential elections. The 1972 data indicated for the first time that inertia and party may have been slightly less potent in determining voting behavior than issues.[18] The SRC has drawn distinctions between "high" and "low" stimulus elections. "Political stimulation in an election derives from several sources: the candidates, particularly those leading the ticket; the policy issues, foreign and domestic; and other circumstances of the moment. The intensity and character of this stimulation vary from one election to the next. There are occasions when none of these components of the world of politics seems important to the electorate, resulting in what we will refer to as a *low-stimulus* election. In other years dramatic

[15] Phillip E. Converse and George Dupeux, "Politicization of the Electorate in France and the United States," in Campbell, et al., *Elections and the Political Order,* p. 280.

[16] Gerald M. Pomper, *Elections in America* (New York: Dodd, Mead, 1968), p. 120. V. O. Key has argued that from simple election figures, misleading impressions develop about the stability of the electorate from election to election. Instead, in his view, "a vast and intricate churning about occurs as millions of voters switch party preferences." In Key, *The Responsible Electorate: Rationality in Presidential Voting, 1936–1960* (Cambridge, Mass.: Harvard University Press, 1966), p. 15.

[17] Arthur H. Miller, Warren E. Miller, Alden S. Raine, Thad A. Brown, "A Majority Party in Disarray: Policy Polarization in the 1972 Election," paper presented to the American Political Science Association, New Orleans, Louisiana, September 1973, p. 89.

[18] Miller, et al., "A Majority Party in Disarray," p. 70.

Table 7. Party Identification from 1952 to 1972 (in percent)

	1952	1954	1956	1958	1960	1962	1964	1966	1968	1970	1972
Democrats	47	47	44	46	46	47	51	45	45	43	40
Independents	22	22	24	19	23	23	22	28	29	31	35
Republicans	27	27	29	29	27	27	24	25	24	25	23
Nothing, don't know	4	4	3	5	4	3	2	2	2	1	2
	100	100	100	100	100	100	100	100	100	100	100
	(1,614)*	(1,139)	(1,772)	(1,269)	(3,021)	(1,317)	(1,571)	(1,291)	(1,558)	(1,507)	(2,705)

* Figures in parentheses refer to the number of cases.

SOURCES: This table was drawn from H. T. Reynolds, *Politics and the Common Man* (Homewood, Ill: Dorsey, 1974), p. 161; William H. Flanigan, *Political Behavior of the American Electorate*, 2d ed. (Boston: Allyn and Bacon, 1972), p. 33; 1970 data from CPS 1970 American National Election Study; 1972 data from CPS 1972 American National Election Study.

issues or events may stir a great deal of interest; popular candidates may stimulate widespread enthusiasm. Such an election, in which the electorate feels the combined impact of these various pressures, we will speak of as a high-stimulus election." [19] In high-stimulus elections, weakly identifying partisans and independents propelled by short-term forces, issues and personality—rather than partisanship—are mobilized. It is the presence of these voters that has apparently prevented the Democrats from capturing the presidency in four elections since 1948 despite their commanding lead among "partisans." (The Democrats have received a majority only once in the past seven presidential elections, in 1964.) This may be due in part to the increased likelihood of high-stimulus elections in an era of electronic campaigning. If this is the case one may wish to raise questions about the current relevance of the relationship of "partisanship" and voting—particularly the self-classificatory scale utilized by the SRC for the analysis of national voting (though not necessarily state and local voting where party identification can be a salient influence).[20] In defense of their partisan self-classification scale, researchers at the SRC have noted:

> We have not measured party attachments in terms of the vote or the evaluation of partisan issues precisely because we are interested in exploring the *influence* of party identification on voting behavior. When an independent measure of party identification is used, it is clear that even strong party adherents at times may think and act in contradiction to their party allegiance. We could never establish the conditions under which this will occur if lasting partisan orientations were measured in terms of the behavior they are thought to affect.[21]

The 1972 presidential election had none of the hallmarks of a high-stimulus election. Turnout was low and voters professed little interest in the election or candidates. The Republican candidate for president won an overwhelming majority despite an impressive partisan edge for the Democrats. The forces at work in recent elections may require further analysis because the influence of party identification on voting seems to be weakening.

SOCIETAL CLEAVAGES AND VOTING BEHAVIOR

Other questions about voting behavior remain to be discussed. Why are some people stronger party identifiers than others? What are the salient

---

[19] Campbell, "Surge and Decline: A Study of Electoral Change," in *Elections and the Political Order,* p. 41.

[20] Andrew Cowart, however, has studied state elections utilizing SRC theoretical propositions and found that party voting in senatorial and gubernatorial elections is modified by the incumbency of the individual candidates, often causing partisan defection. "Electoral Choice in the 'American States': Incumbency Effects, Partisan Forces and Divergent Partisan Majorities," *American Political Science Review* 67 (September 1973): 835–53.

[21] Campbell, et al., *The American Voter,* p. 68.

sources of party identification? Traditionally, the answers have appeared to lie in two significant areas: family and school socialization into politics and socioeconomic status. Let us consider each separately.

Family and School Socialization into Politics Most political scientists attribute the major role of political socialization to the family, particularly with regard to the development of partisan identification and perhaps nonidentification as well.[22] One study found that by the fourth grade six out of ten New Haven children stated a partisan preference, usually the same as their parents and often reinforced by the identification of a favored candidate with the same party. However, it was not until the eighth grade that the children were able to supply more content to their preference, e.g., identification of party leaders.[23] A second study found party affiliation developing late in elementary school and a similarly high degree of continuity with parents' partisan identification.[24]

Herbert H. Hyman reviewed a number of studies on political socialization and concluded they "establish very clearly a family correspondence in views that are relevant to matters of political orientation." [25] M. Kent Jennings and Richard Niemi found a 59 percent continuity in transmission of party identification from one category to another.[26] Thus, early commitment to a party is a form of political participation which may aid in structuring the perspective through which children perceive political issues and events.

There are several other aspects of youthful partisan socialization that require further attention. The first is the low saliency that party identification seems to have. Many students feel party choice should be deferred until they are adults. Hess and Torney state: ". . . the school curriculum under-emphasizes the rights and obligations of a citizen to participate in government. The school focuses on the obligation and right to vote but does not offer the child sufficient understanding of procedures open to individuals for legitimately influencing the government. Nor does it adequately explain and emphasize the importance of group action to achieve desirable ends." [27] The second point to be considered here is that independence of party—in the antiparty tradition —appears to be valued especially among older children who are highly intelligent, of higher status groupings.[28] Furthermore, Jennings and Niemi report a weakening of party identification among the young, and a higher percent

---

[22] Frank Sorauf, *Party Politics in America,* 2d ed. (Boston: Little Brown, 1972), p. 143; Herbert Hyman, *Political Socialization* (Glencoe, Ill.: The Free Press, 1959), p. 74.

[23] Fred Greenstein, *Children and Politics* (New Haven, Conn.: Yale University Press, 1965), pp. 71–72.

[24] Hess and Torney, *Political Attitudes in Children,* pp. 92–103.

[25] Hyman, *Political Socialization,* p. 59.

[26] "The Transmission of Political Values from Parent to Child," *American Political Science Review* 62 (March 1968): 173.

[27] Hess and Torney, *Political Attitudes in Children,* p. 218.

[28] Hess and Torney, ibid., p. 127.

of independent voting trends (12 percent more children than parents identified as independent in 1968).[29] One study concludes, "Clearly, children do not see striking differences between the two major political parties, nor does the ability to differentiate between policies of the parties appear to increase markedly during elementary school." [30]

The general lack of interest in parties among youth is reinforced by a lack of discussion of parties in schools. Greenstein states:

> Since as we have seen, there *are* substantial differences in information about a key *informal* aspect of politics—political parties—the possibility arises that classroom instruction may have something to do with equalizing the awareness of formal governmental information. Lessons about "How A Bill Becomes A Law," or "What the Mayor Does," are accepted parts of the grade school curriculum; discussions of partisan politics are less likely to be. Some aspects of partisanship, for example, the nature of differences between parties, are probably considered too controversial and "subjective" to be dealt with in the classroom. Therefore, if this information is not learned in the home and neighborhood, it is probably not learned at all early in childhood.[31]

When teachers do discuss parties, perhaps out of fear of exercising undue "political influence," they stress the idea that parties do not really differ, that good citizens vote for candidates regardless of their party identification, and that children should not identify blindly with the party of their parents.[32] Hence, the *role* of parties is poorly defined and *antiparty* norms are generally stressed. Because of the emphasis in school on the role that the individual as voter can play vis-à-vis his government, disappointment may set in later in life when the vote (the prime instrument of individual participation in government) is recognized as a less than omnipotent political technique.

Antiparty norms and unrealistic political expectations taught in schools may be combined with reports of the increasing tendency toward independent voting in the polity in general. The long-term effects of such socialization in an era of candidate-centered campaign strategies seem to be leading to an increasing uneasiness about identifying with parties among new voters. Recent studies of twelfth graders find that the correlation of the partisan attitudes of high school seniors with their parents' partisan preference is declining, and that these young people are more likely to be independent. It is possible, of course, that the transmission of attitudes is greater than these studies indicate. Though many Americans have retained their party identification, they vote as independents. Perhaps their children, who identify as independents, have

[29] M. Kent Jennings and Richard G. Niemi, "The Transmission of Political Values from Parent to Child," *American Political Science Review* 62 (March 1968): 173.

[30] Hess and Torney, *Political Attitudes in Children*, p. 80.

[31] Greenstein, *Children and Politics*, p. 98.

[32] Hess and Torney, *Political Attitudes in Children*, p. 218.

had political independence transmitted to them by their parents. The children have, however, given up the party tie, which has become increasingly unimportant to their parents.[33]

The Role of Socioeconomic Status Partisan identification in the United States is not based strictly on class or socioeconomic status—which has as its three components education, income, and occupation. Robert Alford estimates that while normally class voting does not rise above 60 percent because of imperfect status crystallization, it is true that the issues which dominate partisan politics relate to the distribution of national wealth, the degree of public ownership, government centralization and the level of regulation of private business.[34] The images of the two major parties in the United States between the 1930s and mid-1960s related to distinctive class bases. The Democrats were seen as "good for the workers" and the Republicans "good for business." Yet in comparing Norwegian and American partisan identification and class, it has been found that Norwegian parties are more clearly demarcated along age, education, and sex lines, while American parties have tended to be more heterogeneous and have tended to blur class distinctions. In Norway, 80 percent of the working class is affiliated with the Labor party and 86 percent of the middle class with the Conservative party; in the United States, where the vast majority of workers saw themselves as Democrats (66 percent) prior to the 1970s,[35] the middle class divided equally between the two major parties. Hence, Norwegian parties are more clearly structured in terms of traditional class conflict and the parties are more clearly delineated ideologically. Nineteen percent of Norwegians say parties are the same or they are not sure; here the comparable percentage is 48 percent.[36]

Today, the economic bases of American parties are changing as the Democrats are for the first time gaining a majority among business and professional people.

If class is only a partial explanation for party identification, we must look to other sources. One is region. As several political scientists have argued, traditional, sectional loyalties—sometimes dating back to the Civil War or earlier—remain significant in determining party affiliation.[37] Ethnicity and religion also account for party affiliations in important ways. Since the period

---

[33] See Chapter 6 for a discussion of the "youth vote."

[34] Robert Alford, "Class Voting in the Anglo-American Political Systems," in S. M. Lipset and Stein Rokkan, eds., *Party Systems and Voter Alignments* (New York: Free Press, 1967), p. 72.

[35] Angus Campbell and Helen Valen, "Party Identification in Norway and the United States," in Campbell, *Elections and the Political Order,* p. 256.

[36] Ibid., pp. 254–58.

[37] See V. O. Key and Frank Munger, "Social Determination and Electoral Decision: The Case of Indiana," in Eugene Burdick and Arthur Brodbeck, eds., *American Voting Behavior* (New York: Free Press, 1959), pp. 281–99; and Thomas A. Flinn, "Continuity and Change in Ohio Politics," *Journal of Politics* 24 (August 1962): 521–44.

1928–32 Catholics have been considered strong Democratic partisans while Protestants have tended to support the Republican party. In 1972, however, Nixon received approximately 52 percent of the Catholic vote [38]—though this did not necessarily carry over to Catholic support for other Republican candidates. Such groups as Jews and blacks have continued to support the Democratic party long after social class and occupational status have undergone important changes. Hubert Humphrey in 1968 received 94 percent of the black vote and over 80 percent of the Jewish vote.[39] McGovern received just over 60 percent of the Jewish vote and over 85 percent of the black vote in 1972.[40] In 1965 nearly half of all Jewish families had yearly incomes of between $7,000 and $15,000 while only a quarter of all American families earned this much, yet they remained strongly Democratic. The Democratic predilection of Jews was clearly demonstrated by their support for an Irishman, James Donovan, when he ran against a liberal Jewish Republican, Jacob Javits, in a 1962 race for the U.S. Senate. Donovan received 47 percent of the Jewish vote in New York.[41]

It should be stressed that American voters have been seen traditionally by most political scientists as nonideological in carefully thought out class or ideological terms. The SRC estimated that in 1956 only 15 percent of the electorate saw parties and candidates in ideological terms. In 1958 only 7 percent of their respondents gave the SRC any discernible issue content in explaining their congressional vote. Several scholars associated with the SRC have, in fact, argued that there is a general impoverishment of political thought in the U.S. and a thinness of public understanding of concrete political alternatives, often reflected in voting. It should be recalled, however, that most SRC studies were conducted in the end of ideology 1950s and early 1960s, and in writing about the 1972 election several people associated with the SRC have modified this view. Voter support for parties appears increasingly issue-oriented in broad interest related terms. In 1972, the SRC asked the following question:

Some people feel that the government in Washington should see to it that every person has a job and a good standard of living. Others think the government should just let each person get ahead on his own. And, of course, other people have opinions somewhere in between. Suppose people who believe that the government should see to it that every person has a job and a good standard of living are at one end of the scale—at point number 1. And suppose that the people who believe that government should let each person get ahead on his own are at the

[38] *Gallup Opinion Index* (December 1972), p. 10. According to the *Congressional Quarterly Weekly Report* 46 (November 1972): 2949, the Catholic vote for Nixon was 59 percent.
[39] Levy and Kramer, *The Ethnic Factor,* pp. 257–58.
[40] Ibid., p. 226.
[41] Ibid., p. 121.

other end—at point number 7. Where would you place yourself on this scale, or haven't you thought about this? [See Table 8.]

Thus those Jews who favor liberal governmental spending (perhaps in line with their tradition of *Zedakah* or charity), find the Democratic party to be most relevant to them; those Protestants who are individualistic and private-enterprise oriented find the Republican party strongly parallel to their inclinations; many immigrant Catholics who were grateful for the assistance proffered them by Democratic administrations during hard times remained loyal to that party for many years. Those blacks who have turned to the Democratic party have done so because of a belief that federal action—a necessity for massive social change—is forthcoming only through election of Democrats to government. From those voters who opposed integration and favored a stronger stand on Vietnam, George Wallace, the American Independent party candidate for president in 1968, received twice as many votes as his national average.[42] Viewed in this way it can be argued that party identification and voting have some important components that are not just psychological but also involve perception of that political symbol that translates self-interest into political action.[43]

THE IMPORTANCE OF PARTY LOYALTY

THE NATIONAL DEMOCRATIC COALITION

Ever since the New Deal, we have accepted the premise that a number of diverse minorities—the poor, blacks, union members, Catholics, Southerners, and city dwellers—make up the rank and file of the national Democratic party and support Democratic candidates for president. Changes within the coalition have, however, taken place and continue to take place. In some cases the groups have changed in size, in other cases support has fluctuated within the groups. In the pages that follow we will consider voting in *national* elections and continuing or declining partisan loyalty as reflected in *national* elections. Many of the generalizations about national voting behavior are *not* transferable to state and local politics.

Contributions from two groups to the national Democratic coalition appear relatively constant. In 1952, 28 percent of Democratic votes came from individuals whose family income fell below the $3,000 level; in 1968, their

---

[42] William H. Flanigan, *Political Behavior of the American Electorate* (Boston: Allyn and Bacon, 1968), p. 122.

[43] Peter B. Natchez, "Images of Voting: The Social Psychologists," *Public Policy* 18 (Summer 1970): 581.

Table 8. Opinions on Government's Role in Providing Jobs, by Party Affiliation (in percent)

Government	Strong Democrat	Weak Democrat	Independent Leaning Democrat	Independent	Independent Leaning Republican	Weak Republican	Strong Republican
Government should see to a job and a guaranteed standard of living.							
1.00	27.7	14.8	10.6	11.1	8.7	6.3	8.9
2.00	8.8	5.2	9.7	4.8	5.8	4.8	1.0
3.00	8.8	14.4	14.2	19.0	8.7	7.1	5.0
4.00	27.7	22.3	23.9	16.7	23.1	23.8	27.7
5.00	10.1	16.6	13.3	15.9	15.4	14.3	16.8
6.00	4.7	7.9	9.7	11.9	18.3	18.3	10.9
Government should let each individual get ahead on his own.							
7.00	12.2	18.8	18.6	20.6	20.2	25.4	29.7
TOTAL	100	100	100	100	100	100	100
	(148)*	(229)	(113)	(126)	(104)	(126)	(101)

* Figures in parentheses refer to the number of cases.

SOURCE: The Center for Political Studies (C.P.S.) of the University of Michigan data made available through the Inter-University Consortium for Political Research (I.C.P.R.).

contribution declined to 12 percent of the Democratic total. The main reason for the shrinking contribution is the restrictive definition of poverty at the $3,000 annual level. In 1952, 36 percent of the population had a family income at that level; in 1968, 16 percent fell short of that mark. Much of the decrease is due to gains in total income. Consideration of inflation and a more reasonable definition of poverty would reveal that the poor's contribution to the Democratic coalition has been stable. Catholic support of the Democratic party also remained constant in the 1950s and 1960s. Although Catholics have consistently represented a quarter of the population they provide close to 40 percent of the Democratic vote. However, in 1972 Nixon took a majority of the Catholic vote. It is important to keep figures from the 1972 presidential election in their proper perspective. There was a convergence in the vote of various groups in the American polity. That is, Nixon picked up support among all groups (see Table 9). Often in places where McGovern did most poorly, his Democratic running mates did very well. (See Chapter 6 for additional discussion of this phenomenon.)

Support from three components of the coalition weakened in the 1960s. In the 1950s over a third of the Democratic support for president came from union families, but by 1968 the figure fell to 28 percent, and it declined further in the 1972 presidential election. Throughout the 1950s and 1960s Southern voters provided about one-quarter of all Democratic presidential votes. The South has, however, been moving away from the New Deal coalition. By 1968 it had left the Democratic presidential column, and it did so again in 1972.

Today approximately 10 percent of the population dwells in the nation's twelve largest cities. Since 1956 the central cities have been 15 percent more Democratic than the nation. Declining population in the central cities makes them an important but declining part of the coalition. For example, while in the 1950s the twelve largest cities provided 20 percent of the Democratic party's presidential votes, by 1968 only 15 percent of the Democratic support came from these cities. In 1972, Richard Nixon received 58 percent of the votes cast in the nation's cities. Thus the Democrats were not able to "carry" the urban vote in their contest for the presidency.[44] The only exception to this was McGovern's ability to carry cities (with 55 percent of the vote) with populations of over 500,000.[45]

The greatest gains for the national Democratic party in the last two decades have been among blacks. Black votes totaled 7 percent of the total Democratic votes in 1952. Sixteen years later, black support amounted to 19 percent of the party's total vote. As far as young voters are concerned, through 1968

[44] The above discussion and the pre-1972 data is based upon Robert Axelrod, "Where the Votes Come From: An Analysis of Electoral Coalitions, 1952–1968," *American Political Science Review* 66 (March 1972): 11–20.

[45] "CBS Survey," *National Journal* (November 11, 1972): 1732.

young voters failed to provide strong support for the Democrats. Low turnout, 15 percent below the national average, and weak loyalties resulted in a youth contribution of 14 percent of Democratic party votes, despite the fact that 18 percent of the voting age population was between twenty-one and twenty-nine. The enfranchisement of eighteen-year-olds did not affect the partisan balance in 1972 since voter registration among people aged eighteen to twenty-four was quite low: 61 percent among whites and 48 percent among blacks, and the youth vote split almost equally between both candidates.[46] Thus black voters form the strongest addition to the coalition.

PARTY AND PARTICIPATION

Strong *party identification* based on family background and other sources we have discussed is not sufficient to explain all voting behavior. We still must understand why *political participation* varies in intensity and degree. Probably most significant in determining participation and political interest is, as suggested earlier, socioeconomic status. Those people who have the highest educational achievement levels, the highest incomes, and professional and managerial positions tend to be the most active political participants. (See Tables 10, 11, and 12.) It should not, therefore, be surprising to learn that Republicans, who traditionally have tended to be upper income, voted more than Democrats.[47]

Other sociological categories can provide us with clues to voter participation. Urban dwellers are more likely to vote than rural dwellers who perhaps have more limited opportunities for political interaction. Men tend to participate more than women—probably because many women, in the past, have been socialized into thinking that politics is not a "feminine" activity.[48] Older people, who are more likely to be Republicans than Democrats, participate more than their younger compatriots. Young people tend to be only marginally integrated into their communities, partially because they are more mobile than

[46] *Voting Participation in November, 1972,* P–20, No. 244 (Washington, D.C.: Government Printing Office, 1972); see also *Gallup Opinion Index* (December 1972): 10.

[47] This does not, however, mean that low turnout will necessarily guarantee Republican voting. As turnout declines, independent voting drops and Republicans have at least traditionally suffered proportionately heavier vote losses than Democrats from the group essential to their electoral victory. This is because in the past independents have favored the Republican party over the Democratic party. Phillip E. Converse, "The Concept of a Normal Vote," in Campbell, et al., *Elections and the Political Order,* p. 29.

[48] Greenstein, *Children and Politics,* pp. 118, 127. This was less true in the 1968 and 1972 elections. From 1948 to 1960, however, female voting participation trailed men by 10 percentage points; by the 1960s the differential was only about 3 percent. Mary Costello, "Women Voters," *Editorial Research Reports* (October 11, 1972): 782.

Table 9. Demographic Composition of the Candidates' Support among Whites, 1972 (in percent)

	McGovern Primary Voters	Other Primary Voters	Democrats Voting for McGovern	Democrats Voting for Nixon	All Democrats	McGovern Voters	Nixon Voters
(N)	(67)	(98)	(279)	(262)	(807)	(445)	(1000)
AGE:							
18–24	19	5	19	7	13	19	10
25–29	10	8	10	8	9	14	11
30–59	55	62	47	58	51	48	54
60+	16	25	24	27	27	19	25
Total	100	100	100	100	100	100	100
EDUCATION:							
Grade School	13	18	21	21	25	16	14
High School	45	50	45	55	51	44	49
College	42	31	34	24	24	40	37
INCOME:							
Less than $4,000	12	17	17	16	19	15	12
$4,000–$7,999	22	21	24	21	25	21	19
$8,000–$14,999	45	42	37	43	38	39	41
$15,000 or more	21	20	22	20	18	25	28
SEX:							
Male	40	38	43	42	42	41	47
Female	60	62	57	58	58	59	53
RESIDENCE:							
Urban	33	16	29	21	25	29	21
Suburban	36	41	33	37	35	37	43
Rural	31	43	38	42	40	34	36

Table 9. Demographic Composition of the Candidates' Support among Whites (*cont.*)

	McGovern Primary Voters	Other Primary Voters	Democrats Voting for McGovern	Democrats Voting for Nixon	All Democrats	McGovern Voters	Nixon Voters
REGION:							
Northeast	33	11	25	17	20	29	22
Midwest	30	29	31	23	27	32	32
South	13	41	23	46	37	20	29
West	24	19	21	14	16	19	17
RELIGION:							
Protestant	50	73	53	61	61	57	74
Catholic	41	23	41	38	35	37	25
Jew	9	4	6	1	4	6	1
OCCUPATION:							
White Collar	55	55	49	54	47	54	59
Blue Collar	45	45	51	46	53	46	41
SOCIAL CLASS: [a]							
Working Class	51	59	49	58	58	46	48
Middle Class	49	40	51	42	42	54	52
UNION HOUSEHOLD:							
Yes	38	28	35	28	30	33	23
No	62	72	65	72	70	67	77

[a] Respondent's self-perceived social class.

SOURCE: Miller, et al., "A Majority Party in Disarray," pp. 79–80.

Table 10. Family Income and Participation, 1972 (in percent)

				Income		
	<4,000$	4–7,000$	7–10,000$	10–15,000$	15–20,000$	+20,000$
Voted	56	58.8	64.1	67.4	61.5	77.7
Did Not Vote	44	41.2	35.9	32.6	38.5	22.3
Total	100	100	100	100	100	100
	(234) *	(233)	(273)	(408)	(93)	(193)

* Figures in parentheses refer to the number of cases.

source: The Center for Political Studies (C.P.S.) of the University of Michigan data made available through the Inter-University Consortium for Political Research (I.C.P.R.).

Table 11. Occupation and Voting Participation, 1972 (in percent)

	Occupation							
	Professional	Managers and Officials	Clerical Sales	Craftsmen (Skilled)	Operators (Unskilled)	Unskilled Workers	Laborers	Farmers
Voted	87.4	81.8	78	77.1	67.8	62.1	52	88.4
Did Not Vote	12.6	18.2	22	22.9	32.2	37.9	48	11.6
Total	100	100	100	100	100	100	100	100
	(269)*	(192)	(328)	(214)	(270)	(219)	(50)	(43)

* Figures in parentheses refer to the number of cases.
SOURCE: The Center for Political Studies (C.P.S.) of the University of Michigan data made available through the Inter-University Consortium for Political Research (I.C.P.R.).

Table 12. Education and Voting Participation (in percent)

	Grade School or Less	8th Grade	9–11th Grade	9 + Noncollege	High School	High School + Noncollege	Some College	College
Voted	52.8	62.8	60.2	63.9	74.7	76.5	83.9	89.9
Did Not Vote	47.2	37.2	39.8	36.1	25.3	23.5	16.1	10.1
Total	100	100	100	100	100	100	100	100
	(214)*	(226)	(339)	(72)	(479)	(255)	(379)	(317)

* Figures in parentheses refer to the number of cases.

source: The Center for Political Studies (C.P.S.) of the University of Michigan data made available through the Inter-University Consortium for Political Research (I.C.P.R.).

their elders. Race, education, and religion also influence the intensity of political activity. Jews, who tend to identify with the Democratic party, are more active than Catholics, also Democratic identifiers, who are more active than Protestants, who are most likely to be Republicans, possibly a reflection of respective group cohesion.[49] Blacks and Spanish Americans, most often Democrats, often participate less in electoral politics than whites in neighboring communities, due in part to the belief by the former that the political system has few tangible rewards to offer them as evidenced by their previous experiences with the political system and its reward structure. Party activity in a presidential race as well as in other campaigns can increase turnout perhaps from 5 to 10 percent depending on the nature of the office being contested.[50] Canvassing and voter registration campaigns have often proven useful in increasing turnout in low-income areas. A well-funded and publicized voter registration drive in 1964 in Harlem, for example, was able to register well over 100,000 voters.

Political participation also varies with the importance of the office being contested. While in 1956 the number of voters for president was 62 million, by 1958, in the "mid-term" or off-year congressional elections, only 45.7 million voters went to the polls.[51] Voters who go to the polls to cast their ballots are often overcome by voter "fatigue" and tend to vote less at the bottom of the ticket than at the top. Voting participation is also related to the degree of party competition—the more competitive the party system, the more likely voters are to participate.

Austin Ranney has developed five categories of party competitiveness; one-party Democratic; modified one-party Democratic; two-party; modified one-party Republican; and one-party Republican.[52] If one uses these categories and then looks at voting data for recent elections, it is clear that competitiveness brings out the vote. In one-party "safe" areas, voters often perceive their votes as being of no consequence since election results are all but predetermined. An individual's tendency to vote may also be affected by *cross-pressures.* Someone torn between conflicting political views of a spouse and a union "line" is often likely to "sit out" the election. (See Table 13, p. 116.)

[49] Lester W. Milbrath, *Political Participation: How and Why Do People Get Involved in Politics?* (Chicago: Rand McNally, 1965), p. 137: David Gordon has found that ethnicity has an effect on turnout; the presence of ethnics increases turnouts particularly in nonpartisan cities but in northern cities generally. *American Sociological Review* 35 (August 1970): 665–81.

[50] See William J. Crotty, "Party Effort and Its Impact on the Vote," *American Political Science Review* 65 (June 1971): 443–45.

[51] Angus Campbell, "Surge and Decline: A Study of Electoral Change," in Campbell, et al., *Elections and the Political Order,* p. 51.

[52] Austin Ranney, "Parties in State Politics," in Herbert Jacob and Kenneth N. Vines, eds., *Politics in the American States* (Boston: Little, Brown, 1965), p. 75.

Table 13. Voter Turnout Rates and Competition
(1970 Congressional Elections)

Type of Party System *	Average Turnout Rates (percent)
One-Party Democrat	26.7
Modified One-Party Democrat	38.1
Modified One-Party Republican	54.3
Two-Party	53.0

* In analyzing 1970 congressional voting, no one-party Republican states were found.
SOURCE: Average turnout rates were compiled from data in U.S. Bureau of the Census, *Statistical Abstract of the United States,* 1971, p. 366.

IS THE VOTER RATIONAL?

As suggested earlier, the SRC in its studies of the 1950s and 1960s offered some general conclusions that were disheartening to believers in a national informed electorate. They found that the most committed members of political parties were the most informed and aware and least likely to switch party from election to election. But on the average, most Americans demonstrated limited knowledge of, interest in, and information about political events. As we will see elsewhere in this chapter, other analysts have offered alternative views of voter awareness and rationality.[53]

One example of apparent voter ignorance is the customary preference of voters for incumbent local officials, largely, it appears, because their names are familiar and their opponent's are not.[54] In 1970, when 24 incumbent governors sought reelection, only 7 failed to win another term. Of 35 Senate seats up for election in 1970, incumbents were reelected in 24 and only 7 incumbents were defeated (6 in the November election, 1 in a primary). In four states—Delaware, Ohio, Minnesota, and Florida—the incumbent retired. In a typical year, 1970, there were only 56 newcomers to the House of Representatives (with 435 members). In only 27 cases did newcomers seize seats previously held by the opposite party. In 29 instances newcomers replaced members of their own party who died, retired, or suffered primary defeats. From 1950 to 1966 the average number of newcomers was 70.

---

[53] See discussion of the independent, pp. 124–29.

[54] See Barbara Hinckley, "Incumbency and the Presidential Vote in Senate Elections: Defining Politics of Subpresidential Voting," *American Political Science Review* 64 (September 1970): 841–42.

The degree of American voter ignorance can be documented and apparently can be found at every electoral level in every election year. In the 1968 presidential primary in New Hampshire, a poll found that although Democratic candidate Eugene McCarthy made opposition to the Vietnam war the basis of his electoral campaign, 54 percent of a sample before the primary did not know his position on the war; 17 percent thought he was a "hawk" and only 29 percent identified him correctly as a "dove." [55] In 1962, in Wisconsin, during a campaign clearly centered on tax policy, of the less than 60 percent of the electorate who came to the polls, approximately one-half could not identify either party's position on the policy and one-third made a "wrong" choice in voting vis-à-vis their opinion on tax policy.[56] The SRC found that one-third of the electorate did not know whether Republicans or Democrats controlled the House of Representatives between 1956 and 1958; 20 percent of the sample erroneously gave control to the Republicans. Awareness of party control was no higher among those who voted for than against the party. Fifty percent of the voters had neither heard of nor read anything about the candidates for Congress in their districts; less than one in five thought they knew something about either candidate. Forty-six percent who voted said they knew nothing about either candidate.[57] In 1970, a Gallup Poll showed that only 60 percent of the voters knew the party affiliation of their congressional representative, and only 53 percent knew how he voted on a major bill. In 1952, 55 percent of the American public were not familiar with the name of Richard Nixon, and 68 percent did not know John Sparkman's name, though both had just been nominated as vice-presidential candidates by their respective party conventions.[58]

This information can lead the reader to several conclusions: that the masses are ignorant and foolish and incapable of making rational decisions about complex political phenomena—hence, such decisions should best be left to "experts"; or that when the alternatives presented by the parties and candidates come through indistinctly and without clarity and when the party as a link between the citizen and his government is not providing sufficient information, then it is difficult to expect the voter to make rational choices. In support of the latter perspective, it should be noted that recent studies have found that the public does in fact perceive party differences on those issues that are *salient* to them, and that voter rationality may in fact be the reality of American poli-

[55] Milton J. Rosenberg, Sidney Verba, and Phillip E. Converse, *Vietnam and the Silent Majority: The Dove's Guide* (New York: Harper and Row, 1970), p. 49.

[56] Pomper, *Elections in America,* p. 79.

[57] Donald E. Stokes and Warren E. Miller, "Party Government and the Saliency of Government," in Campbell, et al., *Elections and the Political Order,* pp. 199–200.

[58] Robert E. Lane and David O. Sears, *Public Opinion* (Englewood Cliffs, N.J.: Prentice-Hall, 1964), p. 58.

tics. V. O. Key suggested that "switchers" or floating voters are far more numerous—numbering in the millions—than commonly supposed. According to Key, such voters are apt to vote their judgments of political performance and their vote is consistent with their policy preferences. In his view, the voter is more apt to be rational than some political scientists have believed.[59]

One study found that the Democratic party was clearly preferred as the party best able to handle issues such as medicare, social security, and aid for the poor; the Republicans viewed as best able to handle the Communist threat, take appropriate stands on foreign aid, fiscal policy, and states rights. In 1964, the public clearly perceived Johnson-Goldwater differences on civil rights (95 percent said that Johnson favored civil rights reform, while 84 percent said Goldwater opposed civil rights.) [60] Even the poorly informed pro-McCarthy voters discussed above were indicating their dissatisfaction with policy under the Johnson administration through their ballot. Gerald Pomper, in an article discussing issues and American voters between 1956 and 1968 suggested, on the basis of several works relating to American voters and issues that "previous studies demonstrated not absence of ideology but the absence of the ability to articulate hidden ideology." [61] Pomper himself has found that basic issues have surfaced in American politics, especially since 1964, and that the American voting public understands and responds to the basic issue conflicts.

In an analysis of the 1968 election, with specific reference to the Vietnam war issue, Page and Brody examined the extent of policy voting. They found that policy preferences had little impact on votes for major party candidates, but attribute this not to voter ignorance, but rather to the slight actual difference on Vietnam policy between Humphrey and Nixon. Most voters did perceive candidates McCarthy and Wallace as having substantially diverse views on the war. Examination of 1972 election data reveals "stark issue differences" between McGovern and Nixon voters, along liberal and conservative lines. Hence "when the American people are presented with a clear choice they are able and willing to bring their policy preferences to bear on it." [62]

With these alternatives in mind, let us turn to those Americans who are thought to be least informed and least politically interested, and most likely to switch party preference from election to election (if they vote at all): the nonvoter and the independent voter.

[59] V. O. Key, *The Responsible Electorate,* p. 8. Key's analysis has been criticized as relying too heavily on "soft" poll data, dependent on voter recall of past voting behavior.

[60] David E. Repass, "Issue Salience and Party Choice," *American Political Science Review* 55 (June 1971): 394–95.

[61] Gerald M. Pomper, "From Confusion to Clarity: Issues and American Voters, 1956–1968," *American Political Science Review* 66 (June 1972): 416. Pomper has a very good discussion of the literature on voter rationality in this article, pp. 415–18.

[62] Benjamin I. Page and Richard A. Brody, "Policy Voting and the Electoral Process: The Vietnam War Issue," *American Political Science Review* 66 (September 1972): 993.

THE NONVOTER

In 1968, only 61.6 percent of the electorate voted in the presidential election, and in 1972, 55 percent of the electorate chose to vote.[63] The 1972 figure represents a decline of 9 percent in voting since 1960.

1960—64 percent
1964—62.1 percent
1968—60.7 percent
1972—55 percent

This was true despite the enfranchisement of eighteen-year-olds as well as the abolition of literacy tests, poll taxes, and the passage of the Voting Rights Act of 1965 which applied to the South. The Voting Rights Act of 1965 authorized appointment by the Civil Service Commission of voting "examiners," federal officials who would determine an individual's qualifications to vote and would require enrollment of qualified individuals to vote in all elections.[64]

According to *The Gallup Opinion Index,* in 1972, 45 percent of the potential electorate failed to vote. In the past the United States has exceeded a 60 percent turnout only in presidential elections. This should be compared with an over 80 percent turnout in France and Italy. In Britain, with its parliamentary system, for example, the electoral process involves essentially the election of one candidate for one office as opposed to our system of voting for candidates for numerous offices and positions, as well as in primaries to select party nominees.

We have already suggested that voting and strength of party identification are positively correlated with high socioeconomic status (SES). The converse is also true. Poorer, less educated, and less skilled individuals are less likely to be political participants than the affluent and the educated. However, only a small percentage of the electorate never votes—only about 15 percent.[65] The typical nonvoter, according to William C. Flanigan, is likely to be black, southern, female, young, and have an income half that of the rest of the

---

[63] *Congress and the Nation II* (Washington, D.C.: Congressional Quarterly Service, 1969), p. 362. *Congressional Quarterly Almanac, 1972* (Washington, D.C.: Congressional Quarterly Service, 1972), p. 1012.

[64] Examiners could be appointed by a federal court determining that they were needed to ensure voting rights, or by the attorney general after receiving meritorious complaints from 20 plus residents of a political subdivision of a state. Under the "triggering formula" examiners were to be appointed by the attorney general if (1) literacy tests or similar devices were used for voting qualification on November 1, 1964 or (2) if less than 50 percent of voting-age persons were registered or voted in 1964.

[65] Flanigan, *Political Behavior,* p. 22.

population. The "average" voter is likely to be older, better educated, white, married, well paid, and suburban. "Deprived social conditions or inhibiting cultural values lead to low interest, little concern with, and little information on politics and that in turn leads to non-voting." [66] Thus, the least educated, least well established and poorest Americans are involved in what Schattschneider has called "passive abstention" (a term to be greatly preferred to "apathy" which implies total disinterest) not an isolated social phenomenon—but part of the political condition in the United States.[67] In contrast, in Sweden, in the 1960 election to the Riksdag, 88 percent of working-class males turned out to vote, 91 percent of women workers voted, and 91.1 percent of married women voted. The national turnout was 87.6 percent.[68]

LOW TURNOUT EXPLAINED

We must ask why our turnout is relatively low compared to other Western democracies. There are four possible explanations all of which probably have some validity for different subgroups in the population.

(1) Nonvoters have a high level of satisfaction. This assumption may be challenged because most nonvoters come from the lowest socioeconomic echelons in society—those who would have most to gain from politics if they were able to mobilize.

(2) People who are alienated from society do not vote. Alienation is used here as referring to a sense of disillusionment and cynicism with regard to the political system and politicians. We have seen that *antiparty* feelings are part of the general political socialization in the U.S., but for the majority of Americans, feelings of civic obligations, reference group pressure, and the like induce them to overcome their disaffection. For groups such as the poor and the young, however, socialization into the existing institutions of society is very weak; political affiliation with those groups and organizations, which facilitate wider participation, is to a considerable degree a function of class and education.[69] Hence, some citizens are left with the feeling that they are powerless because politics is controlled by a "group of selfish individuals whose influence is unaffected by elections" and that they have few resources with which to overcome their powerlessness.[70] When a sample of people in a lower income

[66] Flanigan, *Political Behavior,* p. 24.

[67] E. E. Schattschneider, *The Semi-Sovereign People* (New York: Holt, Rinehart and Winston, 1960), pp. 106, 109.

[68] Walter Dean Burnham, *Critical Elections and the Mainsprings of American Politics* (New York: W. W. Norton, 1970), pp. 82–83.

[69] See Robert Lane, *Political Life* (New York: Free Press, 1959), pp. 220–34.

[70] Betty Jo Bailey and Harold Weisman, "Voter Registration Campaigns," in Harold H. Weisman, ed., *Community Development in the Mobilization for Youth Experience* (New York: Associated Press, 1969), p. 100.

area in New York City was asked: "Do you think it (an election) will affect you personally or the way you and your family lives?" the responses were: a lot 8 percent, a little 30 percent, no effect 62 percent.[71] Such persons are often too absorbed in day-to-day problems to think of mobilizing for effective political influence. A good example may be found in black and Puerto Rican registration and voting in New York City where approximately 35 percent of that potential electorate votes. Black and Puerto Rican turnout is on the decline in New York where poor, minority group voters complain of complete unfamiliarity with most public officials, candidates, and the nature of the offices being contested.[72] The U.S. Bureau of the Census has estimated that in the 1972 presidential election 25 percent of eligible blacks and 38 percent of eligible voters of Spanish origin chose to exercise their franchise. A comparable figure for white voters was over 60 percent.

(3) Registration and other electoral mechanisms make voting difficult for many people. There have been barriers erected to voting participation both by party leaders who wish to maintain dominance over a controllable group of followers and by "reformers" who have sought, through a tightening of registration procedures, to make voting an act of individual commitment. These problems have been reduced somewhat as a result of the passage of the Twenty-Sixth Amendment and the 1970 Voting Rights Act, which added minority groups and the young to the voting rolls.[73]

Students of political participation have found that since the nineteenth century there has been a decline in voting turnout in the United States.[74] In the latter part of the nineteenth century, the turnout of eligible voters was usually between 75 and 88 percent. Part of this alteration seems to have derived from the change from automatic registration requirements to laws requiring individual registration. Also, as suffrage was extended, people with relatively low turnout rates (such as women) were added to the ranks of the eligible. Other Western democracies—France, Great Britain, Canada—which employ

[71] Ibid.

[72] Arthur Klebanoff, "Gubernatorial Elections in New York State," *City Almanac*, no. 3 (October 1970): 9. Bailey and Weisman, "Voter Registration Campaigns," in Weisman, ed., *Community Development*. A 1972 Gallup Poll, however, found that for the first time as many nonwhites as whites are registering, especially in the South.

[73] Among other things the Voting Rights Act of 1970 provided that any person could vote in a presidential election in the place in which he had lived for thirty days immediately prior to a presidential election, and lowered from twenty-one to eighteen the voting age for all federal, state, and local elections, effective January 1, 1971, "except as required by the Constitution." It also extended the Voting Rights Act of 1965 for five more years. *Congressional Quarterly Almanac: 1970* (Washington, D.C.: Congressional Quarterly Service, 1971): 192–93.

On June 30, 1971, the Twenty-Sixth Amendment was ratified. The amendment stated that "The rights of citizens of the United States, who are 18 years of age or older, to vote shall be denied or abridged by the United States or by any state on account of age." (This amendment included federal, state, and local elections.)

[74] Stanley Kelley, Jr., Richard F. Ayres, and William G. Bowers, "Registration and Voting: Putting First Things First," *American Political Science Review* 61 (June 1967): 374.

automatic registration, have far larger voting turnouts; 77.4 percent, 77.6 percent, and 74.3 percent respectively.[75] Registration requirements have been a means of controlling opposition. The study of New York City's Lower East Side mentioned earlier found "ample evidence of diffuse hostility against minority group members who were trying to register. Specific obstacles as well as legal violations existed to discourage registration, and there was also actual ignorance and incompetence on the part of some of the inspectors." [76] (A subsequent minority group registration campaign elicited increased harassment, incompetence, and violation of the law at local registration places.)

The burden of responsibility to register and vote in the U.S. is placed on the individual rather than on the political system. Thus there is no automatic inclusion on the voting rolls through mail registration or by the Canadian method—door to door canvassing by representatives of each party—which has been 97 percent effective according to one account.[77] Other registration possibilities that are not utilized in the U.S. include registering voters at factories and other much used institutions. All of these mechanisms would facilitate participation and most would place the burden of responsibility for voter registration on the government, not the citizen.

It is possible that the importance of the vote has itself been diluted in the eyes of citizens by rule manipulation in the states: "rotten boroughs"; gerrymandering, obstacles to third-party contestation; scheduling of key state elections in off election years—the effect has been antipolitical and antipartisan.[78] A table of nonvoters in 1972 demonstrates that 28 percent of the nonvoters "sat out" that election out of "disinterest" in politics (see Table 14).

(4) Procedural factors may also relate to low voting turnout. For example, the type of ballot affects voting. The "party column" (or Indiana) ballot lists candidates in rows by party affiliation, usually with a circle or lever to facilitate straight ticket voting; the "office block" (or Massachusetts) ballot lists candidates for each contest in blocks or groups, often alphabetically, and sometimes even without a party label. "The Office Block ballot significantly increases voter fatigue (voters are less likely to complete their ballots) . . . the more complex the design of the ballot, the greater the tendency for voters to neglect races at the bottom of the ticket." [79]

Clearly American parties have been ineffective in mobilizing voter support.

[75] Ibid.
[76] Bailey, "Voter Registration Campaigns," in Weisman, ed., *Community Development*, p. 90.
[77] *New York Times*, November 3, 1971, p. 24.
[78] Burnham, *Critical Elections*, pp. 93–94. Both "rotten boroughs" and gerrymandering involve attempts to draw district lines in order to maximize political advantage for a specific group, candidate, or party.
[79] Jack L. Walker, "Ballot Forms and Voter Fatigue: An Analysis of the Office Block and Party Column Ballots," *Midwest Journal of Political Science* 10 (November 1966): 462.

Certainly those who are sick or disabled or otherwise housebound could be assisted to the polls by party workers. Finally, a twenty-four hour polling day, perhaps on weekends or holidays, could help to make the vote more important and accessible in the eyes of citizens.

For those dissatisfied with parties and electoral politics, there is little comfort in the idea expressed by some analysts "that the kind of issue that stimulates political participation in politics is also the kind of issue likely to create wide cleavage in society . . . there is doubt that the society as a whole would

---

Table 14. The Nonvoter, 1972 (in percent)

38	Did not bother or prevented by residence requirements
28	Not interested in politics
10	Didn't like either candidate
10	Sick or disabled
7	Could not leave job or working two shifts
7	Away from home/traveling
100	

SOURCE: *The Gallup Opinion Index* (December 1972), p. 11.

---

benefit if intense interest and active involvement in politics become widespread throughout the population." [80]

Because it is clear that electoral participation is in considerable measure a function of class and status, ways must be found to include groups that have lower-class status and tend not to participate in politics. The alternatives to increasing participation lie in the direction of continued alienation and extremism. Lipset has written, "a state in which a large part of the population is apathetic, uninterested, and unaware is one in which consent cannot be taken for granted and in which consensus may actually be weak." [81]

---

[80] Milbrath, *Political Participation,* p. 147. See also Herbert McCloskey, "Consensus and Ideology in American Politics," *American Political Science Review* 58 (June 1964): 361–79 for the view that "democratic viability is saved by the fact that those who are most confused about political ideas are also likely to be politically apathetic and without significant influence." He too sees the passivity of large groups as a positive factor.

[81] Lipset, *Political Man,* p. 226.

THE INDEPENDENT VOTER

A group of voters viewed by many scholars associated with the SRC as "irrational" during the 1950s and 1960s were the "independent" voters. According to many SRC studies, at least prior to the 1972 election and the surge in independent registrations the independent was the least informed, interested, and likely to vote of all voters. There have, however, been many elections where the role of the independent has been pivotal. As one can see in Table 15, the independent voter altered the course of the 1968 election. Furthermore, the independent vote has shifted dramatically in every election since 1956.

The American ideal of the independent voter as concerned, nonpartisan out of interest, carefully weighing political alternatives, well informed, etc., was, according to the SRC studies of the 1950s and 1960s without a peer in the real world (see Table 16, p. 126). The American independent was an apathetic political citizen similar in type to the nonvoter.

Several more recent studies seem to have provided some modification for these early SRC findings. V. O. Key in *The Responsible Electorate* argued that the average voter is not a fool and that those people who switch from party to party in a given election do so because of policy preferences. When policy preference and party record are incongruent, the voter is apt to defect.[82] Usually this vote represents a vote against the "ins." Key divided the electorate into three different groupings based not solely on party identification: "switchers," who change their party vote from one election to another; "stand patters," who vote for the same party in successive elections; and "new voters." It is the first group that some analysts now view as the new independent in contrast to the independent of the 1950s and 1960s presented by the SRC studies of that era. The new independent, who we will discuss further in later chapters, is essentially issue-oriented and concerned with candidates' positions rather than with party identification. Current data indicates that independent voters tend to be young and well-educated, with potentially high social status and class position.

Support for Key's view of the independent has been forthcoming from several sources. For one thing, it has become evident that increasing numbers of people, particularly Jews and white-collar Catholics classify (though do not necessarily register) themselves increasingly as independents rather than partisans: white-collar white Southerners, 49 percent; Jews, 45 percent; white-collar Catholics, 38 percent.[83] The number of self-classified independents in the electorate has risen from 6 million in 1960 to 25 million in 1971, an increase of

---

[82] Key, *The Responsible Electorate*, pp. 59, 148.
[83] Flanigan, *Political Behavior*, p. 54.

Table 15. Vote for President—Party Identifiers Only

Percent of [1] Population Self- Identified As Independent	Candidate's [2] Percent of Independent Vote	Candidate's [3] Percent of Popular Vote	Candidate's Percent of [4] Popular Vote Coming Only from Party Identifiers
1952 22			
Stevenson (D)	33	44.4	37.1
Eisenhower (R)	67	55.1	40.4
1956 24			
Stevenson (D)	27	42.0	35.5
Eisenhower (R)	73	57.4	39.9
1960 23			
Kennedy (D)	46	49.7	39.1
Nixon (R)	54	49.5	37.1
1964 22			
Johnson (D)	66	61.1	46.6
Goldwater (R)	34	38.5	31.0
1968 29			
Humphrey (D)	32	42.7	34.4
Nixon (R)	47	43.4	29.8
Wallace (AIP)	21	13.5	7.4

[1] Estimate from Survey Research Center data cited in Flanigan, *Political Behavior,* p. 33.

[2] Ibid., p. 45.

[3] *Statistical Abstract,* 1971, p. 349. Figures for each election do not add to 100 percent due to the omission of minor party candidates.

[4] This figure was arrived at by multiplying columns one and two and subtracting the product from column three. Column four represents the percent of total popular votes which came from individuals' identifying with either major party. The figure represents an estimate—since equal turnout was assumed by independents.

over 400 percent.[84] In 1968, for the first time in recent years, independent voters led those who viewed themselves as Republican partisans.

Perhaps even more significant for the future of the electoral system is political self-classification in the eighteen- to twenty-one-year-old groups. In 1972 the Republicans were truly a dismal third among this age group, with Democrats and independents running neck and neck; Democrats, 42 percent; Republicans, 16 percent; and independents, 42 percent. Among college stu-

[84] Frederick G. Dutton, "As the Parties Decline," *New York Times,* May 1972, p. 37.

dents, over 50 percent viewed themselves as independents in the early 1970s.[85] It is becoming more difficult to justify the view that all independents are apolitical. A recent study by David Repass showed that next to strong Republicans, independents are most concerned with the issues, with Democrats trailing far behind and looking like indifferent citizens by comparison.[86] The new independent (currently greatly in vogue) seems more to approximate the "model" of the independent as antiparty Americans would like to think of

---

Table 16. The Distribution of Partisans and Independents in 1952, 1956, 1960, 1964, and 1968 (in percent)

	1952	1956	1960	1964	1968
Strong Democrats	19	19	19	25	19
Weak Democrats	21	20	22	23	23
Independents	19	21	19	18	25
Weak Republicans	12	13	13	13	14
Strong Republicans	13	14	14	11	9
Never Voted	16	14	11	10	10
Total	100	101	98	100	100
	(1614)*	(1762)	(1923)	(1440)	(1559)

* Figures in parentheses refer to the number of cases.
SOURCE: Survey Research Center, University of Michigan.

---

him—informed and highly issue-oriented in making his voting decision. (See Table 17.)

The findings regarding independent voters are particularly significant because political scientists have long believed that party identification is formed early in life and does not change easily or often. A word of caution might, however, be in order. Louis Bean has argued for the consistency of voting behavior, stressing the basic strength of the Democratic party. He argues that party loyalties are not rapidly disappearing and that independent voters are not in the ascendancy.[87] Thus, many so-called independents are "concealed partisans"—who Bean estimates as 70 percent Democrat voters and 30 percent Republican voters, based largely on parental partisanship. Bean believes that only 9 percent of the electorate is truly independent, i.e., switching back and

---

[85] Dutton, "As the Parties Decline."
[86] Repass, "Issue Salience and Party Choice," p. 398.
[87] Quoted by William Shannon, "What Chance for McGovern?" *New York Times,* August 13, 1972, Section 4, p. 13.

Table 17. Party Identification (in percent)

Number of Issues Mentioned	Strong Democrat	Weak Democrat	Independent	Weak Republican	Strong Republican
0–1 Low	33	35	26	28	13
2–3	52	47	44	46	42
4–6 High	15	18	30	26	45
Index (Percent High; Percent Low)	− 18	− 17	+ 4	− 2	+ 32
	(394)*	(363)	(314)	(194)	(156)

* Figures in parentheses refer to the number of cases.
SOURCE: Repass, "Issue Salience and Party Choice," p. 398.

forth between parties and forgetting family background.[88] It is also possible that the newly inflated ranks of independents are peopled by Democrats and Republicans in transition, for whom independent status is but a halfway house for new partisan identification.

There is a second element of independent identification important to note. A post-1968 presidential election study found that 45 percent of Republicans and 47 percent of Democrats split their tickets while just 25 percent of independents voted a straight ticket.[89] A post-1972 study by *The Gallup Opinion Index* found that 60 percent of all voters split their tickets. This raises two points: (1) the relevance of partisan self-classification as a key to identification and (2) the relevance of party identification in voting in what appears to be a changing political milieu. Walter DeVries and Lance Tarrance suggest that there is a discrepancy between self-perception and voting behavior that seems to be of considerable significance. The number of straight ticket votes has declined from 80 percent before World War II to 40 percent in 1972.[90] A political profile of Michigan in 1970 showed the following:

Self-Identification	Voting Behavior
Republican 30%	Straight Republican 25%
Democrat 45%	Straight Democrat 40%
Independent 25%	Split Ticket 35%

Source: DeVries and Tarrance, *The Ticket Splitter*, p. 102.

The DeVries-Tarrance study shows the ticket splitter to be younger, better educated, more suburban, Catholic, of white-collar occupational status, media rather than party or peer group oriented in voting, and more politically active than the average voter.[91] DeVries and Tarrance emphasize that their view of the independent is a behavioral rather than perceptual one. Further, they contend that traditional ways of looking at voting behavior, party identification, SES, group affiliation, etc., are inadequate to explain current political trends. Their view is upheld by Repass, who indicates that where issue partisanship (on several salient issues) conflicts with party identification, the former often overcomes long-term party loyalties. In fact, many citizens may be reducing the role of party identification on voting to zero.

[88] Ibid.
[89] Walter DeVries and Lance Tarrance, *The Ticket Splitter* (Grand Rapids, Mich.: William B. Eerdmans, 1972), p. 14.
[90] Ibid., p. 22.
[91] Ibid., pp. 14–15.

THE INDEPENDENT VOTER   129

The view that nonvoters and independent voters may be rational and discriminating citizens is one thought with which to close this chapter. In the next chapter, we will examine the nature of change and continuity in American politics and attempt to determine whether a realignment based in part upon rational and discriminating voter choice is likely to arise to challenge the current party alignment.

6

The Changing Nature of Political Alignments

In order to gain a better perspective for our discussion of changes in voter identification and party alignment, and the factors possibly leading to modification of the partisan alignments that have prevailed in the United States since Franklin D. Roosevelt's first presidential victory in 1932, it may be instructive to examine some of the events from 1968 to 1972 that appear to portend change for the last decades of the twentieth century.

In the 1968 presidential election there were some interesting shifts in voting patterns among groups that previously had strongly identified as Democrats. These shifts were reinforced to some extent in the 1972 presidential election. Increased numbers of voters are identifying as independents, and some groups, though retaining their party registrations, are less inclined to maintain strong identity with their traditional party. In this chapter we will discuss briefly the SRC's classification of presidential elections, and then examine some of the voting patterns of groups that seem to be modifying partisan loyalties. These conditions of loosening party loyalty fit well into the perspective of antiparty-ism in America. Finally, we will consider the meaning of current changes for the future of the two-party system.

CLASSIFICATION OF PRESIDENTIAL ELECTIONS

Let us look first at the SRC's classification schema for presidential elections and see if we can make any determination as to whether or not American political parties are in the process of changes that fit into the classification format.[1]

The SRC's classification of presidential elections is based upon "the outcome of the elections and the degree of continuity or change in electoral cleavage." [2] Three basic types of presidential elections have been defined, each one premised on the proposition that one party is dominant among partisan identifiers at a certain period in time.

The first is the *maintaining election;* ". . . one in which the pattern of partisan attachment prevailing in the preceding period persists and is the primary influence on forces governing the voter." Examples are to be found in the 1948, 1960, and 1964 elections when the dominant Democrats maintained their control of the White House.

The second type of election is the *deviating election.* "In a deviating election the basic division of partisan loyalties is not seriously disturbed, but the attitude forces on the vote are such as to bring about the defeat of the majority party." Personality rather than significant policy polarization causes vote switching. Examples are to be found in the Eisenhower elections of 1952 and 1956. In 1952, although the Democrats led the Republicans 3–2 among partisan identifiers, Eisenhower, a Republican, was elected amidst considerable ticket splitting. In the case of Eisenhower, his military experience and popular appeal seemed to the public to augur well for an end to the Korean War and to provide a firm hand to clean out corruption from government. Yet, in 1954, the Democrats gained control of Congress, a control they have since retained.

It is generally agreed that there have been five major party systems in American history—1800, 1828, 1860, 1896, and 1932; each of the last three signaled by a *critical* election. A *realigning,* or *critical election* is one usually brought about by a social or economic crisis. In a realigning election, popular feeling associated with politics becomes sufficiently intense so that the basic partisan commitments of a portion of the electorate change. A new party becomes dominant as movements take place in both directions. V. O. Key identified two critical elections, each one associated with a national crisis. In 1932 large numbers of low-income individuals were converted to the Democratic party as a result of the Depression. In 1896, following the economic difficulties of the early 1890s, a new division between the parties appeared and

---

[1] The SRC's classification of elections is an extension of V. O. Key's theory of critical elections. V. O. Key defines critical elections as an election type in which the depth and intensity of electoral involvement are high; in which more or less profound readjustments occur in the relations of power within the community; and in which new and durable electoral groupings are formed. Campbell and associates describe the same phenomena in that they both refer to intense involvement and alterations in the basic electoral coalitions. Key pointed to one category, then the authors of *The American Voter* built upon Key's base and suggested a three-way classification of elections that incorporated "critical" elections as their "realigning" elections. See V. O. Key, "A Theory of Critical Elections," *Journal of Politics* 17 (February 1955): 4. See also Angus Campbell, Phillip Converse, Warren Miller, and Donald Stokes, *The American Voter* (New York: John Wiley, 1964).

[2] Gerald Pomper, *Elections in America* (New York: Dodd, Mead, 1964), p. 104.

large numbers of voters shifted to the Republican party. Key writes that in 1896, "the Democratic defeat was so demoralizing and so thorough that the party could make little headway in regrouping until 1916." [3]

A critical election, though it occurs in just one year, may be viewed most accurately within a "secular"—or long-term—realigning period. The changes leading to the realignment are based more on ideology, polarization, and class than the other types of elections discussed. Burnham has suggested that in a realigning period, ideological polarization occurs within and between the major parties, and there is an increase in voter participation due to frustration and discontent.[4] It is Burnham's theory that in the past, critical elections have served as short-lived but intense disruptions of traditional voting patterns— signaled by third-party revolts and stresses in the socioeconomic system. According to Burnham, party realignment is essential because it acts as a catalyst for systemic change, permitting the government to respond to mass political demands and to redefine the agenda and processes of American politics. It is however, Burnham's contention that the crucial ingredients for the realignment that would produce America's "sixth-party system" may today be lacking. Our party system may be beyond the possibility of critical realignment because (a) of the dissolution of party-related identification—as evidenced by ticket splitting, independence, decline of machines, etc.—and (b) the absence of a crystallizing issue, such as a great disaster. In the absence of realignment, each future election would be dominated by short-term forces: media, candidate charisma, etc. In other words, according to Burnham an electorate disaggregated beyond a certain point would make critical realignment or "tension management" impossible.

Realignments may result from organic change in the party system or a reallocation of the line of party cleavage. Or, they may occur due to demographic changes in the voting population, such as the addition of women, youth, and blacks or the individual conversion of voters because of changes in their lives or perceptions of politics.[5] "Generational" theories may account for some of the latter conversions. According to some analysts, the cyclical nature of realignments, every thirty-six years or so, may be explained by the presence of a new political generation whose ties to the party identifications created by great issues of the past become increasingly tenuous.[6]

Gerald Pomper has added a fourth category to this classification system, the *converting election,* which refers to the dominant party being returned to

---

[3] Key, "A Theory of Critical Elections," p. 11.

[4] William Dean Burnham, *Critical Elections and the Mainsprings of American Politics* (New York: W.W. Norton, 1970), pp. 7–8.

[5] See James L. Sundquist, *Dynamics of the Party System: Alignment and Realignment of Parties in the United States* (Washington, D.C.: The Brookings Institution, 1973), pp. 6–7.

[6] See Kevin Phillips, *The Emerging Republican Majority* (Garden City, N.Y.: Doubleday, 1970), p. 37. See also Paul R. Abramson, "Generational Change in American Electoral Behavior," *American Political Science Review* 68 (March 1974): 93 for the finding that the relationship between partisanship and social class has declined, largely as a result of generational change.

power by a different voter coalition.[7] An example was the Van Buren election in 1836 when the Democrats were returned to power on the basis of a new voter cleavage.

Some observers thought of 1964 as the beginning of a realigning or a converting period, noting that the geographical distribution of the votes of the parties shifted rather sharply. Thus the Republican, Barry Goldwater, received enough votes in five of the thirteen southern states to gain over 50 percent of the South's electoral votes in the formerly Democratic South, and in once Republican Maine, two-thirds of the votes went to Democrat Lyndon Baines Johnson—as did the votes in forty-four other states. If, however, one looks at voting data from 1960 to 1972 such a change becomes less evident, and such an explanation becomes more difficult to accept. The fact is that in only one region, the South, did Goldwater do so well as to cause a shift from the Democratic to the Republican column. Furthermore, in 1968 Hubert Humphrey received over 50 percent of the vote—or even a plurality of the

Table 18. Presidential Vote by Region, 1968 (in percent)

	Nixon	Humphrey	Wallace
East	42.6	50.5	6.9
South	35.9	31.8	32.3
Midwest	46.9	43.9	9.2
West	48.8	44.1	7.1

SOURCE: *Congressional Quarterly Weekly Report* (November 8, 1968): 3071.

vote—in only one geographic region, the East. (See Table 18.) Of course, 1972 saw the Republicans victorious in every state except Massachusetts and the District of Columbia. These data seem to provide some evidence to disprove the hypothesis that 1964 represented the beginning of a converting period. Some additional points should be made while trying to put this hypothesis to rest. First, in both 1968 and 1972, the strength of the Democratic party, as evidenced by electoral college votes, was down significantly from 1960 and 1964 levels. (See Table 19.) Also, while in 1964 the Democrats gained considerable support from the rich and the middle-class voters, this trend has not continued among the rich (note the 1968 Democratic party campaign deficit of $9 million) although it has continued to a considerable extent among the educated middle class. There was a sharp rise in ticket splitting in 1964, and a fairly large percentage of voters moved for issue-oriented reasons of a short-term candidate related nature, from the Republican to the Democratic candi-

[7] Pomper, *Elections in America,* pp. 104–11.

Table 19. Total Electoral Votes: 1956–1972

	1956	1960	1964	1968	1972
Democrats	74	303	486	191	17
Republicans	457	219	52	302	521
American Independent	N.A.	N.A.	N.A.	45	—

SOURCE: 1956–1968 ibid.; 1972 data from *New York Times,* November 9, 1972, p. 1.

date for president. Such behavior did not represent more permanent shifts in partisan loyalties, and has persisted in both directions for the past decade. Ideological and issue differences between the voters and Goldwater explain a sizable portion of the Republican shifts to the Democratic party presidential candidate in 1964. Goldwater was a minority candidate even in the Republican party. For example, the SRC estimated that 40 percent of the Republicans they interviewed who had been supporters of Nelson Rockefeller ultimately voted for Johnson. Again in 1972 apparently issue disagreements led to massive defection among Democratic identifiers from McGovern to the Republican candidate, Richard Nixon.

1968 to 1972 in Electoral Perspective

We do not accept the notion that 1964 was the beginning of a conversion or realignment in American partisan politics. Rather it seems that since 1964 there has been an increasing willingness among voters to split their tickets and to vote for a candidate regardless of his party identification. Also members of some groups, whom we have long associated as strong partisan identifiers, seem to be loosening their partisan loyalties in keeping with the American antiparty tradition. We will address ourselves to these groups and their voting behavior elsewhere in this chapter.[8] If one classifies the 1968 and 1972 presidential elections in terms of the SRC typology and Pomper's modification, then they were "deviating" elections. Continued flux and instability, not necessarily realignment, seem to be the outlook of the future. Let us first consider the 1968 election and then move ahead to 1972.

TRENDS AND ISSUES

What changes have appeared on the political scene? The first is the success of the third-party candidacy of George Wallace in 1968.

[8] See pp. 142–63.

Table 20. Southern Republican Office-Holding, 1972

Republican Governors	3	(of 11)
Republican Senators	7	(of 22)
Republican Congressmen	33	(of 108)
Republican State Legislators	227	(of 1783)

SOURCE: Computed from *Congressional Quarterly Almanac,* 1972, pp. 1024–27, *Statistical Abstract,* 1973, p. 377, and *The Book of the States: 1974–75* (Lexington, Ky.: The Council of State Governments, 1974), p. 68, Table 3.

George Wallace, running for president as the candidate of the American Independent party in 1968 received the most votes ever by a third-party candidate for president. He received 9,906,473 votes, which translated into forty-five electoral votes, and 13.6 percent of the votes cast in that election. (In 1924 the Progressives received a larger percentage of the total vote—16.6 percent—but the total vote was smaller. In 1912 Theodore Roosevelt received eighty-eight electoral votes, but fewer popular votes and came in second in the presidential race.) Most of Wallace's votes would have gone to Richard Nixon had the former not been running (as apparently occurred in 1972). The formerly "Solid South," which had been 81 percent Democratic in 1932 and 72 percent Democratic in 1944, was 31 percent Democratic in 1968 and 30 percent Democratic in 1972. In 1968, the Republican and American Independent candidates won away the traditional Southern Democratic voter; in 1972 the Republican candidate carried the entire South with almost 70 percent of the vote.

Southern Republicans have done particularly well in gaining lower-level offices in what was once strictly Democratic territory (see Table 20).

The second major change is that while voters have demonstrated considerable variability in electoral behavior, there has been a tendency for people to support the Democratic party at the nonpresidential level.

Forty percent of Nixon's Republican votes in 1968 came from people who had supported Johnson in 1964. However, while the Republicans captured the White House in 1968, the Republican proportion of votes in the election for the House of Representatives increased by only 2 percent, from 43 percent to 45 percent. This was the first time in 120 years that a winning first-term president did not carry at least one House of Congress, and occurred when the Democratic party's proportion of the votes cast for president dropped from 61 percent in 1964 to less than 43 percent in 1968.[9] A similar situation occurred again in 1972.

[9] U.S. Bureau of the Census, *Statistical Abstract of the United States, 1971* (Washington, D.C.: 1971), p. 349.

At the state level in 1969, twenty states had split governments, with the governor and legislatures being of different parties. By 1970, the Republican party, which had captured the White House two years earlier, lost 11 governors and 220 state legislative seats to the Democrats.[10] Also, the Democratic party ran 3.4 percent above their total 1968 vote for the House of Representatives. No clear trends emerged as incumbent liberal Democrats from Tennessee (Albert Gore) and Maryland (Joseph Tydings) lost their Senate seats to their more conservative opponents, while liberal Democrats from Illinois (Adlai Stevenson III) and California (John Tunney) were elected as first-term senators. But, while New York reelected Nelson Rockefeller, a Republican, who had developed a conservative image in his state, South Carolina elected John West, Florida, Reuben Askew, and Georgia, Jimmy Carter, all of whom had campaigned as liberals. In the instances where liberals were elected, often it was the case that blacks and a growing educated white middle class were successful in getting out the vote.

In 1972, despite Nixon's overwhelming victory, the Democrats retained control of both Houses of Congress and were victorious in eleven gubernatorial contests (the Republicans won seven governor's seats).[11] Thus the Republican presidential candidate emerged victorious without being able to spread his wings of victory to others of his party. In part this may be due to the increased number of voters who appear to be ticket splitting and the increase in the number of people who self-identify as "independents," and thus feel no compulsion to vote a party line.[12] In part, too, the Nixon victory was the result of an anti-McGovern vote. It is possible that another Democrat might have been able to mobilize the necessary support among Democrats to defeat Nixon.

The Democrats did well in the other contested elections. They gained one additional state governorship, majorities in two additional state legislatures,[13] and two more senators to augment their Senate majority. Furthermore, many of the Democrats who were successful contenders in 1972 were political liberals. Thus of the thirteen newly elected U.S. senators, eight were Democrats, and five were Republicans. Four of the thirteen new senators were more liberal than the incumbent Republicans they replaced. A fifth Democrat, James Abourezk of South Dakota, replaced retiring Karl Mundt—a Republican —another case of a liberal replacing a conservative. Of the thirteen incumbents who were defeated, their replacements represented a net gain of two liberals. Also, the president ran ahead of his senatorial and gubernatorial ticketmates in most states. He received more votes than twenty-six of the Republican senatorial candidates; he ran behind seven Republican senatorial contenders.

---

[10] Congressional Quarterly, *Current American Government* (Spring 1971): 14, 19; *Statistical Abstract*, 1971, pp. 359, 362.

[11] *Congressional Quarterly Almanac* 28 (1972): 1026.

[12] See Chapter 5 for a discussion of ticket splitting.

[13] *Congressional Quarterly Almanac* 28 (1972): 1071.

Of the seven senatorial candidates he trailed, six were liberal or moderate in their political orientations.[14]

The results of the 1974 midterm elections which strengthened the Democratic majorities indicate that there is little evidence for perceiving an "emerging conservative Republican majority" as the new dominant political mode.

Voters have continued to display relatively little interest in elections, as suggested in Chapter 5. The voter turnout in 1968 was low but dropped even lower in 1972. In 1964, 70,645,000 people voted for president. In 1968, the comparable figure was 73,212,000 and in 1972 only 76,025,000 voters voted for president. This occurred although the potential electorate had increased in this period from 112,250,000 to 139,642,000.[15] In some instances, statewide elections attracted a larger number of voters than the presidential race, an apparent indication of voter disenchantment with both presidential candidates.

During this period, the increasing political importance of the suburbs, whose elected representatives tend to adopt a "moderate" stance on issues, became apparent. A *Congressional Quarterly* study of 194 rapidly growing suburban counties showed that in the three presidential elections in the decade of the 1960s the "Republican candidates received a higher percentage of the vote in growth areas than they did nationally." These suburban counties' portion of the total popular vote increased from 18.6 percent of the national vote in 1960 to 22.5 percent in 1968. By 1972 they cast about 25 percent of the total vote for president. Suburban Republican strength is reflected by the data included in Table 21, which presents the nature of presidential voting in 194 rapid growth suburban counties.

Congressional representation also reflects the increased political importance of the suburbs. After the reapportionment that followed the 1970 census, approximately 291 congressmen (of 435) came from metropolitan areas. Of these congressmen, 129 have predominantly suburban districts, 100 predominantly "central city" districts and 62 a "mixture." Although Republican strength is growing in the suburbs, there is no reason to believe these areas will be solidly conservative. Robert Lehne's analysis of congressional voting patterns reveals that "while suburbs are conservative in relation to voting behavior of the central cities they are definitely liberal in comparison to rural representatives."[16] Lehne finds little support for the view that suburban congressmen are antigovernment conservatives. While Republican party strength has been a fact in the suburbs, it is unlikely that the GOP will dominate politics in this area.

[14] *Congressional Quarterly Weekly Report* 30 (November 11, 1972): 2985.
[15] Data for 1964 and 1968 are from Phillips, *The Emerging Republican Majority,* pp. 366–67; data for 1972 are from *Congressional Quarterly Almanac* 28 (1972): 1012. In 1974 only 38 percent of the eligible electorate voted—the lowest turnout since 1946, *New York Times,* November 10, 1974, Sect. 4, p. 1.
[16] Robert Lehne, "Warming Up for 1972," *Transaction* 8 (September 1971): 79.

Table 21. Suburban Voting, 1960–1968

	1960		1964		1968	
	Vote (Percent)	Counties Carried	Vote (Percent)	Counties Carried	Vote (Percent)	Counties Carried
Republican	54.0	127	42.3	45	49.0	133
Democratic	45.8	66	57.7	149	38.8	43
Other	.2	1			12.2	18

SOURCE: *Congressional Quarterly Weekly Report* (September 4, 1971): 1883.

The saliency of controversial issues has increased. In addition to the traditional economic issues, which have tended to draw voters to the Democratic party, elections at all levels of American politics have seen the addition of potent new issues. For example, the late 1960s and early 1970s saw the infusion into campaigns of Vietnam and the "Social Issue" [17]—a term whose synonym "law and order" combined voter hostility to crime, racial and other unrest, and the changing life-styles of those labeled the "counterculture."

In 1968, 40 percent of the voters said they saw Vietnam as the most important issue, but perceived no difference between Humphrey and Nixon on this issue.[18] Also, the whole question of "law and order" or the "Social Issue" captured headlines during the election campaign. This concern for "law and order" continued on into 1969 and 1970, too. In 1969, "law and order" candidates for municipal positions—the mayoralty in particular—were elected in Los Angeles and Minneapolis. In nonpartisan Los Angeles, Sam Yorty, the incumbent mayor, who was represented as a "law and order" candidate, was opposed by Tom Bradley, a black, liberal policeman. When the ballots were counted in 1969, Yorty received 53.25 percent of the total vote and Bradley received 46.76 percent of the vote. The only groups that provided majority support for Bradley were the blacks and the Jews. Mexican-Americans and non-Jewish whites rallied to Yorty.[19]

At the same time that conservative mayors were being elected in some cities, however, liberal mayoral candidates were successful elsewhere. Thus, Atlanta elected a liberal mayor, Sam Massell, and New York City elected John Lindsay for a second term. Lindsay did, however, lose the Republican primary to a more conservative rival, John Marchi, and won the general election with only 42 percent of the vote. If one looks at the ethnic breakdown of the vote in New York City it becomes apparent that the only groups that provided majority support for the liberal incumbent, Lindsay, in his race against conservative Mario Procaccino, Democrat, and John Marchi, Republican/Conservative, were the blacks and the Puerto Ricans. The Italians, Irish, and Jews, the other large ethnic blocs in New York City supported the more conservative candidates (see Table 22). The year 1970 seems to have marked at least the temporary demise of the "Social Issue." Democrats appeared to have taken the advice of those who urged them to support "law with justice." The cooptation of the issue by most Democrats prevented it from becoming a polarizing force which could benefit Republican "hard liners." In 1972, the "Social Issue"

---

[17] This term was coined by Richard M. Scammon and Ben J. Wattenberg, *The Real Majority* (New York: Coward, McCann and Geohegan, 1970), pp. 35–44.

[18] See Phillip E. Converse, Warren E. Miller, Jerrold Rusk, and Arthur Wolfe, "Continuity and Change in American Politics: Parties and Issues in the 1968 Election," *American Political Science Review* 63 (December 1969): 1085; Milton Rosenberg, Sidney Verba, Phillip E. Converse, *Vietnam and the Silent Majority: The Dove's Guide* (New York: Harper and Row, 1970), p. 50.

[19] Richard L. Maullin, "Los Angeles Liberalism," *Transaction* 8 (May 1971): 48.

Table 22. Ethnic Vote Breakdown in New York City's Mayoralty Race, 1969 (in percent)

	Lindsay	Procaccino	Marchi
Jews	44	44	12
Negroes	80	13	7
Italians	15	55	30
Puerto Ricans	64	27	9
Irish	26	26	48

SOURCE: Peter Kihss, "Poor and Rich, Not Middle Class, The Key to Lindsay Re-election," *New York Times,* November 6, 1969, p. 37.

may have enjoyed a partial renaissance in response to the candidacy of George McGovern.

McGovern ran as a candidate favoring increased federal government expenditures for social welfare services, as well as a decrease in military expenditures and a massive revamping of the federal tax structure. In part, he was perceived by many to be the candidate of "acid, amnesty, and abortion." However, according to the Gallup organization the major issues of the 1972 presidential campaign were the Vietnam War and inflation (along with the high cost of living). Twenty-seven percent of the Gallup sample chose these two separate issues as the most significant in October 1972.[20]

Data from the Center for Political Studies (formerly SRC) indicates that issues had an "exceptionally potent effect in the 1972 elections" largely because McGovern was quite distant from the population's policy preferences on almost all issues.[21] The "war" and "social" issues contributed significantly to voting patterns. What the Michigan researchers have termed "short-term" forces—issues and personality—dominated electoral choice in 1972.

---

[20] The question asked by Gallup organization pollers to the sample population was: "What do you think is the most important issue facing the country today?" The responses were, in addition to the Vietnam War and inflation: general international problems (9 percent); drug use/abuse (8 percent); crime/lawlessness (8 percent); pollution/the environment (4 percent); poverty/welfare (3 percent); corruption in government (3 percent); lack of national unity/purpose (2 percent); problems of youth (2 percent); moral problems/lack of religion (2 percent); miscellaneous/and other responses (9 percent); no opinion (2 percent). "The Gallup Poll," *The Gallup Opinion Index* (Insert into October 1972 Index for release, October 8, 1972).

[21] Arthur H. Miller, Warren E. Miller, Alden S. Raine, Thad A. Brown, "A Majority Party in Disarray: Policy Polarization in the 1972 Election" (Unpublished Paper, American Political Science Association, 1973), p. 18.

Racial polarization, one component of the "Social Issue," has continued to be prominent in voting trends throughout this period.

According to the *Gallup Opinion Index* in 1968 Hubert Humphrey received 86 percent of all black votes, but received only 38 percent of the white votes (McGovern received 87 percent of the black votes and 32 percent of the white vote)—indicating a high degree of racial polarization. Almost one-third of the whites who voted in 1968 switched their party vote from the 1964 election. The 48 percent differential between blacks and whites supporting Humphrey reflected the largest cleavage between groups in the recent history of western democracies. The differential of 55 percent between the races in 1972 represented an even greater degree of racial polarization, indicating the continuation of tensions. In 1973, moderating trends seemed in order. Liberal (and often black) mayors were elected in many cities—Los Angeles, Detroit, Atlanta, New York, Minneapolis, and other major urban centers. In Philadelphia, candidates backed by conservative Mayor Rizzo (himself not a candidate for reelection) suffered several setbacks at the polls.

Thus far, then, none of the potentially realigning issues that cut across party lines and polarize the population, have led to new partisan coalitions. This has largely been due to two factors; the failure of the populace to cluster or polarize around one key issue or ideology and the ability of both parties to "neutralize" potent issues by straddling a middle position. It also seems clear from these results that voter preference for the Democrats has not waned. In 1939, 42 percent of the voters self-identified Democratic; in 1973, 42 percent of the voters still identified themselves as Democrats.[22] Though some conditions for realignment may be present, issue changes are greatly in evidence, as is mass discontent. There is more movement *away* from than *across* party lines.[23]

While long-standing partisan differences remain between sociological groupings defined on ethnic, religious, and economic lines, voters seem more likely to vote regardless of party label. Thus while members of some ethnic and economic groups may be moving away from their traditional Democratic loyalties they are usually not registering as Republicans. They are, however, increasingly likely to split their tickets—as are members of other groups of American voters. In 1972 among the families of unskilled workers, 61 percent preferred Democratic congressional candidates, while only 39 percent preferred McGovern. Among skilled workers figures indicate 52 percent as Democratic voters and 25 percent as McGovern voters. For the economic

[22] John G. Stewart, *One Last Chance* (New York: Praeger, 1974), p. 99.
[23] Michigan researchers report a significant decrease in popular respect for and trust in government and public officials. By 1972, those who thought government operated in a manner more beneficial to special interests than the general public had increased 30 percent (to 58 percent) from 1964.

group with family income between $7,000 and $10,000, 48 percent of the voters preferred the Democratic congressional candidate while only 26 percent preferred McGovern.[24]

THE SHIFTING GROUPS

Now that we have suggested the fluidity of contemporary voting patterns, let us examine the changing and potential role of three crucial groups of Americans that are central to these partisan shifts. These three groups, often seen as vital to the maintenance of Democratic coalition, are the white working class, the nonwhite minorities, and the young.

THE WHITE WORKING CLASS

Working-Class Whites as an Economic Group We have already determined that one-fifth of all family units of four can be classified as poor, and that 41.5

Table 23. Population by Ethnic Origin, 1969

Total	198,214,000	Polish	4,021,000
English	19,060,000	Russian	2,152,000
German	19,961,000	Spanish	9,230,000
Irish	13,282,000	Other	105,633,000
Italian	7,239,000	Not Reported	17,635,000

SOURCE: *Statistical Abstract*, 1971, p. 28.

percent of the family units of four in this country can be classified as subaffluent. (See Chapter 2.) A large portion of the subaffluent group are of Irish, Italian, Slavic, and German ancestry (see Table 23) and are involved in blue-collar work. In 1971 the average weekly take-home pay for an industrial worker with three dependents was $109. 54 (after taxes) in private nonagricultural employment,[25] creating a high degree of economic insecurity. In the past, few children of the working class attended college. Furthermore, working-class "ethnics" tended to be more firmly committed to family and neighborhood. Economic difficulties have been coupled with a feeling of rejection by the dominant WASP culture, which many ethnic identifiers feel discriminates against their basic values.

[24] Stewart, *One Last Chance*, p. 98.
[25] *Statistical Abstract*, 1971, p. 225.

We will first consider the working class as an economic group, then the separate ethnic-identifying groups that comprise this economic group. Since the white working class—often ethnic-identifying—constitutes such a sizable portion of the electorate, it probably deserves more study by social scientists than it has received in recent years. To date no one is certain whether *ethnicity* (ethnic identification among different nationality groups of Catholics, Jews, and other minority groups) or class is the more salient variable in influencing voting behavior among members of these groups. It has been suggested that the American working class never developed a socialistic, class-based party similar to those that exist in Europe. However, there was, between the depression of the 1930s and 1966, a reasonably firm alliance that developed between the Democratic party and organized labor. To the extent that labor acted as a party within a party, it had certain similarities with the socialist labor coalitions in Europe.[26] This interrelationship between labor and the Democratic party has, however, dissipated within the past several years. Thus in 1972 George Meany, international president of the AFL-CIO, was able to persuade the executive council, by a vote of 27 to 3, to withhold that organization's endorsement of any presidential candidate; and the Teamsters Union endorsed Richard Nixon, the Republican incumbent.[27] Even in 1968, as we have previously noted, organized labor did not overwhelmingly support Hubert Humphrey at the polls despite unions' endorsements.

In 1968, the appeal of George Wallace to white skilled workers was great. His vote getting ability among the working class was undeniable (ethnic identifiers and WASP blue-collar workers supported Wallace in significant numbers). Though labor voted 56 percent for the Democrats, another 15 percent of the working-class voters considered defecting from the Democratic party until the last minute. Several studies have found that perceptions of worsening economic conditions for the working class combined with strong working-class consciousness often were linked with pro-Wallace support.[28]

Also, organized workers were perhaps dissuaded from pro-Wallace voting by the efforts of the AFL-CIO to gain increased support for Humphrey, the candidate most favorable to the leadership of the labor union movement. It seemed clear by 1968 that labor was no longer the cohesive force within the Democratic party that it had been in all the years since the Depression. This fact was confirmed in 1972 when union families split 54 percent to 46 percent

---

[26] J. David Greenstone, *Labor in American Politics* (New York: Knopf, 1969), pp. 9–11.

[27] In 1968, the national level committees of labor unions provided $7.1 million to election campaigns (not all presidential) mostly to Democrats. See Herbert Alexander, *Financing the 1968 Election* (Lexington, Mass.: Heath, Lexington, 1971), p. 194. In 1972, labor centered its attention on congressional elections, contributing all $3.7 million of its funds expended to Democrats. *Congressional Quarterly Weekly Report* 30 (October 14, 1972): 643–44.

[28] Seymour Martin Lipset and Earl Raab, *The Politics of Unreason* (New York: Harper and Row, 1970), pp. 364–65.

in favor of President Nixon,[29] as labor leadership remained neutral in the presidential race. It should be emphasized, however, that despite an increasing willingness among members of the working class to vote Republican, Republican identification, as reflected in party registration, has not increased among these voters. Thus in 1939, 46 percent of manual workers self-identified as Democrats, 34 percent as Republicans, and 20 percent as Independents. In 1973, 46 percent identified as Democrats, 20 percent as Republicans, and 34 percent as Independents.[30] It is the increased willingness to buck party entirely that has been evident among this group of voters.

In addition to this voting estrangement from the national Democratic party by organized labor and its leadership, the working class often finds itself alienated from its own political leadership in the local and state Democratic party, particularly in cities where "reformers" have cut sharply into the "old line" party organizations. Part of this alienation can be traced to the different attitudes on social and economic problems to which the middle-class "reformers" and the working class adhere. Organized labor has been affected by the same antileadership views held by other groups in American society and it is no longer evident that labor leaders can automatically "deliver" major segments of "their" workers for liberal or any other causes if, indeed, they ever could.

Working-Class Whites as Ethnic Identifiers It is clear too, that some traditionally Democratic ethnic identifiers are leaving the Democratic fold or at least tending to behave independently of party. Thus among the Irish, with their long-time Democratic tradition, only 41 percent of the people who self-identify as Irish, and who have completed college, say they are Democrats (30 percent Republican; over 25 percent Independent).[31] As the Irish become less concerned with their ethnic heritage, class is likely to become an ever more salient factor affecting electoral behavior. This pattern manifested itself in 1960 when Irish Catholic John F. Kennedy ran neck and neck with Richard Nixon in middle-income Irish sections of New York's Brooklyn and Queens. In 1968, in most northeastern states, Nixon led Humphrey among Irish voters—with Wallace's vote kept to a minimum. At present, however, working-class Irish voters remain Democrats, though not necessarily liberal.[32] Two liberal Irishmen—the late William Fitts Ryan and Paul O'Dwyer—have rarely been able to attract Irish voters in New York. In 1970 a *New York Times* survey found

---

[29] *The Gallup Opinion Index* (December 1972): 10.

[30] Stewart, *One Last Chance,* p. 202.

[31] Mark R. Levy and Michael S. Kramer, *The Ethnic Factor: How America's Minorities Decide Elections* (New York: Touchstone, 1973), p. 126.

[32] Ibid., p. 129.

60 percent of Irish identifiers in New York State planning to vote for Conservative James Buckley for the United States Senate, and Republican Nelson Rockefeller for another term as governor of the state. A similar trend prevailed in Connecticut, where Independent Conservative Thomas Dodd ran against moderate Republican Lowell Weicker and liberal Democrat Joseph Duffy. Duffy trailed the other two candidates among Irish voters. Irish-Americans, like other ethnic groups that are developing more economic security and social fears, are caught between two conflicting forces: Democratic heritage and a changing socioeconomic status.

An ethnic group whose members are largely working class is the Slavic-Americans. In 1967, Gary, Indiana elected its first black mayor. The tally of the votes showed Richard Hatcher, a black and a Democrat, with 39,330 votes, and Joseph Radigan, a white and a Republican with 37,941 votes.[33] The black precincts gave Hatcher 76 percent of their votes while the white precincts gave him only 17 percent of their votes. The highest proportion of votes given by a white precinct to Hatcher was 24 percent in a middle-class neighborhood of the city. The proportion of the votes cast for Hatcher in working-class Polish and Slavic areas was lower; Czech and Greek neighborhoods cast fewer than 10 percent of their ballots for Hatcher.[34] When Republican Robert Taft, Jr., ran against Howard Metzenbaum, Democrat, for the United States Senate in 1970, Taft outpolled Metzenbaum in the Slavic areas of Cleveland. Voting data from the heavily middle European Fourteenth and Fifteenth wards of Cleveland, indicate that Metzenbaum would have won the election if he had been able to outpoll Taft among Cleveland's thousands of ethnic voters. While in 1968 Nixon received 18 percent of the vote in Cleveland's Fourteenth ward, by 1970 Taft polled 36.4 percent of the votes in the same district.[35] However, Milwaukee, Wisconsin, and Buffalo, New York, where Slavic-Americans are present in large numbers, in 1970 saw no significant shift among Slavic-Americans to vote for candidates of the Republican party. Prior to the 1972 election some analysts observed that to date almost no Republicans had gained a majority of Slavic votes, although increasingly, questions of race had been cutting into the normally Democratic Slavic vote. The 1972 presidential vote changed this—at least temporarily. The Polish-American Congress's Ohio Chapter endorsed Mr. Nixon in 1972. In Cleveland's Twenty-third ward,

---

[33] *New York Times,* November 9, 1967, pp. 1, 33.

[34] Ibid.

[35] It should be noted that the Republican candidate for governor received 23.5 percent of the vote in the same election. It is possible to make some conjectural observations about the 13 percent spread of votes among the two Republican candidates in a normally Democratic area. The Democrat running for governor was John Gilligan, of Irish descent. The Democrat running for the senatorial seat was Howard Metzenbaum, a Jew. Perhaps some anti-Semitic feelings were expressed at the polls by some Slavic-identifiers when they cast their votes for Republican Robert Taft. The above voting statistics appeared in *New York Times,* December 9, 1970, pp. 1, 48.

Table 24. Years of School Completed by Persons 25 Years Old and Over, by Age and Ethnic Origin: November, 1969

	Total Number (Thousands)	Completed Four Years of College or More (Percent of Total)	Median Years of School
TOTAL	106,284	11,707	11.0	12.2
English	11,999	1,726	14.4	12.3
German	12,825	1,349	10.5	12.2
Irish	8,630	877	10.2	12.2
Italian	4,683	329	7.0	11.3
Polish	2,769	245	8.8	12.0
Russian	1,584	363	22.9	12.6
Spanish				
Central and South American	273	31	11.2	12.1
Cuban	320	41	12.7	12.1
Mexican	1,909	31	1.6	8.3
Puerto Rican	549	13	2.4	8.4
Other Spanish	766	66	8.7	12.1
All Other	49,286	5,735	11.6	12.2
Not Reporting	10,682	902	8.4	12.0

SOURCE: United States Bureau of the Census, *Current Population Reports, Series P-20, No. 220,* "Ethnic and Educational Attainment: November 1969" (Washington, D.C.: Government Printing Office, 1971), p. 7.

which is 80 percent Slovene and working class, the president received 57 percent of the vote.[36]

Italian voters, according to some analysts, have a strong sense of "ethnic solidarity" and tend to vote for any Italian—regardless of his ideology.[37] This observation must be qualified by class considerations. The more affluent Italian-Americans are less likely to belong to the Democratic party than working-class Italian-Americans, although as yet relatively few Italians have either attended college (see Table 24) or attained high-level white-collar jobs. In 1968—compared to 1960—Nixon's vote getting ability in Italian areas increased by 25 percent giving him about 40 percent of the votes in Italian-American neighborhoods in the latter years. It has been estimated that in 1972 Nixon received close to 80 percent of the Italian vote in some Italian working-class districts in New York City. For example in the Bensonhurst section of Brooklyn, Catholic ethnic voters—largely Italian—gave Nixon 76 percent of the vote.[38] (See Table 25.) In local and state elections there has been a tendency

[36] This was in contrast to his 24 percent voter support in 1968. *Time* Magazine, November 20, 1972, p. 17.

[37] Maurice Goldbloom, "Is There a Backlash Vote?" *Commentary* (August 1969): 22.

[38] *New York Times,* November 9, 1972, p. 26.

Table 25. Minority Group Voting for President, 1960–1972 (in percent)

	1960		1964		1968				1972	
	Kennedy	Nixon	Johnson	Goldwater	Humphrey	Nixon	Wallace	Other	McGov.	Nix.
Spanish speaking*	85	15	90	10	87	10	2	1	—	—
Blacks	75	25	97	3	94	5	1	—	87	13
Jewish	82	18	90	10	83	15	2	—	61	39
Slavic	82	18	80	20	65	23	12	—		
East European										
Irish	75	25	78	22	64	33	3	Catholic Vote	{ 41	59
Italian	75	25	77	23	50	40	10	—		

*Figure based on Mexican-Americans only and does not include the vote from New York's Puerto Rican precincts.
SOURCE: 1960 to 1968 data; Institute for American Research, NBC News, in Congressional Quarterly Weekly Report (March 11, 1972): 533; the 1972 data is based on an NBC election night poll and a CBS election day poll, reported by Congressional Quarterly Weekly Report (November 11, 1972): 2949.

for Italian voters to switch their votes from the Democratic party, the party with which they have traditionally identified, to the Republican party. In 1970 Senator Joseph Tydings was beaten by Republican J. Glenn Beall in Baltimore's Third Ward, with its heavy concentration of Italian voters. (Tydings also did relatively poorly in other ethnic wards.) [39] Similarly in Boston, there was considerable ticket splitting among Italian-Americans in 1970. Thus the Italian-Americans in Boston's North End voted overwhelmingly for Democratic Senator Edward Kennedy, but gave Republican Governor Francis Sargent a substantial minority of their votes (and a narrow majority of their votes in Boston's South End) over his Democratic opponent.

A note on the Jews. Virtually all observers see Jewish-Americans as a primarily liberal Democratic voting bloc. Jews, for example, comprised a disproportionate number of McCarthy campaign workers and "doves" in 1968.[40] This does not, however, mean that there are no class differences among Jews. The increasingly class oriented character of Jewish voters may be an index of one kind of social change that is overtaking the parties today. Increasingly, we find affluent Jews making "liberal" voting choices and working-class Jews, like other working-class groups, making more "conservative" choices. Jews, as a group, however, still remain more liberal than other whites. Though their past devotion to the Democratic party may fall off somewhat, they will probably continue to vote more for Democrats in presidential elections, though not necessarily local elections, than similar income groups. Thus in 1969, conservative mayoralty candidate Yorty received about one-half of the Jewish votes in Los Angeles—running against a liberal black, Thomas Bradley, and in 1973 when these two men contested the mayoralty again, Jewish voters gave Bradley 54 percent of their vote.[41] In 1969 lower-middle and middle-class Jews, especially the elderly or Orthodox, and those in close proximity to black areas and where busing was a key issue, voted for Yorty.[42]

Prior to the 1972 presidential election, reports indicated a movement to Nixon by the "Jewish vote," because of the president's support for Israel and Soviet Jewry. Many Jews did defect from McGovern but a majority continued to support the Democratic candidate: the Jewish votes split 61 percent for McGovern to 39 percent for Nixon.[43] If one breaks this vote down further it is interesting to look at the class variation in voter preference. In Great Neck,

---

[39] *New York Times,* December 9, 1970, p. 48.

[40] Converse, et al., "Continuity and Change," p. 1088.

[41] Bradley won in 1973 and lost in 1969. Data from *Los Angeles Times,* May 30, 1973, p. 1.

[42] See James Wilson and Harold Wilde, "The Urban Mood," *Commentary* (October 1969): 58–59. While Humphrey received 86 percent of the Jewish vote in Los Angeles, Bradley got only 51 percent. See Scammon and Wattenberg, *The Real Majority,* p. 238. Similar trends were present in the 1969 mayoralty race in New York. The election results appeared to herald a "new" coalition of wealthy whites and poor blacks and Puerto Ricans.

[43] NBC Election Night Poll reported in *Congressional Quarterly Weekly Report* 30 (November 11, 1972): 2949.

New York, an affluent community, Jews gave Nixon 32 percent of their vote (compared to 20 percent four years earlier). In an East Flatbush assembly district (Brooklyn, New York), a working-class Jewish population gave Mr. Nixon 51 percent of their vote, while voting by a margin of four to one to reelect their Democratic assemblyman Stanley Steingut.[44]

It seems clear that the ethnic-identifying white working class is no longer the cohesive force within the Democratic party that it had been in all the years since the Depression. Thus, as suggested elsewhere in this chapter, the white working class, made up in part of ethnic-identifiers, which voted heavily Democratic in the years between the Depression and 1966, is increasingly supporting candidates of the Republican party (though a preference for Democratic candidates particularly at the state and local levels remains). There is however no evidence to support the contention that large numbers of these voters have changed their party identification to the Republican party. The willingness to vote for non-Democratic candidates is due in part to the greater issue affinity shared with conservative candidates as white "status anxiety" produces reactions to demands for racial integration and the like. It is likely that especially in the South, "latent" Republicans who have long disliked liberal Democratic policies, may now have "come out." Also the Wallace movement, which had its roots in the South perhaps as far back as the 1948 Dixiecrat challenge, and was clearly premised on opposition to racial integration, grew to have broader implications in local and national politics in the 1970s. Wallace's opposition to school busing, dislike of big business and big labor, and general antiestablishment tone have become dominant themes among key components of the old Democratic coalition: ethnic groups and labor. It should be stressed that Wallace's candidacy—first via a third party, then via Democratic primaries—as well as the results of numerous municipal and state elections, demonstrate that Republicans have no priority on racial and social issue concerns. Given the American antiparty tradition, the increasing willingness of working-class groups to vote for candidates regardless of their party identification is a reflection of an American tradition that is gaining in favor among many groups across the economic and social spectrum.

BLACKS AND OTHER "NEWER" MINORITIES

There are several large as yet unassimilated minority groups in America, who have thus far proven less economically, socially, and politically successful than the immigrants of European stock.[45] We have already suggested the large place occupied by racial fears in the minds of many white voters. Where do

[44] *New York Times*, November 9, 1972, p. 26.
[45] See Chapter 2 for a discussion of the economic and social status of nonwhite Americans.

the blacks and other minority groups stand in the political arena? Have they any chance for increasing their political power? Are they likely to modify or significantly alter chances for party realignment or decline? Most often members of these groups associate themselves with Democratic candidates. As blacks and other nonwhite groups vote in greater numbers, they have the potential—already evidenced in some local electoral arenas—of being a very influential voting bloc. In 1968 and 1972, they represented, as noted above, a sizable portion of the Democratic presidential vote.

There has been a large increase in the number of blacks holding elective office in the United States (see Table 26), but while the number increases yearly, in 1973 blacks comprised only .5 percent—or 2,621—of the more than 500,000 elected officials across the country (as a group they constitute 11 percent of the total population.) [46] About one-half of America's blacks still live in the South—where there has been a dramatic rise in elected black representation since the passage of the 1965 Voting Rights Act. In the eleven southern states there was a total of 1,381 elected black officials in 1973.[47] Most other blacks live in large urban areas—one-third in fifteen major cities.

Blacks, who as a group experience low income, lack of education, and limited employment, in the past have participated minimally in politics, although this trend has sometimes been altered when either an "enemy" (Barry Goldwater in 1964) or a "black brother" contests public office. In 1968, for example, Hubert Humphrey, the Democratic candidate for president, received 86 percent of black votes in the United States, but the turnout among blacks was low—probably because Humphrey did not elicit emotional support among blacks. Humphrey's black vote in the South provided almost half of his total

Table 26. Number of Black Officials in the United States, 1971 and 1973

	1971	1973
Total	1,860	2,621
U.S. and State Legislatures	216	256
City and County Offices	905	1,264
Law Enforcement	274	334
School Board	465	767

SOURCE: *Statistical Abstract,* 1973, p. 378.

[46] U.S. Bureau of the Census, *Statistical Abstract of the United States, 1973* (Washington, D.C.: 1973), pp. 377–78.
[47] Alabama, 149; Arkansas, 141; Florida, 58; Georgia, 104; Louisiana, 130; Mississippi, 152; North Carolina, 112; South Carolina, 99; Tennessee, 71; Texas, 101; Virginia, 62. Ibid.

vote in that region.[48] McGovern's ability to turn out the vote in 1972 among blacks was not as good as Mr. Humphrey's had been in 1968. In Roxbury, a black ghetto area in Boston, Nixon received 4.5 percent of the vote in 1968 and 13.3 percent of the vote in 1972.[49]

Black voter registration in the South increased considerably in the 1960s, due in large measure to the 1965 Voting Rights Act (see Table 27). Thus in 1960, 29.1 percent of eligible blacks were registered to vote compared to 61.1 percent for eligible whites, whereas in 1970, 62 percent of eligible blacks were registered to vote compared to a comparable figure for whites of 69.2 percent. Because of the increased numbers of registered blacks, they have begun to have a significant "swing" impact in some areas. While blacks tend to be Democrats, like the Jews they tend to vote for the more liberal of the candidates put before them. Examples of black influence at the polls, especially in the South, abound. In Alabama in 1970, blacks voted for Albert Brewer in the Democratic gubernatorial primary in his unsuccessful race against George Wallace. In Tennessee, 96 percent of the blacks voted for Democrat Albert Gore in his race against conservative William Brock for the Senate.[50] Elsewhere in the South, in South Carolina, blacks provided the 28,000 vote majority for "moderate" Governor John West when he ran against Republican Albert Watson—in South Carolina blacks comprise approximately 25 percent of the electorate —and in 1970 in Florida and Georgia, black southern voters aided in defeating conservative Republicans in order to aid the election of somewhat more liberal Democrats. Also, blacks have formed third parties in the South. The most notable of these is the National Democratic party of Alabama, which in 1970 elected 109 local officials. Michigan researchers have found considerable support for independent black parties among their black interviewees, particularly in the South.

In the North, black voter power has been deployed in similar manner—but in recent years with far less participation and interest. Black voter turnout has been off in recent elections. Thus in 1964, in northern and western states 72 percent of eligible black voters actually voted while four years later in 1968 black voter participation was down to 64.8 percent. In 1972, 56.6 percent of eligible black voters cast their ballots in the North and the West. These figures compare rather unfavorably to white participation in the same regions as well as nationally. (See Table 28.) One consequence of black voter influence in the

---

[48] Humphrey received 4.5 million votes in the South. In 1968, black registration in the southern states had reached 3,112,000. If an NBC national estimate that 94 percent of all blacks voted for Humphrey is correct, then the black vote in the South provided most of his vote in that region.

[49] *Time* Magazine, November 20, 1972, p. 17. According to Michigan researchers, independent identification has increased more significantly for blacks than for whites, as the former appear to be increasingly dissatisfied with the policies of the Democratic party. Miller, et al., "A Majority Party in Disarray," pp. 85–87.

[50] Levy and Kramer, *The Ethnic Factor*, p. 58.

Table 27. Voter Registration in Eleven Southern States, 1970

	White	Black	Percent of Black Total
Total	16,985	3,357	17
Alabama	1,311	315	19
Arkansas	728	153	17
Florida	2,495	302	11
Georgia	1,615	395	20
Louisiana	1,143	319	22
Mississippi	690	286	29
North Carolina	1,640	305	16
South Carolina	668	221	25
Tennessee	1,600	242	13
Texas	3,599	550	13
Virginia	1,496	269	15

SOURCE: Compiled from *Statistical Abstract,* 1971, p. 36.

southern wing of the Democratic party has been increased defection by whites to the Republican party: that is, strong support by blacks for a candidate may often induce whites to support his opponent. Thus in 1971, when Charles Evers ran for governor of Mississippi, there was an unusually high turnout of both black and white voters—the blacks supporting Evers, who is black, and the whites supporting his victorious opponent, William Waller. It is interesting to note that whereas in 1967 the total vote in the gubernatorial race in Mississippi totaled 448,697, in 1971 the total vote for governor increased to 673,485.[51] This demonstrates both the significant gains and the potential constraints on the power of southern blacks. Also, though blacks can be elected to office in areas where blacks predominate, they have considerable difficulty winning elections in areas where they are not in a very clear majority. There are of course exceptions to this rather general statement. Edward Brooke is a senator from Massachusetts, a state which in 1970 had a total black population of 3.1 percent of its population.[52] Brooke won his first term as a Republican senator, with a comfortable 61 percent of the votes cast, and won reelection in 1972

[51] The 1967 data were reported by Richard M. Scammon, ed., *America Votes 8* (Washington, D.C.: Congressional Affairs Institute, 1970), p. 205; the 1971 data were reported by *New York Times,* November 3, 1971, pp. 1, 32.
[52] *Statistical Abstract,* 1971, p. 27.

Table 28. Reported Voter Participation and Rates, by Race by Regions: 1972, 1970, 1968, 1966

Region and Race	Number of Reported Voters 1972 (Millions)	Percent of Voting Age Population Reporting They Voted			
		1972 *	1970	1968	1966
Total	65,888	63.0	54.6	67.8	55.4
White	60,426	64.5	56.0	69.1	57.1
Black	4,992	52.1	43.5	57.6	41.8
Spanish Origin		37.5	(N.A.)	(N.A.)	(N.A.)
North and West	49,264	66.4	59.0	71.0	60.9
White	46,113	67.5	59.8	71.8	61.8
Black	2,714	56.6	51.4	64.8	52.1
South	16,624	55.4	44.7	60.1	43.0
White	14,313	57.0	46.4	61.9	45.2
Black	2,278	47.8	36.8	51.6	32.9

N.A.—Not Available

*The data for 1972 indicates a figure considerably higher than the rates reported in the press—a figure closer to 55 percent.

SOURCE: The data for 1966, 1968, 1970, and 1972 comes from: United States Bureau of the Census, *Current Population Reports*, Series P-20, No. 244, "Voter Participation in November, 1972" (Washington, D.C.: Government Printing Office, 1972), p. 1. For the 1964 data see: United States Bureau of the Census, *Current Population Reports*, Series P-20, No. 143, "Voter Participation in the National Election: November, 1964" (Washington, D.C.: Government Printing Office, 1965), p. 2.

with 64.6 percent of the votes cast,[53] in a state that has a very low proportion of blacks, and relatively few registered Republicans—43 percent of its registered voters are Democrats, 21 percent Republicans, and 36 percent Independents. However, Massachusetts has a tradition of being liberal. It has a large liberal university population, a liberal Republican party, and Senator Brooke is a moderate, not a militant, black. Elections of blacks in Newark, New Jersey; Gary, Indiana; and Cleveland, Ohio; however, have demonstrated an extraordinary polarization among blacks and whites. In Gary, for example, only 13 percent of the city's overwhelmingly Democratic white voters failed to bolt to the Republicans (6 percent if one omits Jewish sectors) when black Democrat Richard Hatcher ran for mayor in 1967. Black Democrat Carl Stokes was elected in normally Democratic Cleveland by just 1,600 votes in a city of 750,000. Democrats usually have won by a 6 to 1 margin or more in Cleveland, but after Stokes's term of office, Ralph Perk, a Republican, was elected mayor, in a continuation of the white trend away from the Democratic party in that city. In Detroit, black moderate Richard Austin polled only 18 percent of the vote in white areas.[54] In each of these cities, blacks are a majority of the population, and if they mobilize the community behind one candidate, register blacks to vote, and get them out to the polls on election day, they can gain political dominance. Such was the case in Atlanta in 1973 (see Table 29). But, where white votes are necessary, and race—as opposed to other issues—is salient, black candidates may find a rise in polarization and may find it difficult to gain election. The dilemma of blacks in electoral politics and the reaction of whites to black attempts to gain entry through electoral politics has made clear the relevance of race to class and ethnic politics. Gary, Indiana, in 1971, presents a good example of some of the political problems confronting blacks: a portrait of racial fear among whites and demonstration of political power among blacks. Running against a black (in 1967 he was opposed by a white), black Mayor Hatcher received few white votes and an almost solid black vote. In a reversal of national trends, white voter turnout was below average; black turnout was above average.

The *New York Times* reported, "Hatcher's pattern of victory seems as much a confirmation of racial fears among working-class white 'ethnics' as it does a demonstration of the political potency of blacks." Census figures show that 53 percent of Gary's population is black. Hatcher received 58 percent of the vote carrying some black precincts by margins like 518–55 and 471–7, but he received only 9 percent of the vote in the nearly all white Sixth District and

[53] *Congressional Quarterly Almanac* 28 (1972): 1019.

[54] Edward Greer, "The First Year of Black Power in Gary, Indiana" in Greer, ed., *Black Liberation Politics* (Boston: Allyn and Bacon, 1971), p. 217. See also Jeffrey Hadden, Louis H. Masotti, and Victor Thiessen, "The Making of the Negro Mayors, 1967," *Transaction* (January–February 1968): 21–30; *New York Times,* April 20, 1971, p. 21, and November 6, 1969, pp. 1, 38.

Table 29. Cities with 100,000 or More Inhabitants 1970
(Preliminary)

	1970 Population	1970 Percent Black	1960 Percent Black
Atlanta, Ga.	497,000	51.3	38.3
Baltimore, Md.	960,000	46.4	34.7
Birmingham, Ala.	301,000	42.0	39.6
Detroit, Mich.	1,511,000	43.7	28.9
Gary, Ind.	175,000	52.8	38.8
New Orleans, La.	267,000	45.0	37.2
Newark, N.J.	382,000	54.2	34.1
Richmond, Va.	250,000	42.0	41.8
St. Louis, Mo.	622,000	40.9	28.6
Savannah, Ga.	118,000	44.9	35.5
Washington, D.C.	757,000	71.1	53.9

SOURCE: *Statistical Abstract of the United States,* 1971, pp. 21–23.

25 percent in the heavily white First District. Hatcher ran only slightly better than he had in 1967, although this time his chief opponent, Dr. Williams, was also black. However in Los Angeles, where the population is only 17 percent black a black candidate (Thomas Bradley) did receive 47 percent of the vote in 1969. It may be suggested that race and media presentations of "law and order," which Bradley's opponent Yorty emphasized continually, cost Bradley that election.[55] In 1973, when the contest occurred once again, Bradley did emerge victorious, in a clear demonstration that racism need not be paramount in the minds of voters at all times. Further evidence of blacks' ability to win with the help of white voters could be seen in the results of the 1974 elections, when California and Colorado elected blacks as lieutenant governors.

In the 1970s, blacks have developed a new sophistication and independence in politics, largely as a result of black nationalism. Examples are to be found in the Black Congressional Caucus (comprised of black congressmen), the candidacy of Congresswoman Shirley Chisholm for the 1972 Democratic presidential nomination (not supported by most elected black officials), and the National Black Political Convention held in Gary, Indiana in 1972 (which brought pressure to bear on Democratic presidential candidate McGovern).

[55] See Richard L. Maullin, "Los Angeles Liberalism," *Transaction* (May 1971): 48–50. See also Harlan Hahn and Timothy Almy, "Ethnic Politics and Racial Issues: Voting in Los Angeles," *Western Political Quarterly* 24 (December 1971): 729–30, for the view that even though black voters may be remarkably unified, white resistance to black candidates, even for obscure offices, remains great.

Table 30. Age Distribution by Ethnic Origin

	White	Negro	Mexican	Puerto Rican
TOTAL (in thousands)	177,626	22,810	5,023	1,450
Percent	100.0	100.0	100.0	100.0
Under 5	8.3	12.1	13.6	14.7
5–9	9.5	13.0	15.1	17.0
10–17	15.7	18.9	20.4	16.9
18–19	3.5	3.9	4.1	3.0
20–24	8.1	8.4	7.7	9.0
25–34	12.6	11.6	13.6	15.9
35–44	11.3	10.0	11.0	10.3
45–54	11.8	9.2	7.9	5.9
55–64	9.4	6.7	3.4	4.3
65 +	10.0	6.2	3.3	3.0
Median Age	28.6	21.3	18.5	19.0

SOURCE: United States Bureau of the Census, *Current Population Reports,* Series P-20, No. 224, "Selected Characteristics of Persons and Families of Mexican, Puerto Rican, and Other Spanish Origin: March 1971," p. 4.

In local and statewide politics, blacks have exhibited increasing cohesiveness and, therefore, political strength. In Michigan and California, blacks have gained considerable legislative strength and in the states of New York, Ohio, Georgia, and Tennessee, elected black officials have formed caucuses to exercise greater strength politically. In 1972, at the Democratic nominating convention, there were 468 black delegates, 95 Chicanos, 34 Puerto Ricans, and 22 Indians, a great increase in the participation of all these groups.[56] At the 1972 Republican Convention, nonwhite minorities did not fare as well.

What, then, is the hope of a coalition among blacks and other nonwhite minority groups? About 5 percent of the American population is of Spanish speaking origin (this population is 80 percent urban)—largely Mexican-American (Chicano), and Puerto Rican. Like blacks, Chicanos and Puerto Ricans tend to support Democrats when they vote. Like the blacks, these groups have low annual incomes (see Table 31), high unemployment rates (see Table 32), and a small middle class, as well as an extremely young population, factors that are linked to their low voting participation. Only in Texas, where the Texas AFL-CIO and other groups mounted a massive registration drive,

[56] *New York Times,* July 9, 1972, pp. 1 and 43 and *Congressional Quarterly Weekly Report* 30 (July 8, 1972): 1642.

Table 31. Income in 1970 of Persons Twenty-five Years Old and Over,
by Sex and Ethnic Origin: March 1971

	Total Population			Spanish Population		
	Total	White	Black	Total	Mexican	Puerto Rican
Median Income Male	$7,891	$8,224	$5,041	$6,222	$6,002	$5,879
Median Income Female	$2,595	$2,665	$2,244	$2,625	$2,204	$3,115

SOURCE: *Current Population Reports,* "Selected Characteristics of Persons and Families of Mexican, Puerto Rican, and Other Spanish Origin: March 1971," p. 6.

did the Spanish turnout increase by 20 percent from 1960 to 1968. In 1968, Puerto Ricans in New York City cast less than half the number of ballots they cast in 1960, but voted 83 percent for Humphrey.[57] In 1972 their voting fell off even further while their support for President Nixon increased. In one Bronx district the vote for Nixon increased from 15 percent in 1968 to 25 percent in 1972.[58]

Until recently, Spanish-Americans have demonstrated less voter sophistication than blacks in terms of independence, mobilization of the vote for Spanish speaking candidates, and ticket splitting. A recent development among Chicanos concentrated in the Southwest has been the creation of local third parties such as *LaRaza Unida* which have achieved political successes in several Texas cities. For the most part, however, Spanish-Americans have even less political power than blacks. In California, Chicanos comprise just under 15 percent of the population but hold less than 2 percent of the state's elective offices (see Table 33). In the Northeast, where most Puerto Ricans are concentrated, they have virtually no political power. Recently, Spanish-Americans have sought to increase their political influence by joining forces between Chicanos and Puerto Ricans, who have their language and Hispanic culture in common.

The question of a "third world" voting coalition remains in some doubt at this time. Conflicts over political and economic rewards among economically marginal groups tend to limit possibilities for a meaningful political coalition,

[57] Levy and Kramer, *The Ethnic Factor,* pp. 79, 91.
[58] *Time* Magazine, November 20, 1972, p. 17.

Table 32. Unemployment Rates for Persons 16–64 Years Old by Age, Sex, and Ethnic Origin: March 1971 (in percent)

Age and Sex	Total Population			Spanish Population		
	Total	White	Black and Other	Total	Mexican	Puerto Rican
MALE		(in percents)				
16–64	6.0	5.6	9.1	8.6	10.1	10.0
16–24	13.6	12.7	20.1	15.2	14.3	25.4
25–44	4.4	4.2	5.9	6.3	7.1	5.0
45–64	3.9	3.9	5.5	8.0	12.2	—
FEMALE						
16–64	7.0	6.5	10.4	9.2	10.1	10.6
16–24	12.5	11.2	22.4	14.4	15.5	—
25–44	6.1	5.8	7.9	8.4	8.9	—
45–64	3.9	3.8	4.6	4.9	5.3	—

SOURCE: *Current Population Reports,* "Selected Characteristics of Persons and Families of Mexican, Puerto Rican, and Other Spanish Origin: March 1971," p. 10.

either within or outside of political parties. In Los Angeles, for example, in 1969, Mayor Yorty received 60 percent of the Mexican-American vote, although his black opponent had counted on Mexican-American support because of the city's long history of racial discrimination against *both* groups.

Table 33. 1970 California Roster of Federal, State, County, and City Officials

Category of Office	Total Number in Office	Total Number of Mexican Americans
Federal Elected and Appointed	525	7(1.3%)
State Legislature and Advisers	195	2(1%)
Executive Office of State	2,291	13(less than 1%)
State Boards Commission Advisers	1,732	47(2.7%)
City and County Government Officials	10,907	241(2.2%)
Total	15,650	310(1.98%)

SOURCE: "Political Participation of Mexican Americans in California" (Reported to the United States Commission on Civil Rights, August 1971), p. 8.

Yorty was able effectively to convince Mexican Americans that they should not associate themselves with the more racially distinct and disliked blacks and that they would not gain if a black (as opposed to Chicano) was elected to high political office.[59] By 1973 the *Los Angeles Times* reported that Bradley was able to gain 51 percent of the Chicano vote—a shift from four years earlier.

There are apparently shared perceptions among the different minority groups. For example, in Gary, Indiana, black candidate Richard Hatcher was able to win the Democratic primary in 1967 with the aid of a large majority of the city's Spanish-American voters [60] and, when studying ethnic voting patterns on a "fair housing" referendum in California, Wolfinger and Greenstein found that Oriental and Mexican-American groups opposed the referendum (meaning they favored open housing) in far greater percentages than other ethnic groups. Sixty-one percent of the Orientals and 53 percent of the Mexican Americans who voted were against the referendum.[61]

Thus, there are possibilities for political coalition on some issues of salience to all "marginal" groups, but there are also difficulties. Each group is pursuing its own nationalistic group goals. Both within the Democratic party (though Orientals who have sought economic as opposed to political influence in the past, tend to be Republicans) and through third-party movements, the groups are attempting to solidify their own ethnic and regional bases and to call upon shared historical experiences. Geographical, historical, ideological, and cultural differences tend to complicate possibilities for third-world coalitions. At the 1972 Democratic National Convention, for example, each nonwhite minority group had its own caucus. However, with the increased participation and representation for heretofore "marginal" groups within major *traditional* party ranks there may begin to be additional momentum by elected party representatives to redress the economic imbalance from which these groups have historically suffered. As nonwhites choose to exercise their franchise in greater numbers their votes alone will make them a force with which many elected officials will have to contend.

---

[59] See Scammon and Wattenberg, *The Real Majority*, pp. 23–37; Goldbloom, "Is There a Backlash Vote?" p. 18; Wilson and Wilde, "The Urban Mood," p. 59.

[60] Greer, "The First Year of Black Power in Gary, Indiana," p. 217.

[61] "Discrimination in housing does not appear to be a major problem at present for either of these groups. The Orientals have attained phenomenal social mobility since the war, while Mexican-Americans frequently complain that their problems are overlooked in the currently fashionable concern for Negroes. Perhaps, for these reasons, various journalists have claimed that these minorities are unduly hostile to Negroes and expressed their feelings by enthusiastic support for Proposition 14. Our data strongly contradict these assertions. . . . While we have far too few cases to permit controls for education, it is still clear that these minorities were much less favorable to the proposition than were whites." Raymond Wolfinger and Fred Greenstein, "The Repeal of Fair Housing: An Analysis of Referendum Voting," *American Political Science Review* 62 (September 1968): 759.

THE YOUTH VOTE

Some observers have suggested that by 1980, a generation of "new voters" over eighteen years of age will make up one-third of the eligible electorate in presidential elections.[62] According to V. O. Key, new voters contribute to change, to flexibility, and to adjustment in the political system.[63] Nonetheless, the suffrage of women over a half century ago appeared to have had no significant impact upon parties and politics, because politics remained an "unfeminine" activity for most women and (for the most part) they failed either to participate fully or with independent judgment, although this is no longer the case. (By 1972, 40 percent of the delegates to the Democratic National Convention were women. Yet, the "women's vote," counted upon by McGovern strategists as a major component of a progressive coalition, failed to develop. According to the *Gallup Opinion Index* women supported Nixon over McGovern 62–38 percent, which was even greater support than that given Nixon by men.) Some analysts have had greater expectations for the eighteen to twenty-one-year-old voters because of their independence. Young voters, both college and noncollege, are perceived as being far more liberal and anxious to foster social change than their parents.

Young voters have had an impact in several local elections. In Berkeley, California (where 10,000 new voters—mostly students—were registered) and in Ann Arbor, Michigan, both "college towns," "radicals" have been elected to local office, and in Texas, student votes have been the major factor in voting in the legalization of liquor consumption. In five university cities voters have voted to legalize liquor and in every case student voters are credited with tipping the balance. In Commerce, Nacogdoches, and Huntsville, Texas, voters legalized off-premises consumption of liquor. In College Station, home of Texas A & M, and in Lubbock, home of Texas Tech, the sale of mixed drinks was legalized; in Lubbock, for example, the measure passed 22,204 to 20,291 while student voting swelled the turnout 18,000 above the previous high. In other college towns Texas students have had success in electing their peers to city councils and school boards.[64]

As far as party identification is concerned, young people prefer to classify themselves as independents, and as many as 40–50 percent have indicated that they are not affiliated with either party (see Table 34). Many young independents are apparently to the left of the Democratic party, and are well educated and well informed in their thinking. Many of the young people who have registered to vote are generally less bound to traditional politics and have less

---

[62] Frederick G. Dutton, *Changing Sources of Power: American Politics in the 1970's* (New York: McGraw-Hill, 1971), p. 16.
[63] V. O. Key, *The Responsible Electorate* (Cambridge, Mass.: Harvard University Press, 1966), p. 105.
[64] *New York Times,* April 16, 1972, p. 39.

interest in party affiliation. While many of their parents have retained their party registration but split their tickets, the newly registered voters often do not bother to register with a party. They split their tickets, as their parents often do, but do not retain the party identification to which many of their parents still cling. Thus young voters are being socialized into our antiparty tradition at a time when many of their elders are asking questions about strict party loyalty.

There are problems however with the concept of a monolithic "youth vote." Young people, because they are less settled and are more mobile (see Table 35), tend to vote less than their elders (see Table 36). The actual size of the potential youth electorate in 1972 was 25 million (a potential vote of 11.2 million, eighteen to twenty-one-year-old voters and 13.9 million, twenty-one to twenty-five-year-old voters). However, registration obstacles have been placed before young people who may wish to vote; there has also been difficulty

Table 34. Age and Party Identification (in percent)

	Age					
	18–20	21–29	30–39	40–49	50–59	60 +
Strong Democrat	8.0	8.1	11.1	16.6	20.6	19.9
Weak Democrat	25.6	24.0	27.7	25.9	26.5	24.2
Independent, Leaning Democrat	16.6	18.0	11.7	8.5	8.9	6.6
Independent	19.1	18.1	14.2	13.4	9.9	8.0
Independent, Leaning Republican	15.1	14.1	12.6	11.0	6.6	6.4
Weak Republican	9.0	9.1	15.0	12.5	16.8	14.4
Strong Republican	4.0	6.9	6.4	11.3	10.2	17.5
Other	1.0	0.4	0.2	0.2	0.0	0.3
Apolitical	1.5	1.3	1.1	0.6	0.5	2.6
Total	100	100	100	100	100	100
	(199) *	(540)	(452)	(471)	(393)	(623)

* Figures in parentheses refer to the number of cases.
SOURCE: The Center for Political Studies (C.P.S.) of the University of Michigan data made available through the Inter-University Consortium for Political Research (I.C.P.R.).

Table 35. Mobility Status of Persons Eighteen to Twenty-four Years Old Between March 1969, and March 1970, by Age (Numbers in Thousands, Resident Population excluding Armed Forces in Barracks)

	Percent Distribution		
Mobility Status	18–24	18–20	21–24
TOTAL NUMBER	22,493	9,974	12,519
TOTAL PERCENT	100.0	100.0	100.0
Same House	60.8	71.1	52.6
Different House in U.S.	36.4	27.8	43.2
Same County	22.6	18.1	26.0
Different County	13.8	9.8	17.0
Same State	6.4	4.6	7.8
Different State	7.4	5.1	9.2
Abroad March 1, 1969	2.8	1.1	4.2

SOURCE: *Statistical Abstract*, 1971, p. 34.

over the question of whether students may vote at their college residences. On Election Day, 1972, 48 percent of the eligible youth appeared at the polls to vote. They split their vote 50–50 between the two candidates.[65]

In addition, young voters tend to resemble older voters, according to a Census Bureau report, in terms of race, residence, and family income—for example, two-thirds are in the work force and only about 30 percent of youth are students. A Gallup Poll indicated that 49 percent of the young workers say they are "middle of the road" (38 percent of the college students); 22 percent radical (43 percent of the students); 21 percent conservative (6 percent more than among students). Hence, some—perhaps even many young voters—tend to deviate from the "liberal" model suggested by some analysts. Also, for large numbers, "independence" camouflages partisan voting patterns. And, George Wallace in 1968 received 13 percent of the vote of the under thirty voters. In the Florida primary in 1972 Wallace received one-third of the votes of first-time voters. One-half of all his voters had less than a high school education, while three-quarters of McGovern's supporters had attended college, indicating a wide chasm between different groups of young people. These factors raise important questions about the direction, solidarity, and strength of the "youth vote" in 1970–80.

It should, however, be noted that 25 percent of the Democratic party

---

[65] Gallup Poll, quoted in the *New York Times*, December 14, 1972, p. 27.

Table 36. Age and Participation (1972)

Age	Voted	Did Not Vote	Not Regist.
18 to 20	48.3	9.9	41.9
21 to 24	50.7	8.8	40.5
25 to 29	57.8	8.3	33.9
30 to 34	61.9	9.3	28.8
35 to 44	66.3	8.5	25.2
45 to 54	70.9	8.4	20.7
55 to 64	70.7	9.5	19.8
65 to 74	68.1	10.3	21.5
75 yrs. and over	55.6	15.1	29.3

SOURCE: Data culled from Bureau of the Census, Department of Commerce, "Reported Voting and Registration of the Population of Voting Age, by Age and Sex: November 1972," *Voter Participation in November, 1972,* Series P-20, No. 244 (Washington, D.C.: Government Printing Office, December 1972), p. 3.

National Convention delegates in 1972 were under thirty years of age and that young people on campuses and elsewhere played a dominant role in the antiwar movement so significant in American politics, in the McCarthy movement, in Democratic politics in 1968, and in the transformation of the rules controlling the 1972 Democratic National Convention under the aegis of the McGovern Commission. Young people today may be more politically active and, because of television and increased education, are dependent on cues other than parental guidance in making their political decisions. Because so many young voters tend to be independent of parties, they may yet have a substantial impact on the future viability of parties in the United States. For the present however, the young are not clearly an activist bloc of votes upon which a liberal candidate can count. McGovern strategists who anticipated a large youth turnout for McGovern (which failed to materialize) failed to take into account the variation in background, education, and the resultant demands made on the political process by an age group that has as much *issue differentiation* as any other group in the electorate.

CONCLUSION

The evidence we have reviewed has indicated that if, in fact, we are in a realigning period, it is likely to be a protracted one. Significant forces: ticket splitting, the rise in "independence," continuous vote switching, the emergence of a new political "generation," the expression of discontent through a potent third party, and the presence of potentially polarizing political issues would all seem to augur the emergence of a "sixth" party system. Yet, while key groups in society—southerners, youth, "ethnics," and labor—have expressed dissatisfaction with traditional party loyalties, the new issues that have arisen have failed to create a major partisan crisis. Neither have they reinforced the existing party system.[66]

This unusual condition is apparently due to the especially cordial antiparty climate in contemporary American politics, which has led to the electoral disaggregation documented by Burnham and others and which seems currently to be continuing unabated. The future relationship between the voter and his party remains obscure; the impact of changing political issues incalculable.

[66] Sundquist, *Dynamics of the Party System*, p. 354.

Introduction
to Chapters 7
and 8

The subject of the next two chapters is state and local party organization. Such clearly antiparty trends as nonpartisanship have enjoyed their greatest success at these levels of government, constraining the development of strong or even any party organization. Because it is widely recognized that whatever power does exist in American parties is to be found at the *bottom,* the analysis of state and local leadership patterns, cohesiveness, and contemporary functions is of greatest significance.

165

7

The Local Party:
Styles of
Political Activism

There is a widespread agreement among political scientists that the sources of political party power—to the extent that any exist—in our fragmented antiparty culture are to be found within the local party organization. Once the bastion of "machine" power, today the local political club, which served as the building block of party influence, appears to have declined in its role. In this chapter, we will first examine the role of the political activists, then look at the historical and current roles of the "machine" in local politics. We will assess the impact of reform and community organization in modifying the contemporary role of local parties. Finally, we will attempt to determine the degree to which political clubs today (and in the past) have met the needs of their constituents for representation and participation.

RECRUITMENT AND ORGANIZATION

Hugh Bone and Austin Ranney define organization activists as: ". . . persons who regularly devote much time and energy to working in political parties or pressure groups. They number party leaders and workers from precinct captains to presidential candidates, pressure group leaders, lobbyists, and the like. It is estimated that only ¼ of 1 percent of the population belong in this category." [1] The party leadership corps in state and local politics is comprised of a mixture of activists from committeemen, state and county chairmen, and precinct and district leaders to candidates who seek office using the party label. Activists are a heterogeneous group who defy easy categorization. Although they are representative of all groups in the American populace, several salient features stand out among them. Activists are distinguished from the population as a whole by relatively high social status and higher education. Activists tend to come from families who are politically active, have a high sense of personal efficacy, and have an interest in power.[2] In these respects, they are often not representative of their constituencies. For example, in 1967 the median income of Knox County (Tennessee) was $5,755; but the majority of activists there had incomes in the $7,000–15,000 range.[3] In addition, a recent study showed that over 50 percent of state party chairmen held advanced educational degrees. As far as religious background is concerned, Democratic state chairmen are more likely to be Catholic than Protestant. The reverse is true for Republican state chairmen.[4] Also, traditionally, Republicans tended to come more from white-collar backgrounds, while Democrats came more from blue-collar backgrounds. This has never been entirely true since the dominant or majority party within an area has often attracted the more

[1] Hugh A. Bone and Austin Ranney, *Politics and Voters,* 3d ed. (New York: McGraw-Hill, 1971), pp. 3–4. The activity dimensions of political behavior are classified by Bone and Ranney in the following manner:

Organization activists	(¼ of 1%) of adult population
Organization contributors	(5%) of adult population work in campaigns, attend rallies, contribute money
Opinion leaders	(25%) of adult population regularly "talk politics"
Voters	(25 to 35%) of adult population only vote
Nonvoters	(30 to 40%) of adult population vote infrequently or never
Apoliticals	(3 to 7%) of adult population are devoid of knowledge or interest in political affairs

[2] See Lewis Bowman and G. R. Boynton, "Recruitment Patterns among Local Party Officials: A Model and Some Preliminary Findings in Selected Locales," *American Political Science Review* 60 (September 1966): 669; Robert H. Salisbury, "The Urban Party Organization," *Public Opinion Quarterly* 29 (Winter 1965–66): 550–64.

[3] M. Margaret Conway and Frank B. Feigert, "Motivation, Incentive Systems and the Political Party Organization," *American Political Science Review* 62 (December 1968): 1162–63. See also William J. Crotty, "The Social Attributes of Party Organizational Activists in a Transitional Political System," *Western Political Quarterly* 20 (September 1967): 674.

[4] Charles W. Wiggins and William L. Turk, "State Party Chairmen: A Profile," *Western Political Quarterly* 23 (June 1970): 323.

affluent and better educated leadership.[5] At the present time, for example, the Democratic party leadership is clearly as well educated as Republican party leadership. This was made abundantly clear at the 1972 national convention. (See Chapter 11 for a discussion of this phenomenon.) Finally, a disproportionate percentage of activists are lawyers who tend to view politics as a route to rapid economic success.

In the past party politics was used to move up out of the lower class. For today's disadvantaged groups, however, party activism does not seem to be playing a major role in facilitating rapid upward mobility. Thus, social mobility appears to be a prior condition for political progress for blacks in contemporary America, whereas for earlier groups party politics may have been an alternative to education as a means of gaining social mobility. For example, a 1969 study found that 78 percent of black politicians in New York City were college graduates, indicating that they had achieved some social status prior to their active participation in party politics.[6]

A group that has achieved only moderate success through political activism is women. Women are found in disproportionate numbers at the lower ranks of party organization, where they perform the traditional party functions of canvassing and other precinct work; but are usually blocked from high party office by sex role typing. In 1970 only three state party chairmen were women.[7]

Activists have a variety of reasons for becoming interested in party politics. Most indicate that they were asked to participate by friends, that they became interested in a specific party campaign or candidate, or that they were motivated by a concern with matters of public policy. For a lesser number, an explicit desire to obtain a job or make business contacts is relevant. Most party politicians have had some political experience and many have been candidates (or aspire to be) for public office, indicating a significant degree of political ambition among them.

A recent Gallup Poll questioning parents on their views relating to politics as a career for their children indicated that only 23 percent of American parents want their children to enter politics. "Only a minority of people are socialized positively for politics during the years of development into adulthood. They are more likely to be protected from party careers than urged to consider them. . . . In evaluating the careerists who do become involved in

[5] Samuel Patterson, "Characteristics of Party Leaders," *Western Political Quarterly* 16 (June 1963): 332–52; see also Gerald Pomper, "New Jersey County Chairmen," *Western Political Quarterly* 18 (March 1965): 189.

[6] George Martin Furniss, "The Political Assimilation of Negroes in New York City," Ph.D. dissertation, Columbia University, 1969, pp. 386–89, 413.

[7] Wiggins and Turk, "State Party Chairmen," p. 322. Women seem to be moving into state legislative posts with increasing frequency, however. Though still a small percentage, as of 1974 they represent 7.1 percent of the total in 26 states surveyed; up from 5.2 percent in the 1972 sessions. *New York Times,* November 7, 1974, p. 1.

one of our American parties, then, it is necessary to realize that the people are behaving contrary to prevailing public mores." [8] This may explain the relatively small number of party activists in American politics, despite the existence of a relatively "open" party structure at the bottom.

THE "MACHINE" IN LOCAL POLITICS

Peter Clark and James Q. Wilson have suggested three incentives for participation in local party clubs: (1) solidary (or social)—the reason that most people join most organizations, (2) purposive—or ideological and/or programmatic, and (3) material—self-interest via jobs or favors.[9] In practice, however, recent studies have indicated a mix between material self-interest, desire for social interaction, and policy orientation as incentives for political participation and work among activists.[10]

There can be little doubt that the urban "machine" which flourished in many (largely eastern) American cities in the first half of the twentieth century, and which was based on material incentives, was one of the most creative and influential political organizations known in the world. "Machine" was an accurate label because of the nature of the interdependent parts of the party system: the precinct captain who built up a loyal following that would support him, his leader (the "boss"), and the party. The boss's continued power and influence depended on the precinct leader and his ability effectively to control votes. The precinct leader's position was similarly dependent and voters' favors, jobs, etc., depended on the party's continued monopoly of political rewards. Traditional machine politicians rarely held official elective positions, but preferred to maintain their influence from party posts. Even today, in Albany, New York, where there is still an old-time machine, the mayor remains subservient to the county machine.

It is clear that the machine was organized in large measure to enhance selfish motives; that is, getting and maintaining political power and material rewards for a few political leaders. George Washington Plunkitt, the boss of New York City's Tammany Hall machine noted that he made his fortune in politics by buying property with the advance knowledge that a subway line would be

[8] Samuel Eldersveld, *Political Parties: A Behavioral Analysis* (Chicago: Rand McNally, 1964), p. 168.

[9] Peter B. Clark and James Q. Wilson, "Incentive Systems: A Theory of Organizations," *Administrative Science Quarterly* 6 (September 1961): 134–37.

[10] Dennis S. Ippolito, "Political Perspectives of Suburban Party Leaders," *Social Science Quarterly* 49 (March 1969): 2800–15; Conway and Feigert, "Motivation, Incentive Systems, and the Political Party Organization," pp. 1159–73.

coming into the area, thus enhancing the value of the real estate. He distinguished between honest graft and dishonest graft. Dishonest graft referred to corruption. Honest graft was simply, in Plunkitt's words, "I seen my opportunities and I took 'em." [11] This was what Robert Merton labeled the *manifest* function of the machine. "Manifest functions are those objective consequences contributing to the adjustment or adaptation of the system which are intended and recognized by participants in the system." [12] Merton also pointed to the *latent* functions of the machine—"those which are neither intended nor recognized." Let us consider six latent functions of the machine in an attempt to determine whether that much maligned institution performed any significant functions for its constituents.

LATENT FUNCTIONS IN HISTORICAL PERSPECTIVE

1. The machine provided important services for the immigrants who were streaming to the United States. It aided them in securing essential welfare services including housing, food, employment, and ultimately—some would say—in easing the difficulties of urbanization in an alien land. But this function can be overstated. Jacob Riis, writing in 1890, commented on the horrendous conditions of the poor—housing, sanitation, and education—and the political clubs' indifference to these social needs. Referring to "Boss" Tweed and his machine, he wrote:

So Tammany came back. The Health Department is wrecked. The police force is worse than before . . . and we are back in the muck. [13]

2. The machine facilitated political participation and through it, significant segments of the "masses" become socialized into the American political system. Granted the machine's political socialization process was not direct, it did provide access to the political system and the immigrants gradually learned how to participate. Their grandchildren, years later, who were fully assimilated into American society as a result of their parents and their grandparents efforts, could look with disdain upon the early immigrant socialization to the political system. Anticipating this disdain, Riis wrote:

[11] William Riordan, *Plunkitt of Tammany Hall* (New York: McClure and Phillips, 1905), p. 3.
[12] Robert Merton, *Social Theory and Social Structure,* 1968 enlarged ed. (Glencoe, Ill.: The Free Press, 1957), pp. 105, 115–20.
[13] Jacob Riis, *How the Other Half Lives,* reprinted in Francesco Cordasco, ed., *Jacob Riis Revisited* (Garden City, N.Y.: Doubleday Anchor, 1968), p. 408.

He came here for a chance to live. Of politics, social ethics, he knows nothing. Government in his old home existed only for oppression. Why should he not attach himself with his whole loyal soul to the plan of government in his new home that offers to boost him into the place of his wildest ambition, a "job on the streets," that is, in the Street Cleaning Department—and asks no other return than that he shall vote as directed? Vote! Not only he, but his cousins and brothers and uncles will vote as they are told, to get Pietro the job he covets. If it pleases the other man, what is it to him for whom he votes? . . . With his vote he could buy what to him seemed wealth. In the muddle of ideas, that was the one which stood out. When citizen papers were offered for $12.50, he bought them quickly, and got his job on the street.[14]

3. The machine—organized as it usually was around ethnic identity—provided a mechanism for social mobility among coethnics. It did so by securing political jobs, "protection" for fledgling business enterprises, and other "preferments" or special favors. Thus,

. . . The successful patronage seeker is well aware that government must bank its money, insure its property, and construct office buildings—all on a noncompetitive basis, because bank and insurance rates are uniform and there are no subjective standards for architecture and construction.[15]

4. The machine was an indigenous political movement. Its local leadership lived in the community, spoke the language of community residents, and knew the people in the community. This may have served to "personalize" politics and make it more meaningful for the participants. An example of the tone of this political style is conveyed by William F. Whyte in *Street Corner Society*.

When people wanted help from the organization, they would come right up here to the office [of the political club]. Matt [the boss] would be in here every morning from nine to eleven, and if you couldn't see him then, you could find him in the ward almost any other time. If a man came in to ask Matt for a job, Matt would listen to him and then tell him he'd see what he could do; he should come back in a couple of days. That could give Matt time to get in touch with the precinct captain and find out all about the man. If he didn't vote in the last election, he was out. Matt wouldn't do anything for him—that is, unless he could show that he was so sick he couldn't get to the polls.[16]

---

[14] Ibid., pp. 365–66.
[15] Martin Tolchin and Susan Tolchin, *To the Victor* (New York: Random House, 1971), p. 14.
[16] Quoted originally in William F. Whyte, *Street Corner Society*, enlarged ed. (Chicago: University of Chicago Press, 1955), p. 194, and cited by Raymond E. Wolfinger, "Why Political Machines Have Not Withered Away and Other Revisionist Thoughts," *Journal of Politics* 34 (1972): 388–89.

5. The machine served to blunt class identity by stressing ethnic identity instead. The immigrants had a "desire for cultural-religious as well as political, and perhaps at times economic, self-protection." [17] This brought immigrants of like background together, and among them there would be some who would use party politics to reenact, machine style, the story of Horatio Alger.

6. The machine centralized politics and made it clear who had the power and who was responsible for political decisions. Robert Merton has suggested that:

> The key structural function of the Boss is to organize, centralize, and maintain in good working conditions the "scattered fragments of power" which are at present dispersed through our political organization. By the centralized organization of political power, the Boss and his apparatus can satisfy the needs of diverse subgroups in a larger community which are not politically satisfied by legally devised and culturally approved social structures. [18]

THE MACHINE IN CONTEMPORARY POLITICS

There is widespread feeling that the machine of yesteryear no longer exists and that this is a good thing because the institution as well as the patronage and the overt power orientation upon which it rested, were inherently evil. One reason for the machine's *decline* (although not death, as we will demonstrate below) was the corruption and unbridled selfishness to which it gave rise. Incompetence, mismanagement, and waste of public resources occurred under the tutelage of the machine. Indignant reformers arose to decry "bossism" in many cities—sometimes seeking to democratize the party system, sometimes seeking to destroy it.

At least *seven* reasons have been advanced to explain the decline of the urban machine.

1. To a considerable extent, civil service regulations, which provided for merit as opposed to patronage appointments, took their toll of the clubs' support. It has been reported that from 1962–1964 in the territory of New York's once proud Tammany Hall, most political jobs paid less than $5,000 a year and endured for only between six months and two years. [19] Though it

---

[17] Elmer E. Cornwell, "Bosses, Machines and Ethnic Groups," *Annals* 353 (May 1964): 29.

[18] Merton, *Social Theory and Social Structure,* p. 126.

[19] Edward N. Costikyan, *Behind Closed Doors* (New York: Harcourt, Brace, 1966), pp. 265–66. Well over half of American cities have complete civil service coverage for their employees. See Raymond E. Wolfinger and John Osgood Field, "Political Ethos and the Structure of City Government," *American Political Science Review* 60 (June 1966): 314–15.

is a temptation, however, one should not overestimate the influence of the civil service in local politics. There is still patronage! Thus, it was estimated that under New York's reform mayor, John V. Lindsay, the 1969 New York City budget allocation for outside consultants was $75 million, there were nearly 75,000 "noncompetitive" jobs, and the mayor controlled tremendous patronage through his control of the municipal agencies that grant zoning variances.[20] However, unions, which have gained pensions, higher salaries, and significant workers' benefits, can provide for greater security for their members than can patronage positions.

2. The federal government, through its welfare and social legislation (especially social security insurance and Medicare and Medicaid), has expanded the services clubs used to offer to more people than the club could serve. One should note, however, that big government may lead to more impersonal and bureaucratized service delivery.

3. The age of technology has brought with it the need for more "experts" in government, a trend reinforced by the reformers' demands for good government, which requires the use of qualified personnel (this is discussed in greater detail later in the chapter).

4. Some political observers have argued that the media have obviated the need for personal political contact, although this is not as yet clear. What is clear is that districts have grown in population and streets are considered unsafe in many urban areas, making club directed precinct efforts more difficult.

5. The relative affluence of many Americans, some of whom may have been aided in their socioeconomic ascent by the machine, has turned them against it. Now that they have more leisure time and education, they have developed a greater interest in politics and they want to participate themselves. They do not want to have others—that is, the machine—participate for them. (See Chapter 2 for a more complete discussion of this phenomenon.)

6. Some analysts have argued that the disappearance of large numbers of immigrants from American cities has been a major cause of the machine's decline. This seems, however, patently untrue. Migration patterns of blacks, Puerto Ricans, and Chicanos, who increasingly occupy our inner cities, parallel those of earlier groups in direction if not in place of origin. Nearly 4.5

[20] Martin and Susan Tolchin, "How Lindsay Learned the Patronage Lesson," *New York Magazine* (March 29, 1971): 48.

million blacks left the rural South and settled in northern cities in the thirty years between 1940 and 1970. Today, these groups comprise a majority of the city's poor.[21] Urban party organization is not declining because it lacks a clientele. The question of its viability rests on whether the current potential clientele can utilize the party organization in order to gain a fairer share of society's resources.

7. It is not even clear how much parties—through the machine—contributed to the process and progress of groups' success in the past. Some groups—notably Italians and Poles—were less able to gain political or economic power through political organization than the Irish. It is clear that in the 1970s the machine, as a centralizing political device, no longer exists in many places. Though there are clearly exceptions—Chicago being the prime example—power has become increasingly fragmented within the urban area as elsewhere in the political system. Reformers, using primaries and television, and community organization, have tried to share in the stakes of politics. Hence, the party is no longer the sole route to political power.

Party organizations, as this discussion of the machine makes clear, have never been interested in public policy per se unless it has involved their own maintenance of power (e.g., such questions as zoning, tax assessments, redistricting and appointments to political office). Parties do continue to play a key role in manipulating traditional material incentives—jobs, favors, personnel, and contracts—to the extent that the opportunities still exist. Furthermore, one might want to argue that there may be more need than ever for what Costikyan cites as the party leader's job:

> Basically, the leader cushions the impact of government upon his constituents and provides a pipeline for his constituency to the bureaucracy at the heart of every urban center.[22]

Perhaps there is still a role for politics—machine-style—even for reformers. The McGovern and McCarthy campaigns have demonstrated that in the "new politics" nothing succeeds as well as the old door-to-door canvassing.

---

[21] In 1970, 21 percent of the population of central cities in the United States was black, while 5 percent of the suburban population was black. The median income of white families was $10,672 in 1971 and $6,440 for blacks. If one isolates the North and West—where blacks live primarily in central cities—white median income was $11,057 in 1971, and black median income in 1971 was $7,596. The black median income was 69 percent of the white median income in these two regions. A comparable figure for the South was 56 percent—with white median income $9,706 and black median income $5,414. United States Department of Commerce, Bureau of the Census, *The Social and Economic Status of the Black Population in the United States, 1971,* P-23, no. 42 (Washington, D.C.: Government Printing Office, July 1972), pp. 15, 23, 32.

[22] Costikyan, *Behind Closed Doors,* p. 92.

The personalization and humanization offered by the party is in greater demand as bureaucracies have proliferated and the urban citizen feels powerless and alienated. Also, "the professional and business middle class is as eager for patronage today as groups were 50 or 75 years ago—perhaps more so than ever—as lawyers seek judicial positions and businessmen seek contracts and favors increasingly available through proliferating programs and bureaucracies." [23] Limitations on civil service in practice have been observed by students of urban politics. As noted earlier, New York's "reform" Mayor Lindsay (1965–73) joined with Chicago's machine Mayor Daley in increasing provisional positions and noncompetitive jobs on the city's roster and was not beyond using consultants and contract bidding to provide political favors. Upon his election in 1965, Lindsay also rewarded his campaign aides by placing most of them on the city payroll. [24] As Susan and Martin Tolchin point out, the difference between Daley and Lindsay was in their rhetoric, their organizational skills, and the nature of those chosen for rewards. In Chicago, the unions and real estate and highway developers have been politically involved by the Daley machine, whose success in coopting such key interests has been sufficient to prevent crippling strikes and to provide innovative architecture and roads. [25] Chicago under Daley, however efficiently run, nevertheless remains a machine with a closed political system and absolute political rule extending to all aspects of urban life. In New York, Lindsay rewarded the black and Puerto Rican poor and various professionals (e.g., academic consultants) in order to solidify his political support. Lindsay also sought to establish little city halls in order to create party-like organizations under mayoral control. He had some success, although the election in 1973 of a Democratic mayor (Abraham Beame), with strong organizational support may obviate the necessity for some of Lindsay's personal efforts to seek a cohesive organizational base.

The real question about machines and patronage is not their imminent demise—which is not apparent—but how this kind of politics can be reconciled with good and competent government. Patronage reinforces nonideological politics and may encourage politicians to compromise the public interest for private gain. Nevertheless, the machine provides much of the governing as well as the selfishness in politics. Perhaps those who work the hardest should be rewarded and is this not the best way to assure continuity in politics? Reformers who rail against "bossism" in politics may be missing the point. ". . . In a city where the power is in the bureaucracy, the locus of corruption must also be there. And the discretionary exercise of power by bureaucrats is to be

[23] Wolfinger, "Why Political Machines Have Not Withered Away," p. 396.
[24] Tolchin and Tolchin, To the Victor, pp. 64–65. Lindsay was elected initially with "fusion" support from the Republican and Liberal parties in 1965, and with third-party Liberal support only in 1969. At the conclusion of his term, Lindsay became a Democrat.
[25] See Mike Royko, Boss (New York: New American Library, 1971).

feared and needs to be dealt with at least as much as—probably far more than—Boss Tweed's successors." [26] Bureaucracies are the "new machines" with no control by popular authority. Party organizations, built on a mass base, as was the machine (although contemporary political organizations ought not be and cannot be replicas of the old machine) might serve to redress the balance of power between the rulers and the ruled. In the absence of a machine structure to advance group interests through the maintenance of power and provision of material benefits, how can low-income groups be organized?

THE REFORM ANTITHESIS

The traditional nuclear party organization prized party loyalty, and some private gains were made via party by first- and second-generation Americans. Newer recruits to the urban political arena often profess greater concern with "reform" of party and political structures and with public policy and ideology, as they frown upon "diehard" party loyalty. Reform politics, which has appeared with cyclical regularity in urban America, is not a monolithic movement. Subsumed under the reform umbrella are the intraparty reform movements in city (and sometimes state) politics—the New Democratic Coalition (NDC) in New York is one, and California Democratic Clubs (CDC) another; third parties with reformist inclinations (the Democratic Farmer Labor party in Minnesota, and Liberal and Conservative parties in New York); the "no party" systems of some suburban areas; the nonpartisan politics utilized by over two-thirds of American cities with mean populations of 25,000.[27] Let us consider each separately and assess its impact on local party organization.

URBAN REFORM MOVEMENTS

The reform or amateur politician has appeared periodically in city politics —often trying to gain control of the party mechanism—to provide an alternative to the traditional clubhouse style typified by the machine. There have been two major reform approaches within it: populist and progressive. The populists stress grass-roots control and direct democracy; the progressives, better leadership.[28] Both forms can be seen today within the reform movement. In the past, reform movements have tended to be short-lived, nonpatronage

---

[26] Costikyan, *Behind Closed Doors,* p. 307.
[27] Fred Greenstein, "The Changing Pattern of Urban Politics," *Annals* 353 (May 1964): 2–13.
[28] James Q. Wilson, *The Amateur Democrat* (Chicago: University of Chicago Press, 1966), p. 26.

oriented, and noninstitutionalized in terms of a concrete political philosophy. Today's intraparty reformers often tend to be affluent, educated, relatively young, and interested in social as well as political interaction. In this regard, the reform groups do not differ from the traditional political machines that held parties, dances, and Fourth of July picnics. The social interests of young single reformers have tended to create a considerable transient club population. A disproportionately large percentage of these reformers are women.[29] Members of reform clubs are often more policy-oriented than traditional politicians, though reform and liberalism are not necessarily synonymous. Reformers *may* be conservative or indifferent to controversial urban issues. While reformers often lack an integrated political program, they do tend to agree that government should be dominated by the "best qualified," and that "good government" ideals of honesty, efficiency, and impartiality should prevail.[30] Reformers also seek to maximize popular participation both in party and government; this aim, however, is often in conflict with their goal of "expertise" in politics. The effect of the latter is, of course, to limit the mass role in decision making. Reformers tend to favor such political procedures as at-large elections, "blue ribbon" juries, appointment of judges to office, and master planning. Support for these largely procedural changes is buttressed by a common belief that political leadership should be drawn from the reformist middle class. Thus, the reform leadership often believes that from their active participation in politics there will emerge a clear sense of the "public interest." Opposition to patronage jobs as political rewards is usually a major reform plank because such jobs are perceived as inevitably involving compromise of political principles. Community service, then, becomes a major means of binding constituents to reform clubs. At the present time, most reform clubs are comprised of ethnic and religious groups marginal to traditional urban politics such as middle-class Jews and WASPs. Insofar as these groups have not been integrated into many political machines, they may be motivated by an "out" desire to get "in" to the urban political process, as much as by ideological conviction. "Reform" then has provided an alternative route to political office for the ambitious and has on occasion brought change to the urban political process.

The intraparty reform movement of most recent vintage received impetus from Adlai Stevenson's candidacy in 1952 (in the Democratic party) and was aided by the direct primary, which made it possible to contest established political leadership. Increased affluence and the already weakened political machine made possible the political and social climate necessary for reform.

[29] See Francis Carney, *The Rise of the Democratic Clubs in California* (New Brunswick, N.J.: Eagleton Foundation, 1968), p. 7; Wilson, *The Amateur Democrat,* pp. 165–68; and Bert Swanson, Robert Hirschfield, and Blanche Blank, "A Profile of Political Activists in Manhattan," *Western Political Quarterly* 15 (September 1962): 494.
[30] See Wilson, *The Amateur Democrat,* Chapter 12.

Generally, however, reformers have not been able to dominate even local political organizations. In New York City, where they have played an active role, especially in Manhattan but also in the Bronx and Brooklyn, reformers have never been able to control local county organizations. Francis Carney does credit reform with rebuilding the two-party system in California through revitalization of the Democratic party.[31] But reform groups operate on a statewide level in California; and, thus, there is less preoccupation with local concerns and organization. The rhetoric of reform is antileadership in orientation, emphasizing total democratization; its thrust tends to be antiorganizational. An example of this may be seen in the failure of most New York City Democratic reformers to abide by the decision of the "people" in the 1969 Democratic party primary. They preferred to support Liberal (third-party) mayoral candidate John V. Lindsay, as opposed to a conservative Democrat, Mario Procaccino, selected by party voters.

Reformers have had difficulty putting together cohesive organizations. Within the clubs themselves, intraparty democracy tends to prevail and executive authority is "frowned" upon. New York City's experience with a succession of reform movements: the Committee of Democratic Voters (CDV), Committee for Democratic Alternatives (CDA), and NDC is instructive. Each disintegrated due to friction between old reformers and reform insurgents; these successive failures are an indication of the difficulty of institutionalizing cohesive reform organization when organization and leadership are frowned upon. The traditional political function of nominating and endorsing candidates becomes difficult, if not impossible, under these circumstances. The NDC (a national reform movement with a branch in New York), the latest of New York's reform institutions, has initiated a policy of endorsing candidates, especially in primaries, for city and state political office. Such support could at least in theory be crucial. The group has, however, been wracked by acrimony at policy conventions and has thus far not been able to deliver its vote to their preferred candidates. Nor has reform been able to involve lower socioeconomic classes or minority groups. This is due probably to their excessive insistence on total commitment to abstract and procedural goals that are often irrelevant to the poor. Michael Pesce, for example, comments that "when white middle class reformers seek to activate the Italo-American blue collar community their action is read as patronizing, as asking us to fight battles in their interest." [32] He contends that reformers have a tendency to identify with the plight of geographically distant groups, such as the concern of New York reformers for southwestern migrant workers, while they neglect urban workers in their own midst.

---

[31] Carney, *Democratic Clubs in California,* p. 16.
[32] Michael Pesce, "Blue Collar Reform," in Michael Wenk, S. M. Tomasi, and Geno Baroni, eds., *Pieces of a Dream* (New York: Center for Migration Studies, 1972), p. 163.

Reform to a certain extent has aided in the advent of government by experts—with the domination of city politics by autonomous bureaucracies—a form which often is less responsive to demands of the people than the old machine whose faults reformers lament. While it is an exaggeration to see the battle of reform versus machine politics as a classic reenactment of the class struggle, it is nonetheless possible that the working class and the poor have lost out since the advent of reform. As Pesce puts it:

> Social and economic ethnic exclusion . . . has become to a frightening degree the property of the liberal political philosophy behind much of the movement when it purports to improve the conditions under which lower income people live. The reform rejection of working people whose cultural tastes and social attitudes do not correspond to desirable middle class attributes, again and again leads reformers to dismiss the blue collar ethnic class as a political force and to operate against its interest whenever reform does take power.[33]

Blacks and other urban minorities experience similar difficulties in relating to reform. In general, they oppose the reformers' desire to "change the rules of the game" just as they are coming to gain access to power in urban areas. There is, for example, very little enthusiasm expressed by black leaders for appointment of judges by blue ribbon commissions. Their antipathy to this method of judicial selection is rooted in their fear that blacks will be excluded from the elite recommending bodies; hence, from the judicial positions. Contemporary reformers have equal difficulty dealing with black separatism as a basis for political recognition and power. The black demand for proportional material benefits is clearly antithetical to the antipatronage, propublic interest (the latter concept is often left undefined) thrust of the reform movement. The above discussion needs one modification. In some cities there has been a loose political alliance between blacks and some upper-status (reformist) whites. Thus some upper-class whites in New York City were supportive of black demands for community controlled schools. In such school districts the controlling position of the existing white-dominated merit system would decline with community control.[34]

Finally, the often strong issue and policy orientation of the reform movement makes political compromise difficult and thus reduces the ability of local

---

[33] Ibid., pp. 170–71. See Pesce's article for a useful account of one successful ethnic blue-collar reform movement.

[34] John V. Lindsay, then mayor of New York City, and a candidate who had been supported by the reformist white upper-middle class, and by nonwhites, reflected the views of many who had voted for him when, in discussing school decentralization, he said: "This response is more than an experiment in political democracy, although it clearly does make institutions more responsive to the citizenry. It also gives promise of ending the image of the schools as separate from a child or a parent's neighborhood. There is hope for our schools—all of them . . . only if they can rebuild links to the neighborhoods. . . ." Quoted by Mario Fantini, Marilyn Gittell, and Richard Magat, *Community Control and Urban Schools* (New York: Praeger, 1970), p. 121.

parties to achieve broad-based coalition. It has been argued that reform has resulted in "anti-party pluralism, the politics of disintegration rather than accommodation between separate groups." [35]

THE ROLE OF ISSUE-ORIENTED THIRD PARTIES

There have been very few effective third parties in the United States either locally or nationally, if by effective one means successful election of candidates to public office. Though there have been numerous issue-oriented third parties in the United States, spanning the political spectrum from the Communist party on the left to the Nazi party on the right, most of the third parties have not attempted to replace the two major parties. They have acted essentially as interest groups making demands on the political system. There are (and have been in the past), however, some issue-oriented third parties, such as New York's Liberal and Conservative parties and Minnesota's Farmer Labor party, which have had more success in achieving at least some of their political goals relating to the party system than has the intraparty reform movement. Such third parties share with the intraparty reformers the goal of producing change within the two major parties. As a general rule, however, third-party movements seek to achieve such change outside the major parties, operating almost as pressure groups trying to affect the party system. New York's Liberal party, with a miniscule party registration, has been able to influence nominations and elections in both New York City and New York State, by polling enough votes to insure the victory or defeat of a (usually Democratic) candidate. In 1966, for example, the addition of Liberal candidate Franklin D. Roosevelt, Jr.'s votes to Democrat Frank O'Connor's would have made the latter governor of New York. Instead, Nelson Rockefeller was reelected. Third parties such as the Liberals usually vary their political strategy, sometimes endorsing major party candidates, sometimes nominating their own candidates. The New York Conservative party is a right-wing offshoot of the Republicans, as the Liberals have been the left wing of the Democrats. The Conservative party has proven its extraordinary vote-getting ability not only by electing James Buckley to the U.S. Senate from New York State in 1970 in a field which included a Democrat and an incumbent Republican senator, but also by providing the margin of victory for twenty-three state assemblymen and four state senators to the New York State legislature in the same year. "The future of the New York Republican Party has become increasingly intertwined with the prospects and predilections of the currently nonaligned Conservative Party." [36]

[35] Theodore J. Lowi, *At the Pleasure of the Mayor* (Glencoe, Ill.: The Free Press, 1964), pp. 205, 224.

[36] Arthur Klebanoff, "Gubernatorial Elections in New York State," *City Almanac* (October 1970), p. 9.

New York is almost unique among the states in having vital third and fourth parties. They exist largely because of electoral laws that permit minor party endorsements of major party candidates. These cross-endorsements have increased in number to the point where it is unusual for a candidate to bear only a single party label. Without this electoral input, minor parties providing viable alternatives could readily lose their bargaining power and influence, and would probably disappear as they have in most other states. Some third parties, like the Wisconsin Progressive party (1934–46) and the Minnesota Farmer Labor party, acted as extralegal voluntary organizations trying to impact the existing parties from outside. These third parties were reformist in their belief in no patronage and in maintaining a large card-carrying, dues-paying membership.[37] Both of these parties had brief periods of electoral success, and then dissolved. The Farmer Labor party merged with the Democratic party in Minnesota, and in Wisconsin, when the Progressive party dissolved, supporters of the Progressives joined both of the remaining two major parties. Such prominent politicians as Hubert Humphrey and Eugene McCarthy were leaders of the Minnesota group.

NONPARTISANSHIP

Nonpartisanship is an extreme form of antipartyism; it requires that no candidate be identified on the ballot by party label. Nonpartisanship has, as suggested, been a preferred electoral system in a large number of American cities, especially outside of the Northeast. Although some cities (Boston) have only nominal nonpartisan systems, others (Minneapolis and Los Angeles) seem to be genuine in their loyalties to no-partyism. Over one-half of the total number of offices in the United States are filled in this manner; hence, nonpartisanship is *a* (if not *the*) dominant municipal form. Inasmuch as nonpartisan elections are widely used, there are a variety of nonpartisan forms operative in the American political system.[38]

Nonpartisanship is seen by many political scientists as having negative

---

[37] See Leon Epstein, *Politics in Wisconsin,* pp. 77–81; also John Fenton, *Midwest Politics* (New York: Holt, Rinehart and Winston, 1966), p. 87.

[38] Charles Adrian has developed a typology of nonpartisan elections in which he was able to isolate four basic types of nonpartisan election types:
Type I—Elections where the only candidates who normally have any chance of being elected are those supported directly by a major political organization.
Type II—Elections where slates of candidates are supported by various groups, including political party organizations.
Type III—Elections where slates of candidates are supported by various interest groups, but political party organizations have little or no part in campaigns, or are active only sporadically.
Type IV—Elections where neither political parties nor slates of candidates are important in campaigns.
Charles R. Adrian, "A Typology of Non-partisan Elections," *Western Political Quarterly* 12 (June 1959): 452–57.

consequences for the party system. These negative factors can be classified into two broad areas. One set of consequences relates to the voters, the other to the maintenance and continuation of the political system. It is argued that voters, especially lower-class voters, tend to turn out in lower numbers for nonpartisan elections, and members of minority groups tend to gain less representation through nonpartisan elections than through ward-based partisan electoral systems.[39] "The non-partisan election is biased against the poorly educated voter. Its rationale is based upon the assumption that all voters can discriminate among the candidates—a most difficult chore, even for the educated, especially where the candidates may number 50 in city council elections. Most voters don't even know the candidates' names, let alone their policy position." [40] Predominantly middle- and upper-class Republican areas tend to have higher voter turnout in nonpartisan elections than poorer, often Democratic sections—and the former thereby gain an increased political role. In the absence of the guiding "cue giving" role of the party, the media may gain a larger voice in nonpartisan election campaigns.[41] Also, some commentators have contended that in nonpartisan elections incumbency and ethnic identity tend to become more significant than in partisan races. The latter may of course have polarizing effects upon the political system. Nonpartisanship is thought to limit channels for recruitment to the larger political system and because of its emphasis on conformity, create stability and conservatism. In addition, these elections are seen to be disorganized, with candidates forced to rely on independent financing and ad hoc coalitions.

Those who support nonpartisanship tend to distrust politicians and parties and feel that most problems in the urban arena are essentially "nonpolitical" and thus can be best handled administratively. They feel that local politics does not lend itself to a partisan approach.[42] They believe that voters do not need party guidance on the ballot; that the individual should arrive at his political decisions on his own without the mediation of extraneous groups.

The question that comes to mind at this point is whether or not nonpartisanship, where it is operative, has produced a political system significantly different from the dominant partisan system. In some ostensibly nonpartisan cities, the two traditional parties continue in fact to confront one another. Furthermore, the allegations that nonpartisanship increases the role of the middle-class Republicans, depresses lower-class voter turnout and participation in politics, increases the role of the press and powerful interest groups in politics,

---

[39] Robert Lineberry and Edmund P. Fowler, "Reformism and Public Policies in American Cities," *American Political Science Review* 61 (September 1967): 708; and James Q. Wilson and Edward Banfield, *City Politics* (New York: Vintage Press, 1963), pp. 159–61.

[40] Fred Barbaro, "Political Brokers," *Society* 9 (September–October 1972): 45.

[41] See also M. Margaret Conway, "Voter Information Sources in a Nonpartisan Local Election," *Western Political Quarterly* 21 (March 1968): 76.

[42] Eugene Lee, *The Politics of Non-partisanship* (Berkeley: University of California Press, 1960), pp. 28–31.

insulates local politics from the national political scene, is prone to reelecting incumbents, leads to ethnic polarization, and lessens meaningful discussion of policy issues, are allegations that can also be raised regarding the effects of one-party domination of some major American cities and the fragmentation that exists in others. While some differences may exist between partisan and nonpartisan electoral systems, electoral turnout is generally greatest among the middle class, incumbents are usually reelected, racial and ethnic polarization is not unique to or even more likely to occur in nonpartisan cities. Compare, for example, Thomas Bradley's election figures in nonpartisan Los Angeles (1969 and 1973) with Carl Stokes's in partisan Cleveland. At the peak of Stokes's popularity, he received 17 percent of the white vote in "Democratic" Cleveland. In 1969 Bradley received 41 percent of the white vote in nonpartisan Los Angeles.[43] It seems, in fact, that our antiparty two partyism shares many defects associated with nonpartisanship and it is often difficult to differentiate the effects of the two electoral mechanisms.

As suburbia continues to dominate American residential patterns, it is well to recall the words of Robert Wood:

> The existence of comfortable majorities in most suburbs and the growing tendency toward independent voting de-emphasizes parties and more especially dampens the flames of partisan politics.[44]

The no-party politics of suburbia is an extension of the reform movements discussed above: a refusal to recognize the existence of permanent cleavages in the citizenry, a reaction against the excesses of partisanship and patronage, and a distaste for factionalism. According to Wood and others, this kind of nonpartisanship is linked to high voter turnout (in national elections) and issue orientation. In suburbia, the classic mode of direct popular participation unfettered by party ties lives. In part this mode has been operative because of the higher socioeconomic status and independence of many suburban populations. Today suburban populations are socially and economically mixed; but at least in local elections, the tradition of nonpartisanship survives.

THE COMMUNITY REVOLUTION—TOWARD A NEW PARTY SYSTEM?

We have traced the decline, though not disappearance, of machine politics through its reform and nonpartisan antithesis. What, then, is likely to be the

[43] Thomas Pettigrew, "When a Black Candidate Runs for Mayor: Race and Voting Behavior," in H. Hahn, ed., *People and Politics in Urban Society* (Beverly Hills, Calif.: Sage Publications, 1972), pp. 101–2.
[44] Robert Wood, *Suburbia: Its People and Its Politics* (Cambridge, Mass.: Houghton, Mifflin, 1958), p. 152.

future of the political party in urban America? In the past, "the political clubs were the chief modes of communication and control" in the city.[45] Today, to a very considerable extent, this system has broken down and those who seek power and resources must try to develop new mechanisms or revitalize the old. Among ghetto populations neighborhood government and control gained impetus from the War on Poverty. Through block associations, parent organizations, community planning boards, auxiliary police, and the like, larger numbers of the city's poor are being drawn into the political arena. Some of the programs offer the poor limited power over budgets and patronage and could, if nurtured carefully, provide the basis for new party-oriented political organizations. However, numerous barriers remain:

1. The distrust of politicians and parties by the poor who see the "system" and those who join it as traitors and oppressors.

2. Power today no longer resides in the city as it once did. It is increasingly located in the federal government. Revenue sharing may reverse this trend to some degree, but here again the paradox of the poor occurs. Rewards through revenue sharing will accrue to the well organized; the poor are not well organized; in fact, that is precisely their problem.

3. Because of bureaucratization and increased fragmentation of urban politics it would be difficult to gain control of more than one decision-making apparatus at a time. Thus, there are often separate education, welfare, health, and police bureaucracies in American cities and counties, rather than the centralized structure that could be "captured" in the days of the machine. Perhaps the centralized political machine no longer has a raison d'être in our ultraspecialized society.

4. There is as yet no indication that anything more than a cadre of would-be politicos has been created through the new "community system." Many of the newer leaders have been co-opted into city, state, and even federal politics where they can no longer effectively relate as representatives for their poor constituents.

5. Competing groups—churches, party clubs, etc.—within poor communities have not as yet been united by quests for ethnic or racial power.

In *Black Power,* Stokely Carmichael and Charles Hamilton list several things that a viable party would do for black people:

[45] Virginia Held and Daniel Bell, "The Community Revolution," *The Public Interest* (Summer 1969): 146.

a. voter education.
b. voter registration and mobilization.
c. poll watching.
d. patronage—day-to-day, bread and butter help to black people in need.[46]

Frances Piven and Richard Cloward add that "greater black influence . . . depends on strong local organization capable of promoting electoral participation and assuring discipline." [47] These writers and others agree that a new mass-based machine could be relevant to the low-income people who increasingly populate America's urban areas. Whether the "new urban majority"— the poor and the nonwhite—can, or should attempt to resurrect the old style of party organization remains a key question in assessing the future of parties in American politics.[48]

[46] Stokely Carmichael and Charles Hamilton, *Black Power* (New York: Vintage, 1966), pp. 119–20.
    [47] "What Chance for Black Power?" *New Republic* 158 (March 30, 1968): 19–23. See also Alan Altschuler, *Community Control* (New York: Pegasus, 1970).
    [48] Joyce Gelb, "Blacks, Blocs, and Ballots: The Relevance of Party Politics to the Negro," *Polity* 3 (September 1970): 44–69; Marian Palley, et al., "Subcommunity Leadership in a Black Ghetto: A Study of Newark, N.J.," *Urban Affairs Quarterly* (March 1970): 291–312.

8

The State Party Connection

It is evident from our previous discussion that party organization is not central to many aspects of local politics. The next question to consider is the extent to which party plays a substantial role in state politics. A key point to be examined in this chapter is the nature of the state party as a link between local and national parties and politics. In order to develop these themes, a discussion of the Connecticut Democratic party from 1946 to 1970 and California "no-party politics" from 1913 to the present is included. Connecticut's Democratic party during this twenty-five-year period was a very strong, cohesive, and disciplined organization, while in California, antiparty trends have dominated throughout most of the twentieth century. The contrasting of the Connecticut and California party organizations will help clarify the differing roles and functions played by state parties.

PARTY STRUCTURE

Although state party organizations vary in both actual form—set by state law—and in power relationships, there is a general organizational form that seems to be followed by both parties in each of the separate states. State party organizations have a state committee, a state chairman, and often an office staff located at the state capitol. State committee membership is usually determined by party primaries or by state party conventions. Most often membership on state committees is allotted to counties, though there are occasions when other subdivisions in a state will be awarded seats. The party chairman serves at the head of the state committee. The chairman is most frequently selected by an election held by the state committee membership. Sometimes the party gubernatorial candidate dictates the chairman's selection. The state committee's functions include the direction of campaigns and fund raising for the party's statewide candidates. Increasingly, however, as candidates are selected by primaries and open conventions, personal campaign organizations have developed independent of the party's state committee. Still, ward or precinct leaders will often be called upon by candidates to "get out the vote" on Election Day.

The party organizations at different levels are quite independent of each other. State party organizations are not responsive to national party organization—insofar as the latter is operative—and local organizations are not usually responsive to state organizations. The local party chairmen and committee members, selected by the registered party members in a district, cannot be removed from office by the state or national party committees even if they campaign for the candidates of the opposition party. It is at the local and county levels that the only real cohesiveness in party organization exists. "The nation's 3,000 Republican and 3,000 Democratic county chairmen probably constitute the most important building blocks in party organization in America. Yet, each higher level or organization, to accomplish its ends, must obtain the collaboration of the lower layer or layers of organization. That collaboration comes about, to the extent that it does come about, through a sense of common cause rather than by the exercise of command." [1]

Given the limited power of the state party it is not surprising that there have been very few state party "bosses" in recent American history. *But* there have been some and they have used some of the same techniques of dispensing patronage as local political bosses. Generally however there are many self-generating forces and too much organizational incoherence for an elite center to exist in state party politics. This means that authority is not centralized at the state level, nor frequently at any other level of party organization, but rather is scattered haphazardly at various strata of the party structure. [2]

State parties can perhaps be described most accurately as organizational links between local parties, where some actual power resides, and the national party. (See Table 37.)

[1] V. O. Key, *Politics, Parties, and Pressure Groups* (New York: Thomas Y. Crowell, 1964), p. 316.

[2] Samuel Eldersveld, *Political Parties: A Behavioral Analysis* (Chicago: Rand McNally, 1964), p. 527. What Samuel Eldersveld has described as "stratarchy" is a relevant model. The notion of "stratarchy" implies that the party is a structure whose power and influence is diluted through the many layers of party organization.

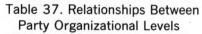

Table 37. Relationships Between
Party Organizational Levels

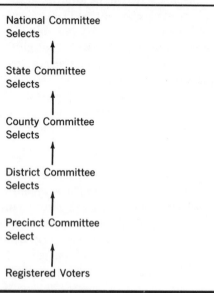

National Committee
Selects

↑

State Committee
Selects

↑

County Committee
Selects

↑

District Committee
Selects

↑

Precinct Committee
Select

↑

Registered Voters

The position of the state party in American politics in many ways reflects the relative position of the states in the national, state, and local political power relationships. In 1934 Charles Merriam made the following observation about the states:

> In many instances the state is a fifth wheel as far as city government is concerned. The state will neither grant autonomy to the cities, nor will it assume the burden of administrative supervision over them. The state will neither rule, nor permit anyone else to rule over the metropolitan regions.[3]

It would be difficult to dispute Merriam's contention of over forty years ago. As the states remain as organizational links, so, too, do the state parties play this role—the latter coming into their own at the national nominating conventions when state delegations attend the convention (though the delegates with the primary system and the open convention system increasingly represent local districts).[4] The role of the state as a weak link in government and the

---

[3] Charles E. Merriam, "The Federal Government Recognizes the Cities," *National Municipal Review* 23 (February 1934): 108.

[4] Democratic National Committee, *Report of the Commission on Delegate Selection and Party Structure* (Washington, D.C.: March 1, 1974), mimeo. The 1974 *Report* of the Democratic party would require that three-quarters of the delegates represent districts no larger than congressional districts.

state party as a weak link in the party system has been brought about by a series of phenomena, the most significant apparently being the unwillingness or inability of state governments to program and fund for urban units. This has been reinforced by a history of malapportionment in state legislatures, which led to rural dominance in state decision making, and more recently (since 1964, and the Supreme Court decision in *Reynolds* v. *Sims*)[5] to the increasing dominance of suburban representatives in state legislative bodies, who like their rural predecessors are not entirely sympathetic to urban problems, especially if redistribution of public resources or increased taxes is involved. As a result the federal government, with its superior resources, has stepped in to aid directly in urban program planning and development. In fiscal year 1972 federal aid to states and localities amounted to over $35 billion, 24.3 percent of all state and local revenues.[6] Yet, as a percentage of local general revenues, state financial assistance increased from 28.4 in 1962 to 32.4 in 1967. In other words, state aid is the source of one of every three local revenue dollars.[7] Thus, the limited role of the state, and by extension the state parties, is not a necessary or permanent condition. States have potential power of great magnitude insofar as they contribute significant funds to local governing units.

A STRONG PARTY MODEL: THE CASE OF CONNECTICUT

Although it is difficult to discuss all of the styles of state party politics in contemporary America within the confines of one chapter, it will be useful nevertheless to consider two contrasting models: the strong Democratic party organization system of Connecticut and the "no-party" system of California. The Connecticut Democratic party in the years following World War II (and until very recently) was perhaps the strongest and most cohesive state political organization in the United States; few other state parties could match its discipline.

In Connecticut, state rules, especially regarding nominations, facilitated strong party organization. There was also strong party competition, ideological agreement within the parties, and a tradition of party strength.[8] The rules helped establish the environment for strengthening the party by a single-minded leader, the Democrat's state chairman, John Bailey.

---

[5] 377 U.S. 533 (1964).

[6] *Statistical Abstract of the United States,* 1973 (Washington, D.C.: Government Printing Office, 1973), p. 289.

[7] Advisory Commission on Intergovernmental Relations, *State Involvement in Federal-Local Grant Programs* (Washington, D.C.: Government Printing Office, 1970), p. 14.

[8] Duane Lockard, "Legislative Politics in Connecticut," *American Political Science Review* 48 (March 1954): 166–73. This discussion relies heavily on Joseph I. Lieberman, *The Power Broker* (Boston: Houghton Mifflin, 1968) and Michael Barone, Grant Ujifusa, and Douglas Matthews, *Almanac of American Politics, 1974* (Boston: Gambit, 1974).

Until the 1970s, both the Democratic and Republican parties were dominated by unusually strong leadership. The leadership of the Democratic party in particular was able to manage its legislative delegations in the state capitol, and was able as well to maintain control of a majority of delegates at state nominating conventions—where major statewide nominees for public office are selected. There were several factors that contributed to the power of the Democratic organization and its leader.

1. All nominations for office were made in convention; Connecticut was a very late comer to the primary system. Prior to the 1930s, the State of Connecticut was Republican dominated. But in the 1930s, the ethnic-identifying members of the working class began to vote and voted primarily for Franklin D. Roosevelt and the Democrats; the businessmen and the Yankee Protestants voted Republican. In 1946, John Bailey became chairman of the state Democratic party. Recognizing the continued need of the Democratic party for ethnic votes, he made a point of fielding ethnically balanced tickets and supporting legislative programs to the liking of ethnic groups. At the same time, he groomed potentially strong candidates—regardless of their ethnic ties—such as Abe Ribicoff for public office. By utilizing this type of candidate selection strategy without the encumbrance of a primary system, the Democrats were able to control the governorship and the resultant patronage from 1954 to 1970.

2. The existence of the straight-ticket lever on the voting machine assisted strong party leadership. Until the 1960s Connecticut voters could activate a voting machine only by voting a straight ticket. After so activating the machine they could, if they so desired, split their tickets. Very few voters, however, bothered to split their tickets. For example in 1956, President Eisenhower, a Republican, carried Connecticut and six Republican congressmen and no Democrats won. In 1958, Abe Ribicoff, a Democrat, was elected governor of Connecticut. This time, six Democrats and no Republicans were elected to Congress.

3. John Bailey made the state chairman's position a full-time job. He divided the state into six regions, moved around, and met with one regional grouping every week. Upon assuming the state chairmanship, Bailey began issuing regular statements on Republican party actions—in both the state legislature and in the state house. He thus was able to put the Republican party on the defensive within just several months of assuming party leadership. In keeping with his decision to make the state chairmanship a full-time job, Bailey met daily with the Democratic State Caucus. In this way, he was able to maintain close and ongoing ties with the legislature via the Democratic lawmakers.

4. Bailey worked well with the big-city bosses and became the "first among equals." They supported him; he consulted with them and gave them each a voice in candidate selection. By working with the city organizations the potential for factionalism within the state party was sharply reduced. "They gave him absolute legislative support, but he gave them patronage and places on the state ticket." [9]

Because John Bailey always remembered his political debts, by 1948 he was able to control a substantial number of delegate votes at the Connecticut State Democratic Convention. Just two years after assuming the state chairmanship, Bailey united the Democrats—who had been split into factions for many years.

5. As far as the selection of policy positions was concerned, Bailey responded to the labor and ethnic groups that provided an essential base for the maintenance of the organization's voting strength by supporting liberal platforms and progressive legislation.

The 1960s, however, saw changes in the rules, and party organizations began to get weaker as the decade wore on. The straight ticket voting lever was eliminated. Also, nominees selected by state conventions could be challenged in primary by any candidate who received at least 20 percent of the convention votes. Still, it was not until 1970 that a Democratic party convention choice was challenged in the primary and defeated in the primary. And, not until 1972 (with the exception of a three-way U.S. Senate race in 1970), did Connecticut voters begin to split their tickets as much as voters in other states. It apparently took time to change political behavior patterns that had been so well established.

By way of summary it can be suggested that a strong Democratic party organization developed in Connecticut because of the interplay of a leader with his environment. The question that remains is whether Connecticut's model can be replicated. Perhaps it can be if a potentially strong leader, who is willing to make the state party chairmanship a full-time job, appears on the scene. An environment with a tradition of reasonably strong party organization, election laws which foster party nomination of candidates (and straight ticket voting), and reasonable issue agreement within the party (especially within the legislative party) can be utilized by a determined leader to unite disparate elements through judicious use of patronage and endorsements. These conditions are no longer all available in Connecticut, and the party organization's control over the state's Democrats has been reduced (though not eliminated entirely). Groups and individuals not included in the party's decision-making process increasingly want to participate. Some younger Democrats also feel that the party leadership needs to be rejuvenated. The results of these feelings

[9] Lieberman, *The Power Broker,* p. 340.

have been manifested by a fall-off of a "solid" Democratic bloc vote in Connecticut in the decade of the seventies. This sentiment was expressed very well by one observer of Connecticut politics who wrote:

> . . . For more than two decades, John M. Bailey has been its unquestioned leader. He became Connecticut Democratic chairman in 1946, and stayed on in that post after 1961 when he was appointed Democratic National Chairman. . . . The Bailey machine is a traditional one in its commitment to organization maintenance more than to substantive programs, in its pragmatism, in its fear of issues, in that it does not see in politics an instrument for social change. . . ." [10]

A WEAK PARTY MODEL: THE CASE OF CALIFORNIA

California parties may best be described as having atrophied in an atmosphere of nonpartisanship and antipartyism. However, while strong party organization in Connecticut has faltered in recent years, California has seen a partial return to two-party politics as party identity and organization have been strengthened somewhat. [11]

California's antiparty tradition is rooted in a variety of sociopolitical conditions:

1. The Progressive movement in California during the years of 1910–20 was able to gain passage of several measures that greatly weakened party organization in the state. Among these were the direct primary and the provision for *cross-filing.* The latter provided that a candidate need not be a registered member of the party in which he sought nomination for office. This provision in particular muted partisanship among voters (as a majority of legislators entered primaries of both major parties and won), destroyed party caucuses, and created a power vacuum into which wealthy special interest groups moved. The end result was to create a special kind of nonpartisanship in state elections. [12] Though cross-filing was abolished in 1954, other state laws governing party organization and activity continue to weaken political parties in California. These laws prevent parties from endorsing candidates prior to primaries, maintain a comprehensive merit system, and provide for the detailed regulation of party organization by state law which creates an unadapta-

---

[10] Everett Carll Ladd, Jr., *Ideology in America* (Ithaca, N.Y.: Cornell University Press, 1969), p. 130.

[11] This discussion relies heavily upon Bernard L. Hyink, Seyom Brown, and Ernest W. Thacker, *Politics and Government in California,* 8th ed. (New York: Thomas Y. Crowell, 1973), and Joseph P. Harris, *California Politics,* 4th ed. (San Francisco: Chandler, 1967).

[12] In the early 1940s, 80 percent of the assembly seats and 90 percent in the state senate were won by cross-filing. Winston W. Crouch, John C. Bollens, Stanley Scott, *California Government and Politics,* 5th ed. (Englewood Cliffs, N.J.: Prentice-Hall, 1972), p. 63.

ble, inflexible structure. State and county party committees have little power and cannot enforce discipline due to lack of patronage and leadership.

2. In California, all municipal elections are held on a nonpartisan basis (as are county and selected judicial elections). One effect of the removal of local politics from the partisan arena has been to inhibit the formation of strong grass-roots precinct organizations that can nominate and campaign for candidates.

3. A further factor preventing the development of cohesive party organization has been the heterogeneity of regions in this diverse state. From the northern liberal Bay area surrounding San Francisco to the southern California conservative aerospace sunbelt to the interior agricultural plateau, the diversity of cultures and political ideologies makes one inclusive party organization difficult to maintain.

4. Additional problems for parties in California include the apparently large number of independent voters who have for a long time practiced split ticket voting. Although the Democrats have had a substantial lead in party registration in the state since 1934, such registration has for the most part been a result of habit and not necessarily party loyalty reflected in voting (apparently many migrants to California brought their Democratic party affiliation with them). Also, voting a straight ticket is prevented by the Office Block Ballot in California. The consequences of these conditions have been to create an environment in which candidates tend to mute party appeals and run virtually nonpartisan, candidate centered campaigns. It is no accident that California, an early precursor of so many antiparty trends, was the first state in which the extensive use of public relations firms and the "new political technology" was utilized as a substitute for party centered campaigns. (See Chapters 3 and 4 for a further discussion of these trends.)

Since the late 1950s *some* of the worst abuses of antipartyism have been modified in California. Unofficial party organizations, particularly the California Democratic Council (CDC), have created a network of local clubs that were coordinated into a statewide party organization.[13] This group endorses candidates before the primary and provides many traditional campaign services. In addition, the legislature has become more partisan since the elimination of cross-filing. This trend was reinforced when the Democrats took over the state administration for the first time in many years in 1959. At that time

[13] The Republicans have had such a group, the California Republican Assembly, since 1932, though it has lost much of its former influence in recent years. See Harris, *California Politics,* pp. 49–53.

party caucuses and whips—long defunct—were revived, although they remain more active among Democrats than Republicans. Party activity in both houses of the state legislature remained strong under the overtly partisan Republican administration of Governor Reagan (1965–1973).

The California experience, like that in Connecticut, illustrates the relevance of political culture and state electoral laws to the development of party organization in a given state.

Many states fall somewhere between the strong party structure described in Connecticut and the loose or even nonexistent party organization characteristic of California. Let us examine some of the specific functions played by state parties in the electoral and governmental process, in order more clearly to evaluate party influence and cohesion.

STATE AND LOCAL PARTIES IN THE ELECTION PROCESS

CANDIDATE DESIGNATION

Traditionally, local party organizations have played a dominant role in the nomination of candidates as well as in the selection of delegates to national party conventions. Parties have also played a major role in the mobilization of voters through door-to-door canvassing, distribution of campaign literature, voter registration drives and rallies.

As the Connecticut and California party systems remind us, in the United States, state electoral laws prescribe organizational and party positions and who may hold them. The advent of the *direct primary* in virtually every American state, permitting popular election to determine party candidates, has without doubt reduced the ability of the party to control its nominees. Primaries are used for a variety of purposes in addition to delegate selection for state and national nominating conventions.[14] Political parties nominate state and local candidates for public office and select state and local party leadership through primaries. Primaries come in several different forms (see Table 38). There are *closed* primaries (only registered party members may vote) and *open* primaries (voters may choose the party primary in which they wish to vote). In the latter case, results are obviously far more difficult to control. Voters may "raid" another party's primary in order to select a weak candidate, only to desert him on Election Day as they support their real favorite; or, they may cross their traditional party lines because of sincere interest in the other party's candidate or because the other party is having a particularly interesting race.

[14] For a more complete discussion of delegate primary elections see Chapter 11.

Table 38. Types of Primaries

OPEN PRIMARY

A system wherein the voter decides in which party primary to vote in the privacy of the voting booth. No declaration of party loyalty is required.

CLOSED PRIMARY

A system wherein the voter declares party affiliation prior to the primary election. Only voters affiliated (or registered) with a party may vote in its primary.

MIXED OR "BLANKET" PRIMARY

A system wherein the voter not only does not have to disclose his party affiliation, but in which he may vote in the primary of more than one party—i.e., one nomination in one party, one in another party if he so chooses. (Used in Washington and Alaska.)

NONPARTISAN PRIMARY

A system to reduce the number of candidates running for an elected position to either one person who receives over 50 percent of the vote, or if this does not occur, to two candidates who receive the highest vote in the nonpartisan primary. If no one receives a majority of the votes, the two top candidates will be involved in a run-off election to determine the victor.

In the state of Washington in 1970, for example, thousands of Republicans voted in the Democratic primary to support Senator Henry Jackson and most of these stayed with him in the November general elections. In some states, primaries are preceded by conventions with the convention delegates selected by the voters. The losers in the convention—in some states—can gain a place on the primary ballot by obtaining a certain number of petition signatures throughout the city, county, or state, gaining some percentage of votes at the convention, or by filing a specified fee. Thus, as noted above, in Connecticut a candidate who receives 20 percent of the convention delegate votes can demand a postconvention primary, whereas in Delaware, a candidate who receives 35 percent of the convention delegate votes can demand a primary.[15]

Some states are even more flexible regarding party loyalty than the states which use the open primary system. Voters may cross back and forth from party to party and office to office in the blanket primary, while under the cross-filing system (used until 1954 in California as related above) the same candidate may enter the primary of more than one party. An additional use of the primary has evolved in those cities and states that are nonpartisan and hold primaries without party labels; if no one receives a majority of the votes,

[15] *The Book of the States, 1972–1973* 29 (Lexington, Ky.: The Council of State Governments, 1972), p. 29.

the two top winners participate in a run-off election.[16] These primary forms are progressively more destructive of party leadership and control.

THE PRIMARY'S INFLUENCE ON PARTY CONTROL OVER NOMINATIONS

A number of conditions can result and have resulted from the use of primaries to select nominees to run for state and local, as well as party positions. Let us now consider eight possible results of this process.

1. A losing ticket may be chosen. Deals to insure geographically and ethnically balanced tickets are no longer possible when voters choose candidates in primary elections. In the first seven decades of the twentieth century, prior to the advent of primary elections in New York State, the Democratic ticket was always a balance of ethnic groups. There would be a Jew, an Italian, an Irishman, and a WASP on the ticket. Also, upstate as well as downstate (New York City and its suburbs) would be represented on the ticket. The primary changed all of this. In 1970 when the New York Democrats had to field a slate of candidates for governor, lieutenant governor, U.S. senator, attorney general, and comptroller, the ticket, chosen via primary, had four Jews and one black. They were swamped at the polls on Election Day—and while a causal relationship between the unbalanced ticket and electoral loss cannot be proven—party leaders saw a clear link.

2. Voters may choose a familiar name or vote for other seemingly irrational reasons when confronted by the absence of party labels. For example, voters in a 133 candidate primary in 1969 in California, for the Junior College Board of Trustees, gave their highest number of votes by far to Edmund Brown, Jr., son of the former governor of the state, whose name alone explains his phenomenal success (186,000 votes to the second place winner's 135,000).[17]

3. Only a small percentage of the potential electorate turns out to vote on primary day—meaning that a small, well-organized group (a special interest or party group), which may be unrepresentative of the party as a whole, can dominate the nomination process. A turnout of one-third of the voters registered in parties is considered average for most primaries.[18] The exception to this condition occurs when the only contest for a position actually takes place in the primary. Traditionally in some southern states, where the only meaningful competition for office was in the Democratic party primary, the voter

---

[16] A more complete discussion of nonpartisan elections and primaries is included in Chapter 7.

[17] John A. Mueller, "Choosing among 133 Candidates," *Public Opinion Quarterly* 34 (Fall 1970): 398–99.

[18] Jerry Freidheim, *Where Are the Voters?* (Washington, D.C.: National Press, 1968), p. 46.

turnout for the primary was relatively high—higher in fact than for the general election, which was either uncontested or where there was no real chance of Republican victory.[19]

4. Many candidates may enter the primary, particularly in the dominant party, causing voter confusion and the possibility of a minority candidate with only a small percentage of the vote gaining the nomination. To counter this problem, some states, New York among them, now hold a run-off election if no one receives more than 40 percent of the vote in the first primary to insure that a candidate will be nominated who will have substantial voter support.

5. Candidates who are wealthy may have a great advantage in primaries and some play increasingly significant roles in primary contests. This to some extent contrasts with the old time convention system where numbers of delegates—rather than numbers of dollars—were significant. Pollsters, media, and public relations specialists are for hire by the wealthy and have assumed an increasingly important strategic role, particularly in statewide (as opposed to local precinct and legislative) campaigns. It has been estimated, for example, that total primary election expenses for governor and lieutenant governor in all the states in 1970 totaled almost $25 million.[20]

6. Primaries do permit insurgent candidates who could not win organizational support under other circumstances to gain victory and often do provide a contest between recognizable factions (for example the contests between "reformers" and "regulars" in New York City, Massachusetts, and elsewhere). It is in this manner that they can provide for an orderly process of personnel change within an "open" party organization.

7. It would be inaccurate to assume that insurgents always win primaries and that incumbents have difficulty gaining nomination and election. As in other elections, primaries often produce victory for incumbents. Incumbents most often win because they have organization and political experience—two "commodities" insurgents often lack in their antiorganization drives. To put it in other words, the regulars know who the voters are, who will actually vote, and they know how to get out the vote. Also, they have the support services to get their votes out on Election Day to support the "right" candidates.

8. In many areas, county and state organizations along with their leadership have, as a result of primaries, lost significant power. Also, since they are less

[19] Austin Ranney, "Parties in State Politics," in Herbert Jacob and Kenneth Vines, eds., *Politics in the American States*, 2d ed. (Boston: Little, Brown, 1971), p. 97.
[20] Herbert E. Alexander, *Money in Politics* (Washington, D.C.: Public Affairs Press, 1972), p. 28.

able to use patronage as a device to insure loyalty and discipline—due to the demands of technology and the expansion of the civil service—increasingly in many areas leaders preside over "an unstable conglomerate of conflicting factions." [21] Primaries tend to exacerbate intraparty factionalism and disunity if such conflicts are already present. It is difficult to escape V. O. Key's judgment that "the direct primary has made possible a popular government of sorts—but not innovation in the organization of political leadership superior to a well-ordered party system as an instrument of popular government." [22] Where vigorously contested primaries occur, often parties remain important to candidates' electoral chances primarily as *labels* with which to identify since they have affective value for voters, as well as acting as the *agencies* through which designation is achieved.

None of the above discussion is intended to leave the reader with the impression that the party organization has been destroyed as a political unit in the nominating process in American states and localities. Clearly one can find cases where party pros have adapted to the primary and have put up regular organization slates which have emerged victorious. Perhaps it would be more accurate to suggest that local and state organizations have been opened up by the primary and open convention systems to would-be participants in party politics. Increasingly it is becoming more difficult for one man, the boss, to count on complete control indefinitely. Vice-President Rockefeller, as governor of New York State (1958–73), however, was able to use the power of his office, personality, and wealth to make the New York State Republican party an extension of himself. Rockefeller was able to obtain the nomination of candidates who were opposed by other prominent party members. He made use of patronage; in over fifty of the sixty-two counties in the state, county Republican leaders were in some kind of state-related (payroll) position. Financial support, along with excellent local political relations cemented by frequent personal contacts, were to a considerable extent the secret of Rockefeller's success. As noted earlier, for many years Connecticut Democratic state party chairman, John M. Bailey, was similarly able to persuade reluctant party leaders to back the candidate of his choice. It has, in other words, sometimes been possible to absorb the direct primary into the party.

However, the decline (though not demise) of patronage, development of independent personality oriented power bases, and the presence of primary challenges make such control more difficult to achieve. The observation of one political scientist who called the state party a "hollow shell" has become more realistic than ever before in our history.[23]

[21] See *New York Times,* February 23, 1970, p. 20.
[22] V. O. Key, *American State Politics* (New York: Knopf, 1956), p. 130.
[23] Herbert Jacob, "Dimensions of State Politics," in Alexander Heard, ed., *State Legislatures in American Politics* (Englewood Cliffs, N.J.: Prentice-Hall, 1966), p. 22.

In terms of financial support, local and state parties are also limited in influence. While state and local party organizations raise money largely from "political dinners," candidates often raise their own money for political office (subject to state laws and their circumvention) [24] from friends, relations, special interest groups, and the like. In a system of political finance in which political committees per candidate proliferate because of the decentralizing impact of state electoral laws, while party organization may supply some aid to candidates in marginal or "swing" districts, the bulk of campaign finance tends to emanate from other sources. However, the ultimate vote-getting activities are still often accomplished most effectively and efficiently by local ward or precinct organization workers.

Party organizations may operate most effectively in the electoral process as *interest groups* in state and municipal legislatures, seeking to ensure their party's continuity or assumption of power by affecting registration and election laws and overseeing apportionment of districts through such tactics as gerrymandering (drawing district lines to maximize partisan advantage). This can be done despite the Supreme Court's decision in *Baker* v. *Carr*,[25] which required state legislative apportionment on the basis of the distribution of population, following the notion of "one man, one vote." Four years after the court's decision every state had reapportioned its legislature on the basis of population distribution or was under judicial order to do so.[26] But, despite reapportionment guidelines, calling for "community, contiguity, and compactness," the majority party in the state legislature can normally draw district lines to favor its interests and candidates. Thus, in 1971, the Republican dominated Illinois state legislature chose to eliminate Congressman Abner Mikva's district, forcing him to choose to contest another Democrat, Ralph Metcalfe, in a predominantly black district, or to contest a seat in a Republican suburban district. Mikva, a liberal Democrat, chose the latter option, and he lost—which was apparently the intent of the Republican state legislators in Springfield who drew up the suburban district in an effort to ensure Republican victory.[27]

The thrust of the argument presented here has been that key aspects of elections—both candidate recruitment and fund raising—are increasingly related to factors in addition to party organization. Though party organization may be advantageous for developing voter registration drives and for "bringing

---

[24] Many candidates tend to avoid state electoral laws regulating contributions to political campaigns by establishing "political committees" in Washington, D.C., which has no such restrictions.

[25] 369 U.S. 186 (1962).

[26] Malcolm E. Jewell, "The Changing Political Environment of State Government," in Lee S. Greene, Malcolm E. Jewell, and Daniel R. Grant, eds., *The States and the Metropolis* (University, Ala.: University of Alabama Press, 1968), p. 37.

[27] *Congressional Quarterly Weekly Report* 29 (October 23, 1971): 2180–82; and *Congressional Quarterly Weekly Report* 30 (July 8, 1972): 1661.

out the vote" on Election Day, as more and more nonregulars are nominated by the party membership to run for party office, parallel groups develop to run campaigns. If these groups are successful in winning elections, then the victorious candidates feel no responsibility to the party whose label they carry. Thus, there are strands of *antipartyism* currently surfacing in state and local politics. This kind of antipartyism is not necessarily opposed to political parties as such. Rather, it is opposed to the kind of party organization sustained for over twenty years by John Bailey in Connecticut, which limits access to the political process to those people who are willing to "wait their turn" and follow the "rules of the game" as set down by the organization. Perhaps Daniel P. Moynihan, writing in the early years of the current reform movement, gave us the best representation of this phenomenon:

> At the moment no one characteristic divides the "regular" party men in New York from the "reform" group more than the matter of taking pride in following the chain of command. The "reform" group is composed principally of educated, middle-class career people quite hardened to the struggle for advancement in their professions. Waiting in line to see one's leader seems to such persons slavish and unmanly, the kind of conduct that could only be imposed by a boss. By contrast the "organization" regulars regard it as proper and well-behaved conduct.[28]

THE PARTY AND POLICY MAKING

It has already been suggested that several factors impair the ability of parties to exercise a key role in the policymaking process. Party is only one of the forces to which a representative must be responsible; he owes equal if not greater loyalty to local elements in his constituency, to special interest groups, and to his financial supporters. Party responsibility is particularly limited at the municipal level because of the decline in visible patronage with which to reward the faithful (due to the merit system), and the advent of such antiparty reforms as nonpartisanship, city managers, weak mayor systems, and commission forms of government. Power in the states as well as in the urban areas has become increasingly fragmented, and special interests, together with multiple bureaucracies, now hold the lion's share of municipal and state policymaking power. Hence, parties are only one set of actors in an increasingly competitive political arena.

---

[28] Daniel P. Moynihan, "When the Irish Ran New York," *The Reporter* 24 (June 8, 1961): 32.

THE PARTY AND LEGISLATIVE POLITICS

Some political scientists believe that "in many states, the influence of the party is far greater than in Congress." [29] A party that can influence public policy formulation depends on identifiable and continuous leadership, and leadership control of political advancement and party finances. Connecticut's parties—especially the Democrats under John Bailey—prior to the 1970s had this type of system. It is not clear that these conditions exist in many other of our fifty states—in California even skeletal party organizations did not exist in the legislature until 1959. In analyzing this model of strong party leadership, two factors must be considered:

1. Strong parties tend to exist mostly in the urbanized Northeast and become less and less likely as one moves westward where there is a more pervasive antiparty spirit. Thus, party legislative cohesiveness tends to be higher in New York, Pennsylvania, Rhode Island, Connecticut, and Massachusetts than it is in the United States Congress. It tends to be about the same as Congress in Ohio, Illinois, New Hampshire, and Washington, and lower than that of Congress in Colorado, Missouri, and California. [30]

2. Party cohesion is limited by the separation of powers in the states. This separation has been exacerbated by malapportionment of state legislative districts. Thus, as a result of the 1972 elections, governors in twenty-three states were confronted with either one or both houses of the state legislature dominated by the opposition party. [31] Such "split government" virtually guarantees the absence of cohesive party power. Also, party government is limited by the fact that the governor and his chief administrative assistants (attorney general, secretary of state, et al.), are often elected separately. In only fifteen states are the lieutenant governors and governors elected together as a team. This often creates a contest for power and prestige among the governor and his divided executive, each official attempting to gain his own support, further reducing the possibility of achieving cohesive party power. In some states the governor, like most big city mayors, also confronts powerful and virtually independent state bureaucracies and special regulatory agencies. Many of the states have civil service systems. The merit requirements established by the federal government as a condition of eligibility for receipt of federal grant-in-aid monies have

---

[29] Duane Lockard, *The Politics of State and Local Government* (New York: Macmillan, 1963), p. 281.

[30] Karl Bosworth and James W. Fesler, "Legislators and Governors," in James W. Fesler, ed., *The Fifty States* (New York: Knopf, 1967), p. 289.

[31] "State Legislatures: Democratic Net Gain of Two," *Congressional Quarterly Almanac, 1972,* p. 1071.

produced civil service activity in some states as well as a proliferation of bureaucracies. Hence, the tradition regarding parties and the constitutional system of the state must be examined in order to indicate where party influence is even possible.

In viewing the party as a reference group in the legislative process, it is well to remember that in some instances party voting is rare, in some frequent, in some completely absent.[32] Where legislative control exists, it may reside with the governor, the party's legislative leadership (minority and majority leaders), or a faction. Because legislative party leaders (including the speaker of the lower house) usually are empowered to assign members and bills to committees and to select committee chairmen, they may exercise considerable influence over their colleagues. Many state legislatures have committee systems and seniority systems that resemble closely the national congressional system.[33]

THE GOVERNOR AS LEGISLATIVE LEADER

The governor may assume a key policymaking role if his party has a *majority* of seats in the legislature, but not an *excess* of seats. Legislators are particularly responsive to a governor's programs and policies when all are running for elective office, the prospect of electoral success apparently providing an incentive for party support of a chief executive. Governors may on occasion operate as strong party leaders, as the examples of G. Mennen Williams, who built a vital Democratic organization in Michigan, and Nelson Rockefeller, former governor of New York, indicate. Where such gubernatorial leadership exists, it is usually due to a skillful use of patronage. Perhaps the absence of unified state party organization can be attributed to inefficient use of the patronage that still exists; one observer in Illinois found that "the distribution of state patronage was little related to attempts to build electoral strength," rather it acted more as an employment agency with little regard for the needs of party organization.[34]

Governors are often weakened when there is a constitutional limit on the length of time they can serve. Thus, the governors of nine states can serve for

---

[32] Malcolm E. Jewell and Samuel Patterson, *The Legislative Process in the United States* (New York: Random House, 1966), p. 418.

[33] See Chapter 13 for a discussion of congressional structure. In California, however, neither committee chairmen nor committee majorities are selected on a partisan basis.

[34] Joseph Tucker, "The Administration of a State Patronage System: The Democratic Party in Illinois," *Western Political Quarterly* 22 (November 1969): 79–84; Frank Sorauf, "State Patronage in a Rural County," *American Political Science Review* 50 (December 1956): 1048–50; and Alan Wyner, "Staffing the Governor's Office," in Thad Beyle and J. Oliver Williams, eds., *The American Governor in Behavioral Perspective* (New York: Harper and Row, 1972), pp. 118–25.

just one term and the governors of nineteen states can serve for but two consecutive terms. Leadership can be further weakened by limitations on legislative veto power (eleven governors have no item veto and the governor of North Carolina has no veto), as well as by the "encumbrances" of separation of powers often reinforced by strict constitutional limitations on their executive powers. There are states where none of the above conditions prevail but where political divisions have weakened the governors. A prime example of the latter situation has been Massachusetts. Where political divisions exist the legislators usually owe little in the way of thanks for their office to the governor (incumbent legislators are often reelected because of name familiarity) and the governor in turn often needs the support of opposition party members in order to gain passage of his legislation. Both of these factors tend to dilute party loyalty significantly.[35]

THE LEGISLATIVE PARTY AS A LEGISLATIVE POWER

In some states, the legislative party itself operates as a political unit. In Connecticut, for example, for many years a party caucus met daily, at which the members debated and voted on bills. This vote was binding on all party members. Where caucuses are successful they usually communicate a party position to legislators and seek to insure conformity to it through patronage, the promise of local "pet" projects, choice committee assignments, and support for individual bills, if the mechanism for securing such rewards exists. The caucus can be a powerful instrument only when other ingredients of party unity are present. In the mid-1960s there were only thirteen states in which majority party caucuses met regularly.[36] There are elements of party responsibility present in some state legislatures, although not with any degree of regularity or consistency. Where a high degree of party cohesion does exist within a state legislature, three basic factors are likely to be present.

1. Close interparty competition will be likely to exist within the state. This means that the lowest degree of legislative party cohesion would be expected in states dominated by one party. As noted above, New York, Pennsylvania, Rhode Island, Connecticut, and Massachusetts have had the highest legislative cohesion. They also are two-party competitive states (see Table 39). In sixteen states, there has been one-party control of the governorship for the decade 1960–70; in twenty-five states only one partisan change during this time.[37]

---

[35] This question is discussed in Ranney, "Parties in State Politics," pp. 107–17.
[36] Ibid., p. 87.
[37] Richard M. Scammon, *America Votes,* Volumes 4–9 (Washington, D.C.: Governmental Affairs Institute, 1960, 1962, 1964, 1966, 1968, 1970).

Table 39. Party Competition and Income

States	Party Competition Ranking 1956 to 1970	Per Capita Income Ranking
1. Connecticut	TP	$5,032
2. New York	TP	5,021
3. Nevada	TP	4,895
4. New Jersey	TP	4,832
5. Hawaii	TP	4,797
6. Illinois	TP	4,772
7. Alaska	TP	4,749
8. California	TP	4,677
9. Massachusetts	TP	4,586
10. Delaware	TP	4,570
11. Maryland	MOP-D	4,514
12. Michigan	TP	4,317
13. Ohio	TP	4,154
14. Washington	TP	4,135
15. Pennsylvania	TP	4,127
16. Kansas	MOP-R	4,090
17. Rhode Island	TP	4,077
18. Colorado	TP	4,057
19. Nebraska	TP	3,998
20. Minnesota	TP	3,974
21. Indiana	TP	3,973
22. Oregon	TP	3,920
23. Wisconsin	TP	3,880
24. Missouri	TP	3,877
25. Iowa	MOP-D	3,876
26. Arizona	TP	3,871
27. Virginia	MOP-D	3,866
28. Florida	MOP-D	3,848
29. Wyoming	TP	3,753
30. New Hampshire	MOP-R	3,708
31. Texas	OPD	3,682
32. Vermont	MOP-R	3,610
33. Georgia	OPD	3,547
34. Oklahoma	MOP-D	3,506
35. Montana	TP	3,479
36. South Dakota	MOP-R	3,446
37. Maine	TP	3,419
38. Idaho	TP	3,402
39. Utah	TP	3,395
40. New Mexico	MOP-D	3,394
41. North Carolina	MOP-D	3,387
42. North Dakota	MOP-R	3,383
43. Tennessee	MOP-D	3,325
44. Kentucky	MOP-D	3,288

States	Party Competition Ranking 1956 to 1970	Per Capita Income Ranking
45. Louisiana	OPD	3,248
46. West Virginia	MOP-D	3,228
47. South Carolina	OPD	3,162
48. Alabama	OPD	3,050
49. Arkansas	OPD	3,036
50. Mississippi	OPD *	2,766

* The fourfold classification was used by Ranney, "Parties in State Politics," p. 87.
KEY:
   TP = Two Party   MOP-D = Modified One Party Democratic
   OPD = One Party Democratic   MOP-R = Modified One Party Republican
SOURCE: Per capita income rankings are listed in U.S. Bureau of the Census, *Statistical Abstract of the United States,* 1972, p. 319.

Hence, in a large number of states, a meaningful two-party structure exists only fitfully.

Two-party states tend to be urbanized, have a high median income, have a large percentage of the work force in manufacturing jobs, and have a sizable immigrant population. The relationship between party competitiveness and income is very clear, with little deviation from the high income-high competitiveness, low income-low competitiveness model (see Table 39).

In numerous states the minority party has apparently been revitalized due to reapportionment (*Baker* v. *Carr* and *Reynolds* v. *Sims*) and may produce greater party competition and cohesion in the future.[38]

2. Similarity among districts represented by legislators from the same party tends to produce a significant degree of voting cohesion. Districts whose incomes and degree of urbanization are relatively homogeneous tend to produce legislators who view policy questions alike. In New York, Illinois, Pennsylvania, and other large industrial states with a definable upstate/rural-downstate/metropolitan character, party and legislative polarization tends to occur around these lines. In such states, party cohesion is likely to exist on taxation,

[38] Studies have demonstrated that party members who are least secure, i.e., have won by the lowest plurality of votes, are least loyal to the party. Apparently, such relatively "unsafe" legislators feel that they need to be more responsive to constituency pressures to gain reelection. Thomas A. Flinn, "Party Responsibility in the States: Some Causal Factors," *American Political Science Review* 58 (March 1964): 64–67.

education, welfare, business, and labor; those issues most reflecting the socio-economic status of groups allied with each party.[39]

3. Often, when parties do play a major role in organizing legislative voting, their influence may be felt on technical and trivial matters, and matters that are crucial to the party as an interest group. If no cohesion exists on organizational or structural votes (such as election of the speaker) then there is none at all to be found. Ideology seems to be the *least* important factor in determining party legislative cohesion. Only in states like Connecticut, where recalcitrants have been disciplined (through denial of patronage, promotion, etc.), where the party has controlled the nominating process (Connecticut, as noted elsewhere, was among the last states to adopt the direct primary), and where a party policy has been articulated in the legislature and campaign, has there been significant cohesion both on party-related and policy issues.[40] Rhode Island and Pennsylvania have in the past provided other examples of such cohesion.

Often, however, if party regularity exists, it exists because of custom and habit, not discipline. In addition, key elements of party responsibility are absent even where parties do have legislative influence because "legislative discipline doesn't expound or support a program in advance to the voters." [41] Even in Pennsylvania where there were reasonably strong "parties" in the early 1960s, nonparty, independent views of legislative behavior prevailed among legislators. The legislators only reluctantly acknowledged the party's role in their voting behavior. This is not to say that there is no relationship between party affiliation and policy. One study found that civil rights policy tends to be more liberal when the Democratic party is in legislative control.[42] An analysis of voting in New York revealed that "parties frequently structure legislative voting in such a way that the legislator responds to the party

[39] Thomas Dye, "State Legislative Politics," in Jacob and Vines, eds., *Politics in the American States*, p. 186. However, at least one study of a state with such an urban-rural mix indicated the contrary. In a study of the Delaware House of Representatives during the legislative sessions that took place from 1965 to 1970, it was found that on welfare and social issues, civil liberties and housing, and urban assistance, the suburban-nonmetropolitan alliance was a more salient influence on voting behavior than party identification. John S. Isaacs II, "An Analysis of Voting Behavior in the Delaware House of Representatives 1965–1970," Master's Thesis, University of Delaware, 1971, p. viii.

[40] Lockard, "Legislative Politics in Connecticut," pp. 166–73; also for a more current commentary on Connecticut state politics see Murray S. Steadman, Jr., "Connecticut: The Politics of Urbanization," in George R. Goodwin, Jr., and Victoria Schuck, eds., *Party Politics in New England States* (Durham, N.H.: The New England Center for Continuing Education, n.d.), p. 15.

[41] Frank Sorauf, *Party and Representation* (New York: Atherton Press, 1963), p. 146.

[42] Robert Erikson, "The Relationship between Party Control and Civil Rights Legislation in the American States," *Western Political Quarterly* 24 (March 1971): 180.

position rather than to a well reasoned judgment of his own." [43] Each party in New York operated as a definable bloc: Republicans were opposed to the use of state power and reluctant to approve state programs that would benefit urban areas, while Democrats showed greater liberalism on personal rights questions. This situation may not be caused as much by partisan loyalty as it is affected by the similarities in the constituencies of members of the same party and the policy predispositions of the lawmakers of the same party. Hence, one can argue that a limited linkage exists between party and the performance of elected officials.

FUTURE PROSPECTS

Nonetheless, linkages between parties at the various levels of political organization are essentially missing. "A great gulf yawns in Pennsylvania—and in most other states—between the local constituency parties and the (state) legislative party." [44] Even in states with some party cohesion, there is little to command collaboration between different layers; and in some states, such as California, the structure of statewide parties is very weak.[45] While there is some evidence of professionalization of the state party organization (for example, the Minnesota Democratic Farmer Labor party provided a comprehensive reelection plan combining research, data, and funding for 117 state legislative candidates as of 1968),[46] and some analysts profess to find revitalization of parties even at the *county* level, state and local parties remain isolated from national party politics. The states have remained prominent in national nominating conventions and the electoral college. But the day-to-day relationship between local, state, and national parties remains at best a tenuous one, primarily because the latter two levels exist only fitfully between elections.

Because a significant number of Americans regard political parties with either skepticism or antipathy, it seems unlikely that there will be a rebirth

[43] Wayne Swanson, Elmer Cornwell, Jay Goodman, "Voting in a Non-Partisan Legislative Setting," *Western Political Quarterly* 25 (March 1972): 48. Other studies have demonstrated that party is an important reference group for judges who rely on party for election and tenure on the bench; and conversely, that party is less significant on the bench where elections are bipartisan. David Adamany, "The Party Variable in Judge's Voting: Conceptual Notes and a Case Study," *American Political Science Review* 63 (March 1969): 69.

[44] Sorauf, *Party and Representation*, p. 146.

[45] One should note that there are about 500 counties in the country where there is no Democratic party organization. This phenomenon occurs most often where there are few Democrats. Similarly, Republicans do not organize in some southern counties.

[46] John Saloma and Frederick Sonntag, *Parties* (New York: Knopf, 1972), pp. 168–69. See also the ranking of state legislatures on "functionalism"—staff, facilities, organizational structure, coordination, and continuity—in John Burns, *The Sometime Governments: A Critical Study of the 50 State Legislatures* (New York: Bantam Books, for the Citizens Conference on State Legislatures, 1971), pp. 48–49.

of the John Bailey of Connecticut model of strong state parties. Bailey was able to fashion a strong party organization in Connecticut in part out of a set of prevailing circumstances. Many of these circumstances—such as the absence of primary elections, straight party balloting, issue division between the two major parties—no longer exist in Connecticut. Bailey's control is faltering as more and more people question the right of a few to make decisions for the many within the party, and as Connecticut's middle-class voters behave as middle-class voters do elsewhere: that is, splitting their tickets and increasingly registering as independents. In California, antiparty trends facilitated by electoral laws and popular attitudes have long prevailed. The no-party system that has dominated California politics may serve as a model for similar trends in other states, for it seems unlikely that conditions will permit a strong state leader such as Bailey to counter the increasing antipartyism of America.

Introduction
to Chapters 9,
10, and 11

National parties in the United States perform limited roles as policy makers, leaders, and unifiers. Constitutional factors and popular attitudes opposed to centralized power have prevented the creation and development of strong parties modeled after those in Great Britain and elsewhere.

These truisms of American politics will not be disputed in the pages that follow. The organization of the party will be considered, not to find hidden sources of power, but rather to improve our understanding of how people are selected to run for public office by the two major parties. Since state and local organization have been examined in Chapters 7 and 8 we will concentrate here on the national political party organization. Once the organization per se has been discussed we will look at the major role of the national parties—nominations (and to a lesser extent) elections of people to public office. In this context the primaries and the convention system will be examined, along with the costs of contemporary campaigning, and some of the alternatives that have been proposed to democratize our electoral process. The latter will be considered in the light of the increased costs that have come about due to increased use of technology in campaigns and as responses to demands for increased participation in the campaign process.

9
The Party as Organization

THE TRANSITORY CONDITION OF NATIONAL PARTY ORGANIZATION

Although we are going to discuss the organization of the national political parties in the United States in this section the organizational framework tells us very little about the relative power and position of the actors in the party system. It does show us, however, that power does not flow downward and suggests that for most purposes different levels of party organization do not have formal influence on other levels. Exceptions most often relate to idiosyncratic relationships among individuals. This is the case because the national parties have little power vested in them and possess no real authority over state and local party organizations or elected officials. To posit any long-term political authority in them would be an exercise in myth building. E. P. Herring noted that, "In the federal sphere, our political parties are temporary alliances of local leaders held together by the hope of winning the Presidency." [1] As a consequence, the national Republican party and the national Democratic party—though always maintaining office staffs and national leaders—have traditionally been little more than paper organizations during the years between presidential campaigns.

[1] Pendleton Herring, *The Politics of Democracy: American Parties in Action* (New York: Rinehart and Company, 1940), p. 121.

THE ROLE OF NATIONAL COMMITTEE CHAIRMEN AND STAFF

If we look at the relationships drawn in Figure 1 it becomes clear that the national party organizations are simply structures comprised of committee-men and women from the separate states of the nation, although they are officially elected at one national convention to serve until the next national election. They are selected in fact by their state parties sometimes in primaries, sometimes at state conventions, and can be replaced by their state parties. They have few responsibilities in their national committee posts. Theoretically, the responsibilities of national committeemen and committeewomen include:

> assisting in fund raising for the party
> representing the national party in their states
> assisting in the presidential and vice-presidential campaign in their states
> coordinating the distribution of campaign (paraphernalia) in their states
> serving as "sources of intelligence for the fieldmen sent out by the national committee" in some states, advancing the cause of particular candidates.[2]

Party power clearly resides in the states and especially in the local party organizations. It is here where the process begins—selecting candidates—and it is here that the process ends—working on Election Day to get out the vote. While in theory national committee members frame party policy, in practice their role is far more limited. National committees operate neither as effective links to the voters, state politicians, nor Congress. Often they fail to communicate information to their party constituents; also, they are not in a position to convey citizen concerns to national decision makers.

Perhaps the most important responsibility of the national committee is to call for the national convention. This is a formal act required by the bylaws of both parties. The committee also recommends a slate of candidates for the convention and publishes a list of the distribution of delegates to each state. Information on presidential primaries, state party conventions, and district caucuses is issued by the committee, as well. The national committee is responsible also for setting up the convention—including site selection and the organization of committees necessary for the smoother operation of the convention. The appointment of people to convention committees can be a most important role for the national committee.[3] Appointments to key committees such as the Credentials Committee, Committee on Permanent Organization, Rules Committee, and Resolutions Committee may determine the nature of the party platform, as well as the party's nominees for president and vice-president.

The national chairman of each party is its nominal leader but his power is

---

[2] Adapted from Hugh A. Bone, *American Politics and the Party System,* 4th ed. (New York: McGraw-Hill, 1971), pp. 162–63.
[3] See Chapter 11 for a more complete discussion of the national convention.

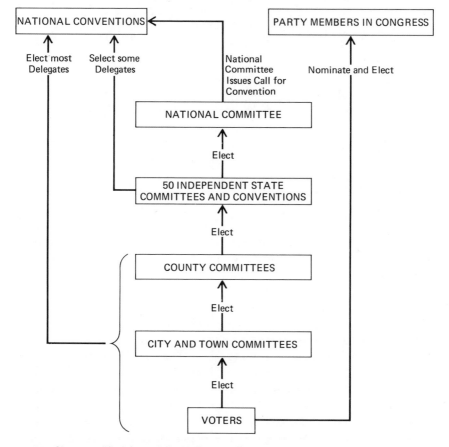

Figure 1. Actual Organization Pattern of National Parties

NATIONAL CONVENTIONS

PARTY MEMBERS IN CONGRESS

Elect most Delegates

Select some Delegates

National Committee Issues Call for Convention

Nominate and Elect

NATIONAL COMMITTEE

Elect

50 INDEPENDENT STATE COMMITTEES AND CONVENTIONS

Elect

COUNTY COMMITTEES

Elect

CITY AND TOWN COMMITTEES

Elect

VOTERS

SOURCE: Chart modified from John H. Fenton, *People and Parties in Politics: Unofficial Makers of Public Policy . . .* (Glenview, Ill.: Scott Foresman, 1966), p. 17.

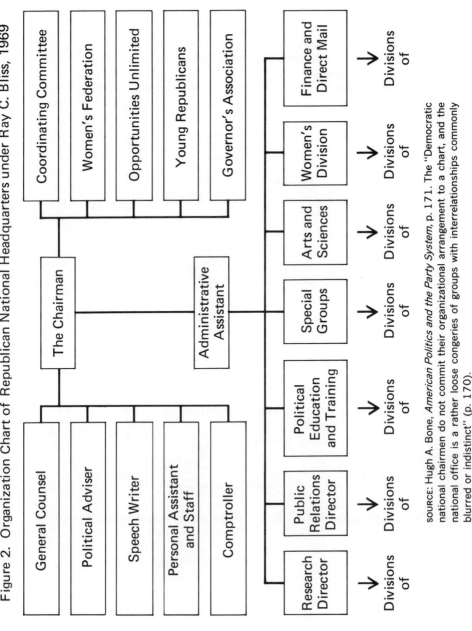

Figure 2. Organization Chart of Republican National Headquarters under Ray C. Bliss, 1969

SOURCE: Hugh A. Bone, *American Politics and the Party System*, p. 171. The "Democratic national chairmen do not commit their organizational arrangement to a chart, and the national office is a rather loose congeries of groups with interrelationships commonly blurred or indistinct" (p. 170).

greatly circumscribed. He is almost always the agent of a stronger party figure or group. In a presidential election year, the candidate designates the chairman of his choice, and an incumbent president may select "his" chairman virtually at will. Under other circumstances, the chairman's selection results from compromise and negotiation among key party leaders.

The leadership of the national committee changes frequently and as a new chairman arrives he must carve out a new position for himself. When the party controls the White House the role of the national chairman and national committee are sharply curtailed. Thus since the 1968 election the Republican National Committee has been in second place to the White House. Often this can cause tensions between the units. In 1970 and 1972 there was, for example, criticism by both Republican candidates for public office, and by some of the staff of the Republican National Committee, of the way the Nixon White House participated in the election campaigns.[4] An apparent casualty of this friction was the incumbent national chairman (as of 1972), Senator Robert Dole, who was replaced by the president's choice (United Nations ambassador) George Bush. In the Democratic party, McGovern's 1972 defeat led inevitably to a new national chairman, a "moderate" acceptable to most party factions.[5] These examples illustrate the fragility of the "power" enjoyed by national party chairmen, who are not independent spokesmen for party policy.

Finally, the staffs of the national committees should be noted. Between presidential election campaigns the paid staff of the Democratic National Committee averages between 60 and 90 people and the paid staff of the Republican National Committee averages between 100 and 120 people.[6] There has been some attempt at institutionalization of the national party organization in recent years, especially in terms of staff and the maintenance of an ongoing party bureaucracy. Consider for a moment the status of the Republican party in the winter of 1974, almost one year prior to an off-year election.[7] There were seven Republican National Committee officials. In addition to a full-time chairman, there was a finance committee chairman, a finance committee executive director, a special assistant to the chairman, a director of political operations, a director of research and state services, and a communications director.[8] Though the size of the paid staff of the committee was smaller than it had been in 1972 there was an ongoing staff with very specific program

---

[4] *Congressional Quarterly Weekly Report* (February 16, 1974): 355.

[5] He was Robert Strauss of Texas, former party treasurer.

[6] Bone, *American Politics,* p. 170. At the beginning of 1974 the Democratic National Committee maintained a paid staff of 60, and the Republican National Committee a staff of 105. *Congressional Quarterly Weekly Report* (February 9, 1974): 297; *Congressional Quarterly Weekly Report* (February 16, 1974): 356.

[7] The discussion of the Republican National Committee in 1974 was drawn heavily from *Congressional Quarterly Weekly Report* (February 16, 1974): 352–56.

[8] Ibid., p. 355.

charges. Among their concerns—other than overcoming the potentially negative side effects of Watergate on the American voters in the 1974 congressional
and state elections—were helping Republican candidates in their 1974 election
bids for congressional and senatorial seats. They provided financial and technical assistance to candidates facing close contests who may have had trouble
raising sufficient funds to run a campaign.[9] Also, they sought to maintain close
coordination among the divisions of the national committee—e.g., finance,
research, minorities, communications—so as to maximize the impact of the
national organization.[10]

The Republican National Committee leadership is concerned, too, with the
need for party building at the state and local levels. But there is a general
consensus among Republicans that there is very little coordination between
the national committee and state parties.[11] The Republican party goal of strong
party organization may be exceedingly difficult to achieve in the foreseeable
future given the antiparty predispositions of so many Americans.

Consider also the institutionalization of the Democratic party organization
in recent years.[12] Ten months prior to the 1974 elections the Democratic
National Committee was staffed by sixty paid employees and twelve unpaid
volunteers. In addition to the national chairman, there was a deputy chairman,
an executive director, a finance chairman, a campaigns director, a research
director, a minorities director, a young Democrats chairman, a delegate selection commission chairwoman, and a charter commission chairman. The
Democrats have been able to sustain interest and some momentum for their
national party during the years between 1972 and 1976 by agreeing to have
a midterm mini-convention in 1974 to consider a proposed draft of a new party
charter—developed between 1972 and 1974—as well as by designating a commission to revise delegate selection procedures for the Democratic National
Conventions.[13]

NATIONAL PARTIES AS COHESIVE FACTORS IN NATIONAL POLITICS

Although the relationship between the party and elected officials is clearly
weak, and although the national parties exercise almost no power over state
and local parties, once every four years the national parties come into the
limelight—at national convention time. This is their *raison d'être* for continued
existence. As E. E. Schattschneider noted:

[9] Ibid., pp. 352–53.
[10] Ibid., p. 353.
[11] Ibid., p. 356.
[12] The discussion of the Democratic National Committee in 1974 relies upon the discussion that
appeared in *Congressional Quarterly Weekly Report* (February 9, 1974): 296–300.
[13] For a discussion of these rules see Chapter 11.

In the tremendously long recesses of the convention the party has no national governing body. . . . The national convention is the least step that can be taken in the direction of party centralization without refusing to make a presidential nomination at all.[14]

Yet, insofar as disparate groups of people are able every four years to come together under a single party banner to nominate and try to elect a candidate for president, the national parties act as cohesive factors in American politics. They are part of the ritual and symbol of American life. They are, however, political transients in the power relationships of the American system.

CONGRESSIONAL AND PRESIDENTIAL PARTIES

Since national parties are mere amalgams of state and local parties they cannot "boss" the president or Congress. There are certainly some local political organizations—as noted elsewhere—that have great power that is dependent upon winning political offices and dispensing jobs and contracts. Jobs and contracts are not distributed by national parties in the same fashion. An accurate graphic representation of the national parties' relationship to political power would look something like a disconnected electrical circuit, with the president and Congress having the power and the parties dangling off without the "juice" being fed in.

Part of the reason for the weakness of the national party organization can be explained by federalism—that is, there are local and state organizations paralleling local and state political structures. It is the local and state government upon which local and state parties depend for a viable existence and not the national parties. Another explanation for the weakness of the national parties can be found in the constitutional separation between the presidential and congressional branches of government. Because members of Congress are not reliant upon the national parties for their nomination and election to office, they do not have to be responsive to policy-related demands made by the national party.[15] Instead they must be responsive to the pressures of interests in their districts—of which party is but one—if they aspire to reelection.

It is in light of these conditions that James MacGregor Burns wrote in his *Deadlock of Democracy* about four-party government in America:

. . . . to see the pattern of power at the national level only in terms of two parties is grossly misleading. The balance between one or two parties, on the one hand, and (at the national level) over a thousand personal parties (one for the President, one for each member of Congress, and at least one for each rival for the office,

---

[14] E. E. Schattschneider, *Party Government* (New York: Rinehart and Company, 1942), p. 158.
[15] See Chapter 12 for a more complete discussion of this relationship.

in both parties), on the other hand, has been struck not in a two-party power system, nor in a multi-party system, but in what is essentially a four-party system. The four national parties are the Presidential Democrats, the Presidential Republicans, the Congressional Democrats, and the Congressional Republicans.[16]

It is likely that Burns's concept can be extended even further into subparties and coalitions within the two parties in each of the houses of Congress.

This condition of separation between the two elective branches of the national government and their relationship to weak national parties could perhaps be minimized if the national parties had functions that related directly to the electoral process for members of Congress. In Great Britain, for example, the national agencies of both the Conservative and Labour parties may veto any candidate selected by a constituency organization, thus depriving the candidate of the official party label, without which chances of being elected are slim. The possibility of having one's nomination vetoed keeps a would-be potential rebel from ignoring party instructions.

Often a *particular* president can retain the voting loyalty of members of his party in Congress, but it is the personality of the president that can do this—by convincing the party members of his position, promising support, or threatening coercion—and not the national party structure. Thus, when President Nixon vetoed vocational-rehabilitation legislation in March 1973, the Democrats were unable to override his veto because the minority leader of the Senate, Hugh Scott (R., Pa.)—who himself had voted for the bill on February 28, 1973—was able to keep the Republicans "in line." But, this was clearly a vote for the president and not for an amorphous national party organization. Such examples tempt one to conclude that when cohesive party organization exists, it may be more a function of personality than of party leadership per se.

LIMITED OPPORTUNITIES FOR PARTICIPATION

Participation in the national parties is limited because, as noted previously, most of the time they are little more than "states of mind." The single most significant source of mass political participation in the national parties is to be found in the delegations from the separate states to both of the national conventions. In 1972 there were 3,016 delegate votes on the separate state delegations to the Democratic National Convention, and 1,348 delegate votes on the delegations to the Republican National Convention. However, these figures underestimate the number of people present because there are alter-

[16] James MacGregor Burns, *The Deadlock of Democracy: Four-Party Politics in America* (Englewood Cliffs, N.J.: Prentice-Hall, 1963), p. 196.

nates at the convention as well as delegates. There were 5,384 delegates and alternates present at the 1972 Democratic convention.[17] Though these figures are substantial, they represent only a small fraction of the total registered voters in the nation. The delegates attend their conventions, casting their votes to approve rules and procedures and to affirm their presidential and vice-presidential preferences. When this work has been completed, they go home. They have no further function in national parties.

The only other major opportunities for participation in the national parties, aside from the roles of committeemen and committeewomen from the separate states, are on the special commissions and committees established by the parties at different points in time to study specific problems. Thus, after the 1972 Democratic party misfortunes in selecting a vice-presidential candidate, the Democratic party established a committee to consider the nomination of vice-presidential candidates. Seventy-five people (hardly mass participation!) were selected to serve on this committee which was chaired by Senator Hubert Humphrey.[18] Several other committees were organized by the Democratic National Committee in response to the party's 1972 White House misfortunes. These included a charter commission and a delegate selection commission.

The proposals of the commission on delegate selection and party structure, which were accepted by the Democratic National Committee on March 1, 1974, and which will be considered by the December 1974 Democratic mini-convention, will, if they are accepted, raise some interesting questions regarding greater participation in national level Democratic party politics, and the effects of such participation upon party cohesion and structure in the years ahead. The report, if it is accepted, instructs: "State Parties (to) take all feasible steps to encourage non-affiliated and new voters to register and enroll as Democrats and to provide simple, easy procedures through which they may do so." [19] To the extent that state Democratic parties will accept and follow this ruling, it is possible that greater participation may result—though caution should be exercised when discussing the relationship between voter registration and active involvement in party politics. As indicated in previous chapters, active involvement in parties, and especially national parties is the exception for the American voter, clearly not the norm. The report of the delegate selection commission of the Democratic party would require that most national convention delegates be selected from districts no larger than congressional districts, and that the delegates to the national convention represent the presidential preferences of the Democrats in their districts—that is, bloc voting

---

[17] *Congressional Quarterly Weekly Report* (July 15, 1972): 1720–21; and *Congressional Quarterly Weekly Report* (August 12, 1972): 1998–2000.

[18] *Congressional Quarterly Weekly Report* (June 23, 1973): 1631.

[19] *Report of the Commission on Delegate Selection and Party Structure as Amended and Adopted by the Democratic National Committee* (Washington, D.C.: Democratic National Committee, March 1, 1974), p. 1.

by delegations, where it is utilized, would be replaced by proportional representation of voter preferences.[20] These changes, if implemented, may bring the national convention closer to Democratic voters. Because of the reduced size of the districts used for delegate selection, a voter's impact on the delegate selection process may be enhanced. Also, because Democratic voter preference would have to be mirrored on the delegations, participation by voters who do not support the leading contenders for presidential nomination may grow. Such voters will have the opportunity to strive for some representation on delegations, and gain a "voice," if not a chance of nomination victory, at the national convention.

[20] Ibid., p. 3.

10

Campaign Finance

Because of the decentralized structure of American parties, it is not surprising that the structure of campaign finance is similarly decentralized. Party committees, including the national committee (discussed in Chapter 9) and congressional campaign committees established by each party in each house of Congress, comprise only one source of campaign funds.[1] Often the most substantial sources of revenue come to independent committees established for the sole purpose of electing a candidate. These organizations are *not* "the party" and they seem to have the effect of detracting from a centralized party structure at the national, state, and local levels. The willingness of many contributors to support candidates, as opposed to political parties, seems to be an off-shoot of the antiparty tradition in the United States. The condition of campaign finance is a classic example of the degree to which candidates for public office increasingly seek to mount efforts independent of party. Hence an examination of this topic provides us with a case study of antiparty politics in America.

In order better to perceive the dimensions of the problems of campaign finance, let us compare the campaign expenditures of Governor Rockefeller and his opponents in New York in 1966 and 1970. In 1966 Rockefeller re-

[1] Such funds may conceivably make a difference in a small state, such as Idaho, but not in a large one like New York.

ported expenditures of $5.2 million; his Democratic opponent, $576,000; the Conservative party candidate, $44,000. In 1970, Republican Rockefeller had 370 employees in his campaign organization, the Democrat, Arthur Goldberg, 35. Rockefeller's effort included the use of three family owned airplanes while Goldberg flew commercial and chartered airlines; Adams, a third-party gubernatorial candidate, traveled by car. Rockefeller's media expenditures alone surpassed the cost of Arthur Goldberg's total campaign by almost $1 million.[2] A large percentage of Rockefeller's expenditures were derived from family sources, including loans from Chase Manhattan Bank, which is headed by a Rockefeller brother.[3] According to James Perry, Rockefeller's campaign demonstrated "the need for money, and more money—a candidate . . . must have it early and spend it often." The role of the party does not seem central to funding this kind of campaign.

In this chapter we will discuss the major problems associated with contemporary campaign finance in the United States as well as the status of existing legislation and the range of proposed options for reform. We will also consider the question of whether the management of campaign finance *in the parties* is possible or desirable in the American antiparty environment. Though the emphasis in this chapter is primarily on national—presidential and congressional—elections, the problems that are raised, and the criticisms of the system leveled by some reform critics against the current campaign finance system can be made against state and local campaign financing processes as well.[4]

SOURCES OF CAMPAIGN FUNDS

THE ROLE OF LARGE CONTRIBUTORS

The role of large campaign contributors came into sharp public focus during the 1972 campaign, when the Committee to Reelect the President, President Nixon's campaign organization, raised substantial sums of money from special interest groups.[5]

[2] Based on *New York Times,* October 25, 1970, p. 60; *New York Times,* October 8, 1970, p. 34; *New York Times,* November 28, 1970, p. 24.
[3] Ibid., about $4.6 million came from his family including $2.8 million from his stepmother.
[4] There have been attempts in some states to pass campaign finance legislation which provides controls on individual contributions and limits on candidate spending.
[5] There were many large contributors to Nixon's campaign: W. Clement Stone of Chicago, chairman of the Combined Insurance Companies of America, $2 million.
Richard Melon Scaife of Pittsburgh, heir to the Melon (sic) National Bank fortune, $1 million. A dozen executives of major oil and gas companies, several at least $600,000.
Walter T. Duncan, land developer of Bryan, Texas, who gave Hubert Humphrey $300,000 and then switched to the Nixon campaign with $305,000.
Arthur K. and Thomas Watson of the International Business Machines family, whose company is engaged in negotiating an antitrust settlement with the Justice Department, more than $300,000.

The *New York Times* carried the following story on January 7, 1973 regarding special interest groups and campaign contributions:

> . . . a year ago Ralph Nader filed a lawsuit here disclosing indisputably that the Agriculture Department, only 24 hours after a group of dairymen had met privately with the President at the White House, had abruptly and inexplicably reversed a previously published decision not to raise the Federal milk price-support level.
>
> Just as indisputably, those dairy farm leaders began the next day to contribute to covert Nixon finance groups an amount that is now estimated to have passed $400,000 by Election Day. The amount was nonetheless a pittance compared with the hundreds of millions the Government price reversal had been worth to dairy farmers.
>
> William A. Powell, president of Mid-America Dairymen, Inc., one of the visitors at the White House, later wrote in a letter, which was disclosed under subpoena, that "whether we like it or not, this is the way the system works." [6]

A large number of all campaign contributions to the 1972 Republican presidential campaign came in the form of large contributions. The comparable figure for the Democrats was estimated to be considerably lower. The involvement of large contributors to presidential campaigns is not a new phenomenon. Herbert Alexander reported that during the 1950s and 1960s the proportion of Republican and Democratic income to national committees derived from individual contributions in excess of $500 was quite high. (See Table 40.)

Large contributions have tended to benefit the Republicans more than the Democrats in recent years, though both parties have received portions of their campaign funds from big contributors. The big contributors represent corporations and unions as well as wealthy individuals.[7] These patterns continued in

---

Ray A. Kroc of Oak Brook, Ill., founder and chairman of the McDonald's Hamburger Chain, Samuel Schulman of Los Angeles, vice-chairman of the National General Corporation, and John J. Louis, Jr., of Chicago, chairman of Combined Communications, Inc., outdoor advertising, each about $255,000.

Foster G. McGaw of Evanston, Ill., founder and chairman of the American Hospital Supply Corporation, and Jack J. Dreyfus, Jr., senior partner in the New York investment firm of Dreyfus & Co., each about $195,000.

Charles and Sam Wyly, president and chairman of the University Computing Center of Dallas, $129,000.

John M. Shaheen of New York, president of Shaheen Natural Resources, Inc., oil refiners, Joseph Segel of Merion, Pa., head of the private Franklin Mint, and Edward J. Daly of Oakland, Calif., chairman of the World Airways Corporations, an overseas charter concern, each about $100,000. *New York Times,* January 7, 1973, Sec. III, p. 22.

[6] Ibid.

[7] This was true, although the Federal Corrupt Practices Act of 1925 forbade corporate and labor contributions. Largely through specially established political "arms," these groups have provided both "hard" money (cash) and "soft" money (indirect subsidies including advertisements, voter registration, and the like). Richard Harris, "Annals of Politics—A Fundamental Hoax," *New Yorker* (August 7, 1971): 50–51.

1972. (See Table 41.) The implications of this kind of fund raising are several. First, Richard Nixon's access to such important contributions gave him a 2 to 1 lead in campaign funds spent over his opponent, George McGovern.[8] Second, the presence of large contributions cannot help but increase the access of the donors to public officials after their election. Hence large contributors often enjoy unparalleled opportunities to pressure effectively for favorable policies, institutionalizing the role played by an elite group whose power is based on wealth. It should be noted that Democratic candidates for Congress and statewide offices sometimes have access to larger campaign contributions

Table 40. Percent of Funds to National Committees in Excess of $500

	1948	1952	1956	1960	1964	1968
Democratic	69	63	44	59	69	61
Republican	74	68	74	58	28	47

SOURCE: Herbert E. Alexander, *Financing the 1968 Election* (Lexington, Mass.: Heath, Lexington Books, 1971), p. 163.

Table 41. Sources of Finance by Group to Nixon, 1972

Financial and Banking Executives	$4,047,000
Oil Executives	1,410,000
Pharmaceutical and Drug Cos.	1,120,000
Government Officials (including ambassadors)	1,011,000
Real Estate Men	1,005,000

SOURCE: *New York Times,* September 30, 1973, p. 61.

than their Republican rivals. In addition, observers have discerned a pronounced pattern of campaign giving to incumbents, even those running unopposed, especially when they occupy key positions in the legislative process.

Many critics seeking reform of the campaign finance system contend that only campaign financing based on small contributions and/or assumption of responsibility for campaign costs by the federal government would dilute the influence of wealthy "special interests." Though there have been some limitations placed on campaign contributors over the years, the constraints they provide have not been uniformly successful.[9]

[8] *New York Times,* October 25, 1972, p. 1.
[9] *Dollar Politics, the Issue of Campaign Spending* (Washington, D.C.: Congressional Quarterly, 1971), p. 15.

THE ROLE OF SMALL CONTRIBUTORS

The demands of reformers of the campaign finance system address themselves in some measure to the sources of campaign funds as well as to *limits* on contributions and spending. Insofar as candidates for public office are often dependent upon a few highly visible large contributors, as noted in the preceding section, candidates may feel some pressure—real or imagined—to act in behalf of the interests of their financial backers when relevant issues arise. When there are larger numbers of small contributors, most of them are unknown to the candidate. Upon successful completion of his campaign he feels no indebtedness for financing his campaign to specific contributors, and he may be more independent of special interests because their influence will have been diluted. Reliance on small contributors would ideally make for a more "open" competitive political process because elected officials would have to be responsive on all issues to many citizens and interest groups. Until the 1960s, efforts to raise money via small contributions were relatively unsuccessful. Since then, however, some new patterns of citizen giving have been discernible.

In recent years successful attempts to raise money from small donors were engendered by Governor George Wallace in 1968 when he ran for president as the candidate of the American Independent party, by Eugene McCarthy in his bid for the Democratic presidential nomination in that year, by Senator Goldwater in the 1964 presidential campaign, and by Senator McGovern in his 1972 presidential race. The year 1964 marked an unusual pattern of small contributions—in amounts of $1 to $500. In 1972, George McGovern raised almost 60 percent of his total campaign support (or $15 million) from between 650,000 and 700,000 Americans. Goldwater, McCarthy, and McGovern, disparate as they may seem, share in common the fact that all were ideologically oriented candidates who attracted the fervent support (including financial) of some backers.

Is this new interest by small contributors in aiding "their" candidates likely to alter the effects of campaign finance significantly? Under the present system, to the extent that average voters cannot make large contributions to political campaigns they are unknown to the political contenders. Hence, it is doubtful that even the 650,000 odd contributors who donated the small sums can ever equal the visibility and consequent access to power enjoyed by large donors.[10]

It should be noted that not every candidate can hope for such mass support. The technique of raising substantial monies from rank-and-file voters requires massive letter writing, newspaper advertisements, telephoning, and speech making. Much of the letter writing and telephoning has been facilitated by

[10] Some fund-raising efforts have actually institutionalized the access of large contributors, e.g., Johnson's President's Club, 1964, for contributions of over $1,000. In this case the fortunate few received certificates and interviews with the president on request.

the use of computer technology—but computer technology is expensive. For example, it was estimated that George McGovern spent $3 million to raise $15 million, thus netting $12 million.[11] In order to carry out a broad-based financial campaign it is necessary also to have a large number of precinct workers to embark on telephone campaigns.

There can be more than one reward gained from this kind of campaigning. In addition to the obvious one of raising money, the outpouring of small contributions provides at least the appearance of broad-based political support for a candidate, and may help build the image of a candidate who is "his own man," unbought by big business or big union interests. One should note however that the three most successful campaigners of this genre in the past ten years have been soundly defeated at the polls on Election Day—Barry Goldwater, George McGovern, and George Wallace. The candidates in question did raise campaign funds but were not able to gain broader appeal due to the ideological positions they held or were perceived to hold. Hence, heartening as these recent trends are, they seem unlikely sources of cash for centrist parties in the traditional American mold.

For the average voter, unless there are substantial changes in the nature of campaign financing, there are currently really only two methods whereby he may influence a candidate and hope to provide a countervailing influence to large individual campaign contributors. First, the voters make the ultimate choice at the polls and thus cannot be totally ignored if a candidate hopes to win, and second, many large contributions come from organizations (e.g., labor unions) which at least purport to represent rank-and-file voters themselves.

OTHER REVENUE SOURCES

Large individual contributions make up a substantial portion of campaign monies. There are, however, other sources of campaign revenue, many of which can also be identified with wealthy individuals and groups. Political dinners can raise substantial sums of money. It has been estimated, by the Citizens Research Foundation, for example, that during the 1968 campaign $43.1 million was raised at fund-raising dinners—$21.5 million by the Republicans, $17.9 million by the Democrats, and $3.6 million by the American Independent party.[12] A Republican $1,000 a plate "Victory 72" dinner in September 1972, held on closed circuit television in twenty-eight cities, reported a total revenue of $4.6 million.[13]

---

[11] *New York Times,* November 26, 1972, p. 48.

[12] *Dollar Politics,* p. 7.

[13] *New York Times,* October 25, 1972, p. 33. Those who bought tickets, according to the *Times,* were among the country's top corporate, manufacturing, banking, financial, and real estate figures.

Loans, often not repaid, comprise another source of large contributions. In 1968, Democrats borrowed $240,177 from a former Chicago underworld figure—Jake "the Barber" Factor—and another $100,000 from the head of MCA Incorporated.[14]

Another source of revenue for political campaigns has, in some states and localities, been payments into party coffers by persons holding political patronage. Thus Martin and Susan Tolchin have noted that: "Parties from big patronage states like Illinois, New York, Indiana, Oklahoma, and Pennsylvania impose a tithe on job holders in order to build a war chest to use at campaign time. In Indiana, for example, where everyone with a patronage job pays 2 percent of his salary to the party, the party in power can "reasonably expect to start a campaign with a war chest of $500,000." [15] Presidential or congressional candidates do not generally raise money this way, but insofar as monies raised by a city help get out the party faithful on Election Day, national candidates can benefit from this fund-raising mechanism.

PROPOSALS FOR REFORM

INCREASED COSTS—THE TECHNOLOGY INFLUENCE

It was estimated that Franklin D. Roosevelt spent $2,245,975 in 1932 to win that election and Richard Nixon spent $48,000,000 to win the presidential election forty years later.[16] The reason for the tremendous increase in campaign costs over the past thirty or forty years can be traced in part to a general inflationary cycle, but it can also be tied to the expanded use of media campaigning, polling, and computer technology—which is extremely costly. The trend toward higher spending has been evident at all electoral levels. Hence expenditures for radio and television advertising rose 57 percent from the off-year 1966 election to that in 1970. Governor Rockefeller's heavy spending in New York in 1970 (discussed above) has been matched by that of other nonpresidential candidates. While it is not clear that money alone can buy electoral victory, further concern in the age of spiraling costs has been raised by the pattern of fund raising in American politics—i.e., the traditional dependence on large contributors.

[14] *New York Times,* June 20, 1971, pp. 1, 37.
[15] Martin and Susan Tolchin, *To the Victor* (New York: Random House, 1971), pp. 116–17.
[16] Herbert Alexander, *Political Financing* (Minneapolis, Minn.: Burgess, 1972), p. 6. Also, see Chapters 3 and 4 for a more complete discussion of the contemporary costs of campaigning. It should be noted that spending on radio and television increased only slightly in 1972, in part because of a new law which required broadcasters to charge their lowest rates for political ads.

BACKGROUND

The structure of regulation of campaign finance has operated in most instances so as to prevent the public from knowing who is giving how much to whom. Basically campaign finance legislation in the United States has had three aims:

1. the limitation and regulation of *donations* made to candidates and their campaign committees;
2. the *limitation of spending* by candidates and their campaign committees;
3. the *disclosure of expenditures* by candidates and their campaign committees.[17]

The history of reform shows clearly that laws—both federal and state—relating to political finance have been developed to prohibit, limit, and restrict ways of getting, giving, and spending. However, as soon as such restrictions were incorporated into law, methods were found to circumvent them.

Meaningful compliance has not been achieved in any of the three areas. Hence, while funding limitations were enacted in the Federal Corrupt Practices Act of 1925 they were virtually ignored. Unions and corporations, barred from contributing outright, continued to do so through such vehicles as labor's COPE (Committee on Political Education) and corporate "dummy" groups such as Chemical Bank of New York's "Fund for Good Government." Candidates often failed to file accurate, or even any, reports of contributions and expenditures.[18]

While individual contributions to campaigns were limited, there was no enforcement. In addition, because contributions to a candidate or political committee working in his behalf were specified by the act, political committees proliferated. In 1972, Senator McGovern alone was known to have had more than 330 finance committees.[19]

Campaign finance legislation was also circumvented in other ways. Because reports had to be filed only for campaigns that crossed state boundaries, candidates hid contributions by raising them in only one state or by establishing "dummy committees" in Washington, D.C., not a state. Special interests and persons associated with them frequently "laundered" campaign contributions earmarked for particular candidates so that voters could not detect them in financial reports the candidates filed. Usually business, labor, and other interests seeking to hide a connection with candidates have passed "earmarked" gifts through one or more intermediaries, especially the Democratic and Republican campaign committees on Capitol Hill. The candidates then listed these committees rather than the original contributors in their filed

[17] *Dollar Politics,* p. 15.
[18] Ibid., pp. 6–7.
[19] *New York Times,* October 1, 1972, Sect. IV, p. 2.

reports. How much earmarked money was contributed in 1972, for example, by sources that effectively bleached out a relationship with candidates is unknown and probably unknowable, but it is believed to be millions of dollars. Candidates feigned ignorance of campaign revenues by putting their aides in charge of money; no campaign expenditures were then reported.[20]

Hence, the source and path of campaign contributions could be obscured; records and reports of spending were unreliable; no offender was ever prosecuted for violation of campaign finance regulations. The public has had little information about and control over funding; the structure of the laws has heightened fund-raising decentralization and led to candidate rather than party oriented revenue-raising efforts. Because of the inadequacies of past legislation and enforcement the need for reform has long been apparent.[21]

THE 1971 REFORMS

The question arises as to whether there are viable alternatives for raising campaign revenue in the United States. In the next several pages we will examine some of the widely mentioned proposals to change the money-raising system for political campaigning. In order to place this problem in some perspective it may be useful to look at an estimate of expenditures in relationship to the cost of government. It has been estimated that $400 million was spent on all political campaigns in 1972.[22] The total federal budget for fiscal year 1972 was approximately $270 billion. Thus total campaign costs in 1972 represented the equivalent of about one-tenth of 1 percent of the federal budget for that year. Looked at in this light, campaign expenditures may not seem to be so great. The problem may be less one of expenditures per se than of inequality of resources for candidates and the public.

One effort at campaign finance regulation came in 1971 with the passage of the Revenue Act of 1971 and the Federal Election Campaign Act of 1971.[23] Briefly, the Federal Election Campaign Act which took effect in April of 1972 eliminated most spending ceilings for candidates for national public office and instituted comprehensive contribution disclosure regulations. In addition, media-related expenditures by candidates were limited. The act also provided for a limit on a candidate's own personal investment in federal elections and required public disclosure of campaign contributions and expenditures of over

[20] See Mark J. Green, James M. Fallows, David R. Zwick, *Who Runs Congress?* (New York: Bantam/Grossman, 1972), pp. 13–16 for a good discussion of evasion of campaign finance laws.

[21] A Gallup Poll in September 1973 found that a majority of the American people (65 percent) favor public financing of elections. See *Integrity in Politics* (Washington, D.C.: Common Cause, December 1973–January 1974), p. 4.

[22] *New York Times,* November 19, 1972, p. 1.

[23] The Republican Committee to Reelect the President (CREEP) apparently raised a substantial portion of its funds prior to this date, resulting in a lawsuit by Common Cause to obtain disclosure.

$100. The Revenue Act of 1971 provided for a new mechanism of fund raising in federal elections. The legislation attempted to broaden the population base that will contribute to political campaigns by providing tax incentives to contributors. The mechanism which was developed provides that contributors to campaigns can receive a tax credit against their federal income tax for 50 percent of their contributions. (The maximum is $12.50 for an individual and $25 for a couple filing a joint return.) As an alternative a campaign contributor may claim as a deduction up to $50 (or $100 on a joint return). An additional provision of the Revenue Act of 1971 was a check-off mechanism for presidential election campaigns. Every taxpayer has the opportunity to designate that $1.00 of his obligated taxes be placed in a fund to subsidize presidential election campaigns. This provision of the law became effective January 1, 1973 and will not affect a presidential campaign until 1976.[24] Under this legislation general funds will be distributed in proportion to check-off totals.[25]

Though the passage of the 1971 reforms was most welcome to many critics of campaign finance legislation in the United States, the new laws did not end criticism of the system. Clearly, glaring inequities in the system remained and were highlighted by the events following the Watergate crisis of 1972. (In 1974 more comprehensive campaign finance regulations were enacted.) Thus one critic of the system suggested that, "The 1971 laws made significant changes in our governance of political financing; they did not make fundamental changes in the nature of the political system. Candidates will still rely on the individual contributions they (or their parties) can raise." [26]

Before consideration of the provisions and the potential impact of the Federal Elections Campaign Act Amendments of 1974, it may be useful to discuss the major proposals for reform of the American campaign finance system. The analysis that follows will be divided into two categories: monetary and structural reforms.[27]

MONETARY REFORMS

Advocates of monetary reform suggest getting people to contribute where they work in conjunction with massive door-to-door solicitations. An alternative or supplementary proposal that has been made would provide for payroll deductions at people's places of employment. Herbert Alexander has estimated

---

[24] This portion of the Revenue Act of 1971 was incorporated into the 1974 law discussed below.

[25] It is interesting to note that a similar check-off provision was passed by Congress and approved by the president in 1966, and was repealed in 1967, just one year later. Alexander, *Political Financing*, p. 41.

[26] Ibid., p. 43.

[27] This is a modification of the categories used by ibid., pp. 44–55. The following section on reforms relies heavily on this material.

that the latter method might raise up to $100 million. There has been some reform of collection techniques with the passage of the Revenue Act of 1971 which provides tax incentives for campaign contributions as well as direct deductions for political party contributions. It is unlikely, however, that our party system can ever produce a funding system entirely dependent on small contributions, in the form of deductions or party membership dues (as in the Netherlands or West Germany). This situation is due at least in part to the general antipartyism of Americans.

STRUCTURAL REFORMS: POLITICAL

Some of the structural reforms suggested include shortening campaigns, shortening the ballot (state/local), eliminating elective judges (state/local), and a nationwide presidential primary. It is the claim of the supporters of these proposals that campaign costs could be curtailed if such reforms were initiated. It is not clear, however, that shorter campaigns would reduce costs since they might lead simply to concentrated spending.

A case clearly can be made for the eliminating of elective judges inasmuch as no evidence supports contentions for the superiority of elective judges over appointive judges—both categories of judges having many outstanding men and women in their ranks. Costs would be reduced in local and state political campaigning if judges did not run for office. (However, since in many areas nominees for elective judicial office do not campaign extensively, this may not be significant.) At the same time, because it is not clear that the vast majority of voters can make meaningful decisions about the competence of members of the bench, abolishing elective judicial posts might not damage the democratic process.

Another structural-political reform considered here is a nationwide presidential primary. Proponents argue that the 1968 presidential primaries cost $45 million [28] and that costs could in fact be reduced since the number of separate organizations could be fewer in number; the physical movement of campaign staffs and candidates could be curtailed; and, the campaign could be single-focused nationally, not multifocused as it is now, in order to attract support in many states. It is further reasoned that if costs were lower, more able candidates who did not have strong financial backing might have a better chance to gain party nominations. At present, it is argued, the cost of primaries wipes out financially all but the most affluent or well-supported potential candidates. These last two arguments can be met with counterarguments. It

---

[28] *Congressional Quarterly Weekly Report* 30 (July 8, 1972): 1650. Current 1972 records indicate that only $13 million was spent in 1972 primaries because of the new campaign regulations discussed above.

is not clear that this change in the form of selection of the presidential nominees would reduce costs, since candidates would have to campaign nationwide. Costs might actually increase because a candidate would have to run two campaigns if nominated: a campaign for nomination and a campaign for election. If the election campaign figure is doubled, than perhaps a picture different from the one drawn by national primary advocates emerges. It can be argued that the present system, despite its inadequacies, may be superior to this alternative. Under the present system, if one can raise the money to wage one successful primary campaign, it is likely that this success will beget the candidate increased financial support. Thus state primaries and conventions may open the field to multiple candidates through electoral victories in individual states. The most recent example of this phenomenon was George McGovern, who after primary victories in New Hampshire and Wisconsin was able to raise additional funds to go on and win the Democratic nomination. It is unlikely that a relative unknown could have made similar gains in a national primary system. (See Chapter 11 for a further discussion of national primaries.)

STRUCTURAL REFORMS: MEDIA USE

Section 315 of the Federal Communications Act states: "If any licensee shall permit any person who is a legally qualified candidate for any public office to use a broadcasting station, he shall afford equal opportunities to all other such candidates for that office in the use of such broadcasting station, and the Commission shall make rules and regulations to carry this provision into effect: Provided, that such licensee shall have no power of censorship over the material broadcast under the provisions of this section. No obligation is hereby imposed upon any licensee to allow the use of its station by any such candidate." (See Chapter 11 for a further discussion of the relevance of this law to campaigns.)

There is an obvious point that comes to light when one looks at Section 315, and that is that "equal opportunity" or "equal time" in reality means equal access to time. There are two different applications of this doctrine. First, there is its application regarding free time, and then there is its relationship to paid time. It is the free time issue that has received the most attention in public debate. A problem arises regarding free time for all of the candidates contesting an elected government position—both major and minor party candidates. Under this concept of equality, if major party candidates demand and receive equal amounts of free time, minor party and independent contenders may then demand that the same time be provided them. Since such time provisions would be very costly, it is most often the case in political contests that free time for candidates is not provided by the networks. This does not preclude news coverage from giving less than impartial treatment to *all* of the candidates aspiring to an elected office.

As far as paid time is concerned, networks must sell time in equal amounts to all candidates for an office. In 1969 the Supreme Court held that: "Because of the scarcity of radio frequencies, the Government is permitted to put restraints on licensees in favor of others whose views should be expressed on this unique medium. But the people as a whole retain their interest in free speech by radio and their collective right to have the medium function consistently with the ends and purposes of the First Amendment. It is the right of the viewers and listeners, not the right of the broadcasters, which is paramount." [29]

Nonetheless, radio and television networks do not always perceive the need for "equal time" in the same manner as candidates, and time is not always readily available even on a paid basis.[30] In addition, candidates must have money to demand access to media time; if they do not have financial resources, they receive limited public visibility. Hence, there are several reforms that have been suggested to cope with the inequities of mass media campaigning. It has been recommended by some analysts that the government pay for all political broadcasts as is the case in Britain and other continental countries where time is allocated on a proportional basis to candidates. Another proposal would permit the stations to deduct income lost as a result of providing free time to candidates from their taxable income. This would ensure truly "equal time" and not merely "equal access" to time, without placing a financial strain on the stations. It would seem that some arrangement, such as those noted above, or greater use of educational television for campaign purposes, would provide for increased participation by more candidates within an electoral arena increasingly circumscribed by the media.

STRUCTURAL REFORMS: FINANCIAL

The proposals for reform of the campaign finance system that have received the greatest public notice have been divided into two categories: there are those proposals which would provide for public financing of campaigns, and others which would establish campaign spending limits. The assumptions that have been made by private citizen reformers as well as by legislative proponents of campaign finance reform have been that the government should provide at least some of the revenue to fund a campaign, and that there should be some

---

[29] *Red Lion Broadcasting Co., Inc., et al.* v. *Federal Communications Commission et al.* 395 U.S. 367 (1969). However, as of October, 1975, the FCC ceased to mandate compliance with the equal time provision.

[30] An example would be the refusal of networks to allow opposition party candidates the right to reply to an incumbent president's press conference during an election period.

mechanism established to curtail spending as well as to control—and disclose—the sources of the funds made available to candidates. It has been assumed that a plan which included these controls would serve to weaken the influence of wealthy special interests by diluting their impact in a sea of small contributors.

Public Financing There is often sharp disagreement on the merits of public financing of campaigns. Its supporters argue that insofar as many potentially good candidates cannot raise the private funds to mount a meaningful campaign, there is a flaw operative in the democratic process. The counterarguments raised by opponents of federal campaign financing suggest: (1) Public financing of elections represents a "raid" on the Treasury unnecessary in our affluent society. (2) Furthermore, it penalizes good fund raisers and in so doing it is an attack on our system of free enterprise. (3) Also, the incumbent national party would have control over the allocation of campaign funds to all candidates, and thus might impair the free operation of the American political system.[31]

A full-fledged reform of the campaign finance system—a fragmented and largely personalized operation—might require a two-pronged approach which will be explored briefly before we examine some of the most often suggested changes of this system. One concern must be with the general elections; another must be with the nominating process—especially primary elections given their increasing costs.

The nominating process may be particularly central to the broader question of campaign finance and its impact upon democratic politics. The problems relating to fund raising encountered by candidates seeking nominations for public office are often more intense than those faced by the prospective candidates once nominated. It is increasingly costly to receive a party's nomination. Many very qualified people are not known well enough, or they are not perceived to be "sure winners" able to inspire sufficient confidence to invest dollars in their nomination efforts. Unless a political aspirant is a known quantity and can elicit monetary support at the outset of his nomination efforts, or unless he can rely on personal wealth or wealthy friends and/or associates, it is often nearly impossible to contest a nomination for public office. Consequently nominations often go to the already known individual—frequently the incumbent—or to a wealthy contender. Clearly this type of condition does not provide for the most "open" of political processes, nor does it encourage participation in the party process by individuals who may be qualified to run for public office but are concerned about financial hurdles. The travail of Senator Fred Harris when he entered the 1972 Democratic "presi-

---

[31] These and other arguments for and against public financing of campaigns appeared in *Congressional Digest* (February 1974): 35.

dential sweepstakes" is a good example of how the financial costs of receiving the nomination force potential candidates out of the running, and may put them into debt. Senator Harris ended his brief involvement in the Democratic nominating process with a debt of $50,000. Though the above discussion has focused upon the presidential nominating process, similar problems often exist for people seeking to contest other elective offices, particularly on a state level.

Primaries do create some problems for advocates of public financing of elections, inasmuch as providing public financing for primary contests (and other preconvention contests) may be fundamentally different from providing subsidies for general election contests because of the problem of deciding which candidates in a primary contest (or a convention process) qualify for such support. The problem is not, however, insurmountable. Casual candidacies can be discouraged by a variety of mechanisms which should make the concept of public funding at all stages of the election process more feasible.

Public financing proposals vary in form but all establish some formula that would provide candidates with public funds for the purpose of ending reliance on large individual and group contributions. Its supporters believe that resources for campaigning should be divided by law among candidates. In addition to providing specific sums of money to candidates, additional forms of public funding might include: a) government subsidies to provide free radio and television time to major contenders for office (including the use of public television); b) reduced mailing costs made available to all (including nonincumbent candidates); and c) government assumption of voter registration and Election Day publicity in order to lessen the costs to parties and candidates of voter mobilization. The latter is of particular interest because the United States is the only mature democracy in the world in which registration and Election Day costs are not paid by the government.[32] Attempts to establish a national system of universal registration of voters for federal elections at government cost have thus far been unable to gain congressional momentum.

Another type of approach has been recommended by Senator Lee Metcalf. He has suggested a voucher plan. Vouchers would be distributed by the government to the voters, who would then turn the vouchers over to their favorite candidates. Candidates would collect their vouchers and redeem them, together with itemized bills, and the government would then defray their expenses. This approach would combine private and public mechanisms—forcing the candidate to mount a grass-roots effort but ultimately relying on government subsidization. This proposal, and others which involve some citizen participation—in addition to government responsibility for expenses—may conform most closely to prevailing American norms.

[32] See Penn Kimball, *The Disconnected* (New York: Columbia University Press, 1972), p. 13.

Spending Limits The second suggested reform of the structure of campaign finance would place ceilings on the amount of money spent to win an election, as well as providing limits on the size of individual contributions. There have, however, been criticisms leveled against restrictions on campaign contributions: (1) they unconstitutionally restrict the right to free expression; (2) it is unfair to keep anyone from supporting a favored candidate with whatever resources he wishes to contribute; and (3) the restriction of large gifts would handicap challengers who are not as well known as the incumbents and who have therefore fewer financial sources to tap.[33] In response to the first objection, nowhere in the Constitution is there a statement providing that a rich person should gain special favors through his ability to make large campaign contributions. As for the second point, a $5,000 limit had been the law for thirty-one years before Congress chose to repeal that ceiling in 1971. As for the final objection to campaign finance limits, this may be the most difficult to answer. The data indicates that 90 percent of all incumbents seeking reelection win in their reelection bids, and that incumbents receive twice as many contributions as do their challengers.[34] Even if this inequity is removed, incumbents will retain advantages in staff, free mailing privileges, and availability of free media publicity via news broadcasts. In addition, the efficacy, as opposed to the legitimacy, of limitations on campaign expenditures may be doubtful. The experience of most Western nations including Britain, whose system of campaign finance is often compared favorably with our own, is that such limitations on contributions and spending tend to be ineffective and unenforced.[35]

THE FEDERAL ELECTIONS CAMPAIGN ACT AMENDMENTS OF 1974

The Federal Elections Campaign Act Amendments of 1974, passed in October 1974, incorporates many, though not all, of the reform concepts discussed above. The 1974 law provides for limits on individual, group, and party *contributions to candidates* for federal office, as well as limits on *expenditures by candidates* for federal office.[36] Individual contributions to a candidate are

---

[33] *Integrity in Politics,* p. 12.

[34] Ibid., p. 12.

[35] Frank Newman, "Money and Elections Law in Britain: Guide for America?" in *Western Political Quarterly* 10 (1957): 585.

[36] This account is drawn from a summary of the Campaign Reform Bill prepared by the Center for Public Financing of Elections in *Congressional Record,* October 10, 1974, H10340–1, and *Washington Post,* October 2, 1974, pp. 1, 3. It should be noted that the limitations on media spending contained in the 1971 legislation have been repealed in this law.

limited to $1,000 for primary and $1,000 for a general election campaign—no more than $25,000 may be contributed by an individual to all candidates for the entire duration of an election campaign. Organizational contributions are limited to $5,000 per candidate per primary and $5,000 per general election. Spending by candidates is limited to $70,000 for House candidates for both nomination and general election campaigns and $150,000 or $.12 per eligible state voter—whichever is more—for senatorial general election campaigns. In senatorial primaries, the limit is $100,000, or $.08 per voter. Candidates are permitted some additional expenditures for fund raising costs under the 1974 law. (National and state parties are permitted to provide candidates for national office with small payments above and beyond the otherwise stated spending limits.) Presidential candidates are limited to spending $20 million in the general election campaign and $10 million in primaries. Perhaps the most innovative provisions of the law relate to the mechanism whereby major party presidential candidates may receive their entire $20 million spending allotment from public funds derived from the Dollar Check-off Fund created by the 1971 act. Candidates who accept such public funding may raise no private funds. Public funds are available also for presidential primaries and national nominating conventions, a recognition of their central role in the presidential election process. Major parties may receive $2 million to finance their conventions and presidential primary candidates may obtain half of their $10 million spending limit from the government, on a 50–50 matching basis, providing they first raise $100,000 in small (under $250) contributions in at least twenty states. The provisions for preconvention campaign funding thus operationalize the concept of matching funds, requiring a candidate to demonstrate broad-based support in order to receive the federal allotment. Such a system, including as it does both small individual contributions and federal subsidies, may prove to be particularly well-suited to the American political culture. In addition to the aforementioned provisions of the 1974 law, the disclosure requirements of the 1971 reform law remain in effect.

Candidates for federal office must establish one central campaign committee through which all expenditures and contributions are to be reported, in order to end the proliferation of committees which have obscured sources of funding in the past. Other notable sections of the 1974 law include the treatment of loans as contributions, prohibition of fund solicitation through franked mail (a privilege previously available to incumbent members of Congress), and reimbursement of minor party expenses proportionate to their percentage of votes. Administration and enforcement of the new law is to be the responsibility of a six-member Federal Elections Commission.

While this campaign finance law is clearly the most sweeping ever passed in America, questions do remain about the degree to which it will alter American campaigning:

1. Because the public subsidies apply only to presidential elections, are congressional and other elections likely to remain dependent on large contributions? [37]

2. Will third parties find it even more difficult to gain a foothold in American politics due to the law's requirement that such parties receive at least 5 percent of the vote in order to obtain a subsidy?

3. Is it possible that office holders who have the advantage of incumbency may find their route to reelection even easier due to restrictions on their challengers' fund-raising ability?

4. How meaningful can attempts be to enforce limits on "in kind" contributions? Are all acts which may aid a candidate (and are worth money) to be limited? If so, what will be the consequences for the tradition of voluntarism which runs deep in American politics?

5. Is it possible that special interest groups will establish multiple campaign organizations and thus circumvent the intent of the law? Similarly, might not the traditional practice of wealthy families contributing via many individual family members continue even under the new law?

6. How vigorous will enforcement be under the aegis of the new Federal Elections Commission? Enforcement of criminal violations will rest with the Justice Department, which demonstrated no zeal for prosecution of earlier violators of campaign finance regulations.

7. How will the 1974 amendments affect the position of parties in the American political system?

CONCLUSION

There has been little discussion of the possibility of centralizing the management of campaign spending in the parties—though the 1974 law does provide for some financial assistance from parties to their designated candidates. It is possible that such centralization might facilitate disclosure, and also less costly campaigning. Considering national politics specifically, if the political parties were to become the central clearing houses for campaign funds, it might be easier to keep them in the public view than it is now to comprehend the multitude of candidates' campaign committees that operate in an election year. Certainly the transfer of the central function of campaigning to the political parties could have the effect of strengthening the role of the parties in American politics. Insofar as candidates for public office would be at least partially dependent on the parties for funding, they would have to be, once elected to public office, more "responsive" to their party regarding legislative or administrative decision making. A more "responsible two-party system" might be created, in which elected public officials represented the views of their parties because they were dependent on their party for election.[38]

Though the above discussion has focused on national-level politics, all of the positions just presented can relate just as easily to state and local politics.

---

[37] There are, however, many states which have enacted their own campaign finance laws—some of which are more stringent than the federal regulations.

[38] There are problems which arise when the question of an elected judiciary is raised. The proponents of responsible party government do not discuss the judiciary when they discuss responsiveness of elected officials to their party.

In the case of the state, state laws could be enacted to give the parties clearing-house functions for state election campaign finance. Similarly, local parties (where they exist) could be given this kind of function for local election races.

Clearly the above is intended in the way of conjecture. Given the tradition of widespread antipartyism in this country and the increasing tendency of voters to register with no party affiliation and to split their tickets on Election Day, it seems unlikely that the parties will assume a central function in campaign finance. In fact, inasmuch as the 1974 law was oriented primarily to candidates—as opposed to parties—it may lead to further fragmentation of the American party system. As a result, we may well move more deeply into an era of antiparty politics in America, with parties continuing to lose ground before virtually "independent" candidate-centered fund raising and campaigning.

11

Parties and the Nominating Process

THE PRESIDENTIAL PRIMARY AND THE STATE CONVENTION PROCESS OF DELEGATE SELECTION

It is evident that the major role of national parties in our antiparty environment is the nominating and to a lesser extent the electing of a president and vice-president. In fact, the national presidential nominating convention is the only time in four years when segments of the state and local parties come together. It is to the nominating process which we will turn our attention now in order to understand better this primary function of the national party in American politics. Election campaigns will *not* be considered in this chapter since the campaign function is *not*—as we have suggested in several places— the function of the national party organization per se.

Before the national conventions can be held it is necessary to select delegates. There are operative in the United States two basic systems for selecting convention delegates—the state primary and the state convention. We will examine both of these procedures beginning with a discussion of the historical development of these two basic selection modes.

HISTORICAL DEVELOPMENT

The earliest nominations for president of the United States—formal methods were not required until 1800—were accomplished by congressional cau-

240

cuses of the two major parties in Congress—the Republicans and the Federalists. The members of each party in Congress met and selected their party's standard bearer for the election campaign. This apparently was not a completely satisfactory method because after six elections the mixed caucus evolved.[1] Whereas the congressional caucus was comprised solely of members of Congress—which meant that if all the representatives of a district were of one party the district had no representation in the caucus of the other party—the mixed caucus achieved representation from all districts. This was accomplished by permitting districts that did not have a member in the congressional delegation in a particular party to choose a member of that party to participate in the caucus selection procedure. The noncongressional representatives to the mixed caucus were selected locally.

This method survived for eight years—from 1824 to 1832—and was ultimately replaced by the national convention. The first national party convention took place in September 1831, in Baltimore, and was held by the Anti-Masonic party. This was followed in December 1831 by a national Republican nominating convention. The convention was not, however, firmly established until 1840, though after 1832 national conventions were held for the purpose of nominating presidential candidates. Once there was a convention, questions arose relating to delegate selection that had not been relevant before its institutionalization. During the early years of the convention (1831–1832) states were invited to send delegates in numbers equivalent to their number of presidential electors. After 1840, there were no fixed rules of representation. Though each state had the same number of votes in convention as it had electoral votes, the size of a state's delegation was determined by each state party, and there were no standard methods for selecting convention delegates. Some states used legislative caucuses, in some states small groups of politicos made the decisions, and in other states delegates were selected by district or state conventions.[2]

In the post-Civil War years a new political form emerged in the South—the *primary election*. The primary (as discussed in Chapter 8) is a preliminary election for the nomination of candidates for office or for the choice of party committeemen or delegates to a party convention, designed to substitute for

---

[1] The above figure is based on:

a) 1788: Washington was selected. There was a general consensus and therefore no caucus. 1792: Same.
b) 1796: There is mixed evidence of caucus (however, not formal).
c) 1800: First year for which there is conclusive evidence of a caucus in both parties.
d) Operative caucuses for 1804, 1808, 1812, 1816, 1820, and 1824.

Data from Frederick W. Dallinger, *Nominations for Executive Office in the United States* (New York: Longmans, Green, 1897), p. 21.

[2] Howard R. Penniman, *Sait's American Parties and Elections*, 4th ed. (New York: Appleton-Century-Crofts, 1948), pp. 277–79.

party conventions. The goal is to increase popular participation. The first primary election of which there is any record was held in Crawford County, Pennsylvania in 1842. Momentum in the primary election movement was, however, realized only when the concept was adopted in South Carolina during the Reconstruction period. The reason for its implementation in the South at this time was its potential for limiting the power of the coastal Bourbon aristocracy in the process of candidate selection within the Democratic party.[3]

The idea of the primary became very attractive to the Progressives of the late nineteenth and early twentieth centuries. The primary is a tool of antipartyism insofar as it has a tendency to reduce the role of the party leadership in the nominating process—which is a central role of the American political parties. In 1903 Wisconsin (where the Progressive movement was strong) became the first state to pass a law establishing primary elections to select delegates to national conventions.[4] The attractiveness of the primary to the Progressives was rooted in their belief that the primary election system would "open up" participation in the selection of candidates to more people. They saw the convention system as controlled by party leaders and often unresponsive to the broader electorate. Progressive support for the primary went along with support for initiatives, referenda, and nonpartisan local elections. By 1910–1916, many states had instituted presidential primaries although within the next few years the fervor for direct election of convention delegates had abated. By 1968, only fifteen states held primaries. In 1972, under the impact of the Democratic party's reform rules that mandated popular participation in delegate selection, the primary enjoyed a partial renaissance: twenty-two states and the District of Columbia (twenty-one states plus Arkansas, which has an optional primary) used the primary to select delegates to attend the national nominating conventions of the two major parties.

States that do not hold primary elections to select national convention delegates generally use either state conventions or some mix of district primaries or conventions and statewide conventions. It is not possible to discuss all of the different states' forms but let us consider the most prevalent styles.

PRIMARIES: WHERE, WHEN, AND HOW

In Chapter 8 the direct primary was examined. A direct primary is a nominating election in which voters choose candidates to run for public office. An indirect primary is a nominating election in which voters choose delegates

---

[3] V. O. Key, *Parties, Politics, and Pressure Groups* (New York: Thomas Y. Crowell, 1946), pp. 372–73.

[4] C. Edward Merriam, *Primary Elections: A Study of the History and Tendencies of Primary Election Legislation* (Chicago: University of Chicago Press, 1909), p. 287. The Wisconsin primary did not, however, apply until adopted by a referendum in 1904.

who are charged with the duty of selecting candidates to run for public office; an example of this is the presidential primary.

In the past, the presidential primary has had an uncertain history.[5] Candidates have not entered all primaries, but have selected primaries in which to participate where they thought they could win or at least could gain by mobilizing important support.[6] There have been candidates who have won virtually all primaries, and have lost the nomination (Kefauver, 1952). There have also been candidates who have lost all the primaries they entered and won the nomination (Hoover, 1928). Some candidates skip primaries completely and win nominations (Humphrey, 1968). These disparities have existed because the primary has taken numerous forms:

1. It may simply be a preference primary—akin to a public poll—with no direct role in selection of the delegates who may be chosen by a separate primary vote or by a state convention.[7]

2. The preferential primary and the delegate selection process may be linked, but the popular vote may or may not be binding on the delegates chosen (who, in any case, are free to vote as they wish after the first convention ballot).

3. The primary may choose a "favorite son" candidate whose selection will be used to bargain for position, favors, etc., at the convention.

4. Delegates may be chosen with no indication on the ballot of their candidate preference.

5. Uncommitted delegates may be chosen and left to determine their own candidate preferences.

In the 1968 Democratic Convention, 40.5 percent of the delegates casting votes were chosen in primaries. Hence, even a candidate gaining a majority of primary votes would have a long way to go in order to gain all the votes needed for nomination.[8]

In a recent study, William Keech has demonstrated that of the presidential nominations since 1936, the front runners at the outset of the campaign have usually won regardless of primaries. This is not to say that primaries have no

[5] Since the states are responsible for running their own elections and thus maintain their separate election codes, no two states have identical procedures for all aspects of the electoral process. In regard to primaries, no two primary systems are exactly alike; this notion of state autonomy in the electoral process derives from the Constitution: Article I, Section 2; and Article I, Section 4.

[6] The classic example was John F. Kennedy in 1960, whose victories in Protestant, rural West Virginia and midwestern Wisconsin (home territory of his rival Humphrey) aided him in gaining the nomination. Theodore White, *The Making of the President, 1960* (New York: Atheneum, 1961), Chapter 4.

[7] In 1968, Eugene McCarthy won the Pennsylvania Democratic preference primary, but the state committee awarded most of the state's delegates to Hubert Humphrey. In New York in 1968, the delegation had 190 votes, 123 elected as members in the states' 41 congressional districts. Sixty-five were selected by the state committee, which failed to allocate a proportional share of seats to pro-McCarthy representatives despite the latter's showing in the primary vote. *New York Times,* June 29, 1968, pp. 1, 15.

[8] *New York Times,* February 10, 1972, p. 24.

value. They can permit relative political unknowns unsupported by the regular party leadership—Henry Cabot Lodge in 1964; Eugene McCarthy in 1968; and George McGovern in 1972—to emerge as front runners, although not always to emerge victorious at the convention. By broadening participation in the delegate selection process, the nominating process is opened to more voters. This system can weaken state and local parties if their selected delegates are not chosen by the voters in the primaries to attend the convention. This process of delegate selection reinforces the antiparty tradition that permeates much of American politics.

In those states which have utilized the convention for delegate selection, the manner in which delegates reach the convention varies from state to state.[9] National delegates selected at state conventions have not reflected an exact demographic distribution of either the general population or registered voters —any more than slates of primary delegates have been reflective of population distribution. District conventions, district primaries, or district party leadership select delegates to state conventions in some states. Also, some states— such as Delaware—designate delegates from districts via district committee and only if their choices are contested will there be a primary election to select state convention delegates who in turn will select national convention delegations. Delegates chosen by conventions may either support a candidate or be officially "noncommitted."

DO SELECTION PROCEDURES MATTER?

One question raised by several generations of political scientists, but satisfactorily answered by none, has been whether or not primaries matter in regard to broadening participation, and in making candidate selection more reflective of voter demands, as opposed to the demands of party leadership. Arguments have been developed in defense of primaries and in opposition to state conventions. The opposing sides can be drawn rather simply. The proprimary group believes that primaries increase voter participation in the nominating process. In contrast, when there are conventions the party regulars control delegate selection, and the "public mood" cannot be readily reflected. Proprimary advocates contend that a broader range of candidates can be presented to the voting public if the system is more open, as it is in the primaries. Either of these results, participation and/or the reflection of the "public mood," are

---

[9] In 1968, twenty-six states and territories selected all their national convention delegates at state conventions. Three other states selected some of their delegates in this manner. The Commission on Party Structure and Delegate Selection, *Mandate for Reform: A Report of the Commission on Party Structure and Delegate Selection to the Democratic National Committee* (Washington, D.C.: Democratic National Committee, 1970). A few states have also used appointment by either party or elected officials to designate delegates.

values in and of themselves, and whatever the monetary costs of running a primary either of these ends justifies such costs. Insofar as these goals weaken strong centralized party organization they are reflective of our antipartyism.

The devotees of the convention system find the above arguments unconvincing. They do not see voter participation increasing sharply as a result of primary elections. They perceive the apathy toward political party activities which most Americans harbor, pointing specifically to the low voter turnout in primaries. They suggest that the high monetary outlays for primary elections (in 1968, $45 million—Democrats, $25 million and Republicans, $20 million—was spent on preconvention activities) [10] are not well spent since the mean turnout in most presidential primaries is only 27 percent.[11] Also, there is no guarantee, they argue, that the results of primaries will any more reflect the voters' wishes than conventions. Since so few people bother to vote in primaries, a small, well organized group of people can control the party's choice of candidate or convention delegates simply by voting. This method, it is reasoned, can destroy the broadly representative nature of parties. Critics of primaries contend that the nomination of George McGovern in 1972 by the Democratic party was in large part the result of a small group of well organized people who participated in the primary process in many states and for a short moment of history succeeded in "taking over" the nominating process of the national Democratic party.[12] It has been argued that the McGovern supporters did not reflect Democratic party voters, since the Democratic party maintained its domination of both state houses and the Senate and the House of Representatives in 1972, but then went on to lose the presidency. However, one point of caution must be raised here. George McGovern received 421.55 of his national convention votes from convention states. So it is clearly possible to mobilize organized support for minority candidates even if a convention system is utilized.

[10] *Congressional Quarterly Weekly Report* 30 (July 8, 1972): 1650. It should be noted that primary costs in 1972 dropped significantly, apparently under the impact of the Election Campaign Act of 1971.

[11] Austin Ranney, "Turnout and Representation in Presidential Primary Elections," *American Political Science Review* 66 (March 1972): 23. For presidential elections, the turnout rate was 62 percent for the same period, 1948–68.

[12] This view is buttressed by the fact that although McGovern gained delegates, he did not necessarily amass huge voter majorities.

	Popular Vote in Primaries
McGovern	4,053,453
Humphrey	4,021,372
Wallace	3,755,424

SOURCE: *Congressional Quarterly Weekly Report* 30 (October 14, 1972): 2641.

As far as delegate selection to national nominating conventions is concerned, if the candidate who succeeds in the primaries is nominated—and there are many recent examples of this not being the case, such as Adlai Stevenson in 1952, Barry Goldwater in 1964, and Hubert Humphrey in 1968—he may have the advantage of a well organized grass-roots organization already operating once the general election campaign gets underway. He may also have the advantage of having a high level of voter name (and issue position) recognition prior to the general election. This can aid a candidate, especially a nonincumbent presidential contender. Certainly it can hinder a candidate too! George McGovern's positions were known to many voters prior to the general election campaign. They were unpopular with many groups in the American voting public. The publicity he and his policy orientations received when he was contesting the primaries with members of his own political party did not help him in his bid for the presidency. In California in May and June 1972, Senator Hubert Humphrey attacked McGovern's positions on national income policy. In a thirty-second television spot Humphrey said: "George McGovern's welfare program is not a job program and will cost taxpayers an extra $72 billion a year. I say welfare should be provided only for those who need it. As President, I'll create what's *really* [emphasis Humphrey's] needed—jobs for the more than six million out of work—over half a million people right here in California. Announcer: Humphrey means more jobs—not more welfare." [13]

Later in the campaign the same theme of fear of changes McGovern might bring was picked up by Nixon's Committee to Reelect the President organization.

TRENDS IN PRESIDENTIAL DELEGATE SELECTION

BACKGROUND

By the time Eugene McCarthy won the New Hampshire primary in March 1968, over half the delegates to the Democratic national convention had already been chosen or were in the process of being chosen. This fact was accentuated by the disappointment of McCarthy's followers over what they deemed to be inadequate representation at the 1968 Democratic convention, and was heightened by the tumultuous disorders that accompanied that convention. In 1969 the Democratic party appointed the Commission on Party Structure and Delegate Selection to change this; to undertake an "examination of the structures and processes used to select delegates to the National Conven-

[13] A Thirty-Second Spot Television Commercial Aired in the California Primary by Hubert Humphrey, from "Spot Commercials: Contrasting Styles," *National Journal* 4 (June 10, 1972): 970.

tion" in order "to give all Democratic voters . . . a full, meaningful and timely opportunity to participate in the selection of delegates, and, thereby, in the decisions of the Convention itself." [14] They made a variety of proposals relating to delegate selection and fair representation. Among the most significant were the recommendations that the party ensure public participation and fair representation (especially for youth, minority groups, and women) in the delegate selection process, select delegates in the year of the election, and abolish the unit rule (or "winner takes all" rule historically used in Democratic primaries and conventions). A consideration of delegate selection procedures is now in order. Since most of the major alterations in methods occurred within the Democratic party, the discussion that follows will focus on the Democrats.

DELEGATE SELECTION PROCEDURES: IMPACT ON 1972 ELECTION

The most immediate result of the Democratic Party Commission report was seen in the composition of the 1972 Democratic nominating convention, and its choice of George McGovern as standard bearer. Since one of the major objectives of the McGovern Commission report was to open up the nominating process, it was not surprising that many people who had never been delegates to previous conventions were selected by their states' parties to attend the convention as designated delegates.[15] In 1968, 34 percent of the delegates had attended at least one previous convention; in 1972 the comparable figure was 16 percent.[16] At earlier conventions, many of the delegates had been party leaders and their designated "faithful," or elected, officials. While in both 1968 and 1972, 32 percent of the delegates were party or elected officials, there was a substantial drop in the number of high-ranking party and elected officials who attended the 1972 convention.[17] Many more women, nonwhites, and people under thirty were in attendance at the latter convention: 38 percent of the 1972 delegates were women, 21 percent of the delegates were under thirty, and 15 percent of the delegates were blacks—compared to 15 percent blacks, 13 percent women, and 4 percent youth under thirty in 1968.[18] The group that lost delegates was apparently the white working class. Less than

[14] The Commission on Party Structure and Delegate Selection, *Mandate for Reform,* pp. 9–10. An additional factor in the reevaluation of delegate selection procedures were contests at the 1964 and 1968 Democratic conventions which challenged delegations on the basis of unfair racial and ethnic exclusion.

[15] There were in fact two commissions established by the party to change convention procedures: the O'Hara Commission on Rules and the McGovern-Fraser Commission on Party Structure and Delegate Selection. We will henceforth refer to both under the rubric "McGovern Commission."

[16] Dennis G. Sullivan, Jeffrey L. Pressman, Benjamin I. Page, and John L. Lyons, *The Politics of Representation* (New York: St. Martins, 1974), p. 24.

[17] Ibid. In 1968, eighty-five congressmen and forty senators attended; in 1972 the comparable figures were forty-nine and fifteen. *Congressional Quarterly Weekly Report* 30 (July 1, 1972): 1574.

[18] *Congressional Quarterly Almanac,* 1972 (Washington, D.C.: Congressional Quarterly, 1972): 1048, and Sullivan, et al., *Politics of Representation,* p. 23.

10 percent of the 1972 delegates were members of unions.[19] These observations on delegate profile would not be complete without a comment on the socioeconomic background of the delegates. The McGovern commission suggested that the convention which nominates the presidential and vice-presidential candidates for the Democratic party should better reflect the composition of the population. However, comparisons of income data for delegates as opposed to the general public indicate relative affluence for the delegates (Table 42). Furthermore, while the median educational achievement level of Americans over twenty-five is 12.2 years,[20] over 39 percent of the delegates to the Democratic convention had some graduate education in their background. A comparable figure for Republicans was 33 percent.[21] On the basis of socioeconomic background variables it can be argued that the delegates to the 1972 convention selected by the more open system encouraged by the party commission report were no more representative of the American people, and perhaps even

Table 42. Income Distribution, 1972 Conventions (in percent)

Income Categories	Income Nationally	Democratic Delegates	Republican Delegates
Under $5,000	18	5	2
$5,000 to $9,999	32	10	5
$10,000 to $14,999	27	20	13
$15,000 to $25,000	18	31	28
Over $25,000	5	32	50

SOURCE: *Washington Post,* August 19, 1972, p. A.10.

somewhat less so than the elected officials, who at earlier conventions had comprised a considerable portion of the delegations. An important casualty of the new rules may have been the "casual" Democrat who votes on Election Day—and whose needs are spoken for by elective party and public officials.

The demands made upon the Republican party for more open delegations to their convention were not as vociferous as they were among the Democrats. But the Republican 1972 convention also had more women, youth, and nonwhites as delegates than had been present at previous conventions. Thus 30.1 percent of the Republican delegates in 1972 were women, 8.7 percent youth

[19] *New York Times,* July 9, 1972, p. 42.
[20] U.S. Bureau of the Census *Statistical Abstract of the United States: 1971* (Washington, D.C., 1971), p. 109.
[21] *Washington Post,* August 19, 1972, p. A. 10.

under thirty, and 6.2 percent nonwhites. Comparable figures for 1968 show 17 percent women, 1 percent youth under thirty, and 1.9 percent nonwhites.[22] The outcome of the Republican convention was a foregone conclusion as soon as President Nixon indicated his desire to stand for reelection in 1972. As a result it would be fruitless to discuss the changes brought by the differences in the sex, age, and racial characteristics of the delegates and their significance on the outcome of the convention. There was an attempt, however, among some of the delegates to change the process of delegate allocation for the 1976 convention. This attempt was unsuccessful—blocked by the conservative majority.

The effect of the McGovern Commission on the total number of (Democratic) primaries held was of some importance. In 1968, fifteen states and Washington, D.C., having a total of 42 percent of the (1,068) delegate votes held primaries to select their delegates to the Democratic National Convention. In 1972, twenty-two states plus the District of Columbia, having 63 percent of the delegate votes (a total of nearly 1,900 delegate votes) held primaries to select their national convention delegates.[23]

In retrospect, perhaps the most interesting outcome of the McGovern Commission report was that even in *convention* states the process of delegate selection was opened to all registered voters and wrested from the control of party leaders. Thus, states such as Iowa, which utilized a state convention to select delegates to the national conventions, saw the Democrats able to reform the system. The following report of the process in Iowa appeared in the *New York Times* on January 26, 1972. It conveys something of the flavor of grass-roots participation in the delegate selection process as it describes:

. . . the nasal voice of Murray Williams, the service man of Montgomery Ward, declaring:

"The Democratic caucus of the First Precinct of Crestin will please come to order. Tonight we will choose six delegates to be sent to the county caucus and then, hopefully, on to the district and state caucuses and finally, to Florida."

What happened in that basement room over the next hour or so is more or less typical of what happened last night in more than 2,000 other basements, parlors, and civic auditoriums scattered all across Iowa, from Dubuque to Council Bluffs, from Britt to Mystic.

In all, 25,000 people were involved, men and women, doctors and day laborers, college students and militant blacks.

---

[22] *Congressional Quarterly Weekly Report* 30 (August 12, 1972): 1998–99. (As was noted elsewhere in this chapter election laws are state laws. In order for a state party to run a primary for delegate selection to a national convention, there must be a state law with that provision. Thus it is not entirely state party responsibility alone that determines whether primaries, conventions, or a mix of the two are used.)

[23] *CQ Guide to Current American Government* (Washington, D.C.: Congressional Quarterly Service, 1972), p. 34.

It may have been the case in 1972 that the most meaningful grass-roots participation was achieved in nonprimary states. Consider also the case of Louisiana.

> In the past, delegate selection in Louisiana was always tightly closed—the Democratic Governor picked the people he wanted. The state party's reluctant response to the McGovern Commission this year was a complicated series of local caucuses. All registered Democrats could participate in the initial stage—meetings in the 105 state legislative districts, held last April 15 [1972]. Delegates were elected at these meetings to the second round of caucuses, held May 13 in the eight Congressional Districts. A total of 40 national convention delegates were elected at these meetings. The 40 met May 20 and chose four more delegates.[24]

Increased participation by blacks and other heretofore marginal groups was also noteworthy. Political participation takes time. It was observed in Chapters 5 and 6 that political participation increases with income and education. "Given this knowledge, it should not be too surprising that the perceived opportunities for increased participation which were an outgrowth of the McGovern commission report were seized upon by voters who were not representative of the population in terms of their socioeconomic status."[25] The Democrats did, however, increase participation among many newcomers to presidential politics: large numbers of people never before involved in politics were chosen as delegates demonstrating that the reforms succeeded in opening up the nominating process to a certain degree. It should be emphasized that the mandatory, self-imposed, Democratic delegate selection reform had far more significant impact than the Republicans' voluntary and less sweeping changes.[26]

Perhaps several final points should be examined now in regard to the likely impact of the McGovern commission recommendations upon future delegate selection procedures within the Democratic party. By way of conjecture we might expect that the day of the "over forty-five white male delegate" as prototype is probably over. However, he is still quite alive; he dominated the 1972 Democratic convention (not in numbers, but in influence), and will probably do so again in 1976. Many more representatives of other groups however, will continue to serve as delegates—as established in 1972. It seems unlikely, however, given the results of the 1972 election, and especially the rules on delegate selection which will be operative for 1976, that the self-consciousness in selecting delegates—to the point that some state delegations attempted to attain demographic characteristics regarding age, race, and sex

---

[24] *New York Times,* June 4, 1972, Sect. IV, p. 4.
[25] It should be noted that often even where candidates put up proportionally balanced delegate states, voters in caucuses or primaries chose unbalanced ones.
[26] *New York Times,* August 20, 1972, p. 50.

which were exact reflections of the state electorate—will continue. Because important constituents of the Democratic party—labor, older "ethnics," and professional politicians—were not represented at the 1972 convention, attempts to assign "quotas" for some groups and not others have been eliminated for the 1976 convention.[27] Furthermore, the opportunities for participation that were heeded by relatively few people and candidates in 1972, though many more than usual, will be better understood by more people and candidates in 1976, and thus there may be more competition for delegate positions within the states. In addition, it may be the case that some "participation fever" may also infect Republicans (who experienced an early variant of the voluntary political style in 1964 when they nominated Barry Goldwater for president).

PROSPECTS FOR 1976

In March 1974 the Commission on Delegate Selection and Party Structure of the Democratic party reported to the Executive Committee of the Democratic National Committee its proposals for delegate selection to the 1976 Democratic National Convention. In part, the selection procedures recommended, which were accepted by the party for the 1976 national convention, could be seen as a reaction to the 1972 convention. The provisions of the report provide for a system in which state parties are encouraged to influence their respective states to hold closed primaries. The effect of this provision would be to foreclose participation by either members of other parties or independent voters who are not registered in any party from the process of delegate selection to the national convention. In a system with only closed primaries, voters who are issue-committed, or candidate-committed, but not party affiliated (i.e., prone to strong antiparty attitudes) will have less of an opportunity to influence the outcome of the delegate selection process.[28] Perhaps more significant, however, in terms of affecting the composition of delegates to the 1976 convention, there are three specific provisions. Firstly, at least 75 percent of the delegates must be selected from districts no larger than congressional districts; also, 25 percent of the delegates may be selected "at large" from a state. The latter is ". . . to encourage the selection of delegations including public officials, party officials, and members of traditionally underrepresented Democratic constituencies. . . ;" those groups whose convention presence is now recognized as vital. Secondly, there will be no unit (or "winner take all") rule permitted to operate within delegations. And thirdly, though an affirmative

---

[27] As suggested above, ranking officeholders were all but absent at the Democratic convention, though most Republican officeholders attended their party's convention.

[28] This reform was a reaction—in part—to the participation of Republicans and nonparty affiliated voters in "open" Democratic primaries, which led to increased support for George Wallace.

action program must be operationalized for both the national party and the state parties, the use of quotas to have a demographically balanced delegate slate has been specifically barred as nonpermissible. There are many other rules and provisions, but insofar as this discussion relates specifically to delegate selection for the 1976 convention these three are the most central to our discussion. Consider now the possible impact of the proposed rules changes.

In primary states the apportionment of delegates must be accomplished in a manner such that at least 75 percent of all delegates are selected from districts no larger than congressional districts. Such a procedure may make it more difficult to organize a state—in the manner that the McGovern supporters did in many states in 1972—to win a slate of delegates. In convention states organization may become more difficult to coalesce too, since delegate slates must reflect proportionally the division of expressed presidential preferences. Also, since there can be no enforced unit rule within conventions, it is possible that given the nature of delegate selection—which will reflect the expressed preferences of the registered voters—it will be very difficult for a candidate for the presidential nomination to come to the convention with a sufficiently large bloc of votes to control the proceedings and eventual nomination.[29]

One further point needs to be raised about the reaction to the 1972 delegate selection process. Though the members of the Democratic party Commission on Delegate Selection and Party Structure were concerned about having a selection process that included groups previously underrepresented in the nominating conventions, they were especially sensitive to the arguments raised about quotas in the aftermath of the 1972 convention. Thus, in order "to encourage full participation by all Democrats, with particular concern for minority groups, native Americans, women, and youth, in the delegate selection process and in all Party affairs, the National and State Democratic Parties shall adopt and implement Affirmative Action Programs. . . . This goal shall not be accomplished either directly or indirectly by the Party's imposition of mandatory quotas at any level of the delegate selection process or in any other Party affairs. . . ." [30] These proposed changes attempt to retain the spirit of the 1972 democratization efforts, while modifying those reforms that were viewed as excessive.

THE NATIONAL NOMINATING CONVENTIONS

The gala event for each of the national parties is their national convention. It is the convention and the campaign that follows, which provide the party with its *raison d'être*. Let us look now at the convention itself.

---

[29] Preferences receiving less than 15 percent of the votes cast for the delegation need not be given any delegates.

[30] Report of The Commission on Delegate Selection and Party Structure (Democratic National Committee, March 1, 1974, mimeo), p. 7.

It has been suggested in the previous pages that despite the attempts to "reform" the convention system in 1972, the delegate profile still was not socioeconomically reflective of the American people. An argument can be made for the position that the social and economic characteristics—as well as age, sex, and race—need not be a mirror reflection of the polity for a convention to be representative. At many conventions, it does not matter who "the bodies" are, in any case, because to a considerable extent the rank-and-file delegate does not make decisions. In many instances, it is the professional politicians—primarily state leaders—who ultimately control the outcome of the conventions.

Conventions have traditionally also been unrepresentative in terms of the "one man, one vote" idea. This is because delegates have represented states and not people. In 1968, for example, the Democrats gave each state three delegates for each of their electoral votes as well as bonuses for each 100,000 votes cast for Johnson in 1964 and votes gained in the electoral college. Bonuses have traditionally been used to reward strong party structures. Because the electoral college vote overrepresents the role of small states, in 1972 the Democrats sought to modify this inequity in selecting delegates by dividing a state's delegation equally on the basis of population and the 1968 Democratic vote. This reform effort was beaten back; in the end 53 percent of the delegates were designated to states on the basis of their electoral college vote while 47 percent of the delegates were distributed on the basis of the Democratic vote in the past three presidential elections. The net result was to leave substantial delegate strength in the hands of smaller states and the South while increasing somewhat the representation of more populous states.

Delegates have traditionally come to conventions committed to a candidate or to a politician who may be a "favorite son" from their state. Many delegates are pledged to vote for a particular candidate for at least the first ballot, and many are pledged for future ballots as well. With regard to rules and procedures at a convention, it is more the rule than the exception that delegations can be "held" by the state leadership to vote as the delegation leadership wishes. In part this has been due to the relatively low level of information delegates have had in the past regarding party affairs. However, not even at the 1972 Democratic National Convention, where many more amateur politicians attended than ever before in recent history, was there complete independence among the delegates. Thus when the McGovern forces needed delegate votes to keep the contested South Carolina delegation intact they were able to garner sufficient votes. This was the case despite the fact that the delegates in question would have been replaced by more women—a cause that had been adopted by large numbers of female McGovern delegates. This example illustrates the degree to which delegates to the 1972 Democratic convention were candidate oriented, even to the exclusion of expressed group goals. As noted previously, the Republican convention also experienced some dissonance which was deflated by the dominant party grouping.

Prior to 1972 one could make a reasonably valid generalization about the attendance at national conventions: that delegates were chosen to attend conventions as rewards for service to the state and local party organizations. People were selected who could be counted upon to cast their votes "correctly" —as determined largely by the state party leadership. Perhaps one of the best anecdotal representations of this political mode was conveyed in the following description. "They had little to do, however, with the real work of the conventions, and like most delegates, Mrs. Brownstein had no illusions about her role. 'I just want somebody to make up my mind for me,' she said in an outburst of candor. This job is more an aliyah—an honor—than anything else. You don't need any special skills.' " [31]

It is not clear that this generalization was valid in 1972. Because of changed procedures, different kinds of people arrived at the convention halls and, as noted earlier, many more amateur political types attended the conventions. Hierarchically run state delegations, which had often dominated earlier conventions, were more difficult to sustain in this environment. Furthermore, a large number of delegates, especially the McGovern delegates at the Democratic convention, were more issue oriented than the previous prototype delegate. Many believed in the causes George McGovern was expounding. Clearly many of these people, who had not previously been involved in party politics, were more committed to the positions expressed by a particular person than to the Democratic party per se. To some extent, some of these participants were political activists but were nonetheless antipartyists. It is doubtful, for example, that all the McGovern supporters would have supported another candidate if the party had nominated one other than George McGovern. A similar phenomenon occurred in 1968 when the Robert Kennedy/Eugene McCarthy delegates were not able to win the nomination for a candidate of their choice. Among the liberal elements of the party who had supported Kennedy or McCarthy, many "sat out" the postelection campaign work.[32] Goldwater's nomination in the Republican party produced a similar reaction. Very few important Republicans supported Goldwater because of their disapproval of his conservative political philosophy.

On the other hand, Richard Daley, a politician motivated by more traditional party oriented concerns, though angered by the 1972 Democratic convention that would not seat his delegation (since it lacked a proper proportion

[31] Martin and Susan Tolchin, *To the Victor: Political Patronage from the Clubhouse to the White House* (New York: Random House, 1971), p. 4.

[32] For example, "Allard K. Lowenstein, a member of the New Democratic Coalition's steering committee, said at the news conference that the group had refused to support Vice-President Humphrey." *New York Times,* August 31, 1968, pp. 1, 9.

of nonwhites, women, or young people), supported the candidacy of George McGovern as the convention's nominee for president.[33]

Clearly then there are now at least two motivations for attending the conventions: reward for service and strongly held political beliefs.

IS THE CONVENTION AN ANTICLIMAX?

A claim can be made that all the convention does is ratify the effects of the candidate's "wheeling and dealing" of the previous four years. Perhaps some examination of a few conventions held in the past several years will put this argument into clearer focus. Since 1960 no major party convention has gone beyond the first ballot. Prior to the 1960 Democratic convention, John F. Kennedy had between 600 and 700 delegate votes assured him.[34] In 1964 Barry Goldwater had 739 Republican delegate votes—or a majority—going into the convention.[35] In the same year Lyndon Johnson, the incumbent Democratic president, had virtually all the delegate votes pledged to him prior to the convention. The year 1968 saw much of the same kind of preconvention commitment with Hubert Humphrey assured of sufficient delegate votes for the nomination, and Richard Nixon having over 700 votes among the 1,333 delegates present at the outset of the Republican convention.[36] Goldwater's nomination was particularly interesting because he enjoyed no broad support even among Republicans. His nomination was ensured by a conservative take-over of local party machinery. It may be argued with some accuracy that like Goldwater's strategists, McGovern supporters succeeded in gaining control of delegate selection machinery, despite the ideological unacceptability of the candidate to much of the party's rank and file.

In 1972, Richard Nixon, the incumbent president, was virtually assured of the nomination, as Johnson had been in 1964; and in 1972 George McGovern and his followers had almost enough delegate votes to capture the Democratic nomination. While the vote was a little closer at this convention than at the conventions of the 1960s, this does not detract from the major point being raised here. Potential candidates must do their political "wheeling and deal-

---

[33] Enthusiasm may not have been as high for McGovern as it might have been for another candidate, but the Daley organization worked for the party candidate or remained neutral in the McGovern race.

[34] New York Times, July 10, 1960, Sec. 4, p. El. Kennedy thus had approximately 38½ percent of the delegates, the largest bloc of votes going into the convention.

[35] New York Times, July 13, 1964, p. 1; see also Judith H. Parris, The Convention Problem (Washington, D.C.: Brookings Institution, 1972), p. 125.

[36] New York Times, August 28, 1968, pp. 1, 30; Congressional Quarterly Almanac, 1968 24 (Washington, D.C.: Congressional Quarterly Service, 1968): 979.

ing" in the four years prior to the convention so that party leadership is responsive to them, and also in the preconvention period when state delegations are being selected by primaries or state and local conventions. In this respect, the national convention is often something of an anticlimax. This trend may underline the importance of nonparty resources—early candidacy, strong personal organization, money, successful polls and media, political personality—in the contest for nomination. The continuation of these tendencies may lead to a further decline in the role played by party leaders in the presidential nominating process.[37]

If, as suggested above, the convention is often an anticlimax with regard to the presidential nomination, it can logically be asked why we incur the expense of national conventions every four years. In many ways the convention acts to counteract our dominant antipartyism sufficiently to keep the parties alive in the four years between the conventions. There are explanations for holding conventions that may not be found to be compelling by all analysts, but which are sufficiently viable so as to have maintained the national conventions as a political form since 1840. Though it is clear that since 1960 the nominations of the parties have all but been reasonably "tied up" prior to the conventions, this has not always been the case. Though Dwight D. Eisenhower was nominated on the first ballot at the 1952 Republican convention, he had only 523 delegate votes *prior* to the convention. Robert Taft, a Republican senator from Ohio, had 491 committed delegate votes.[38] The decision was truly made at the convention as to whom the party would nominate since the differential in committed delegates was only 32, and there were delegates committed neither to Senator Taft nor to General Eisenhower. In the same year the Democrats nominated Adlai Stevenson. Stevenson received only 273 votes on the first ballot; 616 votes were required for the nomination.[39]

In addition to the possibility that someone may be nominated whom "political prophets" did not anticipate, there are other functions of the convention. The convention and the nominating process preceding it act as a *consciousness raiser* for the voting public as well as for party identifiers. Given our basic antiparty attitudes, if the nominating process were not a public "happening" as it is in the United States it seems likely that fewer people would be involved, the range of candidates would be narrower (since candidates can be broken but also made by long campaigns—note George McGovern in 1971–1972),[40] and political awareness regarding the timely issues of politics would more than

---

[37] Nelson Polsby and Aaron B. Wildavsky, *Presidential Elections,* 3d ed. (New York: Charles Scribner's Sons, 1971), p. 159.

[38] Report of an Associated Press Poll in *New York Times,* July 11, 1952, p. 1; the total number of delegate votes at this convention was 1,206. See Herbert Eaton, *Presidential Timber* (New York: The Free Press, 1964), p. 451.

[39] Eaton, *Presidential Timber,* p. 479.

[40] See Chapters 3 and 4 for a further discussion of this phenomenon.

ever be the restricted realm of the affluent and the educated. Insofar as the nominating process culminating in a convention "fires" people about politics it provides an impetus for the polity to think about candidates, parties, and issues, and to vote.[41]

Another significant function of the convention is the unification it provides to otherwise very disparate state and local parties. For example, the Democrats of Georgia and the Democrats of Wisconsin have little reason in the years between conventions to envision themselves as a single political unit. Without the opportunity the convention provides for largely separate political organizations to meet, there would be no national party to work for the election of a presidential candidate. Insofar as the conventions act to bring people together once every four years to nominate a presidential candidate, they play a key role for the parties. An additional point ought not be overlooked. Though the screaming and yelling at the conventions—the circus quality—may appear to serve no useful purpose, and though speeches seem to many people to be a waste of time, all of these occurrences provide the delegates and the party leaders with some of the fuel to keep themselves together for another four years.[42]

It should be noted that the convention may nonetheless become in some instances a battleground for conflicting groups within the party.

In 1948 the Democratic party nominated incumbent President Harry Truman. It was clear that if the convention voted to nominate the president, the South would balk and leave the party, due largely to their opposition to the strong civil rights program espoused by Truman. Truman was nominated: he received 947½ first ballot votes to 263 for Senator Russell of Georgia.[43] The southern delegates left the convention; they met in convention in Birmingham, Alabama, and nominated Strom Thurmond for president on the States' Rights party ticket. The 1948 example suggests that the convention cannot restore unity to a faction-ridden party—as the more recent instances of 1964 (Republicans) and 1968 (Democrats) again remind us.

While the party platform issued by the convention may appear to many to serve no useful purpose, since it is not binding on congressional representatives or even the presidential nominee himself, it provides both a mechanism for compromise and negotiation among delegates and a way of appealing to major

[41] In 1972, the Democratic party convention played this role to a lesser degree than usual, auguring poorly for McGovern's chances in the election. See Miller et al., "A Majority Party in Disarray: Policy Polarization in the 1972 Election," paper presented to the American Political Science Association, New Orleans, Louisiana, September 1973, p. 43.

[42] The Democrats also modified some of these aspects of the convention in 1972. They prohibited "spontaneous" floor demonstrations, limited nominating speeches, and barred favorite son candidacies.

[43] *Congress and the Nation, 1945–1964* (Washington, D.C.: Congressional Quarterly Service, 1965), p. 5. An arena of frequent contention is the Credentials Committee, which resolves questions involving the seating of disputed delegations.

population groups who support the party.[44] Perhaps the best indication of the differences between the Goldwater candidacy in 1964 and that of McGovern in 1972 (it has been noted that both nominations had much in common) lay in the differing approaches of the two candidates to the platform. While Goldwater refused to compromise any of his conservative principles, the McGovern approach was to combine traditional New Deal appeals to the working man with support for innovative approaches to foreign policy (including immediate withdrawal from Vietnam), universal medical care, a guaranteed national income, opposition to big business, and support of "newer" political groupings and issues (embodied, for example, in the call for amnesty for war resisters). Nonetheless, the most radical and controversial ideals espoused by McGovern supporters—abortion on demand, legalization of marijuana, equal rights for homosexuals, unequivocal support for busing, and a $6,500 guaranteed income for all Americans—were abandoned or strongly modified under pressure from McGovern and his aides. Hence, the McGovern delegates engaged in compromise and innovation and upheld the traditional role of the convention platform.

In addition to the platform, the choice of a vice-presidential candidate to "balance" the ticket helps to serve the dual purpose of cementing party support and gaining votes from specific party oriented groups.

Conventions may also provide future candidate hopefuls the opportunity to be seen and heard by the massed leadership corps of the many separate local party organizations. Eugene McCarthy received a strong "push" in 1960 when he gave the nominating speech for Adlai Stevenson at the Democratic convention. Similarly, John F. Kennedy first received national attention when he contested the nomination for vice-president in 1956. Though he lost the nomination to Estes Kefauver (Democratic senator from Tennessee) he received some recognition from party membership that he was able to parlay into the momentum which brought him the 1960 nomination.

More recently the 1968 convention catapulted Senator George McGovern of South Dakota from relative national obscurity to the 1972 Democratic candidate for president. In 1968 when the delegates committed to the late Robert F. Kennedy were looking for a candidate to support, George McGovern emerged as a candidate for these delegates to rally around.

CONCLUSION: THE NATIONAL PRIMARY ALTERNATIVE

A brief discussion of a national primary seems to be in order. We have addressed ourselves to the national party's role in the electoral process—

[44] Some political scientists have not only found considerable differences between the parties' platforms; they have found also a significant correlation between platform pledges and subsequent executive and legislative programs. See Gerald Pomper, *Elections in America: Control and Influence in Democratic Politics* (New York: Dodd, Mead, 1970), pp. 149–70.

specifically at the nominating stage since this seems to be its *raison d'être.* Given some of the limitations of the system, including the costs both in terms of time and money, the often inexact reflection of the polity at conventions due to delegate selection processes, and the low level of general voter interest in the state primaries and conventions, an alternative for the current nominating system has been proposed by some political analysts and some practicing politicos.

Apparently a national primary would be very popular with the American public. According to the Gallup organization, in March 1972, 72 percent of the American people favored a national primary system (in 1968, 76 percent of the people favored this system).[45]

What is the likely form a national primary would take? Briefly, instead of each of the separate states choosing to have primaries, conventions, or some mix thereof at different times, a national primary date would be set and in all states at the same time party primaries would be held to select the party's nominee for president. (Some proposals would eliminate the convention entirely; others would retain it in order to select the vice-presidential nominee and write the platform.)

It is assumed by devotees of this proposal that there would be an increase in voter participation and that since the costs of campaigning would not be high (a questionable point) there would be a likelihood of more, and perhaps better, candidates contending for the presidential nominations of the two major parties. The argument for increased voter participation rests on the assumption that a focused national campaign would attract more attention than the disparate and moving "road shows" that are now the rule in state primary and state convention delegate campaigns. The current mode exists because candidates choose states in which to campaign (in order to maximize their image as "winners") and because they must—given the number of states—move around rapidly from state campaign to state campaign.

Several difficulties seem apparent with regard to a national primary. Name recognition and ethnic and racial factors might prove a significant element in primary victory. Lesser known candidates would not become known gradually as the result of a series of "trial heats" as did McCarthy in 1968 and McGovern in 1972. A nominee unacceptable to the party—a member of an ideologically extreme wing, or a contender with regional support—might be chosen. A candidate could win the nomination with 40 percent of the vote (or even a smaller fraction, if the race were divided many ways), even if 60 percent of those voting selected him as their last choice candidate. Even if there is a run-off provision, it is possible that the top two candidates could be candidates

[45] *Gallup Opinion Index,* April 1972, p. 26. The question asked was: "It has been suggested that Presidential candidates be chosen by the voters in a nationwide primary election instead of by political party conventions at present. Would you favor or oppose this?"

of minority wings of the party. In such situations, the candidate would have no chance of winning the election in November. Entirely missing might be the expertise of party leaders and activists, who bring to the nomination process both a knowledge of and stake in the forces that produce electoral victory.

Money would be a serious problem, particularly if—as seems likely—television would loom even larger in the national primary process. Unless a national primary campaign were linked to spending restrictions, the costs of campaigning would of course be very high. This would effectively eliminate some possible contenders. Even spending limits might cause problems. Each candidate would want to spend up to the allowable limit in each state to win votes. Trends toward personalization of politics and antipartyism would be reinforced in sum.

Two additional points ought to be made here regarding the effect of a national primary system on the party per se. If the national parties are largely instrumentalities for nominating presidential candidates, then the national primary will eliminate them as viable bodies. A winning candidate could totally disdain the party organization, using only its *label* in his election campaign. If the parties are to be respected as part of the symbolism and ritual of American politics, for identifiers and voters, or if one can see a value in conventions in that they bind together disparate state organizations in temporary coalition behind a single presidential candidate, then perhaps we ought to take care to preserve them for the functions—symbolic and actual—they do serve.

Representative Udall has said, "The glue that holds the parties together is the requirement that they meet every four years to resolve differences, choose a candidate and write a platform." [46] Insofar as proposals for a national primary enjoy great popularity, and the operationalizing of such proposals would augment fragmentation within the parties, the antiparty impulse lingers among American voters. Reform of both parties' delegate selection procedures and conventions would seem to be a far better alternative.

[46] *Current American Government* (Washington, D.C.: Congressional Quarterly Service, 1972), p. 32.

Introduction
to Chapters
12 and 13

Responsible party government in the United States does not really exist in national politics—to the delight of some observers and participants and to the dismay of others.* To the extent that a "responsible party system" implies

* See Chapter 14 for a further discussion of responsible party government.

clear-cut party positions and accountability to the public for opposing electoral programs, the American political system falls far short of the model. In this section some of the effects of our antiparty tradition on the role of the political parties in the national policy-making process will be considered. First, the president and the parties, and the bureaucracy and the parties will be examined. In a second chapter the relationships between Congress and the parties will be discussed.

12

Parties and the Executive Branch

The president, "while paying lip service to his party finds himself obliged to bypass it." The modern president can reach the public more effectively through modern communications—these provide him with a "more direct means of contact with the public than the party's many layered relay system." [1] Insofar as Douglas Cater in his book, *Power in Washington,* has drawn an accurate picture of the relationship of the American president to the party system, an examination of the presidency provides us with a good view of antipartyism at work in the American political system.

THE ROLE OF THE PRESIDENT AS PARTY LEADER

The president of the United States has numerous roles to fill, including that of party leader. One expert on the presidency, Clinton Rossiter, suggested that it is the expectation of Americans that the president, having been granted certain powers by the Constitution, will serve as chief of state, chief diplomat, commander-in-chief, chief legislator, and chief executive. Additionally, the president is expected to act as party leader, voice of "all" Americans, leader of "all" Americans, and leader of the "free world." [2] Given these multiple

[1] Douglas Cater, *Power in Washington* (New York: Random House, 1964), p. 12.
[2] Clinton Rossiter, *The American Presidency* (New York: New American Library, 1956, 1960), pp. 13–41.

263

roles, Rossiter argues that the office of the president is a very powerful one.

In the past fifteen years there has been some modification of this view of presidential power by other students of the presidency.[3] Richard Neustadt, for example, wrote that it is not the formal functions of the president that give the occupant of the office power; rather it is how well he is able to persuade other people to do what he wants them to do—given his advantage of being in the office of the presidency. Thus, Neustadt quoted Harry S. Truman as saying:

> I sit here all day trying to persuade people to do the things they ought to have sense enough to do without my persuading them. . . . That's all the powers of the President amount to.[4]

Richard Neudstadt observed that:

> . . . The separateness of institutions and the sharing of authority prescribe the terms on which a President persuades. When one man shares authority with another, but does not gain or lose his job upon the other's whim, his willingness to act upon the urging of the other turns on whether he conceives the action right for him. The essence of a President's persuasive task is to convince such men that what the White House wants of them is what they ought to do for their sake and/or their authority.[5]

The resignation of President Nixon in the summer of 1974, occurring as a result of both judicial and legislative action, appears to reaffirm the concept that no one—not even the president—may rule supreme in our political system.

CONFLICT OF PRESIDENTIAL ROLES

Some of the numerous functions the president must perform are derived from the Constitution; others are derived from custom. The role of the president as party leader is one derived from custom. Since a person cannot fully separate out his multiple roles in life—be he president or factory worker—it is not surprising that often we feel that the man who occupies the White House is using his position as president to the advantage of party. It is hard to know, for example, if a speech to a select group of people in the October just prior

---

[3] Phillipa Strum, *Presidential Powers and American Democracy* (Pacific Palisades, Calif.: Goodyear, 1972), pp. 1–2; also Thomas E. Cronin, "The Textbook Presidency and Political Science," *Congressional Record,* Vol. 116, Part 26, pp. 34915–28, provides a very thorough analysis of the treatment of the presidency in American textbooks.

[4] Richard E. Neustadt, *Presidential Power, the Politics of Leadership* (New York: John Wiley, 1960), pp. 9–10.

[5] Ibid., p. 34.

to Election Day is politically motivated or not. This is particularly so because an incumbent president receives more media coverage than other elected officials. Presidents have often intervened in behalf of their party's candidates both in the nominations process and the general election. In 1962, President Kennedy campaigned for several gubernatorial and congressional candidates and, more covertly, intervened in several primary battles in order to seek to eliminate several conservative Democrats from Congress.[6] As is often the case when a president intervenes in political campaigns, the effort produced meager results. Only two of the (at least) six candidates endorsed by the administration survived through the general election.

In 1970, President Nixon was accused of using the presidency to partisan advantage. The following item written by Stewart Alsop sums up the president's role in the 1970 campaign:

> The President's original "game plan" called for his playing the role of above-the-battle statesman-President throughout. He played the role earnestly and effectively in his European tour and his Vietnam cease-fire speech. He continued to play it on his first campaign foray, into Connecticut. But as the campaign heated up, he visibly and progressively reverted to type, becoming more and more the partisan, non-Presidential, "rocking, socking" candidate of old, while the statesman-President faded into invisibility.
>
> The fading process was completed when the President himself insisted on using a scratchy videotape recording of his Phoenix, Arizona, speech for his final prime-time television pitch the day before the election. This was perhaps his most partisan and least Presidential stump speech. . . .
>
> *A thoroughly partisan candidate-President appeared on the screen—belligerent, sweating, throwing his arms about, shouting to the shouting crowds. Immediately after him appeared the then leading Democratic candidate Ed Muskie, cool, rational, soft-spoken. Thus the roles were neatly reversed—the President was the candidate, the candidate the President. . . .*[7]

The White House virtually directed the 1970 campaign, playing a more overt role than any president since FDR in the 1938 Democratic primaries when the latter had sought to "purge" conservative members from the Democratic party. Nixon himself persuaded twelve congressmen to give up "safe" seats in the House in an all out effort for Republican control of the Senate. He raised $20 million through a special campaign; and then apportioned the funds to facilitate victory for "his" candidates. Nixon and then Vice-President Agnew traveled throughout the country campaigning for those Republican candidates whom they had endorsed. As had been the case for Franklin Roosevelt in 1938, Nixon was unsuccessful in influencing election results. In the end, the Republi-

[6] David Broder, *The Party's Over* (New York: Harper and Row, 1972), p. 37.
[7] Stewart Alsop, "A Defeatable President," *Newsweek* (November 16, 1970): 124.

cans fell 5 short of a majority in the Senate, lost 9 seats in the House, and surrendered 11 governorships and 244 state legislative seats.[8] In 1972 President Nixon stayed off the campaign trail and maintained instead that the work of the president was too time consuming and important to waste campaigning. Again he was criticized—this time by members of his own party who felt that he had deserted them in their time of need.

> . . . Republican leaders wanted Mr. Nixon—especially in Delaware, where two-term Senator Caleb Boggs lost to 29-year-old Democrat Joseph Biden (to help). With Boggs in trouble, State Chairman Gene Bunting personally asked Mr. Nixon twice. Another appeal came from Delaware's most powerful Republican, Tom Evans, co-chairman of the Republican National Committee. But Delaware was never on the schedule.[9]

As of November, the president had campaigned in only ten states. After the election, which had produced a landslide victory for the Republican president while Congress remained firmly in Democratic hands, the party's national chairman criticized the president's indifference to party needs. However, Nixon's attempts to persuade voters to cast a pro*presidential,* rather than pro-*Republican* vote, apparently prevailed.

It seems clear that the role of party leader is a very difficult role for a president to perform. If he actively plays the party leader, he will be criticized for using his office improperly. If he decides not to play party leader, he will be criticized for abandoning his party. He must balance the multiple roles of the presidency in our antiparty environment with great care.

THE PRESIDENT AND CONGRESS

THE PRESIDENT AND PARTY VOTING

In addition to his possible election campaign role, the president must deal with Congress and the party leadership in Congress. Clearly, the president as the nation's chief legislator can enunciate his position on an issue and present his program to Congress. (It is important to note however, that most interaction between the executive branch and Congress does not involve the president directly. Most of the information on programs which Congress receives from the executive branch emanates from the bureaucracy, which is comprised of nonelected officials. See pp. 271–74.) Members of the president's party may speak out and eventually vote counter to his declared position and proposed program because of limited party discipline in the United States. Clinton Rossiter suggested, "Success in the delicate area of executive-legislative rela-

---

[8] Broder, *The Party's Over,* p. 104.
[9] *Washington Post,* November 11, 1972, p. A15.

tions depends on the several variables: the political complexion of President and Congress, the state of the union and of the world around us, the vigor and tact of the President's leadership, and the mood of Congress, which is generally friendly near the beginning of a President's term and rebellious near the end." [10]

Regardless of party, most modern presidents have encountered difficulties from their own party colleagues in gaining congressional support for their programs. By his second term, Franklin Roosevelt found congressional opposition from a coalition including southern Democrats as well as Republicans. The former occupied key positions on the House Rules and Senate Judiciary Committees and were instrumental in blocking FDR's "court packing" plan (an attempt to enlarge the conservative Supreme Court, which was striking down key elements of New Deal legislation). Dwight Eisenhower was opposed by Republican isolationists when he sought to articulate an "internationalist" foreign policy, by Republican critics of his nominees to high public office, and by the Republican chairman of the House Ways and Means Committee who blocked his tax program. John Kennedy could achieve few of his domestic goals during his three years in office due often to opposition from fellow Democrats. Some of Lyndon Johnson's most fervent adversaries (especially regarding his handling of the Vietnam War) in his second term were congressional Democrats. Richard Nixon had difficulty with some members of the Republican party regarding the American role in Vietnam, as well as the appropriate role and extent of government participation and spending in the domestic sphere. Thus, on October 18, 1972, Congress overrode the president's veto on the Federal Water Protection Act Amendments of 1972 (S. 2770)—an extensive environmental protection act.[11] The motion to override the veto carried by a vote of 52 to 12 in the Senate. The Republicans voted 18 yea to 8 nay—nay being a vote in support of Nixon—and the Democrats voted 34 yea to 4 nay. Similarly, the House voted to override the president's veto by a vote of 247 to 23, with Republicans voting 95 yea to 13 nay and Democrats voting 152 yea to 10 nay.[12] President Nixon also encountered serious difficulty from party members on two nominations to the Supreme Court (Clement Haynesworth and G. Harrold Carswell) and the funding of the SST (supersonic transport) by the federal government. Opposition to the Haynesworth nomination centered on questions of financial ethics and an antilabor and anti-civil rights record. The Senate vote for Supreme Court nominee Haynesworth was 45 yea to 55 nay.[13] With considerable Republican defection in this

[10] Rossiter, *The American Presidency*, p. 26.
[11] *Congressional Quarterly Weekly Report* 30 (October 21, 1972): 2754.
[12] *Congressional Quarterly Weekly Report* 30 (October 28, 1972): 2833.
[13] The Carswell vote by party was: Democrats, 17 yea to 38 nay and Republicans, 28 yea to 13 nay. *National Journal* 2 (April 11, 1970): 803. The Haynesworth vote by party was: Democrats, 19 yea to 38 nay, and Republicans, 26 yea to 17 nay. *Congressional Quarterly Guide to American*

instance, none of the three top Republican leaders of the Senate was able to support the president's nominee. Nixon sought to use patronage, favors, and threats to coerce senators to vote in his favor on the Haynesworth decision, which he saw as the fulfillment of a pledge to appoint a southerner to the Court made during his 1968 presidential campaign. But his "actions in the Haynesworth nomination demonstrated that presidential patronage power can often be effective in the form of threats, but the threats are more effective when implied rather than publicly imposed . . . and judiciously applied." [14] Once "regular" Republican senators revealed presidential patronage pressure, the president knew he had lost his votes.

Table 43. Percentage Time Support for President (Nixon)

		Republicans	Democrats
1969–70	Senate	63	46
	House	62	51
1971	Senate	64	40
	House	72	47
1972	Senate	66	44
	House	64	47
1973	Senate	55	30
	House	62	34

SOURCE: *Congressional Quarterly Weekly Report* 31 (September 1973): 2348. *Congressional Quarterly Weekly Report* 30 (January 1, 1972): 32.

Still, comparisons of partisan support for an incumbent president do demonstrate that the president does sometimes provide a focal point for his party. Republicans in both houses supported President Nixon far more than Democrats, although even partisan support for Nixon dropped in the tumultuous post-Watergate period.[15] (See Table 43.) A note of caution is required at this

---

Government, Spring 1970 (Washington, D.C.: Congressional Quarterly Service, 1970), p. 78. Opposition to Carswell was based both on a record of racism and judicial incompetence. Both nominations may be viewed as part of what has been called Nixon's "southern strategy."

[14] Susan and Martin Tolchin, *To the Victor: Political Patronage from the Clubhouse to the White House* (New York: Random House, 1971), p. 281.

[15] His support score in Congress dropped to 43 percent by early 1974—the first time a president lost more support tests than he won. *Congressional Quarterly Weekly Report* 32 (January 19, 1974): 99–102. *CQ* attributes the drop not only to Watergate but also to opposition to Nixon-sponsored program cuts in long-standing social programs.

point. First, the fact that members of a party supported legislation proposed by a president of the same party does not tell us anything about the relative importance of the legislation they chose to support or not support. Also, this information does not indicate the initiator of the legislation. It is possible, therefore, that the president proposed a program he inherited from members of Congress, from a previous president, or from a broad-based coalition of groups that tend to support candidates of his party. Furthermore, the program presented to Congress by the president may have been based on ideas proposed over the years by members of his own party, which over time came to be accepted as part of the issue base of the party. For example, the programs proposed by President Johnson to achieve his "Great Society" had been part of Democratic rhetoric since the New Deal.

TENSIONS BETWEEN THE BRANCHES OF GOVERNMENT

Just as the voting of individuals in Congress in support of a president from their own party cannot be ensured, there can be no guarantee that party leadership in Congress will support the programs of a president of their own party. It was, in fact, the defection of key Republican leaders as well as rank-and-file party members—in the wake of new Watergate revelations—which prompted President Nixon to resign his embattled office in 1974. One of the concerns among Republicans who opposed Nixon's continued incumbency was the fear that he would be a "drag" on party fortunes in the 1974 congressional elections. The differing perspectives of the president and congressmen often are due to the fact that they represent different constituencies for different periods of time. It is likely that, given the fact that the president needs congressional support for his programs, he will consult with congressional party leaders and try to present programs to Congress for which the leadership will be able to muster support. This type of behavior is probably more significant if the president's party controls Congress, than if it is the minority party in Congress. For the first several years of his presidency, Lyndon Johnson was able to work with Congress reasonably well. He held breakfast meetings with Democratic congressional leadership (he had apparently learned his Neustadt well), took them for walks in the White House rose garden, and was often able to influence members of Congress. Thus, when developing a strategy for the passage of the Economic Opportunity Act (War Against Poverty) in 1964, several steps were developed. Johnson wrote in his memoirs:

We induced Representative Phil Landrum [D.] of Georgia to sponsor the bill. Landrum, who I admired, was generally known as a conservative Congressman . . . and I knew he was a thoughtful legislator, amenable to change. When . . .

I first talked about asking Landrum to sponsor the poverty bill, the possibility of his accepting the challenge seemed remote. But the more we discussed it, the more the idea seemed worth trying. Landrum would be a strong and effective leader, and certainly his sponsorship would render the bill considerably more palatable to the Southerners. I talked to Phil about it and found him receptive to the program because he basically was dedicated to the people.

But there remained a serious hurdle. Because of his co-sponsorship of the 1959 Landrum-Griffin Bill, which put certain restrictions on union power, he was regarded as an enemy of labor. Labor support was absolutely fundamental to the success of any poverty bill. I suggested to O'Brien that he and Shriver have a talk with George Meany of the AFL-CIO. Meany and his subordinates were at first incredulous. For years, O'Brien reported to me, the AFL-CIO had been using "Landrum" as a dirty word. And now Phil Landrum was going to father the *poverty bill?* I got in touch with George Meany myself soon after that. In my experience with Meany I knew he could always be counted on to put the interests of his country first. That is precisely what he did this time. My message to him was simple. "After all, it's the result we're after," I told him. Before the poverty bill passed, Landrum and Meany were sitting down together for quiet and friendly talks.[16]

Johnson had the additional advantage of having in Congress numerous freshmen who had ridden into office on his coattails. Still, most presidents understand that congressmen can support them only on issues that will not hurt them "back home," since it is the "people back home" and not some amorphous national party upon whom the member ultimately relies to remain in office.

THE PRESIDENT AND THE NATIONAL COMMITTEE

As suggested in Chapter 9, the national committee of each major party is a nearly powerless institution, whose primary purposes are to raise some campaign funds, act as a symbol for the party, and convene a national convention once every four years to select candidates for president and vice-president. The Republican National Committee during President Nixon's first term of office was headed by Senator Robert Dole (Kansas). Senator Dole was selected by the president for this position and had little exposure as chairman of the committee. After the president's reelection in 1972, at least partially due to the unimpressive races run by Republican candidates for offices other than the presidency, Dole was replaced by George Bush as party chairman. The choice again was the president's, apparently without consulting members of the com-

---

[16] Lyndon Baines Johnson, *The Vantage Point: Perspectives of the Presidency, 1963–1969* (New York: Holt, Rinehart and Winston, 1971), 77–78.

mittee. The person appointed generally matters little since both parties' national committees are nearly powerless. Nixon's predecessor, President Johnson, virtually ignored his national chairman, John Bailey, and established his own personal electoral arm.[17] When a party gains the presidency, its national committee traditionally retires to obscurity.

The national committee is clearly an adjunct of the national party as personified by the president or the presidential candidate.[18] When a party does not control the presidency, the national committee has the potential to be the most visible organ of party organization. Essentially, however, the national head of the party is a symbolic leader who has no independent base of power upon which he can rely. Congress, made up as it is of representatives from different localities, makes little pretense of looking to the national party or its symbol, the national committee. Though there are national forces which affect congressional behavior—including at times the president's preference—the concern with state and local parties and interest groups is often paramount. The national committee does not work for a congressman's reelection. The party back home does!

PRESIDENTIAL POWER VIS-À-VIS PARTY MEMBERS

THE ROLE OF THE PRESIDENT IN ORGANIZING BUREAUCRACY

Although the bureaucracy falls under the organizational jurisdiction of the president, it operates in ways separate and distinct from the presidency. Bureaucracies tend to have lives of their own, independent of a particular set of elected officials. Bureaucracy implies a clear-cut division of "integrated activities which are regarded as duties inherent in an office." [19] Thus, a bureaucratic organization, once it is fully established, maintains a certain rigidity of function, and the person who is functioning within the bureaucratic structure "is only a single cog in an ever-moving mechanism which prescribes him to an essentially fixed route of march." [20] Functions of bureaucratic organizations become routinized and the individuals involved in this routinization develop vested interests.

[17] Bailey had been a major figure in the Kennedy administration who was used to maintain contact with voters and politicians.

[18] Viewed in this context, the Democratic party's replacement of defeated candidate McGovern's national chairperson in 1972 with a new person more acceptable to moderate elements in the party is in line with party tradition.

[19] Robert K. Merton, *Social Theory and Social Action* (New York: The Free Press, 1957), p. 196.

[20] Max Weber, "Bureaucracy," *From Max Weber,* eds., H. H. Gerth and C. Wright Mills (New York: Oxford University Press, 1958), p. 228.

In addition to this potential for inflexibility of action, the self-perpetuation of structures beyond the time of their essential need is a second and often negative factor inherent in bureaucratic organization. Max Weber, the first modern social scientist systematically to examine the nature of bureaucratic organization, suggested that once "it is fully established, bureaucracy is among those social structures which are the hardest to destroy." [21]

In March 1973, there were 2,767,901 nonmilitary employees in the federal service.[22] Most of these people are covered by the civil service and are not subject to the party and personality shifts of politics.[23] They remain in their positions regardless of who is president and which party controls Congress. They are, therefore, loyal to institutions other than parties, and to individuals other than elected officials. The power of the nonelected nonparty-related bureaucracy in contemporary American politics in some ways epitomizes the role of antipartyism in the United States. Inasmuch as the extension of the civil service since its inception in 1883 has sheltered so many governmental participants from "party politics," the institutionalization of "neutral" bureaucracy is a testament to our antiparty attitudes.

Given what has been said thus far about bureaucracy and the civil service protection afforded most members of it, it is clear that many of the departments, agencies, and bureaus of the federal government are not subject to the vicissitudes of party politics. All of this is not, however, to suggest that the bureaucracy is sheltered from politics. Certainly the administrative responsibilities bureaucrats are charged with carrying out are determined by presidential appointees, just as the level of appropriation for services is subject to congressional decision making. However, it is most likely that the interaction of executive bureaucrats with Congress will be with the specialists on the matching congressional committees to whom they will "feed" information, and not with the party leadership or the elected leadership of the Congress. It is also the case that interaction levels are high between concerned client organizations and the responsible bureaucratic agency or bureau. Thus, often there will be exchange of information—as well as personnel—between private groups and bureaucratic groups. Conditions in agriculture will be filtered to departments of the Agriculture Department via agricultural interest groups. Similarly, this information will be channeled to the appropriate congressional

[21] Ibid.

[22] *Federal Civilian Manpower Statistics, Monthly Release* (Bureau of Manpower Information System, U. S. Civil Service Commission, May 1973), p. 4.

[23] One group of people selected by the president includes secretaries, undersecretaries, agency heads, etc. The other group is comprised of career civil servants with high-level appointments. These people are in the "super-grades": positions in grades GS-16, GS-17, and GS-18 of the General Schedule and their salary equivalents. *Positions in Supergrade Levels, A Report on Executive Manpower in the Federal Service,* Subcommittee on Manpower and Civil Service of the Committee on the Post Office and Civil Service, House of Representatives, 92d Cong., 2d sess. (Washington, D.C.: Government Printing Office, 1972), Committee Print No. 92–18.

committees and their staffs. There will be some meshing of ideas and attitudes, and legislation will be introduced into Congress. Two of the three sides of this *policy-making triangle* are made up of nonelected decision makers: individuals who have far less responsibility to the public than party elected officials (see Figure 3).

However, though most jobs in the federal bureaucracy are covered by civil service and thereby immune to the vicissitudes of politics, a number of jobs remain unprotected. These positions provide the president with enough patronage to mold the bureaucracy somewhat in "his image," and to provide political rewards to people who worked in his behalf during the campaign or contributed heavily to it. Hence while the Nixon administration conducted a talent search to find the "best" people to fill vacant government posts those

Figure 3

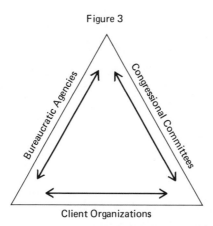

Client Organizations

chosen were predominantly Republicans. Among those rewarded in the Nixon administration were the first attorney general, John Mitchell (Nixon's campaign manager); Robert Finch, veteran of numerous Nixon campaigns, who became secretary of Health, Education and Welfare; and Walter Annenberg, a major campaign contributor, appointed ambassador to England. The top decision makers in government are thus appointed by the president, who may in turn choose to reward his friends and copartisans with key positions.[24] Still, it is well to remember that presidents increasingly seek "experts" for important

---

[24] The total number of appointive executives in the federal government represents a small percentage of the total work force (11,000 of the total work force or less than ½ of 1 percent of a total number of almost 3,000,000). *Executive Manpower in the Federal Service,* U. S. Civil Service Commission, Bureau of Executive Manpower (Washington, D.C.: Government Printing Office, 1972), p. 1.

positions and often award key jobs to nonparty people. For example, Henry Kissinger was selected by President Nixon to be a special adviser on foreign policy and later to be secretary of state despite the fact that he was not a "hard-working" Republican. In addition, there are so many more applicants than there are available positions that thousands of disappointed partisans are inevitable.

PRESIDENTIAL PATRONAGE: ALLOCATION OF RESOURCES

The major source of patronage available to the president lies in the area of expenditures of public monies. The president and his advisers use their discretion to award government contracts and key public works projects. To help favored industrialists and politicians, President Johnson, for example, used the newly created "Model Cities" program. Johnson sometimes chose cities as recipients of model cities grants not on the basis of need, but because of political criteria, formulated to reward towns represented by key congressional committee chairmen.[25] The location of government installations, regional federal offices, and federal recreational areas can be bestowed upon supporters of the president. Such recipients of presidential favor may or may not be members of his party.

THE ROLE OF THE PRESIDENT IN CHOOSING JUDGES

The role of the president in choosing judges is a subject that should be discussed even though there are not thousands of positions to fill. It may be possible to argue that the role of the president in selecting judges runs counter to our antiparty tradition. Insofar as presidents can use judicial appointments as political rewards, antipartyism does not seem to exist. However, judicial terms extend beyond presidential terms. As a result, federal judges, though perhaps political partisans prior to their judicial appointments, need not retain strong party ties after election. In fact, to do so would be contrary to our judicial ethics. Federal judges, inasmuch as they do not have to stand for election, can reach the pinnacle of antipartyism in their behavior.

[25] Among them were Southville, Tennessee (pop. 2,300), represented by Representative Joe L. Evans, chairman of the House Housing and Urban Development Subcommittee on Independent Offices Appropriations; Keville, Kentucky (pop. 5,000), represented by Carl Perkins, chairman of the House Education and Labor Committee; and, Texarkana, Texas (pop. 32,000), represented by Wright Patman, chairman of the House Banking and Currency Committee. This occurred in a program directed at solving *urban* problems. See Susan and Martin Tolchin, *To the Victor*, pp. 289–90.

All federal judges are appointed by the president. This includes justices on the Supreme Court, appointed for life terms (or until a justice decides to retire), judges in the ninety-seven district trial courts, and judges on the eleven courts of appeal. (Judges' terms are for indefinite time periods—"good behavior.") Certainly most cases that come before the federal courts do not carry partisan overtones, but some do. Nonetheless, it may be surprising to learn that of eighty-four judges appointed to the United States Court of Appeals between 1961 and 1964, seventy-nine, or 94 percent were affiliated with the same political party as the president who appointed them. Four out of five appointees had been political activists in their pre-judicial careers.[26] During the forty years preceding 1962, nine out of ten federal court appointees were members of the appointing president's political party.[27]

The fact that the selection of judges—especially Supreme Court justices—can affect major policy areas both in the long and short run is clear. When Franklin Roosevelt was finally able to appoint new judges to the Supreme Court, he altered the Court not only regarding support of New Deal politics. He also initiated a constitutional trend that would dominate for more than three decades: the concern for human rights.[28]

A judicial change in the opposite direction could be seen in the Burger Court, which by 1972 bore little resemblance to its predecessor—the innovative Warren Court of the 1950s and 1960s. Richard Nixon campaigned in 1968 on a slogan of "law and order," and a pledge to alter the liberal Warren Court's rulings, particularly in the area of criminal justice. Once in office, he made good on his promise by appointing four conservative justices to the Supreme Court—when death and retirement made these vacancies available. Nixon's appointees did shift the "balance" on the Court: of seventy cases in the 1972 term, the "Nixon men" voted together on fifty-three.[29] Under the new Court, a more conservative majority has retreated on the rights of criminal suspects and the judicial demands of the poor and has failed to continue the trend of earlier procivil rights rulings. The decision of the Warren Court in *Brown* v. *Board of Education* (1954) set the stage for the desegregation of southern schools (though the movement toward this goal may have been slower than some people had hoped), and helped lead indirectly to more open employment and housing opportunities for some nonwhites in the 1960s and 1970s. An

---

[26] Sheldon Goldman, "Judicial Appointments to the United States Courts of Appeals," *Wisconsin Law Review* (1967), pp. 186–214.

[27] Frank J. Sorauf, *Party Politics in America,* 2d ed. (Boston: Little, Brown, 1972), pp. 377–78.

[28] James F. Simon, *In His Own Image: The Supreme Court in Richard Nixon's America* (New York: David McKay, 1973), p. 18. FDR ultimately achieved his goal of transforming the Court, despite the demise of his Court packing plan, due to accelerated retirement and mortality rates among conservative justices.

[29] Ibid., p. 253. The four Nixon appointees (Burger, Rehnquist, Blackmun, and Powell) plus either Justice White or Stewart usually made up the new majority.

indication of changed judicial perspectives is illustrated by the 1974 decision on school integration in which the Burger Court ruled (5–4) that busing between separate school districts could not be ordered unless all school districts involved were found to have engaged in racial discrimination. The Court found that desegregation does not require racial balance.[30] The dissenting opinions and the civil rights community viewed the decision as highly retrogressive, specifically in terms of the earlier *Brown* decision.

Nonetheless, the Court's independence of presidential power—despite partisan and ideological affinity between judicial appointees and the chief executive—was also demonstrated in the 1974 session. The Supreme Court ruled unanimously (8–0) that President Nixon surrender sixty-four Watergate tapes in compliance with the special prosecutor's request, in the interest of due process. This decision was a major factor precipitating President Nixon's resignation.

Though party ties may blur for some members of the bench over time and in specific cases, it is a paradox that the branch of government most often perceived to be the least partisan of the three major branches of government is, in fact, a source of significant (though not in absolute numbers) partisan patronage for the president.

THE "OUT" PARTY

LACK OF A LOYAL OPPOSITION

While the party that has captured the presidency maintains at least the semblance of an "executive centered coalition" if not a "responsible party," the party "out of power" in the White House has no formal position in the executive branch and no formal leadership. Furthermore, there is rarely one individual in the national party "out of power" who is accepted by most other members as party spokesman. Consider, for example, the case of the Democrats after the 1972 election. As is usually the case, the defeated candidate has many challengers for the role of opposition spokesman. He must compete with prominent senators (sometimes including the elected party leadership), governors, the national chairman, and "elder statesmen" for the power to speak for the party. Only during the period from 1957–1960, when a Republican ruled in the White House, did an opposition party seriously seek a unified voice. During this time the Democratic Advisory Council was active. Even during that period, however, congressional leaders (especially Rayburn and Johnson)

---

[30] *Milliken* v. *Bradley* (July 24, 1974). This ruling may be the result of factors other than the new Court balance alone—including heightened public opinion and legislative and executive pronouncements against busing.

fiercely resisted the effort. The reality of the leaderless "out" party is rein-forced by the nonpolicymaking nature of the national parties and their na-tional committees. To restate the above in a somewhat different manner, there is no institutionalized "loyal opposition" in the United States.[31]

In contrast to the United States, Britain does maintain a loyal opposition that has formal responsibilities.

> The Opposition has a constitutionally recognized role; leader of Her Majesty's Opposition and under recent legislation, some other of its officials too, receive a salary from the State. The Opposition is important because it gives expression to public opinion, and reflects the current public reaction to Government policy; it is the mouthpiece which the Constitution provides for the expression of public opinion, and a Prime Minister must always pay attention to it, however large his majority. . . . The Opposition is always ready to take over the Government at any time, in the event of an electoral swing and a Government defeat, and for this contingency, maintains a "Shadow Cabinet."[32]

Insofar as any relationship exists between the president and the opposition party in the United States, it is usually at the president's request. Thus, if the majority party in Congress is the opposition party, it may be wise to maintain open channels to its congressional leadership, as Eisenhower did during his terms as president. Although his party did have a congressional majority, President Johnson often relied on the assistance of Republican Minority Leader Everett Dirksen to attain his desired legislation. This is not, however, always the case; Richard Nixon tended to ignore the majority Democratic leadership in promoting key bills.

Since there is no loyal opposition and no "Shadow Cabinet," the notion of party program or party spokesman for the opposition party is nonexistent in American politics.

CONCLUSION

The potential for a president to act as a strong party leader affecting public policy decision making is present, but it must not be overstated. The president faces competition from congressional leaders. He must operate also within an

---

[31] For a somewhat different view of the role of the Democratic party during this period see James L. Sundquist, *Politics and Policy* (Washington, D.C.: Brookings Institution, 1968), p. 415. Sund-quist noted that "Despite its deep internal division, the Democratic Party in its opposition years did fulfill its role—it succeeded in defining a concrete program that presented the voters with a true choice in reaching their public decision in November 1960."

[32] Karl Lowenstein, *British Cabinet Government* (New York: Oxford University Press, 1967), pp. 122–23.

executive branch in which the vast majority of personnel preceded him in their positions and will continue in them after his term in office is completed. In the post-Civil War era, President Andrew Johnson came into conflict with a highly partisan Congress dominated by the opposition party. Efforts by Johnson to appoint his friends to federal office and remove his enemies were blocked when Congress enacted the Tenure of Office Act—of dubious constitutionality —in March of 1867. Johnson's violation of the law became the legal basis for a blatantly partisan attempt at impeachment, which failed of conviction by one vote. Later, in 1883, the Pendleton Act was enacted, which provided for the development of a federal civil service. No contemporary president has the power that Johnson had to develop a bureaucracy in his own image!

13

The Party as Policy Maker: Congress

THE PARTY AND CONGRESS

Political parties in the American Congress, though significant for organizational purposes, have no binding ties over their members once the active work of Congress begins. The antiparty tradition seems to have survived well in the congressional atmosphere. Congressional parties are not cohesive units, and members of Congress are not bound by the notion of responsible party government, as an examination of the role of parties in Congress will indicate.

Not all political scientists, it should be noted, concur with this strong a view. James Sundquist, for example, contends that the Democratic party in the 1950s and 1960s behaved at times much like a "responsible party." It did develop a program to which it committed itself—and which it put into effect after winning office.[1] But Sundquist himself acknowledges that the Eighty-seventh Congress elected with President Kennedy made a "shambles" of the party's own domestic program. When a compromise version of the party's program was enacted under President Johnson, it came about at least in part because of congressional remorse regarding Kennedy's assassination.

The view that responsibility to binding party programs is far from reality

[1] James Sundquist, *Politics and Policy: The Eisenhower, Kennedy and Johnson Years* (Washington, D.C.: Brookings Institution, 1968), Chapter 9. See also Gerald Pomper, *Elections in America: Control and Influence in Democratic Politics* (New York: Dodd, Mead, 1970), p. 201. Pomper argues in a similar vein that the platform clarifies the party's position on controversial issues and in turn the victorious party coalitions (legislative and executive) pursue the intentions stated in the party's platform. Pomper does show, however, that such policy content is far less binding than "responsible party" advocates would wish.

279

in the United States Congress ought not to be construed as suggesting that there have been no occasions when members of the same party have voted together, or that there have been no party supported programs that have become law.

One of the reasons that the American party systems are not monolithic, disciplined, and completely cohesive in Congress (in other words, not too strong) is the lack of centralized authoritative party leadership. There are several explanations for this lack of party leadership in Congress. Perhaps the foremost lies in the fragmented nature of congressional leadership—split as it is between committee chairmen and elected party leaders. The latter group is, in addition, handicapped by the absence of formal powers and the inability or unwillingness to utilize meaningful sanctions against recalcitrant party members. Other factors include the nature of election campaigns and the congressmen's eagerness to heed demands of their constituents—and special interests in their districts—often to the total or at least partial exclusion of national party interests and, more specifically in this instance, the wishes of congressional party leadership.

COMPETITION AMONG LEADERS

The absence of coherent party leadership in the Congress is attributable in large measure to the competition between rival spokesmen for party policy.

Committee Leadership There are two sets of leaders within each party in both houses of Congress. They are the party leaders elected by the members of the party caucus, and the committee chairmen, who—until the precedent-breaking actions of the House Democratic membership at the outset of the Ninety-Fourth Congress, when some House chairmen were deposed—were selected by virtue of their seniority on the committee. The latter have been nearly omnipotent in their own special policy areas. The dimensions of the potential problems are seen especially within the majority Democratic party, regarding policy consistency among leaders. In the Senate in 1972, for example, of the seventeen committee chairmen, nine were from states of the old confederacy. They had average ADA scores of 11.6 out of 100 for that year.[2] (The ADA is the Americans for Democratic Action, a liberal interest group that

[2] *Southern Chairman* (Senate)	*ADA Scores*
1. Talmadge (Ga.)	10
2. McClellan (Ark.)	10
3. Stennis (Miss.)	0
4. Sparkman (Ala.)	0
5. R. Long (La.)	15
6. Fulbright (Ark.)	50
7. Ervin (N.C.)	10
8. Jordan (N.C.)	5
9. Eastland (Miss.)	5

SOURCE: "How Special Interest Groups Rated Senators," *Congressional Quarterly Weekly Report* 30 (December 9, 1972): 3111.

ranks members of Congress on their liberalism.) The Senate majority leader was Senator Mike Mansfield of Montana, with an ADA score in 1972 of 80. Hence, the moderately liberal policy statements of Mr. Mansfield were often directly opposed to the policy predispositions of many of the committee chairmen.

Not all committee chairmen have equivalent influence in affecting legislative output. But, until 1975, chairmen held their positions as a result of the seniority system, which provides for almost automatic promotion upon reelection to office. The member of the minority party with the greatest seniority in his party on a committee will be the ranking member of the minority party. If in the next election his party gains control of his house, and if he has retained his seat in congress and is still on the committee, he will most likely become chairman of the committee, and the previous chairman—if he is still in office and still on the committee—will become the ranking minority party member. With the exception of 1946–48 and 1952–54, since 1932 Congress has been organized by the Democratic party. Because of the seniority system it has been likely that chairmen of standing committees will have served in Congress longer than the rank-and-file senator or congressman. The reelection necessary for this feat is easier to accomplish in a reasonably noncompetitive one-party district. Traditionally, this type of district for Democrats has been located in the rural south and in industrial northern cities, and for Republicans in the midwestern farming areas. Also, chairmen have tended to be *older* than most of the members of their own party in Congress.[3] This latter phenomenon need not be bad, but superimposed on the conservative predispositions of many of the Democratic committee chairmen who have controlled the committees of Congress for nearly forty-two years consecutively it can set the very powerful committee chairmen well out of the mainstream of American politics, creating an unrepresentative elite. Thus, in the Ninety-Third Congress, of the seventeen Senate standing committee chairmen, eight were from southern states (47 percent), and the average age of a committee chairman was 64.8 (see Table 44).[4]

Given the great powers of some committee chairmen in determining the nature or even the existence of legislation in a particular area, the reasonably strict method whereby a congressman or senator becomes a chairman of a standing committee is significant. The power of committee chairmen resides

[3] See James C. McCann, "Differential Mortality and the Formation of Political Elites: The Case of the U.S. House of Representatives," *American Sociological Review* 37 (December 1972): 689–700. McCann shows that in addition to the fact that southern Democrats fare well at the polls, they have relatively lower mortality rates than their northern counterparts. This latter condition, he suggests, is an important supplement to their electoral advantage.

[4] Congress itself is hardly representative of America's population; 54 percent of our representatives are lawyers, another 33 percent businessmen or bankers. Women, over half the electorate, comprise only a handful of representatives; there are few young people, blacks, or Hispanic-Americans. Workers are represented by three "labor leaders," *Congressional Quarterly Weekly Report* 31 (January 6, 1973): 15.

Table 44

	Average Age	Percent Southern
Comm. Chrmn.—Senate	64.8	47.0
Senators	55.3	22.0
Comm. Chrmn.—House	65.8	37.0
Congressmen	51.1	24.8
General Population	28.1	24.0

SOURCE: *Congressional Quarterly Weekly Report* 31 (January 6, 1973): 14–20.

---

in several key roles. Since the beginning of the twentieth century, chairmen have had virtually plenary power. The chairman:

a) sets committee meeting times
b) controls the agenda of meetings and appoints subcommittees
c) refers bills to subcommittees of his choice
d) hires most of the committee's professional staff
e) appears before the Rules Committee (in House of Representatives) to defend his committee's action on a bill
f) leads floor debate on bills reported out of his committee
g) serves on Conference Committees to iron out differences in Senate and House versions of a bill.[5]

It is possible for a chairman of a committee to prevent legislation on key policy matters for long periods of time. Thus, Representative Emanuel Celler, who represented a district from Brooklyn, New York, from 1923 to 1972, was chairman of the House Judiciary Committee for twenty-one years and in that capacity was able to prevent consideration of an equal rights for women amendment for the same number of years.

Some committee chairmen have power which far outstrips that of the elected congressional leadership. Consider for a moment the role of the chairman of the House Ways and Means Committee. For many years Democratic Representative Wilbur Mills from Arkansas was chairman of this powerful commit- tee. Ways and Means has three basic policy areas under its jurisdiction: 1) taxes, 2) social security, 3) trade legislation. In addition, from 1911 until 1975, when the Democratic caucus voted to change the rules for making Democratic committee assignment, the Democratic membership of the Ways and Means Committee served as the Committee on Committees, which made committee assignments for the Democratic party in the House of Representa- tives. Beginning with the Ninety-fourth Congress, this important function is being handled by the House Democratic Steering and Policy Committee. For

---

[5] William L. Morrow, *Congressional Committees* (New York: Charles Scribner's Sons, 1969), p. 32.

the Republicans, this often important job is done by the Republican Committee on Committees. Wilbur Mills, as chairman of this committee was not only a power within the committee, but because of the nature of the work of the committee and his own idiosyncratic relationships with members of his committee and other members of Congress, a very powerful man in Congress. He was a leader elected by his constituents in Arkansas and not by his colleagues in the House of Representatives; his seniority gave him a more influential policy input than the elected Democratic leadership in the House of Representatives.

Mills's key role in policy making was seen in the protracted congressional struggle for a "medicare" system in the United States. This example also illustrates the fact that even Mills's power—great as it was—was situational; the flow of influence is two way. One reason it took so long to develop a promedicare majority on the committee was that the American Medical Association concentrated its lobbying power in the home districts of Ways and Means Committee members. But perhaps a more important reason was the firm opposition of Chairman Mills, who had considerable influence over his colleagues. Until 1965, when there was a clear majority for the measure without his vote, Mills refused to discuss any kind of compromise. In 1964 he issued a statement expressing some sympathy with prepaid health insurance for the elderly but said he could not support it because such a program would overtax the Social Security system. When Mills finally switched to support Medicare in 1965, his support proved crucial to the bill's success. By changing from opponent to manager of the bill, Mills assured himself control over the content of the legislation. He encouraged innovation and incorporated more generous benefits into the legislation. Tom Wicker of the *New York Times* noted that Mills became the "architect of victory for Medical care, rather than just another devoted but defeated supporter" of the Kerr-Mills welfare approach.[6]

The Elected Party Leadership Whereas committee chairmen have derived their positions within the congressional system from seniority, there is another set of leaders within each party who gain their position through election by their party colleagues in Congress. The party leaders—majority and minority—and the party whips in each house are selected by their respective parties, as is the Speaker of the House (the only congressional leader mentioned in the Constitution—Article I, Section 2), chosen by his colleagues in the House of Representatives and the president pro tempore of the Senate selected by his fellow senators. The Speaker of the House has been the highest formal official of the House and the majority party since 1789. With the exception of 1919–1925, he has been an important leader since 1869. Elected legislative leaders have been very influential in determining the nature of legislative decisions.

[6] Quoted by Theodore R. Marmor, *The Politics of Medicare* (Chicago: Aldine, 1973), p. 69.

Speaker of the House Joseph Cannon, for example (1903–1911), was extremely powerful. His power was largely derived from his concurrent chairmanship of the House Rules Committee, a power which the Speaker no longer possesses due to legislative action in the early twentieth century. A House revolt stripped the Speaker of much of his power and most of it was transferred to the committee chairmen. (Some observers profess to see a cyclical process operative here; when one figure or group of figures gains too much power, the pendulum swings back.) Still, the Speaker of the House retains powers within Congress that provide potentially for a strong position. Included among the duties currently assigned to the Speaker are those of presiding officer, recognition of speakers on the floor, the control of parliamentary proceedings, interpretation of the rules of the House, referral of bills to committee (often crucial to the fate of legislation), and a key role in the appointment of members to the committees.

While the party leaders—majority and minority leaders in both houses—do not have the institutional responsibilities that provide certain powers to the Speaker of the House, they can have substantial influence over members of their respective parties. The majority leadership emerged as a formal and important position in the House about 1899.

The majority party leaders have a primary responsibility for organizing their party. They make the basic scheduling decisions about business in the House or the Senate, seek to gain desirable attendance on the floor, distribute and collect information, and persuade members (either through bargaining or by applying pressure) to behave in specific ways in relation to individual bills. Today the powers of elected party leaders within Congress are derived from actual legislative duties, but are probably related more to personality. It seems clear that those elected party leaders who have enjoyed influence and success have relied less on the formal powers of their office than on persuasion and political acumen. The role of Lyndon Johnson as Democratic majority leader from 1953 to 1960 is instructive; he used tact and persuasion rather than overt pressure to get his way. Like Republican Speaker of the House Joseph Martin, he never asked his colleagues to vote against their constituents' wishes. Johnson used his limited formal powers to gain more influence. Thus he utilized his role as Steering Committee chairman to put all Democratic senators, even freshmen, on one important committee, building a reservoir of gratitude upon which he could rely when necessary.[7] Choice committee assignments over which he had considerable discretion were used to reward those who voted with him. Johnson could assign members to special committees, arrange travel jaunts, and do other favors for Republicans as well as Democrats. Ultimately, his persuasive ability in large measure was due more to his personal influence than to institutional power.[8]

[7] For a discussion of congressional party committees see p. 285.

[8] This account relies heavily on Ralph K. Huitt, "Democratic Party Leadership in the Senate," *American Political Science Review* 55 (June 1961): 333–44.

While at the outset of the Ninety-third Congress in January 1973, Senator Mansfield, Johnson's successor as Senate Democratic majority leader, was able to alter the liberal-conservative balance on the key Senate Appropriations Committee by having three liberals added to the committee's membership, it is widely recognized that he has a far more limited view of his leadership role than did Johnson.[9] According to Washington observer Elizabeth Drew, both Mansfield and the current Speaker of the House Carl Albert, "operate in similar styles, deferential, laissez faire." When party leaders do take the lead from time to time they do so in response to strong pressure from within their own ranks. The role of elected party leadership since the 1950s is in contrast to the era of the 1950s when Johnson as majority leader in the Senate, and Sam Rayburn as Speaker of the House faced an opposition party president and were able at times to impose considerable order on their congressional parties.[10]

Another set of elected congressional leaders are the whips. It is the duty of the whips to try to ensure that there are enough votes cast to pass laws in the form supported by the party's elected leadership; they are agents of intelligence gathering and communication. Although the whip function was developed in the late nineteenth century by both parties, until the 1930s their activity was sporadic. Since then both parties have developed well-organized whip organizations and the chief whips have therefore become more powerful. Due to the structure of American legislative parties, their power cannot be compared to that of their British counterparts, whose name and role they seek to emulate. Whips, like other party leaders, seek to gain votes by offering favors, including pet projects and help with desired legislation and key committee assignments. In recent years whips have sought increasingly to use their positions as stepping stones to climb up the party hierarchy to the majority or minority leadership.

PARTY COMMITTEES

Although the congressional parties have created numerous caucuses—or conferences—that seek to bind members to an agreed upon party position, on the whole the goal of party unity has not been achieved. There is a bewildering variety of party committees in both houses. In the House, for example, there is a Republican Committee on Committees, a Republican conference, a Republican Policy Committee, and a Republican Research Committee. Connections

[9] The Appropriations Committee is important because all legislation for funding must eventually go to this committee before it can go to the floor of the Senate for a vote. The chairman of the committee is Senator Long of Louisiana, a conservative Democrat.

[10] See Sundquist, *Politics and Policy,* p. 391, for the view that during this period the Democratic party developed a program to which it committed itself and played a "responsible party" role. During Johnson's term as president (1963–68), Everett Dirksen, the Senate minority leader often played a vigorous role as party spokesman.

among such committees are normally fragmented and it may be said safely that under most circumstances none of these committees assumes a commanding role in legislative policy making. Party committees for both parties were recommended by the Joint Committee on the Organization of Congress in 1946. The Joint Committee recommended, "That both the House and the Senate establish formal committees for the determination and expression of majority policy and minority policy. . . ." They recommended also, "That the majority policy committees of the Senate and House serve as a formal council to meet regularly with the Executive . . . to improve relationships between the executive and legislative branches of the Government. . . . The Committee's recommendations [for policy committees] were based on the theory that in a democracy national problems must be handled on a national basis. Only through the expression of the will of the people by their support of political parties on the basis of platform pledges can the majority will be determined. Likewise, the minority viewpoint is also expressed in support of the minority platform." [11]

These proposals, based on the "responsible party" concept, have not produced significant results, except for a major, albeit constrained, role played by the House Republican Policy Committee from 1959–1965. Given the general lack of unanimity on many issues within the two parties, the policy committees, though still in existence and still meeting, have not been able to provide much policy direction for their respective parties. [12] In fact the policy committees reflect the intraparty factionalism inherent within each of the two major congressional parties.

In the late 1950s many of the younger and more liberal Democrats in the House of Representatives felt that the Democratic party Policy Committee did not at all represent their interests or concerns. Thus, in 1959 they developed the Democratic Study Group (DSG), whose primary purpose was to provide organization to advance liberal programs, as a counterforce to the coalition of Republicans and conservative Democrats who had often dominated the legislative arena. The DSG sets forth policy statements for its membership, raises campaign funds, publishes a newsletter, and has developed its own whip system. [13] While this group has enjoyed several notable instances of

[11] U.S. Congress, Senate, Joint Committee on the Organization of Congress, *Senate Report No. 1011,* 79th Cong., 2d Sess., March 4, 1946, p. 13.

[12] During the Ninety-third Congress there were some attempts to strengthen the Democratic caucus in the House of Representatives (see p. 287).

[13] This is a portion of the letter sent to Democratic members of Congress regarding the formation of the DSG.

   Dear Fellow Democrat:
   Democrats in the Congress are being criticized, unfairly at times, for failure to carry out to a greater extent the legislative program spelled out in the Democratic Platform. One reason for lack of success in some of our efforts has been a breakdown of communication among members who favor such a program. . . .
   We have had several meetings and have organized the Democratic Study Group on a

legislative success—including the passage of measures on civil rights and aid to depressed areas—even DSG members have encountered difficulties in achieving consensus on key issues (e.g., the ABM issue of 1970). However, this party within a party has produced some important attempts at congressional reform—including the modification of the seniority system for the selection of committee chairmen and the institution of an electronic system for the recording of teller votes.[14] The membership of the DSG has been increasing—two-thirds of Democrats belong; about seventy are "core" members.[15] Furthermore, the Ninety-third Congress saw a member of the DSG, Representative O'Neill, emerge as House majority leader. It is possible that the DSG may emerge as a "substitute" for strong Democratic party leadership in the House. In the Republican party where the more liberal Republicans found that their policy committee did not represent their interests, their party leadership responded by placing more younger liberal members on the policy committees. Liberal Republican senators are also members of the "Wednesday" club, a membership subgrouping similar to the DSG (although it is not as influential within the Republican party).

Within the House of Representatives, 1973 saw revitalization of the Democratic and Republican caucuses as organizations at which party members thrash out differences, take party positions, and push for reforms (as well as playing their traditional role of making committee assignments).[16] In 1975, the Democratic House caucus altered congressional tradition by unseating several chairmen of important committees. Neither the role of the caucus nor that of a new House Democratic Steering and Policy Committee established by the Democrats in the Ninety-third Congress to set legislative strategy in accordance with party policy, is as yet clear.[17] There is, however, little reason to assume that the lack of party cohesiveness—the nearly virtual absence of

---

preliminary basis. More than seventy members have attended one or more of these meetings. We have established a tentative whip organization. We have elected a temporary steering committee, responsible to the will of a majority of the broad group of participating Members of the House. Of course, we will realize that there will be basic conflicts between individual beliefs and among the interests of the Districts we represent. But these may be resolved in a freer discussion of each others problems than we are able to get from floor debate.

Cited by Mark F. Ferber, "The Formation of the Democratic Study Group," in Nelson Polsby, ed., *Congressional Behavior* (New York: Random House, 1971), p. 257.

[14] See pp. 295–98 below. The DSG does provide the only comprehensive listing of prospective legislation in Congress.

[15] *Current American Government* (Washington, D.C.: Congressional Quarterly Service, Spring 1974), p. 91.

[16] Senate Republicans also caucus weekly to discuss upcoming legislation; their caucuses and policy committees have been given professional staffing. At least one observer sees these groups as contributing to generally high Republican unity. David Broder, *The Party's Over* (New York: Harper and Row, 1972), p. 218.

[17] Steering committees seek to establish the order in which legislation will be considered on the floor of Congress. They also seek to determine floor tactics. The Democratic Steering and Policy Committee in the Ninety-Fourth Congress assumed the role of nominating committee chairmen. In the past, however, steering committees have played a limited role in both houses of Congress.

intraparty discipline—has yet been altered. Perhaps one should note, however, the apparent increase in what may be party cohesion, which has surfaced in the Ninety-third Congress (see Table 45). Thus on the question of impeachment of President Nixon there was considerable Democratic unity long before members of his own party turned against him. Also, one can find apparent party cohesion on some key votes, including measures to limit executive impoundment of funds appropriated by Congress, to enact universal voter registration by mail, and to subsidize presidential primaries from public funds.

Because there are few negative sanctions for not backing the party leadership, party cohesion *qua* party loyalty remains ephemeral. Punishment has been only rarely meted out to legislators even when they bucked their own party to support the presidential candidate of another party. Even in instances of clear party disloyalty negative sanctions have not been always (or even usually) applied. When in 1956, Adam Clayton Powell, the Democratic congressman from Manhattan, endorsed Republican President Eisenhower, he suffered no loss of congressional privileges. Democratic Senator Harry F. Byrd of Virginia endorsed General Eisenhower in 1952, and then remained silent in the 1956 and 1960 campaigns, without any sanctions being taken against him. There have been a few cases where sanctions were applied—specifically the loss of seniority and committee assignments. Congressman John Rarick (Democrat, Louisiana) did lose his seniority in the Democratic party after he supported George Wallace's candidacy in 1968. This kind of punishment is, however, the exception, rather than the rule. Almost the only kinds of sanctions which are directed by party leaders are unfavorable committee assignments, which can make some difference to member's political aspirations.

If one were to discuss the articulation of party policy more accurately, and without the constraints of organization charts, it would be more accurate to suggest that when either congressional party presents policy statements they are often more the statements of party leadership than of rank-and-file congressmen and senators. This is not intended to suggest that there is never similar voting on legislation by members of the same party. There is a *tendency* —to be discussed on pp. 290-92 —for Democrats to vote with Democrats, and Republicans with Republicans. Nonetheless, it seems clear that the number of leaders—those elected by party members as well as the committee chairmen serving as a result of seniority—within Congress makes it very difficult to provide unified party leadership to either party, especially given the wide range of issue-orientations among the various members of each party. In the complex maze which is Congress, the party is at best only one referent for its memberships political aspirations.

The lack of "party responsibility"—as measured by the ability of political parties to take positions and have their members abide by them—in the United States contrasts sharply with the party system in Great Britain. In Great Britain, where nominations, and to a very considerable extent the financing necessary to run a campaign for the House of Commons, derive from the party, if party members buck the parliamentary party they may have difficulty gaining renomination and support for future elections. Thus party voting coherence is higher in Britain than it is in the United States. Karl Lowenstein has noted that, "Party solidarity in England rests on two principles: first, the Prime Minister's power to dissolve Parliament at any time, thus threatening the individual M.P. with loss of his seat in new elections, and secondly (and just as important), the strong party loyalties that exist in England in a more pronounced form than anywhere else." [18]

Table 45. Measures of Party Unity

| Years | Party Vote as Percent of Total | Percent of Party Unity | |
		Democrats	Republicans
1968	32	57	73
1969	34	62	62
1970	32	57	59
1971	40	62	66
1972	33	57	64
1973	41	68	68

KEY: Composite party unity scores show the percentage of the time the average Democrat and Republican voted with his party majority in partisan votes; party unity votes are the roll-call votes in the Senate or the recorded teller votes in the House of Representatives that split the parties—that is, votes in which a majority of voting Democrats opposed a majority of voting Republicans. Votes on which either party divided equally are excluded. SOURCE: *Congressional Quarterly Weekly Report* (February 2, 1974): 210.

The American phenomenon comes into clear focus if one looks at party unity scores, to gauge the amount of time the average Democrat and the average Republican voted with his party majority in disagreement with the other party's majority. (See Table 45.)

One change discernible in 1973 that could portend a rise in future party voting was the decline in party division between northern and southern Democrats, which dropped by 10 percent from the 1972 level. Democratic voting unity in the past has been weakened by the close legislative association between southern Democrats and Republicans. Some of the newer southern Demo-

---

[18] Karl Lowenstein, *British Cabinet Government* (New York: Oxford University Press, 1967), p. 120.

cratic congressmen, who are more "liberal" in outlook, appear to have contributed to the trend toward greater cohesion. Still, generally fewer than 40 percent of the votes in either house of Congress are party votes. Insofar as less than 70 percent of the members of the parties vote with their majority, even on these limited votes, it seems reasonable to examine other variables that influence congressional voting and to ask what role party does play in an individual member's behavior in Congress.

UNDERSTANDING CONGRESSIONAL BEHAVIOR

PARTY INFLUENCE AND CONSTITUENCY INFLUENCE

It may be suggested that in American politics, three different and competing concepts of legislative representation are operative. There is the Burkean view of the representative *as trustee,* which suggests that the representative, once elected, ought to represent his *own* will and judgment; the *instructed delegate* view, which implies that the representative ought to follow his constituency's mandate in matters of policy; and the *responsible party* view, which stresses that representatives ought to follow the dictates of national party leadership.[19] This typology suggests that while the party may play a role in affecting congressional behavior, legislators are by no means responsive only to party organization in performing their jobs. Even though partisanship appears to provide voting coherence on particular legislation, similarities in personal ideology, constituency and group pressures, and the influence of individuals within government may be more significant than party identification alone.

A recent study of congressional behavior suggests that the validity of the notion that "party is the single best predictor" of congressional voting behavior depends upon the policy area being considered.[20] Roger Davidson in his study *The Role of the Congressman* found that over half of the congressmen he interviewed "tended to disagree" or did "disagree" with the statement: "If a bill is important for his party's record, a member should vote with his party even if it costs him some support in his district."

Nonetheless, often leadership can exert influence over some members of Congress. When it is possible, one study found, members of Congress prefer to vote with their party rather than have the party leadership disapprove of their actions. Clearly this phenomenon is not simply a reward and punishment mechanism largely because the party has few rewards and punishments. It is also a state of mind. Congressmen and senators apparently prefer to be loyal,

---

[19] Warren E. Miller and Donald E. Stokes, "Constituency Influence in Congress," *American Political Science Review* 57 (March 1963): 56.

[20] Aage R. Clausen, *How Congressmen Decide* (New York: St. Martin, 1973), p. 95.

and to invoke party loyalty is a sanction in itself.[21] Sometimes party influence is based on friendship patterns, other times on favors owed, or it may relate to a desire to establish a relationship in which some day favors will perhaps be owed. In addition, as people with similar policy predispositions tend to be attracted to the same parties, districts with comparable demographic characteristics (especially racial, urban-rural, and SES) tend to send representatives to Congress from the same party. Thus districts with a predominantly affluent white population are more likely to select Republican congressmen and these representatives are likely to have reasonably similar voting records.

Party influence tends to be greater in more "procedural" issues or those involving party organization of the house in question. On such votes the party line is often strictly upheld. Specifically, these votes deal with procedural questions concerned with, for example, the organization of Congress and the adoption of rules governing the functioning of Congress. They include elections for majority and minority leaders, whips, and the Speaker of the House. But if we return to the broader legislative arena, it may be instructive to look at some of the key issues upon which Congress has decided (or not decided) to take action.[22] Perhaps some of the most interesting votes in the past decade have arisen over questions on welfare reform, antiwar restrictions, and the extension of the Voting Rights Act. On such essentially controversial, visible issues, cohesion based on party loyalty is lower. Party is often a poor guide to voting on such issues; party lines and distinctions become obscured and unclear.[23]

Often the most significant factor that helps to explain why a member deviates from positions taken by the party leadership is the nature of his constituency. Though members of Congress like to vote with the party (even though there is no strict discipline to enforce such behavior), they also wish to be reelected. Warren Miller and Donald Stokes, in a study published in 1963, indicated that a reasonably high positive correlation existed between congressmen's behavior and their perceptions of their constituency's interests. They found correlations between congressmen's own policy views and their perceptions of their constituents' views to be 0.7 for social welfare, 0.6 for foreign involvement, and 0.9 for civil rights.[24] All of these correlations are significant,

[21] Lewis F. Froman and Randell Ripley, "Conditions for Party Leadership," *The American Political Science Review* 59 (March 1965): 59.

[22] Legislation that could influence partisan gains may also produce high cohesion. For example, a 1971 bill to aid the poverty-stricken Democrats by providing a $1 checkoff on tax returns got fifty Democratic votes and was opposed by forty-two Republicans (two Republicans favored the act; five conservative Democrats opposed it). *New York Times,* November 23, 1971, pp. 1, 27.

[23] Froman and Ripley, "Conditions for Party Leadership," pp. 56–61. It should be noted that roll-call votes, until recently the only recorded votes in Congress, which comprised only 10 percent of the total, are the basis for these analyses of congressional behavior.

[24] Miller and Stokes, "Constituency Influence in Congress," p. 51. Other studies have also found that correlation between constituents' views of civil rights and those of congressmen are particularly high.

but it would seem that the civil rights relationship, the highest one, would be the easiest one to explain. In 1958–1959, the period for which this data was collected, the issue saliency of civil rights was particularly high. Thus it would be likely that voters would know the views of the candidates on this issue. As for social welfare, the two parties have had since the 1930s reasonably clearly delineated positions on social welfare programming—with the Democratic party generally more supportive of public sector involvement than the Republican party.[25] Social welfare is probably the issue closest to the responsible party view of congressional behavior—as party labels in this area appear to provide a means by which voters identify candidates with views like their own. It appears even here, however, that the nature of cause and effect relationships is unclear. Organized constituency pressures and differences may produce positions which appear to be party related. An interesting perspective on this question was expressed by Donald Matthews when he said that party affiliation influences a senator in choosing which groups in society he will represent.[26]

The third area of concern, foreign policy, had the lowest correlation coefficient between congressmen's policy views and their perceptions of constituent views. Since we were not involved in any active military actions at the time, the level of concern with this sector of issues was probably lower than for the domestic issues. This area has historically been closest to the Burkean, or trusteeship view of representation. It is possible that if a similar test were performed in 1975, that there might be a higher correlation on some foreign policy issues with a focal point of voter concerns and congressional perception of constituency interest being the Middle East and the military budget.[27]

Even in the absence of strict party discipline it is possible on some key issues to have some notion of the voting behavior of a member of Congress if you know to which party he belongs. It is, however, difficult to infer party effects from the existence of partisan voting alignments, since this requires separating out other factors in the decision-making process. Thus, if you wish to increase the likelihood of predicting a particular legislator's voting patterns, it would be useful to know about the composition of his district as well—to determine the powerful lobbying groups, the nature of the district's economic and demographic base, the national and racial backgrounds of the voters, as well as the

---

[25] See *Congressional Quarterly's Guide to the Congress of the United States* (Washington, D.C. Congressional Quarterly, 1971), p. 529; and Duncan McRae and F. H. Goldner, *Dimensions of Congressional Voting* (New York: Octagon, 1972); Wayne Shannon, *Party, Constituency and Congressional Voting* (Baton Rouge: Louisiana State University Press, 1968); Lewis A. Froman, *Congressmen and Their Constituencies* (Chicago: Rand McNally, 1963).

[26] Donald Matthews, *U.S. Senators and Their World* (Chapel Hill: University of North Carolina Press, 1960), p. 139.

[27] Ibid., p. 56; but a survey by the American Businessmen's Committee on National Priorities found that on withdrawal of troops from Vietnam, nine of the ten congressional leaders surveyed voted contrary to the policy preferences of their constituents. *New York Times,* August 23, 1972. On domestic issues, the correlation between representatives' voting records and constituency preferences was almost as low.

member's own ideological predispositions. Upon examination of the voting record of Democrats from central cities in the Ninety-second Congress, it should not be too surprising to learn that on issues of welfare reform, for example, the passage of H.R. I, 100 percent of the Democrats from congressional delegations of New York City and Chicago voted to accept this legislation, which would have led to increased federal government assumption of welfare costs.

ADDITIONAL INFLUENCES

Additional factors that influence congressional voting have been mentioned only in passing. Such phenomena include interpersonal relationships among congressmen, the influence of the bureaucracy (see pp. 271–74), and the ability of the president to influence members of Congress—especially of his own party—to vote in a particular way.

The role of the president in influencing members of his own party is an interesting phenomenon to observe. It has been noted by Mark Kesselman that, "After a Republican president (Eisenhower) espousing an internationalist foreign policy took office, most representatives whose voting record became more internationalist were Republicans. Nearly all representatives who shifted to more conservative positions, as measured by their roll call votes, were Democrats. The partisan affiliation of the representatives who shifted creates a strong presumption of presidential partisan influence." [28] We know that the president provides an important policy input into the legislative process. He intervenes in day-to-day operations of Congress, personally or through special congressional liaison personnel attempting to influence members of Congress to support (or not support) programs.

But certainly a member of Congress of the same party as the president does not have to abide by his policy wishes. Lyndon Johnson's victories in enacting the Civil Rights Acts of 1964 and 1965 did not have the support of many southern Democrats [29] (although in 1965 Congress did approve 68.9 percent of Johnson's legislation). The president remains a legislative influential insofar as he can influence members of Congress; he can do so either directly or indirectly by going to the people and waiting for the pressure to be brought

[28] Mark Kesselman, "Presidential Leadership in Congress on Foreign Policy: A Replication of a Hypothesis," *Midwest Journal of Political Science* 9 (November 1965): 403–4.
[29] The southern Democratic vote for the Civil Rights Act of 1964 was: Senate southern Democrats, 3 for and 20 against; House southern Democrats, 11 for and 92 against. The Voting Rights Act of 1965 votes were: Senate southern Democrats, 5 for and 17 against; House southern Democrats, 33 for and 60 against. Data for 1964 from *Congress and the Nation, 1945–1964: A Review of Government and Politics* (Washington, D.C.: Congressional Quarterly Service, 1965), pp. 93a, 96a. Data for 1965 from *Congress and the Nation, 1965–1968: A Review of Government and Politics* (Washington, D.C.: Congressional Quarterly Service, 1969), pp. 10a, 15a.

to bear on members of the House of Representatives and the Senate by "the folks back home." Consider this selection from Lyndon Johnson's memoirs:

I spoke about rats in every public forum I could find—in press conferences, in bill-signing ceremonies, in labor conventions, in meetings with Jaycees, in visits to scientific institutes. I recorded dozens of spot announcements for use on radio and television: "If we can spend literally millions to protect our cows from the screwworms, why can't we spend a little money to protect our children from the rats?" I asked my staff to encourage civil rights groups, social service groups, and urban and religious organizations to issue statements condemning the House action.

I argued economics with the conservatives: . . . . "I stressed morality with the moderates: . . . ." I talked politics with the Republicans: "I thought you'd like to know about an article in the current issue of *The Democrat:* its title is something like 'Republicans Laugh as Slum Dwellers Battle Rats': now you can't afford to have us saying things like that, can you?"

On September 20 the House reconsidered its action. With the heat of public indignation upon them, the Republicans had stopped laughing. By a 44-vote margin the House voted to add a rat control amendment to our Partnership for Health bill.[30]

The question of interpersonal relationships within Congress as an influence upon congressional policy outcomes should also be examined. Friendship patterns fostered by seating arrangements, committee assignments, and the need for political reciprocity in favor-giving can influence legislative policy decisions. Alan Fiellin, in his 1962 study of the members of the New York State delegation in the House of Representatives, hypothesized that "House politics is not unintelligibly complex, consisting only of the individual behavior of each of 435 isolated members. Rather, it is much more simply structured through a network of informal groups and relationships. This network provides channels for information exchange, political negotiation, and the formulation of compromises—probably impossible tasks for 435 atomized units." [31] Such relationships are frequently found in state delegations, among those who travel together, eat together, etc. These groupings can act as cue-giving mechanisms within the legislative party, especially on complex or ambiguous matters.

It should be noted also that pressure group activity is a significant and often decisive influence on congressional voting behavior, one too frequently ignored by traditional studies of how congressmen vote. For example, in 1972 a vote amending a bill withdrawing pesticides certified as unsafe from the market,

---

[30] Lyndon Baines Johnson, *The Vantage Point: Perspectives of the Presidency, 1963–1969* (New York: Holt, Rinehart and Winston, 1971), p. 85.
[31] Alan Fiellin, "The Functions of Informal Groups in Legislative Institutions," *The Journal of Politics* 24 (February 1962): 90.

was passed by the Senate with a provision to compensate manufacturers whose products were to be so removed. The Senate vote of 71 to 0 occurred after a concerted campaign by the pesticide industry to compensate the affected manufacturers.[32]

POSSIBILITIES FOR REFORM

The above analysis has suggested that there are multiple influences on members of Congress—party is sometimes one of these influences. In assessing possibilities for reform, it is important to remember that as long as congressional party power remains dispersed and enmeshed in internal cleavages, the party will have difficulty becoming a greater legislative force. The reforms that have been suggested to "remedy" the irresponsibility and complexity of the legislative policy-making process include procedural and constitutional changes. Let us consider each type of legislative reform separately.

PROCEDURAL CHANGES

Many of the critics of the congressional system in the United States point to the procedures that have evolved in Congress and suggest that it is the procedures themselves which make Congress a body unresponsive to the needs and demands of the American population. Most of these observers criticize the slowness with which legislative change occurs—particularly change supported by the more liberal elements in Congress and the rest of society—and they note that some procedural changes, given the present configuration of representation in Congress, might hasten the passage of redistributive legislation. Before examining the procedural changes suggested by critics of the Congress, it should be noted that they might not be making these suggestions for change if key actors were playing different roles. Thus, if committee chairmen were primarily representatives of northern urban areas with liberal predispositions these same critics might be very satisfied with the current set of congressional rules.

The demand for procedural change in Congress has focused primarily in two congressional traditions: the seniority system and the committee system, though other processes are criticized as well.[33] As a liberal reformist Demo-

[32] *Congressional Quarterly Weekly Report* 30 (October 14, 1972): 2637.

[33] The 1972 elections did produce a more liberal tone, particularly in committee chairmanships. Among those retired or defeated were the conservative chairmen of the Rules and D.C. Committees, now replaced by liberals. According to *Congressional Quarterly* the newcomers tend to be liberal on reform, which cuts across party and ideological lines, and was an issue stressed in many victorious congressional campaigns. *Congressional Quarterly Weekly Report* 30 (January 6, 1973): 14. The 1974 election results seemed to indicate a continuation of these liberalizing trends.

cratic coalition has come to play a greater role in the House in particular, some changes have been effected. Many of these changes emanated initially from the Democratic Study Group.

As far as the committee structure itself is concerned, critics of congressional rules who view the committee system as overly cumbersome have long sought an opening-up of the executive, closed sessions of committees. The House, during the Ninety-third Congress, voted to reduce the number of closed (secret) committee sessions, providing that all meetings except those involving national security must be open to the press and public. In addition, "mark-up sessions" in which votes are taken on a bill's different sections must be open unless a roll-call vote is taken to close them.[34] All votes taken in committee are now to be recorded and committees are required to adopt written rules, instead of relying on the chairman's whims, as in the past. The House has also sought to weaken the power of key committees such as the Rules Committee and Ways and Means Committee, which have customarily forced congressmen to accept their legislation as written by placing a "gag rule" barring amendments on outcoming legislation. The new rule provides for floor consideration of specific amendments to bills regardless of the committee's actions.[35]

Alternatives to the seniority system have also been sought. Some have proposed that seniority be eliminated altogether in choosing committee chairmen and that an open election among the members of the committee or party caucus in the majority party determine who shall be chairman. Others who contend that open choice of committee chairmen by the members of the majority party is not a viable alternative to the present system favor a system that minimizes seniority to some extent. Along these lines it has been suggested that a procedure which provides a balance between seniority and the degree of party competitiveness in one's home district might be a better way to choose committee chairmen. Such a system would maximize expertise in the area of policy concern of the committee, possibly accomplished via seniority. It also would provide for a degree of responsiveness to the general public, since it is assumed that party competitiveness in one's own district requires active attention to one's constituents and would bring about more responsive committee chairmen and committee structures.

The rigidities of the seniority system have gradually eroded in the Congress. Thus in January 1973, the Republican party in the Senate voted to change the method of selecting committee chairmen and ranking members of committees solely on the basis of seniority. In the future these positions will be filled

---

[34] *New York Times,* March 8, 1973, p. 1. However, in 1972, Congress continued to hold many meetings in secret, even increasing such meetings during that year. *Congressional Quarterly Guide to Current American Government* (Washington, D.C.: Congressional Quarterly Service, Spring 1973), p. 84.

[35] *New York Times,* February 22, 1973, p. 1. Chairmanships of committees and subcommittees have also been limited to one for each legislator, regardless of seniority.

by vote of the Republicans on the different committees. Also in 1973, for the first time in recent years, House Democratic committee chairmen and ranking members had to win their jobs by majority vote of the full party caucus. All the votes were recorded by secret ballot, consistent with the earlier decision of the caucus that 20 percent of its members could demand a recorded vote. However, although House Democrats placed a procedural obstacle in the path of seniority, they stepped around it and awarded all committee chairmanships to the same members who would have received them if the system had gone untouched. But, in 1975, the House Democrats did not award all chairmanships on the basis of seniority.[36] This appears to be a significant procedural change which could augur the onset of a new system; one in which chairmen must serve as leaders responsible to members of their own congressional party. Nonetheless, the impact of these changes on future party leadership and cohesion is uncertain. It may be that seniority, with its basis in congressional tradition, will not be entirely eliminated—despite decisions to provide such an option. But, knowledge of a system whereby a member's seniority can be passed over may profoundly affect the behavior of chairmen and potential chairmen.

In addition to the seniority system and the committee system, there are other areas of concern for the procedural reformers. Many reform-minded analysts of the congressional system have been pleased to see a change in the methods currently used to tally the votes in both houses of Congress. The House has virtually abolished the practice by which congressmen could avoid having their votes on crucial floor amendments recorded. It is possible that this system of teller voting has increased the opportunities for pressure by party leaders.[37] Now all votes are registered by name so that a member's votes are public knowledge. This change was facilitated through simple mechanization of the teller system. In 1973 an electronic voting system with buttons on members' desks connecting to the teller's (or recorder's desk) was installed in the House.[38]

An additional area for procedural reform in Congress relates to the role of party leadership vis-à-vis the members of their party in their respective houses. At the present time as noted earlier, elected party leaders, given the limitations of their roles, rarely have much opportunity to enforce strong party discipline. If congressional party rules were changed so as to provide the elected leader-

---

[36] In January 1975 the Senate Democrats also voted to select committee chairmen by secret ballot instead of relying upon automatic seniority.

[37] See Froman and Ripley, "Conditions for Party Leadership," p. 60. They contend that party unity is greater on teller votes. The Legislative Reorganization Act of 1970 provided for recorded teller votes for roll calls and quorum calls. Public Law 91-510, Title I, Sec. 120.

[38] Such systems have been installed in the state legislatures of 36 states as well as in the legislatures of Sweden and West Germany. Over 100 years ago, Thomas Edison was awarded a patent for an electrographic vote recorder similar to that installed in the House of Representatives. *Congressional Quarterly Weekly Report* 30 (December 16, 1972): 3155.

ship of the congressional parties with more authoritative power, it is conceivable that party policy committees could make decisions that would be more binding on both committee chairmen and membership. This might reduce the power of committee chairmen who rule by virtue of their seniority and are not necessarily representative of the party in Congress or the nation's voters. This would of course lead to stronger party or "responsible" government which would please some liberal reformers—as long as the policies being formulated by the majority were favorable to their political views.

It is too early to assess the future impact of Democratic and Republican attempts to rebuild party caucuses and policy-making committees on revitalized parties in Congress. Given an historical perspective, however, it seems unlikely that basic structural changes will occur rapidly—though they may emerge over a longer period of time. One final point on the potential for reform of the congressional system needs to be made. In May 1974 the Democratic party caucus voted by secret ballot, 111 to 95, not to consider the proposals brought before it by the House Select Committee on Committees to reorganize the committees of the House of Representatives. The proposed reforms would have reduced the jurisdictions—and influence—of several committees, including the all-powerful Ways and Means Committee. Apparently, many House Democrats—liberals as well as conservatives—were not prepared to reorder the House. Some of the liberals who had in the past been outspoken critics of the existing committee system voted against the proposed reorganization because they feared that a reshuffling of committee responsibilities and membership would dilute liberal strength on some committees. Also, it is important to keep in mind that within the House of Representatives at the time of this vote there were 117 subcommittee chairmen (57 in the Senate). Given the large number of subcommittees many congressmen have chairmanships and may be hesitant to tamper with the existing system which has given them some power.

CONSTITUTIONAL CHANGE

It is possible to argue that a stronger role for the party as policy maker would require constitutional changes via amendment. Short of a major revision of the separation of powers system and new provisions for a parliamentary system combining executive and legislative functions, the basic constitutional change often recommended involves changing two-year terms in the House of Representatives and six-year terms in the Senate to four-year terms, with elections occurring at the same time as the presidential election. Such a change in the present system might in theory at any rate provide us with a system in which both Congress and the president, elected at the same time, would be responsive to similar societal pressures and would more likely represent more similar issue positions. This might alter the balance of power between the branches of government and thus facilitate party government. If the president and Congress were elected at the same time it might be possible for the president to be a more powerful leader for his party in Congress—since many congressmen and senators would be tied to the president's issue positions. A popular president might be able to command electoral support for congressional candidates, which at a later date could be translated into party loyalty.

Though party responsibility might be increased with this system—and certainly the ongoing campaigning most representatives must pursue if they wish to be reelected would be curtailed, there are certain drawbacks to such a proposal. While two-year terms are very short, they require that most representatives remain "in touch" with their constituents, stressing the "instructed delegate" element of our tradition to some degree. If representatives were elected with the president, the House of Representatives might not be as reflective of the differences in our nation.

The pervasive "pluralist" (or "Madisonian") view discussed earlier in this book makes it unlikely that there will be any major change because of the limited role prescribed for parties by the founding fathers and subscribed to today. Events such as Watergate have probably ensured the continuation of a system in which no one branch can easily dominate the entire political process for the foreseeable future; federalism and separation of powers will continue to prevent responsible party government from becoming a reality. It is not clear that any change short of constitutional amendment will increase the role of party or make Congress more responsive to the general public. It is possible of course that if the voters could understand better what Congress was doing, they might force greater party loyalty on their elected representatives, as party could be a more meaningful *cue* to understanding the policy-making process in any legislative body. However, the public apparently has so little information about what happens in Congress "that the irregularity of congressmen and ineffectiveness of the congressional parties have scant impact at the polls." [39]

CONCLUSION

Changes in structure, procedures, or even in the expectations of leadership cannot be expected to foster great changes in the American political system. While some of the reforms discussed above may help to make Congress a little more responsive, a major revitalization of party inspired policy is unlikely in a Congress whose "caucuses have caucuses." In a House of Representatives

---

[39] Donald E. Stokes and Warren E. Miller, "Party Government and the Saliency of Congress," *Public Opinion Quarterly* 26 (Winter 1962): 546.

where there is a black caucus, a liberal caucus, a rural caucus, a burgeoning women's caucus, and other subgroupings within and across party lines, party seems foreordained to take a back seat on many policy issues.[40]

It is important for us to remember the multiple influences on our congressmen and senators. They come from a variety of different backgrounds and districts and many are the products of strong antiparty environments. They are working in a system that calls upon them to be responsive to their constituents and organized pressures, as well as party. Hence, we ought not be too hard on them for oftentimes minimizing the role of the national party in their respective houses as they respond to their perceptions of constituent and other interests.

[40] See Elizabeth Drew, "Why Congress Won't Fight," *New York Times Magazine* (September 23, 1973): 88.

14
Conclusion

We have considered many aspects of political parties in the American political system and the general conclusion that has been reached is that our parties have survived and performed despite the fact that they exist in a strong antiparty environment. Like all American institutions they have responded slowly to changes in the environment. Because, "parties are a dependent variable, institutions whose form and function largely depend on both the society and the constitutional system," the adaptations to change that do take place in American parties have not affected our antiparty predispositions or altered the fact that parties play what is largely a symbolic function.[1]

Parties have not for many years performed the role of "important link" between the government and the people. Changes that may take place in the future will have to be tempered by a series of environmental factors we tend often to overlook if we examine political parties in a vacuum. These environmental forces include the "new political technology," and its effects on information dissemination; the increasing tendency of voters to be "independent" in their voting decisions; and the increasingly politicized role of groups who until very recently were nonparticipants in the political process. Let us review

---

[1] Evron N. Kirkpatrick, "Toward a More Responsible Two Party System: Political Science, Policy Science or Pseudo Science," *American Political Science Review* 65 (December 1971): 976–77.

briefly how these conditions may affect parties and the antiparty tradition that has evolved from the very earliest years of our nation.

THE NEW POLITICAL TECHNOLOGY AND PARTIES

THE EFFECTS OF MEDIA

We have indicated in Chapters 2, 3, and 4 that technology has played a very significant role in affecting our political environment. Information reaches the members of the polity with much greater speed than ever before in our nation's history. Such information leads many of us to take positions on issues that may never before have seemed relevant to our experiences. There is increased diversity in terms of sources of political information: from television to sophisticated advertisements to polls and "scientific" predictions. One clear result of this is an increased unwillingness among voters to accept the "word" of a political party when a voting decision has to be made. The "cue" political parties can provide is not as necessary when we each have an individual store of information to help us make our own political decisions.

The condition fits well into the American political tradition. We have had as a nation an abiding concern with the central role of the individual in society, and the freedom of the individual to make decisions for himself. Technology may have produced a political system close to that called "nonpartisan"; that is, the individual relating to the polity without the intervention of factions. By providing a greater opportunity for the citizenry to respond on the basis of individual choice, and reducing the dependency of the voter on the "cue" role of parties, the media—especially television—have reinforced the American counterpart of the Lockean man.

MORE THOUGHTS ON TECHNOLOGY

There are other aspects of political technology that seem to have reinforced our antiparty tradition. The costs associated with a campaign based on computer analysis, public relations experts, and the media have led political hopefuls to look to groups and individuals in their constituencies (and sometimes outside of their district) to provide the necessary funds to run for public office. To accomplish this feat, political candidates have looked beyond party. They have developed their own fund-raising mechanisms, and they have in numerous instances participated in reducing the role of their party in its central function, the election campaign. The media have further reduced the clout of parties in political campaigns by permitting candidates to reach the voters without door-to-door contacts. It should be noted, however, that while old-style techniques involving citizen contact and district organizations are still extensively utilized in gaining both nomination and election, especially on the local level, even these tactics can be coopted by an individual office seeker or splinter group who may be acting for special, rather than party, interests. The 1964 nomination of Goldwater (Republican) and 1972 selection of McGovern (Democrat) seem to indicate how—on the national level—a corps of dedicated volunteers can assume possession of the party label and use it for their own purposes.

Whatever the techniques employed, the increased cost of campaigning raises an important economic question with very strong political implications: Until there is redistribution of economic resources in the United States, can we expect to have a political system in which meaningful participation is not limited by class and status? What we knew for many years became abundantly clear in the context of the campaign fund-raising scandals of the second Nixon administration: All of the people do not have the same opportunity to influence political decision makers. There is ample evidence that party politics (and all American politics for that matter) is pervaded by class bias. By examining socioeconomic characteristics of voters, party activists, and elected public officials, a pattern of middle-upper-class dominance at all levels of partisan participation becomes clear. Hence, some citizens have better access to political power than others, and this access is measured to a considerable degree by a surrogate measure, "dollars." The money is not contributed necessarily to the party; it is contributed to the candidate. If he is elected, he will have to at least listen to the demands of the financial donors who in fact helped him garner the support of the voter-participants on Election Day.

As far as any change in this condition is concerned, there is legislation that is intended to counter excessive campaign spending and lessen dependence on large contributors. Perhaps in the years to come, campaign finance laws will more *effectively* do the job that the laws in the past have failed to do. Thus, even the comprehensive campaign finance law of 1974 does not provide full public financing of elections. Enforcement of legislation may be difficult. Who, for example, is to be controlled? If the candidate must stay within funding limitations, can I as an individual citizen spend money to help elect the candidate of my choice? If this latter situation is not controlled then even spending limits clamped on campaigns and candidates may not totally change the situation. If citizen's rights to support a candidate of his or her choice—by having a party, a meeting, etc.—are curtailed, then there will be a sharp curtailment of individual rights. Will democracy for the many have been increased or decreased?

Significant inequalities in access to the political system are likely to remain despite the partial public financing and contribution limitations imposed by the 1974 law.

Despite the persistence of unequal access to the political system, meaningful participation may be enhanced by the opportunities provided by technology. (Of course the political process for many Americans may be defined more broadly than parties.) Possibilities for increased expression of political opinions through scientific techniques and media—as yet unexplored—may produce a more responsive set of party leaders and public officials. As suggested elsewhere, many Americans appear to be expressing their interest in and willingness to participate more in political life—both in party and nonparty activities. It might, however, be naïve to expect the beneficiary of political concern and activism among some groups to be a stronger party system. It is unlikely that in this era of specialization we will suddenly shift gears and return in significant numbers to party organization related activities.

TECHNOLOGY AND BUREAUCRACY

One further thought on technology and American political parties. As the trained expert becomes more of a central figure in our postindustrial society —especially since he has the information central to our political decision making—both bureaucrats who work directly for the government and those who are employed within the private sector seem to act as modifiers of the pragmatic political role that parties have played. Clearly, parties have played some role in public policy decision making, although it has been historically *very limited.* It is possible that even this very circumscribed role is being curtailed by the need for expert testimony and special skills. Thus, decisions on how to cope with the energy crisis in 1973–1974 were developed by energy experts in both the private industry and public government sectors. Both parties took back seats to the "experts" and interest group representatives. The intelligence provided by the experts to members of Congress guided Congress in the framing of legislation to try to cope with the problem.

AMERICAN PARTIES IN PERSPECTIVE

IS THERE A ROLE FOR MASS-MEMBERSHIP PARTIES IN THE UNITED STATES?

The antiparty tradition in the United States is being reinforced by the technology of our postindustrial society. An important word in the above sentence is *reinforce.* In point of fact we have always had a strong antiparty tradition. In the early days of the republic there was a clear disdain for political parties among most of the founding fathers, which has been identified in these pages as the Madisonian or "pluralist" view. The Constitution, for example, made no mention of political parties; and it was clearly the intention of many of the framers of that document to contain and limit the majority rather than maximize its potential power. This is crucial because the opportunity to mobilize a majority politically is at least a theoretical aim of the two-party system.

The Madisonians, though distrustful of factions, were cognizant of their reality. Within the Constitution, federalism, separation of powers, and the creation of a large and diverse territorial republic (with ability to expand) were operationalized. Such checks and balances have acted to prevent the formation of a permanent majority—or mass party. It should be noted that when parties did emerge in the United States they arose as congressional factions, not so much by design as by necessity, stemming largely from personality conflicts and irreconcilable political ideas.

The dominant American antipartyism has been reflected in the past half century by the increased use of nonpartisan elections, the rise of internal party reform movements, and an increasing predisposition on the part of voters to cast their votes independently of their party affiliation. Party affiliation has been declining also, as is indicated by the fact that by 1972 there were more registered independents than registered Republicans.[2] Even in the Congress of the United States, party ties are not too strong—constituent interests and ideology often seem to provide a more consistent explanation for congressional voting behavior than party. Furthermore, even the partisan role of the incumbent president is circumscribed by the realities of vertical and horizontal separation of powers. Thus, American parties have, from the beginning, been viewed on a spectrum ranging from total hostility (in the "nonpartisan" view) to mild antipathy.

Only the majoritarian, or property view, was a concept that was spurned by our early political leaders; and today a predisposition to this view is shared by very few Americans. Nonetheless, a proposal by the 1972 Democratic convention to hold biennial party conferences and create a national executive committee ("bigger than any of its officeholders [and] candidates"), recent attempts to institutionalize closed direct primaries in the presidential nominating process, and the efforts by Democrats in general to make the national convention more representative and increase intraparty democracy are tentative, beginning steps along the road toward stronger national party organizations. Even these modest efforts have been greeted with a negative reaction from one editorialist: "a coalition with varied interests and only a political opposition in common is one thing; a party of political theory quite another." In his view, our present nonsystem of parties is preferable to a seemingly unworkable theoretical alternative.[3] Though in 1974 a miniconvention was

[2] A 1974 survey reinforces this analysis, as the Republicans retain third-party status. An August 1974 Gallup Poll found 42 percent Democrats, 34 percent Independents, and 24 percent Republicans. *New York Times,* August 11, 1974, Sect. IV, p. 4.
[3] Robert Bendiner, *New York Times,* February 19, 1973, p. 23.

held by the Democrats, as yet, basic attitudes toward the party do not seem to have been affected.

Even proponents of responsible party government concede we have seen precious little of it in America in the past generations, either at the state, local, or national levels. George Reedy's words are worth recalling in this context:

> The arguments for responsible party government are compelling. But their logic is totally irrelevant . . . those who desire ideological politics must await the day when mechanisms are available which permit coalition at the government level, and thereby relieve our political parties of the necessity of filling this role.[4]

Ultimately, the goal of creating strong parties uniting both the executive and legislative branches within the national party and the state and local levels with the national party, must await a transformation of constitutional and customary practices. Seniority, federalism, local nonpartisanship, and divided governments at all levels are just a few of the factors that will inhibit a massive change in American parties.

ISSUES IN AMERICAN POLITICS

A brief look at the contemporary political scene simply leads one to reiterate what was suggested in the previous section. It is certainly not apparent that mass-based parties are developing in the United States. Antipartyism is a view held by large numbers of people. Perhaps the only mass-based participation emerging in the United States is a mass-based antiparty participation evidenced by low levels of party loyalty on Election Day, and high levels of nonparty registration and voting. This antiparty tendency may be on the rise because of the very character of our parties and our system. As noted elsewhere in this chapter, change comes slowly to American institutions. Americans seem to be developing a greater concern for *issues* as "cues" for voting, as is evidenced by the 1972 election.[5] However, political parties, given their district-level organization, city, county, state, and finally, national organizations, have *not* followed suit. Parties are most often not issue-oriented or ideological. A politically concerned person with strongly felt issue positions (or an all-encompassing ideological world view) may be more attracted to interest groups whose views correspond to his own and who seek to influence political decision makers in terms of specific policies. Interest groups have existed always in this nation. They exist today and perhaps it is to these myriad groups with special concerns that many politically concerned citizens are attracted. Rapidly grow-

---

[4] George Reedy, *The Twilight of the Presidency* (New York: Mentor, 1970), pp. 131–32.
[5] See Chapter 6 for a discussion of the role of issues in 1972 electoral choices.

ing nonpartisan "public interest" groups such as Common Cause (with a reported membership of over 200,000) seem able to attract the membership dues political parties have never been able to obtain. These and other interest groups are perhaps more reflective of increased issue-orientation—especially among people who are most likely to participate, the educated middle and upper classes.[6] It should also be noted that participation in reform movements, protests, and demonstrations indicates that there is no declining interest apparent in the United States in political decision making and the individual's role in influencing this process.

Parties do not take meaningful positions on many issues because the political system almost requires centrist politics to win elections. Given the diversity of interests represented within each party and the experiences of ideological candidates such as Goldwater and McGovern, it is unlikely that parties will become particularly issue-oriented. Students of American parties are confronted with a paradox today. If parties do not change and adapt stronger issue positions in an era of increasing awareness, range, and concern for issues, they are likely to continue to lose ground among the educated, affluent middle class. However, strong issue stands—at least for the time being—will antagonize a sufficiently large number of voters to prevent electoral victory.

NEW GROUPS AND PARTIES

GROUPS SEEKING POLITICAL POWER

There are groups trying to gain access to the American political system that have previously not been able to participate in the political process even in so limited a manner as voting. These groups include blacks, Spanish-speaking Americans, and youth. They are making demands on the political system for meaningful participation. Blacks, for example, are voting in increasing numbers and have been successful in electing mayors in big cities, as well as city, county, and state legislators. They are becoming a political force in many cities and counties with which the established political leaders must reckon. As yet unclear is the extent to which participation via increased voting and office holding will bring any substantive change in the economic conditions that disproportionately afflict nonwhites in this nation. What is interesting is that in this age of political cynicism wrought in a tradition of antiparty politics, blacks and Spanish-speaking Americans are often willing to give parties a chance. (Perhaps this statement does need a modifier attached to it insofar as many local elections in which black candidates have participated have been nonpartisan.)

[6] See Chapter 6 for a discussion of education and its effects on participation.

It is not yet clear whether or not parties can provide the access for these groups to political decision making that will equalize political and economic resources in the United States. Clearly, earlier groups that tried to use parties to gain better positions in society succeeded in many instances—Jews, Italians, Irish—in gaining economic and political mobility. It can be argued, however, that gains made via parties were largely gains for individuals, and that collective "group achievement" resulted from using a variety of techniques, including education and economic entrepreneurship. Party politics, with its job opportunities and decision-making potential, was then just one factor leading to improvements for these earlier groups. When talking of the present decade, however, we must remember that the job opportunities are more limited because of civil service regulations in cities, counties, and states, as well as the national government, and that the requisites of an advanced industrial society often create jobs requiring special skills and expertise. This final condition may limit the party-related opportunities for individual advancement that were available to the politically emerging groups of 50 or 100 years ago and may lead to further denigration of parties.

ARE PARTIES REACTIVE?

Perhaps one final point can be made regarding political parties in the United States. Frank Stanton, vice-chairman of CBS, when discussing politics and political technology, made the following observations:

> . . . the political world is still peering cautiously around the corner of the nineteenth century, pausing only to look back over its shoulder occasionally to the eighteenth. It takes no social historian to observe that if we ran our factories, conducted our communications, and nurtured our health at the same rate of scientific and technical advance as we conduct our political affairs, we would still be taking weeks to make a pair of shoes, delivering the mail by Pony Express, and treating pneumonia by bloodletting.[7]

Perhaps Stanton's observation is credible because we do have such a strong antiparty tradition in the United States based on fear and even hostility to politics and much that is "political." However, insofar as parties can serve the function of nominating candidates for public office—where partisan elec-

---

[7] Frank Stanton, "Science and Democratic Progress," Speech delivered at the commencement exercises, California Institute of Technology, Pasadena, California, June 11, 1965, reprinted in U. S. Senate Subcommittee on Communications of the Committee on Commerce, "Projections— Predictions of Election Results and Political Broadcasting," July 18–20, 1967, pp. 277–78.

tions are held—and if they can continue to provide the citizenry with a linkage (even if it is symbolic) to government, our antiparties will survive; blundering perhaps, but performing essential electoral and symbolic functions in a polity too complex for citizens to take a continuing and sustained interest in politics.

Index

Celler, Emanuel, 282
Center for Political Studies, University of Michigan, 14, 140
Center for the Study of Responsive Law, 29
Chambers, William, 5
checks and balances, 8
Chicanos
  migration patterns of, 173–74
  voting behavior, 97, 156, 157
Chiles, Lawton, 79
Chisholm, Shirley, 155
Citizen's Research Foundation, 84, 226
Civil Rights Act of 1964, 293
Civil Rights Act of 1965, 293
civil rights legislation, 291–93
civil service regulations, 172, 175, 272, 308
Civil War, 9
Clark, Peter, 169
Cleveland, Grover, 9
closed primaries, 194, 195, 251
cloture petition, 297
Cloward, Richard, 185
committee chairmen, congressional, 280–83, 284, 295–98
Committee for Democratic Alternatives (CDA), 178
Committee for Democratic Voters (CDV), 33, 178
Committee on Political Education (COPE), 94, 228
Committee to Reelect the President, 50, 246
Common Cause, 29, 35, 307
communications, 23
Communist party, 180
Community Action Programs (CAP), 39
community revolution, 183–85
computer technology, 27, 65–67, 69, 227
Congress of the United States, 217–18
  bureaucracy and, 272–73
  committee system, 280–83, 295–97
  constitutional change, 299–300
  elected party leadership, 283–90, 298
  political party affiliations, 10–12
  powers of, 17
  president and, 266–70, 293–94, 299

Congress of the United States (*cont.*)
  procedural changes, 295–98
  reform possibilities, 295–300
  seniority system, 281, 287, 295–98
  voting behavior, 290–95
congressional elections
  1954, 131
  1958, 115
  1962, 105, 265
  1970, 80, 81, 85, 116, 145, 180, 265–66
  1972, 116, 136
Connecticut Democratic party, 186, 189–92, 200, 201, 208
consensus system, 17
Conservative party (New York), 176, 180
Constitution of the United States, 7, 305
contributors, campaign finance and, 222–27, 228, 230, 236, 237
conventions. *See* national nominating conventions; state conventions
converting elections, 132–33
Conway, Jack T., 35
Costikyan, Edward, 174
courts of appeal, 275
crime rates, 37
critical elections, 131–32
Cronkite, Walter, 30
cross-filing, 192, 193, 195
cybernetics, 28

Dahl, Robert, 15, 20, 93
Daley, Richard, 33, 175, 254–55
Davidson, Roger, 290
Deadlock of Democracy (Burns), 217–18
delegate selection, 18, 36, 219–20
  1972 presidential election, 247–51, 252
  prospects for 1976, 251–52
  state convention process of, 240–44
  trends in presidential, 246–52
Democratic Charter Commission, 13
Democratic Committee on Committees, 282
Democratic Farmer Labor party, 176, 180, 181, 207
Democratic National Committee, 215, 216
Democratic National Convention
  1948, 257